FORDHAM

FORDHAM
A History and Memoir

Raymond A. Schroth, S.J.

an imprint of
LOYOLAPRESS.

CHICAGO

an imprint of

LOYOLAPRESS.

3441 N. ASHLAND AVENUE
CHICAGO, ILLINOIS 60657

All photographs, except where noted below, are reprinted courtesy of Fordham University Archives.

The photograph of the birthplace of John J. Hughes, S.J., is courtesy of Francis Canavan, S.J.

The photographs of the Seven Blocks of Granite, of Franklin D. Roosevelt and Robert I. Gannon, S.J., and of the bust of Orestes Brownson are courtesy of the William Fox Collection at the Fordham University Archives.

The aerial view of the Rose Hill campus is courtesy of Fairchild Aerial Surveys, Fordham University Archives.

The photograph of Laurence J. McGinley, S.J., is courtesy of Art Green, Fordham University Archives.

The photographs of Timothy Healy, S.J., Leo McLaughlin, S.J., Edward A. Walsh, and Michael Walsh, S.J., and of Pedro Arrupe, S.J., are courtesy of Conrad Waldinger, Fordham University Archives.

The photograph of Claire Hahn is courtesy of Jack Becker.

The photograph of Eileen Markey is courtesy of Eileen Markey.

The photograph of Joseph A. O'Hare, S.J., is reprinted courtesy of Peter Freed.

Interior design by Think Design

Library of Congress Cataloging-in-Publication Data
Schroth, Raymond A.
Fordham: a history and memoir / by Raymond A. Schroth, S.J.
p. cm.
Includes bibliographical references (p.).
ISBN 0-8294-1676-5
1. Fordham University—History. 2. Fordham University—Biography.
I. Title.

LD1811.F52 S357 2002
378.747'275—dc21

2001050545

Printed in the United States
02 03 04 05 06 07 08 09 Bang 10 9 8 7 6 5 4 3 2 1

Table of Contents

Acknowledgments

My list of people to thank is long. For inspiration, one who most stands out appears in these pages. Joseph R. Frese, S.J., was my mentor from my arrival at Fordham when I served his daily Mass on the fourth floor of Dealy Hall. He gave me my topic for my first book, *The Eagle and Brooklyn,* concelebrated my first Mass, and preached at my final vows.

Thomas Hennessy, S.J., Robert Grimes, S.J., Roger Wines, and Msgr. Thomas Shelley generously shared their deep knowledge of Fordham history. Patrice Kane and Vivian Shen, Fordham archivists, generously made their treasures available. Many professionals and friends read parts of the manuscript and offered corrections and suggestions or helped with research: Kate Adams, John Antush, Richard and Bernadette Cieciuch, Tom Curran, Daniel A. Degnan, S.J., John Deedy, Jim Dwyer, Herman Eberhardt and Laura Chmielewski, Susan (Barrera) Fay, Alice Gallin, O.S.U., Don Gillespie, John Harney, David Herndon, Robert H. Hinkle, Jerry Holden, John and Carolyn Holl, Jonah Hulst, Robert Keck, S.J., James R. Kelly, John Kezel, William Lanouette, James Loughran, S.J., Mark Massa, S.J., Morgan Melchiore, Joe Muriana, Paul Nigido, Danny O'Byrne, Nick and Patricia O'Neill, John W. Padberg, S.J., Nicola Pitchford, Peter Reichard, Rene Sanchez, Arthur Schore, Stephen Stuart, David Toolan, S.J., Rupert Wentworth, and Mike Wilson.

Finally, I thank my own Jesuit community at St. Peter's College, where most of this was written, and the staffs of the St. Peter's College library and of the Jesuit villa houses at Cornwall-on-Hudson and Mitchell Farm, where I could interrupt my writing with a swim.

Preface

I do a lot of my thinking on long runs and bike rides, so it was on a ride along the New Jersey shore in the summer of 1996, with my biography, *The American Journey of Eric Sevareid* (1995) behind me, that I decided to try to tell the story of Fordham.

For a number of reasons, I wanted to tell it in a different way, not as the traditional institutional history that tends to concentrate on high administrators, buildings, finances, and distinguished faculty, but rather, as much as possible, through the experiences of students, the young men and women who were shaped by the institution and who carried its spirit into a larger world.

Thus, where the documentation was available, I have told stories of individuals formed by Fordham—a few, such as Denzel Washington and G. Gordon Liddy, famous; some, such as Robert Gould Shaw and James J. Walsh, fairly well known; others, like Michael Nash and Lou Mitchell, less so. Then I also follow their lives for a while after leaving school. Through them, we meet some great teachers, deal with some educational and religious controversies, watch the borough of the Bronx rise and fall, march off to war four times, open Catholic higher education to African Americans and women, and witness what some have considered the loss of Fordham's Catholic identity along with its emergence as a prospering and ambitious institution in the heart of New York City.

I realized that I could not tell these personal stories and also do the complete, definitive history of a large 159-year-old institution, giving due attention to all the graduate and professional schools, each meriting a history of its own. So I have concentrated on Fordham College, the trunk of the tree from which the branches have sprung. It is the historical heart of the university and, until the development of the Lincoln Center campus in the 1960s, the core of its identity. Although there have been Jesuit administrators and teachers at the other schools, Fordham College has been the most "Jesuit" of the several colleges. It is also the one I know best, allowing me to use my own student and faculty experiences as a unifying thread.

Without trying to do too many things at once, I have described Fordham's relationship with the several other worlds it has inhabited. The Bronx has been transformed from a remote farming community into a teeming, sometimes hostile, environment, but a place Fordham would not flee. American Catholic higher education was slowly emerging from its academic ghetto into intellectual competition with its secular neighbors. America itself repeatedly called on Fordham's Catholic young men to demonstrate their patriotism at the cost of their lives. The Catholic Church, after centuries of certitude, was changing, and the Society of Jesus, which first came to America as a missionary order, had established a formidable network of colleges and universities, with a profound impact on both Catholic and American culture.

So the last word on Fordham University remains to be written, but I hope this story will ring true both to those who know it and to those who meet it here for the first time.

RAS
March 2000

Prologue

I ✦

The bright Sunday-in-May dawn breaks over the Bronx. It is 6:30, but much of the campus has been up all night, and some who would have liked to sleep later had been awakened at 4:30 by the mad clanging of the old ship's bell of the aircraft carrier *Junyo.* Presented by Admiral Chester W. Nimitz, blessed by Cardinal Francis Spellman, and first rung by Harry S. Truman in 1946, it hangs in front of the gym. Exuberant seniors coming home high on the beer at Clarke's Bar near the corner of Fordham Road and Webster Avenue and on the thrill of their impending graduation thought it would be fun to wake up the world.

Outside the gates, cars and buses cough, groan, and rumble past the Bronx Botanical Gardens on one side and, a little farther up Fordham Road on the other side, the Bronx Zoo. It is a bustling, graffiti-spattered Spanish neighborhood of 150,000 people, where any one of us could climb the hill on a Saturday afternoon through the chattering crowds to the subway station and never hear the English language once. A few blocks to the south is Belmont, or Little Italy, a tight, colorful enclave surrounded by Spanish and black neighborhoods, a remnant of thirty years ago when it seemed the whole world made the Bronx its home.

It is a neighborhood I have struggled to comprehend in long walks, runs, and bike rides, especially the bike ride that winds through the entire borough and is led by Bronx Borough president Fernando Ferrer. I am left rationally though not yet emotionally convinced that this is my home, this sprawling complex of boom boxers, laborers,

Sunday park picnickers, violent criminals, vandals, Fordham students and their long-suffering families, street hawkers, idealistic teachers and school principals, and street litterers who transform Fordham Road on weekends into the filthiest street in New York.

This neighborhood has also been the home of some of Fordham's best students. As children they gazed from their bedroom windows at the gothic tower of Keating Hall; as young men and women, the campus gate became their door to the world.

It is the campus's loveliest time of the year. The lush green canopy of its elms, oaks, and maples has formed. The flower beds are replanted for the graduation, alumni reunion, and priestly ordination weekends; four new bowers for rose bushes have been set up in the quadrangle across from the 1838 Administration Building and between the late-nineteenth-century Dealy and Hughes Halls. The black and gray squirrels with eyes like cocker spaniels scamper up to visitors as if they have a right to special attention, and even the family of skunks that freely roam the campus at dusk have no idea that they are only 95 percent welcome.

In gray shorts and a gold Loyola University New Orleans sweatshirt, I start a long-planned morning run around the campus. I am operating on four and a half hours of sleep, having been up till 1:00 A.M. with Mary Higgins Clark's *All around the Town,* a quick-read thriller about a little girl, abducted and abused at four, who develops multiple personalities to suppress the memory of her abuse and who may or may not have stabbed her college teacher to death in bed. Ms. Clark, a Fordham graduate, is giving the commencement address today, and it would be bad manners to meet her without having read at least one of her books.

I start from the steps of Hughes Hall, once Fordham Prep and now a residence hall. To the right is Loyola Hall, built in 1928, now home to forty-eight mostly retired Jesuits, a good number struggling with cancer or heart disease, or maneuvering the halls with walkers, five of whom were here when I was a student over forty years ago.

Nearby, between the Jesuit residence and the University Church and surrounded by a hedge, is an old graveyard, the resting place of the original nineteenth-century Jesuits, diocesan seminarians, students, and workmen whose few remains were moved in 1890 from the New

York Botanical Garden property that Fordham originally owned. Here and at other universities, the prominent cemetery gives the students something to feel creepy about at Halloween, and for years the rumor made the rounds of Jesuit colleges that a serial killer had staked out a Jesuit campus graveyard for his next attack. It also allows the fathers the illusion that after death they will never have to leave Fordham.

A few feet away is a mound of dirt, the excavation of the colonial farmhouse of the Rose Hill estate, Fordham Manor. On my left is the sprawling 1950s three-wing, six-house complex of Martyrs' Court. I lived there for two years as an undergraduate and for ten, in A house in the 1970s, as a resident faculty counselor. There one night, a good Jesuit friend with whom I had concelebrated a nightly midnight student Mass brought his student girlfriend to tell me they were to be married. Today they are divorced. There, one night after dinner, I found the corpse of a young man in his room who had died of cancer. On a slip of paper on his desk he had written, "I must be brave." When another much-beloved student died, his roommate reported his continued visible presence in the room.

There, in the 1970s, lived honors students and the editors of the *Ram*. For many Octobers the first big social event of the year was the A house faculty reception, to which the boys sometimes wore tuxes and the girls evening gowns. Students and teachers drank beer together and the floor ran wet and sticky with brew—before the law changed and the campus went dry.

Across the road from C house in Roberts Hall was the former basement office of Prof. Edward Anthony Walsh (1900–73), *Ram* adviser and mentor to generations of journalists. He had never married, so the light burned late in his book-crammed, manuscript-strewn headquarters, where he mumbled out of one side of his mouth as he lit a fresh cigarette in the other side with the glowing butt of one he was about to crush into his tray.

In the 1950s, drawn by the light, we would drift over for a study break or stumble in at midnight on the way back from our Webster Avenue pub crawls to share his Irish whiskey and bask in the presence of this "Great Man" and his late-night cronies. Vaughn Deering might be there, the drama coach who had played Brutus and Cassius when he toured with Otis Skinner, along with the huge perspiring bulk of

Rev. J. Franklin Ewing, S.J., a renowned anthropologist and one of the most authoritative Catholic intellectuals to dare defend the theory of evolution.

I remember the night Ed Walsh entrusted me with a secret mission—to go out and buy a bottle of Scotch for one of the Jesuits, since at that time liquor was not regularly served in the Jesuit community. It was the first bottle of booze I had ever bought, and the errand filled me with both the fear that I might be committing a sin and the pride of having been chosen to bring one of the fathers some joy. On my way back from the North End Liquor Store, up the elm-lined path in the dark, I spied the Jesuit dean of discipline, the black-haired, steely-eyed Thomas Brady, S.J., headed toward me. What if he were to stop me and ask what I was hiding in the brown bag under my coat? We weren't allowed liquor in our rooms. Would I try to save myself by telling the truth and embarrassing one of his fellow priests? He nodded hello. The crisis passed.

I pick up my running pace on the downslope toward the Third Avenue Gate, where the new library—on the "must-do" agenda for the last forty years—is about to open its doors. I cut across the broad expanse of the Martyrs' Court lawn with a glance back to A house looming in the distance and jog around the old, now-abandoned gothic Duane Library and toward the great quadrangle, Edwards Parade. Here on warm days Fordham students play soccer in bright maroon-and-white jerseys, stretch out shirtless in the sun, or fling Frisbees in high arcs and leap like ballet stars to snatch them down in midflight. Here, within a few hours, thousands of us will line up under the gaze of towering Keating Hall—a 1930s centerpiece that students imagine to have been constructed during the Middle Ages—for the commencement exercises.

II —

Upstairs in Spellman Hall, the semicloistered enclave behind Keating where nearly all the nonretired Jesuits now live, Fordham's president, Joseph A. O'Hare, S.J., has been up since 5:30 and is putting his day in order.

O'Hare came to the presidency in 1984 with his doctorate in philosophy from Fordham after teaching philosophy in the Philippine Islands and serving as editor of the Jesuit weekly magazine, *America.* Though a master of the English language, he had never administered anything larger than a magazine staff, and in his early years, one would not have had to look far to find a critic wondering whether his sharp mind and rhetoric sufficiently equipped him to run a two-campus complex of thirteen thousand students, plus faculty and alumni.

His response: he evolved an administrative style in which he wants to know everything that's going on, but lets vice presidents and deans administer the school. Meanwhile, he stresses communication, repeats his key objectives, and projects the image of a public figure who is friend to and committee member for a succession of mayors and civic leaders. On alumni weekends, he shakes the hands and remembers the faces of hundreds—thousands—of alumni under the tents, sometimes joining in the dancing.

He has reason to feel good this morning. The $54 million, 250,000-square-foot library, his major project, is about to open: the *New York Times* will call it "one of the most technologically advanced libraries" in the country (June 1, 1997). He will entertain the faculty and the honorary degree recipients—including Lena Horne and Beverly Sills—on the library's fourth-floor esplanade that overlooks a sweeping lawn ablaze with a copper beach tree. Although the editor of the alternative student publication, *the paper,* has deplored the selection of an "airport bookstore" writer as commencement speaker, O'Hare is confident in his choice.

Most important, Fordham is on a roll. The coming fall will welcome the largest class in Fordham's history in spite of the university's having survived one of its most traumatic years in recent memory. It was not traumatic because of those public disruptions like strikes or no-confidence votes that usually rend the fabric of university life, but, for the most part, because of private pain that inevitably became public.

In August 1996, Fr. O'Hare had a short list of priorities for the year ahead, goals that, if he handled the year well, would give him some satisfaction when this day came around again. Up front, some goals were obvious: finish the new library and plan its dedication. Get a big donor for whom the library might be named. Should President

Clinton be invited to speak? Complete the $150,000,000 capital campaign. Seal the merger, in curriculum and faculty, between the two Fordhams—the traditional Rose Hill College, which to most living alumni was *the* Fordham College, and the College of Liberal Arts at Lincoln Center, established in the 1960s as the more nontraditional (some say bohemian) downtown campus. Somehow he had to do this in a way that would create a consistent Jesuit image for both campuses, but allow each campus its distinctive character.

And he had to deal with the WFUV tower dispute. The New York Botanical Garden had been protesting that the new forty-five story, oil-derrick-like transmission tower for Fordham's 40,000-watt FM radio station would ruin the view. A series of court decisions had ruled in Fordham's favor, but the garden had enlisted its benefactors, such as wealthy socialite Brooke Astor, to deplore the tower's intrusive presence. He also had to put out some brush fires: the political science department was split, ideologically and personally, and could not come up with a chair acceptable to the administration. The American Association of University Professors had been called in.

Finally, O'Hare had to lead the Jesuits as an apostolic community. Some were still smarting from the separation of the "active" and "retired" communities, and some of the retired remained wounded by Fordham's alleged secularization in the 1960s. At that time, in the context of changes in Jesuit education throughout the country, the president, Leo McLaughlin, S.J., had shattered traditions and egos to move Fordham into the mainstream of American higher education. Jesuits had to forfeit power, including the ability to place Jesuits on the faculty without the approval of lay colleagues. Removed from office, McLaughlin went south to teach in a historically black college, but soon left the Jesuits to marry a younger woman. Today, suffering from a stroke and with his spouse deceased, Leo has returned to spend his last days in the New York Province Jesuit infirmary.

III ⌐

The most intractable issue has been the neighborhood. In the 1970s and 1980s, Fordham alumni started sending their sons and daughters to Fairfield, Georgetown, Scranton, Boston College, and Holy Cross. Jesuit education, yes. The Bronx, no. The long walk down Fordham Road from the D train stop on the Grand Concourse to the Fordham Third Avenue gate takes only twelve minutes of clock time, but on a dark, cold, lonely night through garbage-strewn sidewalks, when the only other persons in sight are a solitary band of youths tooling along on their bikes or beat-up gypsy cabs chugging along ominously beside you, it can seem an eternity.

In the 1970s, a Fordham promotional film shot its helicopter-over-the-campus scenes to promote the illusion that Fordham was a sylvan paradise, all Bronx Zoo and Botanical Gardens with barely a glimpse of the burned-out neighborhoods to the south. Then, invoking a new strategy in spite of the occasional stray bullet that made its way through a residence-hall window, Fordham decided the neighborhood was an asset, a real slice of the most exciting city in the world, a roiling pot of ethnic diversity where the new New York, the new America, was coming into being. It taught its students to be cautious, but not fearful, to take responsibility for the neighborhood because it was their own.

Then it happened. Around 4:00 A.M. on Saturday, April 13, 1996, a neighborhood man, Alimir Lekovic, an eighteen-year-old Bosnian immigrant, was attracted to a Fordham junior whom he spotted outside the White Castle burger joint on Fordham Road. He followed her to her off-campus apartment on Bathgate Avenue, attacked her in the stairwell, raped her, slammed her head against the staircase, stole her credit cards, and left her in the basement for dead. Lekovic, whose neighbors told him to turn himself in, was caught within four days; the young woman went into a coma, came out, and went home from Montefiore Medical Center on April 24. But the Fordham community had to deal with its communal trauma in a variety of ways. The attack took place on Spring Preview weekend, when parents brought their teenagers to Fordham to see if this was the right place for them. They were greeted by signs warning that a violent criminal was on the loose.

Eileen Markey, a sophomore from Springfield, Massachusetts, fifth of seven children of Irish parents raised in Queens, had come to Fordham because it was Catholic, Jesuit, and in New York. She was fragile emotionally, having suffered eight months of depression in high school in which "once close and fulfilling friendships decayed into polite acquaintanceships." Because of the Urban Plunge program that introduced incoming freshmen to the Bronx, she considered these littered streets her home. Yet in the days following the attack on the other girl, as Eileen went out to buy cigarettes and stood on the corner of Fordham Road and Hoffman Avenue waiting for the light to change, she found herself cringing from suspicious-looking strangers.

With hundreds of her fellow students, she crammed into the Mass of Healing in the University Church, where Joe O'Hare would preach and try, they thought, to make some sense out of the pain and fear that were tearing them apart. As Markey remembers it, however, the president confessed that he could not explain why this had happened, and with that he won her respect. If he had said God would take care of everything, he would have lost her and all her friends. Rather, she experienced the power of the Mass in a time of tragedy, not foreseeing that it would be the first of a series of such liturgies. For four days, while the girl was in a coma, Eileen sat up with her friends speculating about what kind of a person could do something like this, not condemning, but trying to understand, to see him as a human being.

In spite of the widely publicized crime, Fordham's enrollment rose—partly because of an aggressive admissions staff and bright, sophisticated literature; partly because, in the popular culture, with the rise of sitcoms such as *Seinfeld,* the word was spreading across the country that New York was both safe and "cool" again. Fordham had earned a year of peace.

Then, on Saturday afternoon, October 12, as the football team warmed up for the Homecoming Weekend game against Lafayette, William Tierney, a twenty-year-old junior defensive back, with his family in the stands and his sister waiting to sing the national anthem, fell to his knees. The team doctor and the Fordham Emergency Medical Service were immediately at his side and rushed him to St. Barnabas Hospital. But Bill Tierney was dead.

Fordham canceled the game and all the weekend events and went into mourning for a much-loved, humble kid. He was the team motivator, a volunteer baseball-team manager, and he liked doing little things for other people, like getting them coffee. The stunned crowds filed from the stands over to the chapel for an impromptu memorial Mass. O'Hare spoke and, later the next week, preached the funeral homily in New Jersey; he told 1,300 sobbing young people the last thing they might be expected to welcome at the moment—that, for a Christian, death is a friend. "Death is not something that happens to us. Death is what we do. Death is the signature of life because how we die defines who we are."

Staten Island freshman Vincent Augello came to Fordham because he loved the green campus, because Fordham gave him financial aid, and because Boston College had turned him down. His father, an Italian immigrant who knew the Fordham area from his job as track man for the Metro-North Railroad, which runs along the western border of the campus, had warned him about the neighborhood. Vinny, though still uncomfortable on the late-night walks down Fordham Road, had learned to give it a chance.

He was a very responsible young man who had his priorities straight when, though he had made his high-school football team, he put aside his helmet and shoulder pads—and the broken bones they foreshadowed—and took up the tuba to play in the Monsignor Farrell High School concert and marching band. He discovered that music was not about pushing valves but "performing," about "making your emotions seep out through the bell," bringing the audience to tears. Playing the "Jupiter" section of Gustav Holst's *The Planets,* he knew that giving up football was the best decision he had ever made.

In philosophy and theology classes he was elated to discover that he could actually think, write down his ideas, and get credit for them. Though a volunteer catechism teacher in his parish during high school, he had come to college indifferent toward religion. Now he found that his theology course readings in Sigmund Freud had caught him off guard: Freud's description of God—one who forgives, answers prayers, protects us, and promises everlasting life— met his own, but did that make his God, like Freud's, an "illusion"? Though he continued to go to church, Vinny put his religion in limbo. Meanwhile, he found in his fellow freshmen, the gang on the third floor of Alumni Court North, the best friends he had ever known. They hit the neighborhood pubs, sat on the hall floor and smoked cigars, watched baseball on TV.

And for the first time, he had a close friend who was black. Vinny had grown up "a little prejudiced," with his own distinction between two kinds of black guys: regular blacks and the ones who stood out with their rap music and baggy clothes. But it was impossible to hate Raymond Milward, the Calvin Klein–model handsome, trilingual, nineteen-year-old acting student who was "friends with everybody," who bought all his friends beers on his own birthday.

Then on Friday, February 7, at 11:30 A.M., there was an ambulance outside the residence hall and Ray was carried out on a stretcher. He had had a seizure; his eyes were like glass Christmas tree ornaments. "Don't worry, Vin," he said. "I'll be fine." That night the 3 North gang hit some clubs in Manhattan and got home at 4:00 A.M. to find the door blocked; they could not come in until they had reported to the Medical Center and taken an antibiotic. Upstairs the custodial staff stripped the bedclothes from Raymond's bed and the adjacent rooms and took them to the health station; they cleaned the bathrooms with a highly concentrated disinfectant, scrubbed the walls, ceilings, showers, sinks, and toilet seats, and steam cleaned all the carpets. Raymond had died of bacterial meningitis five minutes after noon.

At the memorial service at the Progressive Community Chapel in Springfield, Massachusetts, Vinny and two busloads of his friends sat shivering and sobbing in their seats as the gospel choir sang "Amazing Grace." Back on campus they consoled one another by crying and hugging; now Vinny, who was beginning to see God not merely as an illusion but as cruel, struggled for something to say to Ray's mother. He nursed his anger, ducked outside, smoked a cigarette, and looked for Ray's mom. Today, more than the impact of Ray's death, Vinny remembers the mother's smile, the brilliant light radiating from her face. "He's all right," she said. "He's with God." The God who had stolen his friend became the Spirit, the Christ, shining through this woman.

Three nights later, a popular junior from Port Chester, New York, Patrick McNeill, after apparently having had too much to drink, walked out of the Dapper Dog Bar on 92nd Street and Second Avenue in Manhattan and disappeared.

The disappearance of Patrick McNeill was for many reasons very different from the university community tragedy in which the usual mechanisms of support—discussion groups, the nearness of priests and psychological counselors, campus ministry prayer services—can play a decisive role. If Fordham had been late-nineteenth-century London, the obvious solution would have been to call in Sherlock Holmes, who would have found the young man suffering from amnesia in an apartment in Brooklyn, having been abducted by high-school enemies determined to settle a score. But reality is more brutal—and often simpler—than detective fiction.

In the weeks that followed, as family, friends, and police spread out through Manhattan and Queens posting fliers and tracking down false leads and sightings, the boy's understandably distraught father accused Fordham of not doing enough, and the university replied that it could not disrupt the lives of students to join the search when the expertise and authority rested with the New York police. An investigative journalist published an article in *New York* magazine (March 31, 1997) indicating that McNeill was a troubled young man, more so than his family and friends portrayed.

People who drown in New York Harbor during the winter sink and stay down. In spring, when the temperature warms, gasses form in the body and it floats to the surface in mid-April or early May. Seven police boats tour the Harlem and East Rivers and haul the bodies out, and the scuba teams, swimming in a murk so dark they only know a body when they bump into it, search for those that fail to float. Corpses tend to accumulate between the Manhattan and Williamsburg Bridges. On April 7, Captain Aldo Anderson of the Army Corps of Engineers saw a corpse at 10:00 A.M. He told the *New York Times* (May 18, 1997), "The water was easy so we could see a hump I thought was a dog."

Father O'Hare and the director of Fordham's security drove to Port Chester to deliver the news to the family. Insofar as a coroner's report can solve a mystery, Pat McNeill tumbled into the East River the night he staggered out of the Dapper Dog. There were no signs of violence and there was a "moderate" amount of alcohol in his system.

For Patrick's funeral, 1,200 people flocked to the Corpus Christi Church in Port Chester, 750 of whom had to watch from video monitors in the gym next door, with another 50 mourners in the street. About 16 Fordham students made the list of invitees allowed into the church. The cardinal sent a personal representative, who said a few words at the end. Five Fordham Jesuits, including O'Hare, concelebrated. At the end of Mass, Patrick McNeill Sr., displaying remarkable control considering the anguish he had endured, eulogized his son, thanked those in Port Chester who had sacrificed in the search for his boy, and cataloged his son's loves—his father, his mother, his sister, his neighbors, etc. He did not mention Fordham.

IV ⚊

Fordham senior Eric Montroy, small but quick, had worked his way up to captain of the football team at Buffalo's Canisius High School. He had chosen Fordham over SUNY Buffalo and Syracuse University and came in not as a scholarship superstar, but as a kid whose high school teachers had given him a love of language, critical thinking, and public service. In no time he was president of the environmental club and on his way to Guatemala, after boning up on Guatemalan history, for his sophomore spring break. As he remembers, it was the first time he had experienced tension "between patriotism and critical reality," and according to his reading, it was not right that the United States should "start a civil war just so John Foster Dulles can sell more bananas."

Eric became the gentlest, most peaceable of radical protesters. Handing out anti-Disney fliers on the Buffalo Mall because of Disney's unfair labor practices or protesting General Electric's recruiting at Fordham because the company was a big polluter, he always did so politely. When he objected to United States Marine Corps recruiters in the campus center, Eric made it clear he respected the marines as individuals, he just didn't believe in what they did. His ability to see things clearly through a Christian prism, however, took a few blows in the first semester of his junior year in Professor Nicola Pitchford's course on postmodern British fiction.

Nicola Pitchford, a striking presence in the classroom and at small dinners where she socialized with students, was young, tall, and beautiful, and it was both her first year at Fordham and her first opportunity to teach such a bright group of students at this high level.

She had gone to Pomona College and had her doctorate from the University of Wisconsin. There her research had centered on British fiction and the problem of making meaning and ethical judgments in a multicultural society that is composed of a broad variety of divergent ethical systems. As a Quaker, she was drawn to Fordham because she saw it as a place where an English teacher could deal with religious and ethical concerns.

She may not have foreseen the degree to which postmodernism is a hand grenade thrown into a room full of young people raised on the traditional certainties of the Catholic faith. The philosophy behind the novels on the reading list asked how one could make any ethical claims at all in a relativistic context. It imposed a theory of skepticism against any one answer to a moral problem. She sensed the confusion in the class and warned them: there were no answers to some of the questions raised.

Postmodernism, as Eric saw it, subverted the rational scheme on which he had built many of his religious convictions, and now after class he staggered home at the end of the day wondering whether he could believe in anything at all.

Eileen Markey was taking the same course with the same results. They loved it. It was the best course they'd had. But it was wiping out their deepest convictions. All the students did all the readings—ten novels—but the readings implied that there was no one reality, no standard, that everything was up for grabs. But, asked Eileen, who had plunged back into depression, if there is no meaning or logic, how can Salman Rushdie write a novel as meaningful and logical as *Midnight's Children*? Eileen became a "heartbreak student," the pupil who is obviously bright but breaks the teacher's heart by missing class and failing to hand in her papers. The sophomore dean, Sister Mary Callaghan, called her in regularly and Eileen loved her: "She doesn't give you any breaks, but she's very, very, understanding."

In this depressed and confused state, both Eileen and Eric joined Fordham's Operation Outreach Christmas trip to work with the destitute and dying at Mother Teresa's hospice in Calcutta. Preparation for the trip in the company of kindred spirits began to convince Eileen that perhaps she did belong to this college community that was challenging her with unanswerable questions.

Along with about a hundred other visiting students, the ten Fordham students, most of whom were very intellectual, plunged into very nonintellectual toil in one of the city's several missions—for boys, for the mentally ill, for the poor and dying—that are sponsored by religious orders. In a routine of prayer and work that began with Mass at 6:00 A.M. and ended with adoration of the Eucharist and group reflection before turning in, they touched and nursed their fellow human beings on the most basic level.

Daily they changed and washed bedclothes soiled and caked with vomit and diarrhea from the night before. They led their patients—dying of hepatitis and malnutrition, afflicted with lice, aged between twenty and sixty but looking much older—to the baths, undressed them, bathed them, then brought them out into the sun to dry. In the afternoons, they would sit with the dying and talk—or rather listen to what were, as far as the Americans could tell, the stories of their lives—and hold their hands and massage their dry, cracked bodies with coconut and mustard oil. Eileen knew that back home assisting anyone over the age of two to go to the bathroom would turn her off, but here she could plunge her hands into filth and think nothing of it, because of the cycle of prayer.

Eric developed an affection for a blind Bengali poet named Joe with whom he sat and hugged and tried to talk. Until the day when he found Joe gone and the attendant said bluntly, "They took the body out." That's right, Eric realized, it was just the body, not the person, so unlike the falseness of American funeral homes where they put makeup on the corpses. Some days he helped bury the dead and was humbled, overwhelmed by the privilege of carrying the corpse of someone he had never known.

Ironically, both Eileen and Eric began to work their way out of their "rational" crises of faith through more experiential, "irrational" leaps of faith. Mother Teresa's Missionaries of Charity liked to decorate their walls with little signs with wise sayings, such as "Sometimes you have to get lost to find the right path." Eric found support in those little sayings and in the writings of the Jesuit retreat giver Anthony DeMello, in the Spiritual Exercises of Saint Ignatius Loyola, and in liberation theology. They were also welcome to visit Mother Teresa herself—a very tiny woman with worn feet, smooth hands, and very beautiful blue eyes—for a few minutes in the afternoon, but Eileen passed that up. Eileen had nothing to say to her and hesitated to take up Mother's time just so she could go home and say, "As I said to Mother Teresa . . ."

V

Nevertheless, both came home to Fordham with a lot to say in *the paper*, the to-the-left journal founded by a group of students who had taken my personal journalism course in the 1970s. Eileen wrote a column about exploring the Bronx, and Eric, consistent with his membership in the pacifist club, Pax Christi, found an issue that might make him less popular with his senior class, but on which he could not stay silent.

The USS *Intrepid* is an old World War II aircraft carrier docked at the end of 46th Street in the Hudson River. It is one of three remaining from the twenty-four "fast carriers" built between 1943 and 1945 to carry the war to Japan. It is 898 feet long, displaces 42,000 tons, carried 110 aircraft, was once the floating home of 3,500 officers and men, and it had shot down or bombed 577 enemy places and sunk 106 enemy ships. Recommissioned in 1954, it helped blockade Cuba during the Cuban Missile Crisis and did three tours off Vietnam during that war. In 1982, it was sold to a private company and transformed into a commercial enterprise, the USS *Intrepid* Sea-Air-Space Museum. But today, its deck cluttered with aircraft and missiles from every war and its interior redesigned with exhibits in cases and weapons dangling from the ceiling, it is much more—or less—than the standard memorial or military museum. It's a party place, catering hall, and disco that attracts 450,000 visitors a year.

To the parents and grandparents of the class of 1997, the *Intrepid* conjures up images of "The Good War," the world rescued from Hitler and Hirohito by the sacrifices of brave men. To them, a pre-postmodern generation, and Fordham graduates from the late 1940s and 1950s, certain symbols, such as the flag and even the *Enola Gay*, represent the triumph of good over evil.

To the grunge fringe of the postmodern generation X and some of their contemporaries, symbols mean nothing. To pierce ears, eyebrows, noses, tongues, nipples, and nostrils, or wear a cross around your neck or tattoo a Celtic cross or the Blessed Virgin Mary on your chest or bicep, or plaster Nazi paraphernalia, Confederate flags, or sexy rock group posters featuring scantily clad women on your wall means nothing. Cardinal Spellman blessed and Harry Truman rang Fordham's bell outside the gym that Admiral Nimitz had given as a memorial to the World War II dead. Today students ring it when they win football games or when they're drunk.

To someone whose conscience has been formed by Pax Christi meetings, symbols are everything. The cross is not something you hang around your neck to look cool, and the Eucharist is not, as the media often call it, "a wafer," but Christ present in the group and in the individual. And the USS *Intrepid*—warship, museum, dance hall— is a floating hunk of promilitary, pro-war propaganda.

The Fordham Senior Week Committee decided to hold its senior ball on the USS *Intrepid* deck. It was relatively cheap, in Manhattan— and, you know, cool. Eric Montroy wrote respectfully in *the paper* (February 18, 1997) that the decision, "in our postmodern age of blurred realities," had "turned a normally joyous prospect into a sour and stressful moral investigation." Seniors who, in conscience, did not think that students at a Catholic-Jesuit university should dance on a death-ship would not be able to attend the ball.

A younger Jesuit, John Dear, a peace activist who had already served a prison sentence for his anti–nuclear weapons protests and who was teaching one course in the theology department, published a long letter in *the paper* and personally called O'Hare, demanding that he, as president, move the dance. O'Hare, who doesn't run the university by making lower-echelon decisions, took the call, listened with as much patience as he could muster, and hung up on him. In the *National Catholic Reporter* (May 2, 1997), Dear argued that the committee's decision to dance on the *Intrepid* proved that Fordham had failed as a Jesuit institution.

Eric's column earned a little praise and much scorn. One student wrote that her only "stressful decision" was deciding on a dress. Another suggested, in the *Ram,* that they should have the ball in the church. At an open meeting, with the Senior Week Committee—and John Dear and me—present, there was, I thought, an extraordinarily thoughtful airing of views. But the committee chair's declaration, "We didn't think anyone would be upset," threw Eileen Markey into a funk. It meant that her group of friends had been even more marginalized over the past three years than she had ever suspected and that they had had little or no impact on the basic heart of the campus. But the committee was willing to reconsider if they could come up with an alternative spot and get their *Intrepid* deposit back. In fact, O'Hare himself wanted to help them make the change.

On Good Friday, about fifteen Fordham students joined the one thousand New Yorkers, led by Pax Christi, who in recent years on this day have re-created the traditional stations of the cross by proceeding from the United Nations across town to the *Intrepid,* where they have demonstrated and risked arrest. Eileen Markey was preparing to read a public letter from Pax Christi to O'Hare, Fordham College Dean Joseph McShane, S.J., and the Senior Week Committee when a police officer told her to put her hands behind her back, cuffed her, took a Polaroid photo, and put her in the paddy wagon. Arrested with her were her father, who had come down from Springfield to be with her, John Dear, philosophy professor James Marsh, and Daniel Berrigan, S.J. Eileen knew that her arrest would never move the ball; she just thought someone should stand up for principle. For her, the dissenters were the "men and women for others" whom the Jesuits had claimed they wanted to let loose on the world. In the holding pen, Dan Berrigan asked her if this was her first arrest. She said yes.

He wished her many more.

The cost of moving the dance, over $33,000, was too much. The protesters were not bitter, just tired. The night they got the news, about forty of them—described by someone as Fordham's total liberal population—gathered at an off-campus apartment on Hoffman Avenue. They sat out in the backyard and started a bonfire of old boards and boxes; they played guitars, lit a few joints, drank beer and red wine, beat bongo drums as the smoke ascended into the still Bronx night air, and celebrated Eileen Markey's birthday. The night of the ball, they met again in a suite at the Times Square Marriott Marquis for an alternative party, then joined the revelers from the *Intrepid* at a Manhattan nightclub in the early morning hours.

VI ⤙

I keep running, past Spellman Hall, past Keating, and there it is: at the far end of the football field, the unfinished tower, our half-built super-Erector set, built to transmit WFUV's unique programming of folk music and the Sunday Mass into distant Connecticut and New Jersey. We had built it there because environmentalists said the traditional radio tower atop Keating was a health hazard. Now they wanted us to move and redesign it so it would be skinny and less noticeable? I run in the garden and never notice the tower, but I'm not a good judge in this dispute.

I need breakfast. It will be a long day. As assistant dean, I will be a marshal, keeping the graduating seniors in line. When I signal Eric Montroy to climb the steps and accept his degree, we'll hug. When the young woman who was assaulted a year ago comes forward, Joe McShane will hand her her diploma and embrace her as well.

The year had been exceptional in that, in the public eye, much of the education had been in a training of the emotions, in grieving, in honing the moral sense, all of these among Fordham's goals since the beginning. It had been like other years in that students and faculty, generally happy with each other, had achieved a level of excellence.

Many other things of varying degrees of seriousness had happened as well. A Lincoln Center professor was sanctioned for surreptitiously videotaping female students' feet in the library. Students for Choice were required to leave the annual Club Fair. Marijuana use reportedly increased. Thousands of students spent infinite hours talking into their cellular phones, playing video games, listening to music on their portable CD players, drinking beer, playing basketball, hanging out, working part-time jobs—and going to class, writing papers, and reading books. The political science department got a chair. Some great Jesuits passed away. And Leo McLaughlin died among his Jesuit brothers and was eulogized in the University Church by the former assistant general of the Society of Jesus, Vincent O'Keefe, S.J.

Joe O'Hare, who began the year setting his goals as a fund-raiser and civic leader, had spent much of it as a pastor, praying in hospital emergency rooms, putting in eighteen- to twenty-hour days like some of his student-affairs staff, reaching for words and gestures that ease public and private pain. He would tell the graduates that they had been "tested by sorrow" and learned "how fragile is the gift of life."

Mary Higgins Clark would compare college life to a suspense novel. The best first line for a mystery novel, she would say, is "A shot rang out." For a graduation, "The graduate knew that from the moment the diploma was placed in his or her hand, nothing would ever be the same."

1.

Michael Nash Arrives

I ⁓

When young Michael Nash and his five companions climbed down from their New York and Harlem Railroad car at the Fordham station on Sunday evening, August 9, 1846, he was not quite twenty-one years old, the age at which today most Bronx Fordham graduates are heading for law school or graduate study or are looking south, toward Manhattan towers, with dreams of careers in finance or the media. Lincoln Center graduates are looking in all directions, and a good number on both campuses are setting dates for their weddings.

The weary six had just traveled through an America at war—a nation at a turning point in its history. President James K. Polk, a Democrat swept into office by a wave of national expansionism called manifest destiny, had set his sights on the vast territories known as California and Oregon, and in April, American troops had crossed the border from recently annexed Texas into Mexico.

To the north, a short walk from Concord, Massachusetts, young Henry David Thoreau had settled into a little cabin built with his own hands on Walden Pond, where he raised beans, measured the depth of the water, lamented the surge of industrialization personified in the railroad that roared by within earshot, scoffed at the telegraph that had been set up two years before, and recorded the voices of frogs, the reverberations of the church bells, and his conversations with visitors in his notebooks. Twenty miles south of the Fordham station, young Walt Whitman sat on the porch of his office at the *Brooklyn Eagle* and watched the ferry pull into the Fulton Street dock just a few yards away.

II ⌁

But Michael Nash, up until a few months before, had not been that sure of what he intended to do with his life.

Born in County Kilkenny in 1825, he had come to America in 1830 with his father, James Nash, who was making a trip to investigate a family legacy in Kentucky that, depending on what the father discovered, the Nashes might accept or turn down. Michael's older brother Thomas had been slated for the trip, but three days before sailing, their mother refused to part with her first son, so, since the ticket had already been bought, the family sent little Michael in his place.

The voyage to New York took forty-three days, followed by eleven days on steamboats, canal boats, stagecoaches, and railroads in uninterrupted travel to Louisville, where James Nash evaluated the farmland that had been bequeathed to him and decided that it was too far from priests and the Mass. He decided he should turn it down.

By 1832, the seven-year-old Michael had determined that he wanted to stay in America for reasons not very clear to himself except that perhaps he would head out for the frontier and become an Indian scout. His father not only agreed with this, but as James Nash boarded the riverboat that would take him away from his son up the Ohio River to Pittsburgh and the boy tried to change his mind, James Nash refused to let his son so easily switch a very young man's first major decision.

Besides, James Nash had handed his son over to Fr. Quinn, the vicar general of the diocese of Bardstown. As Michael's guardian, Fr. Quinn would take charge of his schooling for two years and then, perhaps, send him home to Ireland. After placing the boy for five years in a little academy run by a semiretired priest in a church basement, Fr. Quinn transferred Michael to St. Joseph's College, which was run at the time by diocesan priests, in Bardstown, about forty miles southeast of Louisville.

III ⚊

Prior to the suppression of the Society of Jesus in 1773 by Pope Clement XIV and the rulers of several European countries, the Society had 669 schools or colleges spread over every country of Europe and across the world. In France, there had been 91 colleges and 20 seminaries with forty thousand students, manned by three thousand Jesuits. Following the restoration in 1814, Jesuits strove to reevangelize France, specifically through eight minor seminaries, with the hope that their spirituality might revitalize French Catholicism with a new breed of young priests. But the July Revolution of 1830, which replaced Charles X with the "citizen king," Louis Philippe, threw the Jesuits into disfavor for a while; they were forced out of their minor seminaries, and a good many turned their eyes abroad to missionary work in Algeria, China, Canada, Louisiana, and Kentucky. A group of Paris Jesuits, responding belatedly to Bishop Flaget's invitation to Bardstown, sailed by way of the West Indies and New Orleans and up the Mississippi River to Bardstown, only to discover that St. Joseph's had been set up without them.

While the journey to Bardstown had been an ordeal, young Michael Nash loved the trip. The stagecoach horses, changed every ten miles and always in prime condition, galloped along the turnpike and, having set out at 4:00 A.M., arrived at Bardstown that evening.

Michael was delighted with St Joseph's "tastily laid out campus," but discipline was lax and during his 1840–41 Christmas vacation he made another of those snap decisions—this time to drop out of school and become a brass finisher. Fortunately, there was a providential visit from Fr. William Stack Murphy, S.J., president of St. Mary's College, which was situated on a farm near Lebanon, about twenty miles southeast of Bardstown. Fr. Murphy convinced Fr. Quinn to intervene and entrust Michael to the Jesuits. It was a close call; he would have learned a trade, but unless the hot temper that his peers considered his outstanding characteristic got him in trouble, he would have disappeared from history, assuming that being a Fordham founder makes one part of history.

From the start Michael was at home at St. Mary's, with its pretentious front gate and half-dozen brick buildings, and its kindly Fr. Murphy, who greeted them like a father. In its crowded, curtainless dormitories the boys slept two to a bedstead, separated by a board, with tin wash basins by the beds.

The school, it seems, was not prospering. Its enrollment was evaporating—from 180 in 1836 to 78 ten years later, and only half of those were Catholics. The Catholic boys in the Sodality went to Mass every morning, though it was not required, and the others began their studies after prayer in common. Michael was drawn into the Sodality by one of the more interesting Jesuits of that time. Fr. Thomas Legouais, consistent with the philosophy of the French province from which he had come, presented the Sodality as a family to which the boys would want to belong.

Fr. Legouais had been born in prison to a noble French family during the Reign of Terror. After practicing law in Paris, he joined the Sulpicians, then the Jesuits in 1821. After teaching theology in France and Spain, he was assigned in 1832 to the Kentucky Mission. In an 1857 photograph of St. John's College faculty, his face is gaunt and tight, with high cheekbones and deep, hollow eyes. Frail and delicate, less than five feet tall, described as "a pygmy" or a "veritable dwarf" though well proportioned, he did not allow his size to limit his effectiveness. Even so, he was so small that he needed a boost to mount his horse and was sometimes mistaken for a child. One parent visiting St. Mary's saw him saying Mass and stormed into the head office scandalized that the Jesuits had allowed a little boy to celebrate a liturgy!

We can deduce from Michael Nash's account of his own life—which was preserved in a memoir, some letters, and an obituary in the Jesuit historical quarterly, *Woodstock Letters*—that though described as brave and naturally pugnacious, opinionated, and inclined to lash out sharply at those with whom he disagreed, something in his personality made Nash attractive to older priests. During Michael's 1843 summer vacation, Bishop Guy Chabrat, coadjutor of the ailing Louisville bishop Benedict Joseph Flaget, suggested that Michael and his peers not return to the Jesuits at St. Mary's but finish their studies at a different seminary. That same summer Fr. Murphy, the dean of the college, called him in for a conference and plainly asked what he intended to do with his life. Nash didn't know. In April 1845, Murphy tried again, telling Nash he thought he was "called," and Nash put on the Jesuit habit. When Nash was tempted to leave during the novitiate, his novice master handed him a letter that had just arrived from a Christian Brother in Ireland urging him to "put his hand on his breast" and like a man say, "Lord, what wilt thou have me do?" Michael consulted Murphy, who simply assured him that joining the Jesuits was the way to save his soul.

IV —

Meanwhile, events in New York that would change Michael Nash's life had come to a head. The fiery Irish immigrant Bishop John J. Hughes had taken over the diocese after his mentor, Bishop John Dubois, had died from a series of strokes in 1842. John Hughes had sailed from Ireland with his father at seventeen and worked as a gardener and overseer of slaves at John Dubois's Mount Saint Mary's boarding school in Emmitsburg, Maryland, until, at twenty-three, he badgered Dubois into accepting him into the seminary. Ordained for Philadelphia in 1826, he had moved to New York as a coadjutor bishop in 1838. From the moment of his arrival, Hughes was overwhelmed by concern that the Catholics of New York City and its suburbs were increasingly threatened by a bigoted Protestant majority.

In an 1840 fund-raising letter to the Leopoldine Society of Vienna, which he was about to visit on a European begging tour, Hughes estimated the Catholic population of the greater New York diocese, which comprised all of New York State and northern New Jersey, at 200,000 souls, with forty-nine churches staffed by fifty-six priests. The Catholic population had grown dramatically since the repeal of the Dutch and British colonial anti-Catholic exclusionary laws in 1789 and more dramatically with the early waves of prefamine Irish and German immigrants.

Hughes's goal was one church for every two thousand souls. Recent studies put New York City's 1840 Catholic population at between 75,000 and 90,000, or between 25 and 30 percent of the city's 300,000 residents. Most Irish worked as laborers and domestic servants, the least skilled and least prosperous levels of the population. As a result and as if in mockery of Hughes's goal, the average parish size was 8,500, and in the densest Irish ward a single church might try to accommodate 20,000 people. In general, German Catholic parishes were well organized, the Irish ones less so. If all the Irish had been practicing their religion, only half would have been able to get into church, but contrary to the contemporary impression, not all the nineteenth-century Irish, in either Ireland or New York, were devout. In Ireland itself, the church also lacked the resources and manpower to reach its people, particularly in rural areas.

Hughes was determined to educate his parishioners and safeguard their faith. First, he would get them to the sacraments, for which he needed proper vestments and chalices, the accoutrements of worship. Then he would establish a vast network of parallel Catholic institutions—churches, hospitals, orphanages, and schools—to bolster the faith of his flock. By 1845, he had won a national reputation and had become a hero to the New York Irish by smashing his adversaries in one controversy after another: lay trusteeism, public education, and the nativist movement.

In 1839, when the lay trustees of old St. Patrick's cathedral claimed, according to civil law, the authority to appoint as director of the parish school a priest whom Bishop Dubois had suspended, coadjutor Bishop Hughes, a marvelous and fearless debater, confronted the trustees at a public meeting and appealed over their heads to the parishioners. As he told a friend the next day, "I recalled to them the glory of their fathers in Ireland battling for three hundred years against the abused civil power of the British government" and warned them that "the sainted spirits" of their ancestors were looking down from heaven "ready to disavow and disown them if . . . they allowed pygmies among themselves to filch away rights of the church that their glorious ancestors would not yield but with their lives to the persecuting giant of the British Empire." Many in the audience wept. The power of the trustees was broken. As Hughes gloated, "They were dead." The young Hughes had brought with him from Ireland a profound hatred of all things British, an emotion that stayed with him all his life, and he correctly presumed that his flock shared that hatred.

In 1840, to break the power of the Public School Society—a Presbyterian-dominated association that administered the public-school system, which was suffused with a bland, nondenominational but often anti-Catholic kind of Christianity—Hughes appeared before the Common Council of the City of New York and argued for over three hours for public funds for Catholic schools. Rejected, Hughes organized lay Catholics politically and petitioned the state legislature in Albany in 1841. When Democrats failed to support his proposed legislation, he had New York Catholics organize their own political party, called the Carroll Hall ticket, and in two elections they endorsed sympathetic Democrats and ran candidates of their own. In 1842, the legislature passed the McCay bill, which expressly forbade funds for religious schools but also replaced the Public School Society with elected school boards in New York City. As if to prove that this was a Catholic victory, a mob of angry Protestants stoned Hughes's residence.

Throughout the 1840s, Protestant anger against the flood of Irish immigrants grew more intense and peaked in 1844 when the American Nativist Party elected James Harper mayor of New York. On election night, 1,200 nativists marched through Catholic neighborhoods waving "No Popery" banners, and 3,000 to 4,000 Catholics, having heard that the marchers were headed toward the cathedral, armed themselves and stood in the churchyard, though the attack never came.

Nativist marchers in Philadelphia were said to be bringing to New York an American flag that they claimed to have rescued from Irishmen who had desecrated it. Hughes went to city hall and told the outgoing mayor, Robert Morris, that "if a single Catholic church were burned in New York, the city would become a second Moscow"—a reference to the burning of Moscow in 1812 during the Napoleonic invasion. On May 11, 1844, an editorial by Hughes in the *Freeman's Journal,* the Catholic paper that Hughes controlled, left no doubt that Catholics by the thousands—"cool, collected, armed to the teeth, and with firm determination, after taking as many lives as they could in defense of their property"—were ready to give up, if necessary, their own lives for the same cause.

Hughes's vision, however, was not mere militant "ghetto Catholicism," but was part of a grand worldview inspired by the Irish cardinal Paul Cullen. According to Cullen, the Irish, and particularly the American Irish, who a few years later were able to escape the ravages of the famine would, in revenge against the British, make the Catholic faith the dominant religion in both America and the world.

V

Although Hughes made his national reputation as a fighting politician, his principal commitment was to education. His flock were sheep without enough shepherds, or with shepherds too poorly trained to be priests, so Hughes was determined to build a seminary and a college, one modeled on Mount St. Mary's College and Seminary in Emmitsburg. Hughes would aim his college at the New York Catholic elite, the sons of the wealthy in danger of losing their faith by being educated with and by Protestants.

In the 1830s, there were only nine Catholic colleges in the whole country: five in the South, four in the West, and not a one in the Northeast. Two Jesuit schools had been established in New York—one in 1684 and another, Fr. Anthony Kohlmann's New York Literary Institute, in 1808, on the site of the present-day St. Patrick's Cathedral—but they had lasted only a few years. In 1813, there were only fifty Jesuits in the United States. When it came down to staffing either Kohlmann's school or Georgetown College, Georgetown's 1789 founder, ex-Jesuit archbishop John Carroll, made it clear to the Jesuits that Kohlmann's would have to fold. To Kohlmann, this was an early example of a theme that would return in the twentieth century: prejudice against New York. In Kohlmann's opinion, New York was worth more than all the other states together.

Bishop Dubois's first attempt at a college, established at Nyack in 1833, burned down before the eyes of a cheering crowd of Protestants in 1837. Next, Hughes planned a college in Brooklyn, and when his benefactor failed to donate the Brooklyn property, he decided to build a college and seminary at Lafargeville, in the Thousand Islands near the Canadian border. Predictably, it was a terrible failure. What sensible young man, seminarian or not, wanted to spend $112 tuition plus $8 for washing and mending to live in the snow belt, three hundred miles from New York, in a school where the catalog warned that "unconquerable indolence or insubordination" would lead to dismissal?

Hughes closed the Lafargeville St. Vincent de Paul Seminary in 1840. The year before, he had purchased Rose Hill, an estate of approximately 106 acres in southern Westchester, "in the Manor of Fordham, in the Town and County of Westchester," from a New York City merchant named Andrew Carrigan. Hughes paid $29,750 for the property and then spent $10,000 to renovate the half-finished 1838 manor house. The lovely, sylvan plot was a subdivision of the former Fordham Manor. With a farm and bounded by the Bronx River on the east and a stream called Mill Brook on the west, it seemed near enough to the city (about ten miles) to attract city boys but far enough away to keep them out of trouble.

Hughes opened a seminary there called St. Joseph's in September 1840. There were about twenty students, of whom fewer than fourteen had been retained from Lafargeville. One teacher, a diocesan priest Hughes had recruited in Europe, taught all the subjects. When the college itself, named for St. John the Baptist, opened formally on June 21, 1841, John Hughes's forty-fourth birthday, there were six students. It was a start. But in no way did Hughes have the resources to run this school. He had asked the Jesuits for help, but because they had already committed themselves to Georgetown in the Maryland Province and to St. Mary's in Lebanon, Kentucky, the superior in Rome had to turn him down. Hughes specifically did not want Maryland Jesuits because they would make his school a poor cousin to Georgetown.

Administering the school from Manhattan, Hughes ran through four diocesan priest presidents in five years. The first, Rev. Dr. John McCloskey, who went on to succeed Hughes as bishop of New York and was named the first American cardinal, lasted one year. His successor, Ambrose Manahan, was an autocrat. A young faculty member, Fr. John B. Harley, felt obliged to appeal to Hughes. "What was before the home of harmony and happiness is now the abode of discord and unhappiness," he wrote in February 1843. "Mr. Manahan has come among us, full to overflowing of wild and useless schemes:

schemes that are not at all suited to the character and wants of the institution." The seminarians, he said, were on the brink of rebellion, and New York risked losing them to another diocese.

Frustrated, Harley offered Hughes his resignation. Rather than accept it, Hughes fired Manahan and put the twenty-seven-year-old Harley in charge. Harley restored order, but in 1845 fell ill. Though Hughes took him to London, Dublin, and Paris in search of medical help, Harley never recovered and died at thirty in 1846. His place was taken by Fr. James Roosevelt Bayley, nephew of Elizabeth Bayley Seton, the second American saint, and distant cousin of Theodore and Franklin D. Roosevelt.

Bayley had been an Episcopalian pastor in Harlem, but was converted by conversations with McCloskey. He was baptized in Rome, entered the Sulpicians in Paris, and ordained by Hughes in New York in 1844 prior to being named vice president of St. John's. There he supervised the building of the new seminary right next to the college, now called St. John's Hall, with its little Gothic turrets in the roof disguising the original chimneys that allowed for an open fireplace in each room. Then, right next to St. John's, the seminary church was completed in 1845.

Frustrated by the turnover in his administration, Hughes wrote again to the Jesuits superior general in Rome, Rev. John Roothaan, S.J., with another plea for help. He entrusted his letter to Fr. Peter DeSmet, S.J., the famous missionary to the American Indians, whom Hughes had met on his way to Europe in the summer of 1843.

Hughes predicted that within another twenty years his diocese would become an Episcopal See with each division larger than all of Belgium but that "thousands of souls must perish for want of the bread of life. This is a critical time for the Church in America—this is the important period for laying the foundations in every kind of religious establishment that will grow with the growth of this young American Empire." Roothaan replied that he just didn't have the troops, nor could he close the Kentucky Mission.

Little did he know that the Kentucky Mission was falling apart. During the fifteen years of Jesuit direction, the school had expanded and had influence, but they had been plagued by up-and-down enrollment and all kinds of mishaps. Nor did young Kentucky "gentlemen" live up to the myth of their gentlemanliness. In 1833, two students angry over being disciplined burned down their dormitory. In 1835, a fight between two students ended in a stabbing, and the Jesuits had to institute a ban against bearing arms. But the boys had ready access to Kentucky moonshine, and boozing rival gangs of armed students threatened one another. In 1836, one drunk student pulled his pistol on a Jesuit.

Hughes however, on a hunch, started writing to Kentucky. Fortunately, Hughes's interest coincided with the American travels of the French provincial, Fr. Clement Boulanger, S.J., whom Roothaan had delegated to visit the Jesuit houses in Kentucky and evaluate the viability of their work.

VI ⚊

News came to St. Mary's the following fall that for several ostensible reasons—the hostility of Bishop Chabrat; St. Mary's flagging enrollment, which had fallen to seventy-eight in 1846; and its depressing isolation from the city—the Jesuits were closing out this project. They were moving their whole operation, at the invitation of John Hughes, to St. John's College in New York. Michael Nash, whose life would be radically transformed by their decision, had neither made the required Jesuit thirty-day retreat nor taken his first vows. Nevertheless, consistent with the Society's rule to be ready to travel instantly from one place to the next whenever God's glory seemed to beckon, by summer he was ready to go.

Actually, the reasons for the move were more complex and reflected the broader ambitions of the Jesuits in moving to New York. Jean-Baptiste Hus, assistant to Fr. Boulanger during his decisive visitation, spelled out the many reasons in a memo to superiors. They reflected the principles of St. Ignatius Loyola in searching for the *magis,* the "greater good," in choosing apostolic opportunities.

The big attraction was that there was no Catholic college in New York, and Fordham's proximity to the city would give the fathers and scholastics a host of apostolic opportunities to preach, hear confessions, and teach catechism. New York families were in a better social position than those in Kentucky; here was a chance to teach sons of families with influence, and to influence, through their seminary, the future priests of this dynamic, expanding diocese. Finally, New York was closer than Kentucky to Canada, France, and Rome, to which young Jesuits could be sent to study and beg. Though Hus's reasoning was fundamentally sound, it sowed the seeds of future problems. Hughes had not invited the Jesuits in order for them to spread their wings in the big city. He did not want them competing for funds or for popularity with his diocesan priests.

Old Bishop Flaget, at eighty-three, was personally saddened by the departure. Ironically, his letter offering the French Jesuits St. Joseph's at Bardstown years ago had gone astray, and he had given the Jesuits St. Mary's in its place. Now they were leaving him. Two years later, to his joy, a contingent of Jesuits from St. Louis would arrive to take charge of St. Joseph's and remain there until 1868. After the departure of the Jesuits, St. Mary's reverted to the diocesan clergy. In 1893, it was consolidated with St. Joseph's of Bardstown and it became a seminary in 1929. In 1971, it was sold to hippies from San Francisco, who in time left for Oregon. In 1984, it became—and remains—a minimum-security prison. All the Jesuit-era buildings are gone.

During the summer of 1846, a total of twenty-eight Jesuits—twelve priests, eleven brothers, and five scholastics—in bands of a half dozen, made the ten- to eleven-day trek from Kentucky, up the Ohio River by steamboat, then by stagecoach and railroad to what is now the Bronx. They made the move in stages. A vanguard of president-designate Fr. Augustus J. Thebaud and Fr. Murphy arrived on April 28, followed on July 18 by Fr. John Larkin, who was to be the dean. Four bands, each with a leader, left Kentucky between July 21 and July 31. We don't know how they transported all their baggage. We know they shipped their library, the great majority of their books being scriptural, theological, and classical literary works in French and Latin.

They brought their laboratory equipment and zoological speci-mens, and we do know that they brought a clock big enough for its chimes to be heard all over the campus. It tolled the news whenever one of the fathers died. It had been sent from Paris to Bardstown and, moved north, was now one of those symbolic links with the past that alumni love to remember. They also shipped a corpse. Fr. Eugene Maguire, who died of cholera at thirty-three in 1833 in Kentucky, could not be left behind, so they shipped him north and interred him as an early resident in the Jesuit graveyard near the Bronx River to the north.

Because of their individual histories, these Jesuits were an odd, polyglot crew. Some had been born in Ireland, but for various reasons had entered the Society and been trained in France with its unique French version of Jesuit spirituality. Others were Frenchmen still smarting from the anticlericalism of the French Revolution and the Society's generation-long suppression in Europe. They were working out their vocations as missionaries and as members of the newly formed New York–Canada mission in a land where, they well knew, the French Jesuits Isaac Jogues, René Goupil, and John de La Lande had been massacred by savages, as they were then considered.

The New York–Canada Jesuits, having come from France, were jurisdictionally distinct from the Maryland Jesuits, whose former member, Archbishop John Carroll, had opened Georgetown in 1789; the New York Jesuits, not too pure to harbor a sense of rivalry with their Maryland brothers, strove to keep their institutions unspoiled by Maryland traditions.

Only fifteen years before, their twenty-seven-year-old fellow-Catholic countryman Alexis de Tocqueville, had toured America to study at its grass roots the process of democracy that was spreading with an inexorable inevitability back toward France. He had found Catholicism very much alive in spite of the widespread defections from the faith during the colonial period. When he arrived in New York he wrote to his mother on Sunday, May 15, 1831, that he had heard a sermon in a Catholic church on grace, in English, and understood it. Catholics had five churches and twenty thousand faithful, he reported, and he predicted that their numbers would multiply quickly and spread into the wilderness.

But for all the goodwill on both sides, there is a motif to the French Jesuit–Fordham story that jars the contemporary Jesuit's concept of the intellectual apostolate. The early Jesuits seemed always to be packing their bags to take on something else that needed to be done—such as start a parish or found another college a few miles from this one. From the start they wanted a parish in New York that Hughes, his mind set totally on the school question, did not want to give them.

Today, a Jesuit who arrives at Fordham knows that his particular ascetical challenge is to hunker down and produce scholarly books and articles so he can win tenure and thus stay there indefinitely, most likely until he dies. In 1846, few of the founders were scholars in the contemporary sense or fluent in English. They were zealous work-horses, ready to pour themselves out doing what they were told until they were whisked off within a few years to one of the other Jesuit schools and parishes multiplying throughout New York and New Jersey or until they dropped.

In the mid-nineteenth century, the American Jesuits operated what one historian has referred to as "staging areas" from which their missionaries fanned out across the country and established schools. They were called colleges then, but, in today's terminology, they were actually academies, high schools, or prep schools from which, if the students persevered the seven or eight years necessary for a bachelor's degree, colleges and universities grew.

The first was Georgetown, whose roots were in the English Jesuits. Referred to as "gentlemen of Maryland," many of them came to America prior to the worldwide suppression of the Society and, like Carroll, carried on as diocesan clergy until the Society's restoration in 1814. Belgian Jesuits, trained at Georgetown, established St. Louis University in 1818, as well as other schools in the Midwest. Xavier, in Cincinnati, opened in 1831, and Holy Cross, in Worcester, Ohio, in 1843. Italian Jesuits started schools in the far west after the 1850s, and German Jesuits started schools around the Great Lakes after the 1860s. The French worked in Kentucky until they moved north to Canada and New York City, forming the hybrid New York–Canada Mission.

As R. Emmett Curran says in his history of Georgetown, the antebellum period during which the Jesuits moved to Fordham was one of "rapid, exuberant expansion in the number of colleges in the United States." Hundreds were founded between 1830 and 1861, of which nearly three hundred became permanent or long-lived institutions of higher learning. Seventeen of the thirty-one Catholic colleges founded survived the Civil War. Their students were largely, sometimes mostly, Protestant, but partly in response to nativism, they became more exclusively Catholic colleges. Thus, says Curran, the "ghetto" school evolved and became the dominant kind of Catholic college by the late nineteenth century.

VII ⤙

Michael Nash's band of six, under the leadership of Fr. John Ryan, left St. Mary's on the Feast of Saint Ignatius, July 31, and made their way north by way of Louisville, Cincinnati, Wheeling, and Pittsburgh, their steamer running aground again and again. They then traveled by stage to Cumberland, Maryland, and by train across the Potomac at Harpers Ferry, and on to New York. There they bought tickets at the New York and Harlem Railroad office on Center Street across from City Hall Park. A horse-drawn car conveyed them to the Broome Street and Bowery office, where what Michael termed a "very diminutive engine" was hooked up to the cars.

Diminutive it may have been, but the railroad, established in 1832 to move freight and passengers between lower Manhattan and the fashionable farming suburb of Harlem, was gradually changing the face of New York and would become decisive in the history of Fordham. Fourteen years earlier, the only way to move between New York's urban heart and the countryside was by steamboat up and down the Hudson or the East River, or by stagecoach, which in bad weather over primitive roads could take all day.

The train chugged up the Bowery, passing vacant lots—some fenced in as beer gardens—all along the way. Above 14th Street, they noticed, there were no sidewalks. At Yorkville, they sped through a tunnel cut out of rock then over the Harlem River to Mott Haven. Between Mott Haven and Fordham they saw only one house, one of the farm buildings of the late Gouverneur Morris, Federalist and diplomat, cousin of a signer of the Declaration of Independence, and lord of one of the four manors. The manors were feudal-style, township-sized territories—including Pelham to the northeast, Fordham to the west, and Philipsburgh to the north—into which the area now known as the

Bronx and Westchester counties had been divided in the eighteenth century. The Fordham stop, because of construction still underway between there and the White Plains terminal, was on that day the end of the line.

At first, they had to look hard to find the college. Straight ahead and south of the college grounds was the gate to a little Episcopalian college, now closed, on the farm estate of a Rev. Dr. Powell. Next to it was the Rose Hill gate and a long, curved footpath. A stone wall, with a row of oxheart cherry trees, stretched out to the east as the borderline between the Rose Hill and Powell estates. On the left, a ravine led down to the railroad tracks, where the Mill Brook stream, gone underground in the twentieth century, marked the western border of the property. On the western side of the railroad tracks that ran along the edge of the campus rose a steep hill dotted with the few houses that identified this lonely spot as a town.

Before them a vast, splendid, oval-shaped lawn swept up to the door of the square stone manor house, which had been built in 1838. The college's principal building, it had a student chapel on the first floor, a study hall, a refectory, and wings sprouting out to the north and south. Other brick wings and buildings in the back held dormitories, laboratories, and recreation rooms.

North of the lawn and just to the west of the now-completed chapel stood the three-story brownstone known then as St. Joseph's Seminary, now as St. John's Hall. Beyond these, farther to the west, was a square stone blockhouse, later called the Pill Box, occupied by William Rodrigue and his wife. Rodrigue, whose socially prominent family had fled Santo Domingo to escape a slave rebellion, had befriended Hughes when the bishop was a priest in Philadelphia. When Rodrigue married Hughes's sister Margaret and the couple followed him to New York, Hughes installed him at St. John's as a mathematics teacher. He was also the college architect, designer of his own little house in 1840, the college church built between in 1844–46, and St. John's Hall.

Rodrigue's influence was more critical in another way. When Hughes had worked as overseer of a handful of slaves at Mount Saint Mary's, he was appalled enough by what he saw to compose a little antislavery verse, including the line, "And chase foul bondage from the southern plain." But the horror stories around the dinner table with the Rodrigues about their memories of the slave rebellion in Santo Domingo made the bishop wary of abolitionism, and while Hughes could acknowledge that slavery was an evil, he could never take a strong stand against it.

Slightly to the left of the main building, surrounded by a clump of majestic elms, stood the campus's sentimental centerpiece, the original old manor house, more a cottage than a mansion. Even in the early nineteenth century this old edifice was referred to as George Washington's Headquarters, although his real headquarters had been on the Gouverneur Morris estate a few miles south. Fordham people also liked to believe that this was the house that appeared in James Fenimore Cooper's novel *The Spy.*

Its real genealogy was more prosaic. In 1678, the original lord of Fordham Manor, John Archer, an unpopular landowner whose overbearing ways kept him in steady conflict with his tenants, had sold off parts of his 3,900-acre holdings. This included a 102-acre tract described as "the great plain by the Bronx River," just south of the present Botanical Gardens, which Archer sold to an Englishman, Roger Barton. Barton sold it to a Dutchman, Reyer Michielsen, who passed it to his son-in-law, Benjamin Corsa. To expand the property, Corsa borrowed money from Robert Watts.

When Corsa died in 1770, his son Isaac took over the estate, but during the Revolution, Isaac sided with the British while his brother Andrew served as a guide for Washington's army, which camped near Corsa's orchard. The Corsas lost the property when Isaac fled to Nova Scotia and Robert Watts pressed for payment of his debt. Watts's brother John bought it at auction in 1787 and named it Rose Hill after their ancestral home near Edinburgh. The property changed hands about ten times over the next years, until its last resident, in 1836–38, Dr. Horatio Moat, built the new manor house that is today's administration building. Recent excavations suggest that the old manor house dates from the early 1690s. In 1846, it was inhabited by a few Sisters of Charity, who took care of the refectory, the infirmary, and the small boys.

With the arrival of Michael's band, the hegira from Kentucky was complete. New Jesuits from various parts of the northeast and Canada would continue to dribble in for months, until by Christmas the community would number forty-seven Jesuits—sixteen priests, eighteen scholastics, and thirteen brothers. Although the record books were kept in Latin and French, English was established as the official community language. From the day of his arrival the previous spring, the rector-designate, Fr. Thebaud, had made his presence felt, though acting behind the scenes because Hughes did not want the legislature, which was about to approve St. John's charter, to know he had sold the school to Jesuits.

VIII

Thebaud, at thirty-nine, was in many ways an ideal man to guide St. John's College through the transition from local diocesan seminary and college into a Jesuit institution. Short and rotund, with a high forehead, he was a scientist and philosopher bursting with energy and with the intellectual curiosity that goaded him to explore Kentucky's Mammoth Cave and experiment with hot-air balloons. Ordained a diocesan priest in Brittany, as were several of his colleagues, he shifted to the Jesuits to become a missionary.

Arriving at St. Mary's in 1839, he first dedicated his days to learning English. Every day he read and wrote English in his room until nine or ten; then he found a silent spot in the woods by a stream where, as a scientist, he could study the crawfish, the yellow birds, bluebirds, woodpeckers, and robin redbreasts. He studied the climate, the effect of the heat on plants and persons.

He admired the handsome Kentucky men, one of whom, he said, was eight feet tall. He found it ironic that though they might have a splendid appearance, they were physically weak and died young. He saw both anti-Catholicism and slavery, which gave him much to think about. He taught physics, chemistry, and botany. He wrote books entitled *The Church and the Moral World* and *The Irish Race,* several novels, and several volumes of recollections that were published after his death. He was prudent, a practical planner, and got along well with the mercurial Bishop Hughes, who would later grumble that importing the Jesuits had been a major mistake.

Thebaud had convinced the outgoing president, Rev. James Roosevelt Bayley, to have a spring 1846 commencement ceremony, for it was the school's fifth year and this was their first graduating class. In the tradition of Kentucky hospitality, the school provided a lunch for the guests; apparently the Bronx neighbors got wind of the free food and trekked up the path, encamped on the lawn, and wandered through the college buildings and church.

So two months later, we might imagine, Thebaud, accompanied by the young diocesan seminarians who had been serving as prefects and teachers, greeted Fr. Ryan's party at the "Mansion" and led them on a brief campus tour, including a stroll over to the church, where the evening sun setting over the Hudson River shone through six new stained-glass windows. Originally the gift of Louis Philippe, whose 1830 accession to the throne had in part precipitated these Jesuits' departure from France, they had been intended for old St. Patrick's Cathedral in lower Manhattan, but they didn't fit, so Hughes moved them to the Bronx. Tagging along among the welcoming seminarians was the young Bernard McQuaid, who would become, in 1868, the first bishop of Rochester. In the words of one historian, he would be "an ironhanded diocesan autocrat, in the John Hughes chief executive officer mold of the Irish-American bishop." He was also known as a "progressive conservative," reluctant during the First Vatican Council to support the doctrine on papal infallibility.

Behind the seminary, the Corsa farm stretched to the north and east. Down the slope from the Rodrigue house, on the edge of a swamp near the railroad, sat the college pond, a rectangular body of water two hundred feet long, twenty feet wide, and three feet deep, where cattle drank, muskrats, turtles, and small fish made their homes, and from which the workmen and brothers hauled water for their kitchen and washbasins when the cisterns ran dry.

All this was Michael Nash's new home, and one in which his new superior immediately put him to work. As frequently happens in missionary territory, the missionaries had taken on a task slated to overwhelm them from the start. They were attempting to administer and staff four institutions in the same place at the same time: a diocesan seminary, a Jesuit scholasticate, a Jesuit novitiate, and, lest we forget, a college for Catholic boys from New York and, it turned out, from Latin America as well. Inevitably then, the whole house took its order and lifestyle from the novitiate, with its restrictions and spiritual obligations.

A number of boys—some of them too far from their homes in Mexico, Cuba, South America, the West Indies, and the Southern states to return, and some from Brooklyn and New York—were spending their summer vacation at Rose Hill, and Thebaud made Michael their prefect. "Without exception they were the worst boys I had ever met," Michael wrote later. "Wild boys, and reckless boys I had met in St. Joseph's and St. Mary's Colleges, and in the schools of Louisville, but they were also gentlemen, sons of families of standing in society. Those of whom I had now charge, especially the New York and Brooklyn boys, did not possess the remotest instinct of gentlemen."

McQuaid gave him some practical advice on how to manage the "indescribable set" that had fallen into his hands, and it must have helped. In September, Nash was put in charge of all their recreations. On a typical day he accompanied the boys to the refectory, monitored their behavior in the dormitory, presided at morning chapel and in the study hall, taught for two hours, and meanwhile was expected to study for his own courses in rhetoric. He was expected to be a full-time seminarian and a full-time workhorse. Like generations of Jesuit scholastics before and after him, he couldn't do it all, but he did it anyway. It was that kind of energy and total immersion in student life that for a century or so would define Fordham and many schools like it as particularly "Jesuit" institutions. When that resource—that energy—would be exhausted, they would have to take their identity from something else.

2.
A Visit from Mr. Poe

I ~

In the 1950s, on the corner of 190th Street and Webster Avenue, parallel to the old New York and Harlem Railroad (later, N.Y. Central) tracks and the Third Avenue elevated subway tracks that clattered up the western border of Fordham campus at that time, stood a bar called Poe's Raven. It was not the most popular college hangout—that was either the Decatur, two blocks up 194th on the left, or the Webster Bar and Grill, "the Web," about a block south on Webster Avenue. The Web was an "elite" hangout, because beers there cost fifteen cents rather than the ten cents up the street, and the Web was the hangout of the two student drinking clubs named for their literary heroes, the Hemingways and the Faulkners. No, they did not vie to outdrink one another, as if Papa Hemingway could put away more Rheingolds than that Southerner; it was merely a rubric for getting together and dignifying the gathering with an intellectual cover, and an excuse to talk about literature when we weren't doing our homework.

The Raven was something else. It had a back room with tables and chairs and trellised walls, as if somehow the guests were not sitting in a Bronx pub but in a European garden. The feature of the front room was the gorgeous old marble bar, which would clank when you put your glass down. The story was that this was the place where Edgar Allan Poe had written "The Raven," the one piece of literature all of us knew from either grammar school or high school. Looking around the little room, at its high ceiling and dark wood, we could well imagine this story to be true. It was also a public place that Fordham students did not control. From time to time, townies, Irish boys from up the block who did not go to college, locked wits and fists with Fordham students as they punched each other out on the street outside the Raven's swinging doors.

Occasionally on weekend afternoons, as if visiting a shrine, we climbed the hill to Kingsbridge Avenue and Poe Park, to which the original Poe cottage, the one Poe had lived in during the 1840s, had been moved. It had a rundown look. There was nothing awesome about it; it was just a neglected artifact in a neighborhood that was beginning to fade.

II ⌐

In June 1846, as the Jesuits were moving from Kentucky to Rose Hill, Edgar Allan Poe moved into a Bronx cottage. He paid one hundred dollars a month rent to John Valentine, who had paid a thousand dollars for this hilltop acre to Richard Corsa, whose family had also owned the St. John's property.

The poet found the new St. John's College, especially under the direction of the Jesuits, a most congenial place. The campus was not more than a twenty-minute walk down the hill from the sparsely settled neighborhood where he and his ailing wife, Virginia, along with Virginia's mother, Mrs. Maria Clemm, had settled into a small, white three-room cottage in the Kingsbridge section.

Poe was thirty-seven, just over five feet tall, about 110 pounds, pale and thin, with thin hair, a balloonlike head, watery eyes, and a tongue that tended to protrude when he spoke. He was also desperate and starving. Virginia, twenty-four, tiny and frail, with dark hair and big dark eyes, was dying of tuberculosis. Her mother, tall, strong, and resourceful, lived in a tiny room upstairs and seemed to be the main force holding the household together. Poe, often laid low by his own illnesses, struggled to compose what he considered his masterpiece, a "spiritual testament," the long prose poem *Eureka,* while pacing up and down the cottage floor and corresponding with editors in an attempt to sell his shorter works.

Literary friends brought them food and clothing. One visitor found the cottage simple and immaculate, surrounded by cherry trees, and high enough to overlook the lovely grounds of St. John's College at the foot of the hill. The poet was in a good mood. He had just received a letter from Elizabeth Barrett Browning, who informed him that his new poem, "The Raven," had filled its London readers with terror, and he had just captured a bobolink. He had put it in a cage and was determined to domesticate it and enjoy its "bell-like" songs.

The good mood did not last. Virginia died January 30, 1847. They laid her out in a white dress in a coffin on the writing stand between the living-room windows, and then Poe, wearing his old West Point military cloak, and the mourners bore the casket that bleak, winter day to the Valentines' vault in the Old Dutch Reformed Church. As the weeks went by, Poe was trapped in the cottage with his protective mother-in-law and haunted by memories of his dead wife. Some nights neighbors found him in the churchyard, covered with snow and moaning outside Virginia's tomb.

Eventually he found solace in long walks. At four in the morning, he would stroll west to the aqueduct bridge, High Bridge, whose granite arches, 145 feet high, stretched across the Harlem River. Often Poe escaped to St. John's.

Passing no more than a few dozen houses and farms along the way, he could saunter down the gradual slope of what is now Kingsbridge Road, which then extended to the New York and Harlem railroad tracks. Past the train stop, it became long, straight Union Avenue—later called Pelham Avenue and, later still, East Fordham Road. There, depending on how he felt, he would stop off at the bar of the Old Fordham Hotel, pick up his mail, and have a drink. If the hotel did not distract him, he would continue on to St. John's.

To a degree not fully understood in his time, Poe suffered from depression, an illness aggravated by alcohol. Usually, Poe could stay sober for long periods of time, but sometimes only one drink could throw him into an uncontrollable mood. If he stayed too long at the hotel, a neighbor would take him by the arm and, on winter nights, guide him through the snow up the hill to his cottage home.

Once past the hotel, he crossed the tracks and, like the arriving Jesuits a few years before, turned left (north) through the college gate and went up the path that encircled the great lawn, right to the stone mansion's front door.

When Poe came in the early evening, around six, he arrived in time for the Angelus. The great bells in the tower of the college church, which also served as the local Our Lady of Mercy parish, rung out in the traditional prayer: "The Angel of the Lord appeared unto Mary, and she was conceived of the Holy Ghost." *Bongbongbong—Bongbongbong—Bongbongbong!* With the bell tower just a few yards away, he would not just hear the bells but also feel their vibrations as their tolling fled the tower and sent some trembling shivers through his fragile frame. A glass of wine with the fathers would calm his nerves.

There's a large bell in the Fordham archives that once hung in the church and that, tradition says, inspired Poe's famous poem "The Bells." Unfortunately for the tradition, contemporaries and scholars have a list of competing churches, such as the Church of the Ascension and Grace Church, in lower Manhattan near the house of Poe's friend Mrs. Schew, who claims he wrote the first two verses there. According to another tradition, this bell hung in the cupola of the mansion and called students to class and meals.

Poe liked the Jesuits, as he told a friend, because they were "highly cultivated gentlemen and scholars, they smoked and they drank, and played cards, and never said a word about religion." His favorites were the learned and versatile president Auguste J. Thebaud and a young Canadian, Edward Doucet, who, even though a twenty-three-year-old scholastic and dormitory prefect at the time of Poe's visits, somehow became the lonely poet's spiritual confidant. Why would Poe unburden himself to this much younger man? Probably because the gentle Doucet had at twenty-three the same personal qualities that in later years made him well known as a counselor and confessor—discretion, a straightforward manner, and enormous sympathy. The Jesuits had witnessed Poe's ordeal and had seen him dragging himself home from New York, sometimes at the edge of despair, having failed to sell a manuscript. He had poured some of his sorrow into his poem "Annabel Lee." Some he shared with Doucet as they walked around the college grounds—which were then much larger and graced with hills, woods, and rock formations—and conversed in French.

After their walks, the fathers turned Poe loose in their library, where he sometimes lingered so late they would offer him a bed for the night. If—and this happened only rarely—he joined the fathers in a glass of wine and his symptoms began to appear, someone would gently offer an arm and say, "Come, Poe, we will go home now."

III ⌐

By the time of Poe's visits, St. John's was fairly well established, although the community had gone through a series of major and minor growing pains in its first two years.

The questions of which and how many Jesuits constituted the original founding fathers—the Jesuits who launched the college-seminary in its first and second years—are like the question of who constituted the famous football Seven Blocks of Granite in the 1930s, when, with Vince Lombardi on the team, Fordham was briefly a football power. With replacements, the "seven" became "ten," depending on who measured what and when. Fr. Robert I. Gannon's *Up to the Present* (1967) records that twenty-eight Jesuits (twelve priests, eleven brothers, and five scholastics) made the move from Kentucky to New York. By the end of 1846 there were fifty-three Jesuits in the community. Fr. Thomas Hennessy calculates (1997) that by fall 1846, there were forty-seven Jesuits on board. Of these, twenty-five were working at St. John's College, and eighteen of these had come up from Kentucky.

Of the others, some were community-support men, or seminarians in their studies; some were, in a sense, missionaries, using Fordham as a springboard or, in medieval terms, as a monastery from which they could sally forth on missionary expeditions, get toeholds in New York, and found parishes and even another college. Of the twenty-five, fifteen were faculty or administrators and ten helped with other work. The seminarians, such as Michael Nash, did double duty—their own studies plus dormitory and study hall proctoring. Of the original forty-seven, six left the Society—not an exceptionally high dropout rate considering the hardships of the life, the inherent instability of a mixed-culture community where members were constantly coming and going, and the temptations and opportunities offered by that bustling city ten miles to the south. Of the remaining forty-one, nineteen were French, eleven Irish, six Canadian, three German, and only three American, with one each from England, Spain, Belgium, Haiti, and Czechoslovakia.

Though French was the native language of the great majority, following the Jesuit rule that the official language of the house must be the language of the country meant that table readings and recreational conversation were supposed to be in English. Until the 1870s, however, the fathers kept their official house diaries in French or Latin, and whatever the rule, we can easily imagine them reverting to French among themselves. Friendship groups form naturally on the basis of one's native tongue.

We can also guess something of the tone of their community life from their relative youth. The average age of the faculty was thirty-eight, and of the nonfaculty, forty-eight. Several who had transferred to the Jesuits from the diocesan priesthood had been Jesuits for only a few years, and some who had been recently ordained had not yet taken their final vows. Also, although the proximity of young seminarians can throw a damper on community life if the older members are forced to conform to a restrictive seminary-like lifestyle, the campus atmosphere—especially with 150 or so boys running around—must have exuded life and energy. Above all, there was the pioneer spirit, the excitement of founding something new that would perhaps last for centuries.

Within the original group, four administrators, who also worked as classroom teachers, made the early decisions that set St. John's on its course.

Thebaud, in addition to his wonderful curiosity and natural scientist's keen powers of observation, also had the historian's sense to see himself and his enterprise in the larger context of the events of his time. Like his countryman de Tocqueville, he observed everything in his surroundings and kept notes on all he saw. He saw St. John's College in relation to New York, which had grown spectacularly as a business and political center since he had first walked up Broadway in 1838, and in relation to the flood of Irish immigrants changing the religious and economic face of the city. He was also convinced from his experiences in the South that although the more educated upper class in the Northeast was becoming more tolerant, Protestants didn't like Catholics, and religious leaders in his position could not be shy in fighting back against bigotry from the pulpit or in public print. Meanwhile, he also taught botany and led his students through the fields and forests that now constitute the New York Botanical Garden, naming and describing every weed, flower, shrub, and herb to his awestruck boys.

Fr. Clement Boulanger, S.J., who had been provincial superior of the newly restored Jesuits in France from 1842 to 1845, came to America as the Jesuit general's official visitor in 1845 and was the man who initially sealed the deal with Hughes to buy Fordham for $40,000. In 1846, at the age of fifty-five, he set himself up at Fordham, made it the headquarters for the New York–Canada Mission, and became a professor of moral theology.

When young William Stack Murphy's uncle, the bishop of Cork, refused to let him join the Jesuits because he had "other plans" for him, William moved to France, went to a Jesuit school, and joined the Society there in 1823. Sent to the American missions, he arrived at St. Mary's in Kentucky in 1836, became dean and president-rector, and moved to Fordham in April 1846 as the other half of Fr. Thebaud's advance guard. Even at forty-three, his hair was perfectly white, and his thin, spare frame and thoughtful eyes heightened by glasses gave him the look of an intellectual. He spoke French, Spanish, Irish, and Italian, taught Greek and Hebrew, and spoke English without a trace of an Irish brogue. Both Fordham and the Society of Jesus continually moved him in and out of administrative posts, including a period in the early 1850s in St. Louis, where he was sent to control and direct the expansion of St. Louis University. But he suffered from a chronic dyspepsia that from time to time forced him to give up leadership or teaching positions.

Father John Larkin, S.J., though he was at Fordham only four years—1846–47 as dean and 1851–54 as president—was the kind of outstanding character whom students remember because of the force of his presence and personality. A lot of his reputation was due to his appearance: he was strikingly handsome, with a big head of brown, silky, wavy hair and a resounding voice, and he was huge, weighing in at over three hundred pounds. John R. G. Hassard, who was a student while Larkin was president, recalled that no man could speak of Larkin "without a quickening pulse." He wrote in *The Fordham Monthly* (December 1886), "A great many of the Jesuits were fine-looking men, but none of us had ever seen just such a type of masculine beauty as this big, rosy Englishman. . . . Although his face was too full, the exquisite outlines of his classical features were preserved: he had the mouth of a young Greek god; in his eye there was a singular union of mildness and penetration."

Reading between the lines of documents from the 1850s, we can see that—as any twentieth-century alumnus could testify—not all the students loved all the Jesuits all the time. But Hassard, writing many years later, recalls the skill with which Larkin the rhetorician could play with inflections of the language to achieve a special effect. Most of all, he remembers Larkin's good humor. Though strict, he allowed boys to have fun. Above all, he took time out of rhetoric class to talk about life. He molded character. Years later, one of his former students, dying of consumption, was consoled by the prospect of seeing Fr. Larkin in heaven.

Where had Larkin come from? Born in Ravensworth, County Durham, England, in 1801, son of an Irish innkeeper, he was educated at Ushaw College. When Ushaw authorities judged him not suited for the priesthood, he went off to sea at the age of fifteen, sailing to Hindustan and other eastern ports. Soon fed up with the seafaring life, he went into business in London, where he caught the eye of the bishop of Mauritius, who, struck by his good looks and manners, appointed him his secretary and took him home with him. After a few years on that distant island, young Larkin sailed to Europe, where he entered the Sulpician seminary in Paris, joined that religious order, was transferred to America, and was ordained in Baltimore in 1827. Sent to Montreal College, he taught Latin, Greek, and philosophy with perhaps too much success, in that, by 1832, the bishop of Upper Canada was seeking to name Larkin his coadjutor. Larkin wormed his way out of the appointment by claiming he was unfit.

In 1839, Larkin seized upon the retreat given by Fr. Pierre Chazelle, superior of the Jesuit Mission in Kentucky, to join the Society of Jesus, along with the seminarian William Gockeln, who also became a Fordham founder and president. In Kentucky, Larkin became headmaster of a small, short-lived Jesuit school and gained a wide reputation as a preacher. According to one story, in 1843 when ex-President John Quincy Adams suddenly canceled his address to the Louisville Mercantile Library Association, Larkin filled in for him with a lengthy oration on genius. Clearly, here was a talent made for New York.

Whatever Larkin's bulk, he and Thebaud moved quickly to size up St. John's academic situation and prepare some reforms. Thebaud had no illusions about the quality of education that American Catholic colleges had been offering. He considered St. Mary's, from which he had just come, as little better than a grammar school. There and at other schools, men taught who had no idea how to teach, partly because Catholics had not been allowed to open schools for many years in the colonies and because seminarians were forced to teach while undergoing their own training in philosophy and theology.

For one year, Thebaud and Larkin left the old system in place and watched it operate. Thebaud had been told it was an exact duplication of the system at Emmitsburg, where both Bishop Hughes and Rev. Harley, St. John's most recent president, had been educated. It was also chaotic. So many teachers were trying to teach so many things to students at various stages of development that the boys could get no continuity in their education. Shuttled from one class to another every forty-five minutes, no one teacher had time to get to know the students or care about them individually.

By January 1847, the Jesuits decided that to obtain the bachelor of arts degree, a boy would have to be able to read with ease the works of Cicero or Livy, Virgil or Horace, and Demosthenes or Homer, and to pass exams in arithmetic, algebra, geometry, and trigonometry. And rather than have each professor teach one branch of study, one teacher would teach all the liberal arts to his class for a year, and the boys would move less often.

Finally, the St. John's standard curriculum was replaced by one borrowed from the Georgetown catalog and based on the traditional Jesuit *Ratio Studiorum* originally published in 1599. The *Ratio,* in Thebaud's scheme, was not a dead letter from the sixteenth century, but a dynamic document, revised each generation by Jesuit general congregations. It is basically a list of very practical pedagogical rules, some of which Fordham professors still stress today. For example:

- Pray to God for knowledge; but meanwhile study as if he would not grant your prayer without hard, studious effort on your part.

- Distribute your day into hours, so as to have a definite time for your tasks.

- Interrupt long and difficult study with some healthy recreation.

- Do not be tardy for class, nor go to it like a slave driven to the mill, but arrive early if possible so as to be ready and eager to begin the day's work.

- After leaving the classroom, do not immediately banish all thought of the day's lessons, but ruminate over them or discuss them with your fellow students.

- Do not limit your efforts to prescribed study; with the teacher's counsel you can easily undertake further work of reading, writing, and memorizing.

By 1839, the Georgetown fathers had established a *Ratio*-based structure that, with some variations, would hold in American Jesuit schools till the end of the century. The junior division lasted four years and included grammar and Latin. The senior division of poetry (humanities), rhetoric, and philosophy lasted three years. Completion of these earned an undergraduate degree. A second year of philosophy merited a master of arts. Fordham's French fathers, however, called the humanities "Belles Lettres" and required more French courses. They also continued the "commercial" track, the nineteenth-century precursor to the business school, as an alternative to the Latin-based classical curriculum. By the Civil War, 23 percent of Fordham students were in the commercial course; by 1881, 38 percent.

Throughout the adaptations, philosophy was supposed to remain the crown of a boy's education with five lectures a week, each lecture consisting of an hour and a half in the morning and another hour in the afternoon. Supposedly, these lectures were presented in Latin. According to the catalog, the philosophy year included semipublic disputations in which students debated the important questions in the presence of the faculty, but several realities forced them to retreat from these standards. First, few students stayed the full seven years that would bring them to this intellectual climax. Second, few transfer students could handle the Latin, and remedial courses could not bring them up to snuff. Finally, as more students flowed in from Latin America, a sizable portion of the student body didn't know English, much less Latin. When we reflect on the phenomenon that some of the Jesuits had not mastered English either, we can only speculate on the level of communication at early Fordham.

IV

What was the underlying essence of the education that the first generation of Fordham Jesuits tried to instill?

John O'Malley, S.J., in a chapter of *The First Jesuits* (1993) on the 1548 founding of the first Jesuit school in Messina, Italy, lists ten characteristics that seem to account for the initial success of what became an international Jesuit system of education.

1. The schools, because they were endowed, charged no tuition.

2. They welcomed students from every social class.

3. The curriculum stressed character formation.

4. The Jesuits saw "humanism" and Thomistic theology as compatible.

5. The curriculum made students progress in an orderly fashion from class to class.

6. Learning had to be active: students had to write, speak, recite, debate, and put on shows.

7. The religious program moved students from pious practice to an inner appropriation of spiritual values.

8. To instill a deeper spirituality they adopted the confraternity —a spiritual club—or a sodality.

9. They applied these principles to their international network, but adapted to local customs.

10. Jesuits loved their students, knew them as individuals, and tried to influence them by example rather than by words.

Though steeped in these international principles, Fordham's main influence was, in a word, French. But one word is not enough. These principles were in some ways quickly and in others only gradually adapted to America in Kentucky and New York. The curriculum and, above all, the spirit of early Fordham were derived from the Jesuit colleges in France that flourished between the restoration of the Society in 1815 and their suppression by an anticlerical French government in 1880.

If this seems like a long time ago and remote from or irrelevant to contemporary Jesuit higher education, the reminiscences of anyone who attended a Jesuit prep school such as St. Joseph's Prep in Philadelphia or St. Peter's Prep in Jersey City in the 1940s, or Fordham College in the 1950s, or an old Jesuit novitiate such as St. Andrew-on-Hudson in the late 1950s prior to the influence of Vatican II would instantly recognize the transplanted mid-nineteenth-century French regime.

First, immediately following the restoration, the French colleges were not colleges, strictly speaking, but minor seminaries sponsored by the local bishop with the hope that the young men would become the vanguard of a new French clergy who would reevangelize what had become, since the Revolution, an overwhelmingly secular society. In actuality, they were boarding schools for upper-class Catholic boys, most of whom had no intention of becoming priests. Their parents, however, agreed with the French hierarchy and the Jesuits that only religious schools would save their youth and

Christian France from the corrupting influence of both the teachers and the pupils in state schools.

As a result, there is an element of "crisis," of an embattled stance, in Jesuit education from the beginning. So many of the courses—particularly philosophy and history, as well as religion—were geared to demonstrating the ultimate truth of Christianity and the errors of its adversaries, from Rousseau and Voltaire in the eighteenth century to John Dewey in the mid-twentieth. For Auguste Thebaud, a principal adversary was Thomas Paine, whose *Age of Reason* was the gospel of American atheism, and as Thebaud traveled through nineteenth-century America, he measured the religious atmosphere by gauging Paine's lingering influence.

A graduate from 1849, writing in 1891, remembers Fr. Isidore Daubresse—who had been assigned in 1846, at the age of thirty-six, to teach theology in the seminary—as someone who had looked more deeply into the problems of life "than we could ever hope to" and had then deliberately become a saint. He was both kind and inflexible. His true majesty asserted itself in "condemning false theologians in the classroom." "Truth, absolute truth, must be the student's standard—he must find it, look at it in the daylight, live by it and die by it," said alumnus H. H. Dodge fifty years after the classroom experience.

With a similar goal, but in a different spirit, a Fordham Jesuit ethics professor in 1955, cramming in a list of previously unmentioned "adversaries" in the last days of the semester, would tick them off, with about ten minutes on each, and conclude, "So much for Thomas Hobbes." Yet this professor, Edward McNally, S.J., was revered by his students because, whatever his certitudes, his sharp mind did not shrink from ambiguity. His best students would press him with moral dilemmas—partly to get his answers but also to watch his mind work on new material. One day a student asked whether it was "licit for a Catholic movie actor to play the role of a rapist." Fr. McNally's brother, Stephen McNally, had in fact just played a rapist in the film *Johnny Belinda*. He replied, "You may leave the room."

Whatever the ambiguities of their status, the French schools that were the original models for the American schools fulfilled their seminary role fairly well: an average of about one-fifth of the graduates went on to become priests. In that spirit, for many years, until the precipitous drop in vocations in the mid-1960s, the cream of the graduating classes of American Jesuit high schools often joined the Society, and for many years during the nineteenth century, Fordham proudly published the list of graduates who became priests and Jesuits. Indeed, one of the students from 1846 became a Fordham president.

Second, because the French colleges were seminaries and wanted to seize the boy in childhood, the course of studies, compared to today's colleges, was very long—from seven to ten years, with the youngest students in France being from seven to ten years old. The practical result of the long course of studies and the different economic conditions of the American context, though the youngest students were a little older at both Kentucky and Fordham, was a heavy turnover and a considerable age span among the students.

There is plenty of evidence that early Fordham students, who were strictly supervised, were not always happy, and few restless young Americans wanted to spend all their youthful years in rustic Westchester. The system also called for another form of enforced segregation within the student body. Though boarders and day students took the same classes, they were kept apart during recreation, lest the day students corrupt the boarders, many of whom were from Southern states and from Latin America, with their city ways. The different age groups lived in separate dormitories and swam in separate swimming spots on the Bronx River bank. We can imagine that this rigid separation—similar to the separation of novices and juniors in Jesuit seminaries—must have been hard to enforce when everyone lived within a few yards of one another, within a half-dozen buildings, on this isolated campus with its farm and woods.

Of the subjects taught—Latin, Greek, grammar, literature, rhetoric, philosophy, history, geography, mathematics, and religion—although philosophy was the crown, Latin was officially considered the most important. In *Colleges in Controversy: The Jesuit Schools in France from Revival to Suppression, 1815–1880* (1969), John Padberg, S.J., explains why Latin was at the heart of French Jesuit nineteenth-century educational philosophy.

> It meant for them, first, the adamantine conviction that the Latin
> and Greek literature of classical antiquity presented universal

values for human development. The moral values developed
by antiquity were, they maintained, radically incomplete
and inadequate in themselves, and needed the advent of
Christianity for their completion. But the literary and artistic
values of classical culture presented fixed and immutable
standards of the highest perfection. By long and intimate
contact with those masterpieces of the human spirit, and
through them with the classical culture in which those values
were embodied, students were ideally to acquire for themselves
personal but objective standards by which to appraise, to
accept or reject, works of literature or art (169).

This insistence on Latin held until the pre-Vatican II mid-
twentieth century. In effect, Latin was an endurance test, a rite of
passage to manhood for boys between the ages of seven and seventeen.
Its justification evolved in attempts to satisfy each new generation of
restless schoolboys: Latin exercised the muscles of the mind; knowing
Latin made other languages come easily; Latin was fun; Latin is
useful when you go to Rome and have to read inscriptions on ancient
monuments. An unexpressed though likely reason for keeping it in its
honored place was that Latin was, after all, the language of the liturgy
and the Roman Church, and the "best" Jesuit graduates would need it
in the seminary.

Again, although Latin was supposed to be the spoken language of
the classroom, particularly in philosophy—as it was in Jesuit seminaries
until the 1960s—it is hard to determine how much this was so.
Memoirists in the student magazine, the *Monthly* in the 1890s like to
pepper their sentimental essays with Latin phrases, but they never
reminisce about talking Latin in class, which should have been a
memorable experience. In effect, by the later part of the century, since
the commercial course was taught in English, it's hard to imagine the
other courses holding the line.

Third, the distinctive Jesuit teaching method stressed logic and
rhetoric, *eloquentia perfecta,* the ability to express oneself in and outside
the classroom; emulation, competition for prizes, rank, and public
recognition in both sports and academics; imitation, development of
a literary style by copying the style of the masters; and the prelection,
wherein the teacher devoted the last part of the class period to a

preview of the next day's assignment. He not only explained the Latin text of, for example, Cicero's *De Amicitia* but actually led the class through much of the translation, pointing out the ablative absolutes and filling in biographical material on Cicero. The alert boy furiously scribbled down the prelection and began his homework with a head start, knowing he would be called upon to recite and explain the text at 8:00 the next morning. When the Fordham campus included what is now part of the Bronx Botanical Gardens, the professors took their students into the hills and valleys of the countryside to exercise their lungs and vocal chords as they declaimed their adolescent masterpieces to the rocks and trees.

Fourth, although religion was taught formally only twice a week, religious faith permeated every aspect of the students' lives. The theory was that moral training took place, not in the classroom, but through the controlled atmosphere of the institution. Attendance at daily Mass was required of all students at Jesuit institutions until the late 1950s. The Sodality of the Blessed Virgin Mary, traditionally one of the first student clubs established at Jesuit schools, set apart, often by invitation, an elite group of young men to receive more intensive spiritual development through retreats, meditation, and the daily examination of conscience.

Often this device would bring the school's natural leaders under more direct and personal Jesuit influence. In the 1950s, for example, the Fordham sodality prefect was for a brief time a scholastic, Avery Dulles, S.J., son of John Foster Dulles, President Eisenhower's secretary of state. Some of the sodality members were also leaders of the liberal-leaning National Federation of Catholic College Students, the Association of Catholic Trade Unionists, and the Fordham Young Democrats.

Furthermore, from the beginning, nearly all the teachers were Jesuits, whether they were prepared to teach or not. William Rodrigue taught drawing, penmanship, and civil engineering through the 1850s. However, one of the Jesuits' first decisions, after a year, was to fire a layman, Mr. Stallo, a teacher of chemistry and physics, who was also a "secular infidel." Thus, all the role models—a term not yet invented in 1846—for the boys were celibate men in long black robes, all with their individual quirks and idiosyncrasies as well as talents and virtues.

Corporal punishment was common in schools throughout the country. To allow the Jesuits to appear as often as possible in positive roles, the Society's policy forbad Jesuits to administer corporal punishment but hired laymen to whip the boys who broke the rules. This, like other wise policies, wasn't always followed, and in one case the general of the Society had to intervene and sanction French Jesuits who applied the rod. Students visiting the old Jesuit graveyard in the 1880s paused over the grave of Fr. Fitzpatrick, who had been a Fordham student before joining the Society. They remember him because as "First Prefect of the First Division in stormy times," he often administered the "old strap." Fordham Jesuits beat students in the earliest years, and as this is written, there are Fordham alumni still living who recall having to bend over and submit to a father's whip. Many will laugh and say they deserved it; some will not.

Fifth, the Jesuit school was modeled on the family. When Fr. Laurence J. McGinley, S.J., president from 1949 to 1963, addressed an assembly in his rich, cultivated baritone as "members of the Fordham family," he was not indulging in Jesuit rhetoric, but expressing a commitment to a century-old tradition. The rector-president, for better or worse, was the father of both the Jesuit community and the students. His leadership style would depend on his personality, but he was as personally responsible for the lives of his subjects as was a parent. This responsibility for personal care—called *cura personalis*—flowed through his administration and faculty, down through the seminarians who, besides studying their own philosophy, lived in the dormitories and served as ever-present surveillants of the students' lives.

The seminarians' role was complex: they were instructors, tutors, watchdogs, disciplinarians, spiritual mentors, and friends. At the same time, they were human beings of limited experience, understandably not always up to the tasks imposed on them. The French writer Hippolyte Taine, in *Carnets de voyage: Notes sur la province, 1863–1865* (1897), explains why his friends send their sons to the Jesuit school at Metz. Because it is "stylish," "because good contacts are made there," and because "the Fathers makes themselves comrades of the students, while [in the Lycee] the professor is cold and the surveillant is an enemy. . . . They gain the friendship of the students, become their comrades, walk around with them arm in arm on the playing fields during recreation, etc. The children love them and once grown up, they come back to see them."

But young Jesuits often broke under the workload. John Padberg, S.J., recounts the example of one, Paul Brucker, at Metz in 1865. He was proctor for ninety students in the study hall, dormitory, recreation grounds, chapel, and afternoon walks; he taught history to seventy-five, and German to forty-five. In April he collapsed. The doctor said, "Well, he is simply at the end of his rope, this young man. Make him sleep for a week."

V ⁓

Even though St. John's had only four students ready to graduate in July 1847—Thomas Dolan, Andrew Smith, S. M. Rosecrans, and P. McCarron—Thebaud and Larkin decided to make a big show of it. The New York and Harlem Railroad obliged them by running an extra 1:00 P.M. six-car train to transport the New York crowds to the event. Rosecrans, future bishop and brother of the Civil War general, was a Thebaud favorite. He had converted to Catholicism before coming to St. John's, and his decision to become a priest convinced Thebaud, an admirer of the American convert-journalist-philosopher Orestes Brownson, that America might actually raise up a clergy to support a truly American—as opposed to immigrant—church.

Over two thousand guests—including politicians, army officers, and, according to the *New York Herald* (July 16), "hundreds of pretty girls, beautiful young ladies, and good-looking matrons"—gathered under a huge tent set up on the lawn in front of what is now St. John's Hall. Archbishop Hughes, Thebaud, Larkin, Murphy, and others looked on as a brilliant student named Charles DeBull delivered a formal oration. Other students spoke on Russian history, Daniel O'Connell, and chivalry. Finally Larkin, in prose as rotund as his girth, solemnly admonished the graduates that in receiving their degrees they receive them not from St. John's but from the Republic. Therefore "they should show themselves on all occasions, in word and deed, friends of law and order, defenders of truth and justice, supporters of sound morality."

For the time being, these were Larkin's last words to Fordham. Since their arrival, the Fordham fathers, once they had finished their classes, had been looking for work and opportunities in the city, and though Fordham was barely off the ground, they felt ready to establish a new parish and college downtown, a day school that would reach those sons of the best families in Brooklyn, New York, and New Jersey who declined to board at Rose Hill. So Larkin was dispatched—as he often told the story—with only fifty cents in his pocket: twenty for his one-way train fare, twenty-five to ship his trunk, and five to found a school.

He begged and borrowed $18,000 to purchase an abandoned Universalist church and house on Elizabeth Street near Walker Street, renovated the basement into six classrooms, and hired an artist who had given him $5,000 for safekeeping to paint murals on the walls and ceiling. By September, he had assembled a Jesuit community of four priests, three scholastics, and one brother, including young Michael Nash, who in his reminiscences leaves no hardship unrecorded.

For a while they lived without furniture or cooking utensils and on bread and water unless a kind neighbor brought them some meat. When Michael arrived in September they had finally bought beds, and breakfast had improved to bread and coffee, but without butter or milk. But the school opened in October 1847 with 120 students. Parishioners flocked to the church to admire the murals and be uplifted by Larkin's oratory, and the fathers heard confessions morning and night, until they dropped from exhaustion.

In November, Nash was laid low for eight days with fever and spent another eight days recuperating in Astoria and at Fordham. Two lay brothers responsible for feeding the group abandoned the community in despair.

When the house and church-school burned down in January 1848, Larkin refused Boulanger's directive to return to Fordham to recoup. He announced, to stunned followers, who thought the tragedy had unhinged his mind, that the school would reopen the next day at St. James's Church, the parish of a former Jesuit priest, Fr. Smith, who had turned his back on the Society but would now come to their aid.

At St. James's the band again drove themselves to exhaustion. "Only God and those who have experienced it know how hard a life it was!" wrote Nash. Yet, though they arrived at work drenched with rain and taught all day in wet clothes, they did not get sick that winter. Father Smith, however, worn down with fund-raising for his Jesuit comrades, collapsed and died. His successor, caring for the sick, contracted typhus and perished also. The effort to found this new college was becoming a complicated mess.

On June 1, 1848, in the midst of their ordeal, Nash answered the door to find there three priests and four brothers who had just arrived, after a month at sea, from France, desperate for rest and food. Nash gave them beer, which they had apparently never tasted before. One of the new missionaries was Brother Julius Mace, an accomplished musician who had studied piano at the Paris Conservatory, attracting the attention of the composer Louis Gottschalk, until some bitter disappointment led him to join the Society. He had come to New York in search of humble obscurity. Having arrived, he immediately wandered out into the city and got lost—till he arrived at Fordham, seventeen miles away, late at night. Brother Mace stayed there until he died fifty years later. He taught music and played the organ, during which he often fell asleep, scoured pots in the scullery, and chopped wood. His fingers grew stiff and his various illnesses bent him almost double, but he never complained.

The brilliant Larkin, meanwhile, was determined to use every skill he had to pull his project out of the hole. Because of his eloquence and his imposing presence, Larkin was a most talented fund-raiser. One day in the Jesuit dining room he proclaimed "Deo Gratias"—permission to speak during their otherwise silent meals—pulled two apples out of his pockets, and regaled his brothers with a tale of how an old woman selling apples on the Bowery had stopped him on the street.

"The Lord be praised!" she cried out. "Oh, Father," she said, "if I had some money to give you! But I am a poor widow with five children whom I must support by my apples. Something I can give and I hope will have all the blessings of the widow's mite. You must take the two finest apples in my basket." With stories like this, Larkin was becoming a phenomenon. Within a week he raised $6,000 to rebuild the burned-out church, only to discover that Bishop Hughes had decreed that no one in New York, with the exception of the Sisters of Mercy, was to collect alms.

Larkin, it seemed, wanted a church where the Jesuits could preach and hear confessions (i.e., have opportunities for influence) without the responsibilities of a parish (i. e., the marriages, baptisms, funerals, and paperwork), the often dull, routine work that is the basis of the church's sacramental life but that ties the priests down to the local neighborhood and, shall we say, cramps their style.

Tension between the Jesuits and their original sponsor had already begun to form. The good Fr. Smith had, before his death, gained Hughes's permission for one special collection throughout the city on behalf of the Jesuits, at which Smith himself would preach. When the day for the collection came, Smith had already passed away, so Larkin himself mounted the pulpit. It had been Fr. Smith's last wish, he intoned, that the parishioners should give alms generously with the hope of releasing Smith's suffering soul from the pains of purgatory. As Nash remembers the day, "The impression was great. The idea of his being yet in pain, and the thought of their being able to release him produced such an effect that the father had to cease his sermon. The alms were abundant—our reputation again rose."

This was part of the problem. Larkin's successor, Fr. John Ryan, selected a new site, the center of a block between 15th and 16th Streets and 5th and 6th Avenues, for a church and school and, with Nash in tow, called on Hughes in order to accept Hughes's conditions. The Jesuits would not staff their parish with more fathers than the other churches of the diocese. Nor would the church have more confessionals. If they had more priests, they would also have had more time to prepare their sermons and thus embarrass Hughes's parish priests who were less educated and already overworked. Furthermore, said Hughes, he didn't want the church called the "Holy Name," because that was reminiscent of the "Gesu," the baroque Jesuit church in Rome that, in Hughes's mind, was "outshining St. Peter's." They should name it after a Jesuit saint—like St. Francis Xavier.

Ground was broken in July 1849 for the College of St. Francis Xavier, and the architect was William Rodrigue.

Larkin, meanwhile, was in Europe. There was something about the way he carried himself that made his colleagues think Larkin was bound to be a bishop. The bishops of Canada remembered him well from his years in Montreal, and when the bishop of Toronto died, they unanimously nominated him for the position in January 1848, partly because he was English. Although a document arrived from Rome in February 1849 appointing him, Larkin fought it with all his energy. There were too few English-speaking Jesuits in New York, he argued, for him to be spared. In Europe, he convinced Jesuit superiors to beg the pope to excuse him. He remained in England, preaching and doing his tertianship—the final period of Jesuit spiritual formation preceding final vows—until called back to New York to become president of Fordham in 1851.

Michael Nash, meanwhile, having played his part in founding Xavier, returned to Fordham in 1852 to begin his philosophical studies and, inevitably, to slave away as a prefect during student recreations, in the refectory, and in the dormitory. He survived to begin his theology in September 1855, but by July 1856 he was so broken down that the college physician diagnosed him as suffering from consumption and predicted that he could not live another year. They sent him to France to die.

3.

Brownson, Hughes, and Shaw

Little Robert Gould Shaw is mad. He's a fiery, precocious, head-strong young fellow with, at thirteen, a strong sense of right and wrong—particularly when he feels that he himself has been wronged. This October 20, 1850, he's sitting in the St. John's College study hall, his head down over his work, writing the obligatory weekly letter to his mother. All the other boys are fooling around: they're stamping their feet and letting out those whoops and yells that boys know make the prefect mad, especially when the prefect is a young and nervous Jesuit without the force of personality that intimidates bad boys. The other boys are being bad and Robert is going to be blamed.

Worst of all, Robert hates Fordham, as St. John's was commonly called from the earliest days. The son of a very wealthy Boston Protestant family, he is stuck in the Bronx because his uncle, Coolidge Shaw, who had converted to Catholicism and joined the Jesuits, had talked his parents, Francis and Sarah, into sending him here. The family could easily afford the $200 tuition that St. John's was now charging (though the average laborer's wage at the time was about $300 a year), so they delivered Robert in June with all the equipment the catalog prescribed: three winter and three summer suits, six shirts, six pairs of pants, six pairs of stockings, six handkerchiefs, six ties, three pairs of shoes or boots, a hat and overcoat, a silver spoon, and a drinking cup marked with his name.

He has 114 fellow students, some of them—the well-behaved ones—seminarians from St. Joseph's, and many from the deep South and Latin America. They all live under a French and Victorian disciplinary system calculated to protect their virtue and, as a by-product, instill resentment as well. No one may leave the grounds without a prefect. Parents from the New York area may visit only once in three months and are warned to make their visits as rare as possible. Mail from persons other than the student's parents may be opened by school administrators; books, papers, and periodicals other than those approved by the Jesuits are forbidden. There is a Christmas vacation, but no spring or Easter break.

Years later, many students from the same time will remember St. John's fondly—the long walks on the beautiful, wooded grounds, swimming in the nearby Bronx River, skating on the campus ponds in winter, and the games of handball, cricket, and an early form of baseball called rounders. Robert is not one of them. His first letter home, June 3, 1850, says plainly, "I wish I hadn't been sent here at all. . . . I'm sure I shan't want to come here after vacation, for I hate it like everything." The other boys broke the bridge and strings of his beloved violin. A neighbor's farm dog attacked him as he returned to the campus from an excursion to New York to meet his mother. He abhors the thought of being whipped, especially when the punishment is unjust, and he often dreams of running away, inspired by a classmate who ran away and got a job working on a Hudson River sloop for a month. Sometimes Robert's homesickness makes him break down and cry in front of the other boys, many of whom he despises because they are lazy, and when they don't do their homework, the teacher blames and chastises the whole class. Nothing angers Robert more than being punished for something he didn't do.

So today, when he asks the prefect's permission to leave the room and the prefect replies, "Go and don't come back," Robert is indignant. He didn't do anything and he's being thrown out. Wandering the corridors, he bumps into Fr. Thebaud, who asks why he isn't in class and sends him back to the study hall. The prefect, feeling his authority has been challenged or that Robert is lying, sends Robert back to Thebaud for a note. Thebaud is not in his office, but Robert encounters him on the grounds. See Fr. Regnier, says Thebaud, for the note.

August Regnier came to Fordham in 1846 as a twenty-six-year-old theology student, was ordained the following year, and is now prefect of discipline. When Robert walks in, Regnier presumes he has been sent to receive a whipping and reaches for his switch. Robert, his resentment boiling, quickly talks his way out of a punishment and gains reentrance to the study hall. There, the prefect, more frustrated than ever by his failure to control the boys, jumps down from his pulpit and stalks the room, looming over the miscreants who pretend to be busy when he passes but make noises behind his back.

Robert and Fordham survive the next three months. But if those months, viewed now through the prism of Robert's letters, seem bleak, they are typical of—actually tamer than—the atmosphere in other boarding schools, both Catholic and secular, all over America. In 1833 and 1850, Georgetown was convulsed by student rebellions, and between 1830 and 1860 it expelled eighty-five students.

At Fordham, Robert gets sick and vomits. The boys catch squirrels in traps and half-drown them in barrels of water "to tame them." A Syrian priest visits, says Mass, sings the liturgy in a squeaky voice, delivers a talk in Greek, and asks the boys to donate money for his church. They do. New ventilators are installed in the dormitories to warm the whole building by steam heat, but they don't work. The smoke goes back up into the dormitories, and all the boys get sick. When a big black cat runs wild in the study hall, the boys panic and jump up on their desks; when the cat runs up the wall, a boy hits it in the head and kills it. In mid-December, the boys are in a steady state of rebellion. They throw ink around the study hall and get some on the prefect, make as much noise as they can there and in the dining room, and sabotage one another's bunks—including the prefect's—so that they break and collapse.

In January, the Shaws granted Robert his freedom and took him to Europe where, the following October, he enrolled in a boarding school in Neuchâtel, Switzerland. There he began to mature, to learn more about the wider world than school in the Bronx had allowed. His parents had long been leading abolitionists, and he read Harriet

Beecher Stowe's *Uncle Tom's Cabin* (1852) and *A Key to Uncle Tom's Cabin* (1853) repeatedly and probed his parents in letters, many written in French, for their thoughts. But he made up his own mind on everything.

Within the next few years he grew to his full height of five feet five inches, was slim and delicate enough to go to a fancy ball in 1855, one time as a joke, dressed as a woman. He gave some time to his studies, attended the theater or opera nightly, and worried a bit about what to do with the rest of his life. He knew he was not going to be a "reformer," he was not very interested in politics, he was not an abolitionist, and though he occasionally attended a variety of church services, he was not devoted to religion. He was convinced that the Jesuits, whom he never forgave, resented that he had not converted to Catholicism like his uncle. He would go to Harvard. Or maybe he would go to West Point.

II ⌐

A few old documents give us a rare glimpse into the personal lives and minds of Shaw's contemporaries. One, found in the archives, is an album of photographic portraits, each about the size of a playing card, of individual students taken in the 1850s and 1870s. Some are identified with little inscriptions or affectionate notes, such as "Remember me in your prayers, yours truly, Maurice O'Gorman, b. 5 Aug '58 / Jan 25, '71." Another says, "P. L. Kean, in memoriam. November 1856 / 19 Mar 1873, Fordham." The stiff studio portraits feature the boys, very young, in formal suits too big for them. Faces grim, each stands with his hand on a chair or stuck in his coat like Napoleon. Or he sits at a table with his hand pressed on a book. A few sport long beards, moustaches, or muttonchops; most are clean shaven. Their complexions are pale or swarthy. Nearly all look like old men in little boys' bodies.

In three short-lived Rose Hill student publications we see their minds at work. *The Goose-Quill* (1854–55), *The Critic* (Sept.–Dec. 1856), and *The Collegian* (Sept. 1859–April 1860) were the only vehicles of student expression until the *Monthly* appeared in 1882. Appearing twice monthly, they were not publications in the strict sense, since they were not printed but rather transcribed by hand on eight-by-twelve-inch two-column lined paper and posted in the reading room, described as a dingy place in the cellar with a few old newspapers and a couple of torn magazines. The editors and contributors were anonymous, with Greek or Latin or comic pseudonyms. The aspiring writers would simply drop their masterpieces in the reading room letter box and wait to see their little poem or essay appear if the editors found it worthy.

Actually, the "secret" force and transcriber behind *The Goose-Quill* was the modest and unassuming John R. G. Hassard, who was also the secretary of the newly formed (1854) St. John's Debating Society, which argued as their first topic whether or not "Christian nations," as they assumed the Western powers to be, could side with the Turks in the Crimean War. John, who was eighteen, had converted from Episcopalianism to Catholicism three years before, under the influence of his High Church Episcopal curate, who had himself converted in 1849.

One editor of the *Collegian,* called Solon, was particularly snappy in rejecting his contributors. In a series of editorials, he excoriated them for their plagiarism, printing the student poem and source alongside one another. He could also be nasty when he was trying to be nice. After a poem called, "My Mother," that began

My Mother died when I was young
and nothing but a child.
Her pretty face I can recall,
It was so very mild.

Solon noted: "We have inserted your poem in order to encourage, not on account of any extraordinary merit, for it is inferior to most of the poems in the *Collegian*" (December 18, 1859).

Since their guidelines prohibited anything "capable of wounding, in the smallest degree, the feelings of anyone" (*The Goose-Quill*) as well as "reflections on authority" (*The Collegian*), these boys are not crusading journalists, yet occasional satirical pieces reinforce the frustrated tone of many of Robert Gould Shaw's letters. An "autobiography" of a desk describes study-hall mischief—spitball fights, the hysterical cat, Jesuits raiding desks at night to confiscate tobacco. In another piece, a "traveler" gets off the train at the Fordham station, wanders onto the grounds, meets the men in black robes and three-cornered hats and thinks he's in a penitentiary; he meets the boys and thinks he's in a lunatic asylum; he sees the cupola on the mansion house and thinks it's to watch for runaways. A student writes regularly to his city friend and complains of the prefects who confiscated his romance novel just as he was getting to the love scene. One author dedicates his poem to a Jesuit, but although Jesuits are remembered as beloved and venerable by alumni writing in *The Monthly* twenty years later, here they are more likely to appear as disciplinarians, objects of fear.

Only rarely does the world outside the study-hall window intrude. In *The Collegian* three pieces commemorate the death of the historian William Hickling Prescott, and a poem exhorts its readers, "now, when our cities are full," to migrate to the West. A *Collegian* editor looks out the window and sees Poverty—poor people coming onto the grounds to beg for food—and urges his readers to, in their imaginations, enter the hovels and tenements of the poor: "Fellow students, look up to the poor instead of looking down on them, and your path will be smooth throughout life" (September 23, 1859). In a unique reference to international events, an editorial on March 3, 1859, backs Pope Pius IX in his conflict with Napoleon III.

The one evidence that Fordham boys other than Shaw were giving any thought to the most burning issue of the day, apart from the Crimean War, is a report in *The Critic* (September 1856) of a debate on "Whether it is advisable, under existing circumstances, to abolish slavery." In a packed hall, eleven debaters stood and took their turns, alternating affirmative and negative, and spelling out what may well have been a cross section of Catholic thinking on slavery at the time. Those favoring abolition stressed the God-given equality of the races or the equality that could be achieved if both races were educated. One, anticipating Afrocentrism, argued the quality of the Negro race from antiquity as exemplified by Egyptians, Phoenicians, and Carthaginians.

But the first speaker in support of slavery sneered that he "did not feel very solicitous about the descendants of Ham." His colleagues quoted passages from Scripture that supported slavery, and Master

Fitzpatrick spelled out the "destitution and depravity" of the Negro in Africa as contrasted with the superior living conditions of the slaves in the American South. He spoke eloquently of the national progress and economic benefits brought on by slavery, and in imagery that would have been familiar to Archbishop Hughes, who feared a slave revolt, he depicted the riot and confusion that would result from emancipation, which would leave us "gazing at the country crouched at the feet of an infamous tyranny." The boys cheered.

If Hassard's pioneer journal fizzled, his later journalism career did not. After graduation in 1855, he entered St. Joseph's Seminary on the campus, but left in a year because of his health. He served as Archbishop Hughes's secretary until Hughes's death in 1864, and he published a biography of Hughes two years later. After a few months as first editor of *The Catholic World,* he went on to the Chicago *Republican,* and then to the New York *Tribune,* where he was music critic, editorial writer, and managing editor until his death in 1888 after a long struggle with tuberculosis.

Elsewhere, at Fordham, the Larkin administration had a few other problems. When Larkin, an Englishman, canceled the St. Patrick's Day holiday, the Irish students bought cheap marbles as weapons and broke most of the windows in the college. On a more serious level, Mr. Cole, a blacksmith on Kingsbridge Road, warned that the Fordham Heights branch of the anti-immigrant Know-Nothing Party planned to attack and burn the college. The fathers, armed with twelve muskets furnished by the government, planned to defend their property, but Cole's warning frustrated the attack. Most of the rifles fell into the hands of the drama department, but one stayed in the president's office until around 1968, just in case.

III ⌐

Sadly but inevitably, the relationship between the Jesuits and their original sponsor, Archbishop Hughes, was unraveling. The issues that separated them were both large and small. As often happens in extended controversies between strong-willed parties, even when both of them are by profession moral leaders trained by their spirituality to put petty and, above all, material differences aside, the big problems are the underlying issues of ego and will. In the meantime, they fight out the controversy in the language of property rights, footpaths, fences, footnotes to contracts, and who said what to whom behind whose back five or ten years before.

As the dispute developed over five years, even the Jesuit general in Rome became involved, and the Society's reputation for cleverness and diplomacy was considerably dimmed.

The underlying issues go back to the fundamental disagreement as to why the Jesuits were in New York in the first place. Hughes, in his mind, had brought them for a narrowly defined purpose, to conduct a college for the sons of the middle and upper classes, thus protecting future leaders from Protestant-dominated public education, and to run a seminary that would quickly supply him with much-needed priests. To a degree, we know that St. John's was doing this fairly successfully from the way the college's earliest histories and memoirs respectfully list prominent alumni from the earliest classes who became priests and bishops.

The Jesuits' goals, on the other hand, were both pragmatic and broadly ambitious. First, they wanted to escape their losing game in St. Mary's, Kentucky. Then they wanted to branch out into various positions of influence—another college, additional residences and parishes, including a new parish in Yonkers, with an emphasis on preaching and hearing confessions.

Aside from the conflict of wills between the two religious forces, Hughes and the Jesuits fought about four issues. First, Hughes was dissatisfied with the Jesuits' conduct of St. Joseph's Seminary. Second, a clause in the original 1845 contract required the Jesuits to give St. John's back to Hughes if they ever left. The Jesuits called this the "cramping clause," because it prevented them from developing the property and selling it. This led to a dispute over who really owned the property. Hughes said the Jesuits had received the college as a gift, with their agreement to assume its $40,000 debt. The Jesuits said they had bought it and Hughes had made a profit. Third, Hughes kept the title to the church of St. Francis Xavier on 16th Street, whereas the fathers said it should belong to them. Furthermore, Hughes had forbidden the Jesuits to hear men's confessions outside the confessional box, thus impeding the Jesuits' access to influential Catholic leaders. Fourth, the Jesuits said Hughes had promised to give them a church and residence in the city. He had offered them a debt-ridden parish, but no house.

At one stage in 1856, Hughes became so fed up with them that the president of St. John's board of trustees, Mr. Peter Hargous, told the Jesuit president, Remigius I. Tellier, a Piedmontese who succeeded Larkin as president (1854–59), that the best thing for the Jesuits to do was to give the archbishop a year's notice and then get out of town. For his part, Tellier described Hughes in a letter (April 16, 1856) to Fr. Pieter Beckx, the Jesuit general in Rome, as "un esprit extraordinaire de domination; il a besoin de dominer." Orestes A. Brownson wrote later that Hughes once told him, "I will suffer no man in my diocese that I cannot control; I will either put him down, or he shall put me down."

The conflict came to a head in the summer of 1855 when Hughes removed the Jesuit director of his seminary and attempted to replace the Jesuit faculty with his men. Hughes's move should not have come as a surprise. Since 1850, the seminarians had been grumbling with complaints, particularly about living conditions that were detrimental to their health. Actually, the diary of the Jesuit minister during these days includes a long list of students who left because of bad health, yet several notations say the young men *arrived* in bad health or that their health improved while they were there. Yet Fr. Daubresse admitted in an 1855 letter to Boulanger that the cold and dampness of the seminary building had led to the death of one student.

Again, we should place this death in the context of the early nineteenth century when the young were particularly susceptible to seasonal sicknesses such as cholera or choleralike gastrointestinal diseases that swept the country in 1833–34, 1844, and 1848–54. St. John's could not be blamed, Daubresse argued, if the students contracted their diseases over the summer and brought them to Rose Hill.

Daubresse, a man who joined the Jesuits because he was convinced it was the only way to save his soul, was part of the seminary's problem for a number of reasons. Acclaimed for his learning, having taught philosophy in Belgium and canon law in France, he was installed as a St. Joseph's professor though he was unable to speak English well.

Furthermore, both he and his colleague, Fr. Seraphim Schemmel, S.J., were ultraroyalists still in shock from the French Revolution. They were never at home with democratic ideas, and they let the seminarians know it. Years later, although Hughes asked the Jesuit general to allow Daubresse to be made a bishop (denied), Hughes would not allow him to conduct a retreat for young priests because they had such bad memories of him from their seminary days.

The coup moved slowly, however, and Hughes was reduced to asking some Jesuits to stay on. The problem, again, seems to have been that the Jesuits were French, with an authoritarian attitude and rigid piety that did not jibe with the democratic inclinations of these young men from New York and Brooklyn. On May 6, 1856, all but nine of the seminarians simply walked out, beginning a process by which the Jesuits themselves withdrew their own seminarians, except those in regency, and, in 1869, resettled them at Woodstock College, in the remote environs of Baltimore.

Over its twenty years, St. Joseph's Seminary, with a student population averaging between twenty-five and forty and a faculty of three, had never been a major operation. A total of 107 alumni were ordained. A few years later, in 1861—although he later softened his criticism—the rector of the North American College in Rome wrote to Hughes that, based on those who had been sent to Rome, "Fordham Seminary was not only a wretched but a dangerous place for your young men."

There were other disputes about boundary lines as to who—Jesuits, Hughes, the Harlem Railroad—owned what on the borders of the property. Hughes had retained the eight or nine acres that stretched north from the one seminary building and the church, bordered by the railroad on the west and the church on the east. A survey showed, however, that the Rodrigues' stone house was right on the line. Hughes's sister could not step off her front stoop without trespassing on college turf.

To complicate matters, Hughes had made the college chapel, Our Lady of Mercy, a local parish church wherein parishioners had to buy pew rights to enjoy the Jesuit liturgies. As a result, hundreds of churchgoers tramped across the campus and drove their carriages up the road every Sunday.

Hughes, furious at reports that Fordham Jesuits had been maligning him, called a meeting for September 28, 1858, to bring matters to a head. The day before, he had briefly received Fr. William Stack Murphy and Fr. Jean-Baptiste Hus, the new superior of the New York–Canada mission, who had made the mistake of pressing Hughes too hard for what he considered Jesuit rights. The archbishop kept them cooling their heels in the parlor for an hour and a half, then berated Hus in French for demanding his "pound of flesh." He then turned to Murphy, knowing Hus did not speak English, and froze Hus out of the conversation.

The next day, Larkin replaced Hus as an envoy to Hughes, and Thomas Legouais was included as secretary. Two Maryland Jesuits, Charles Stonestreet and John McElroy, were brought in as witnesses because they were friends of Hughes and might be able to mediate. The archbishop laid out his case over several hours. He was convinced the fathers had been undermining him with lies and gossip. When they consulted a lawyer, Charles O'Conor, an outstanding Catholic layman and Hughes's friend, on their property rights, Hughes considered it an insult.

As for the promised church, he had offered them one but they had turned it down because it was in debt. Then, he said, they raised money for a church without his permission. When it burned down, he gave permission for a collection to rebuild, but they abused the privilege by going door-to-door in New York and Brooklyn. They didn't rebuild but took the money to 16th Street and built Xavier. Other aspects of Jesuit behavior irked him more. Given access to parishes, they worked with the pious rich, neglected the poor, and were seen at the theater and opera during Holy Week. The men punished for this portrayed themselves as victims and whined to their parishioners.

McElroy and Stonestreet left the meeting convinced that their fellow Jesuits were at fault, and the Fordham men thought the session had been stacked against them. Legouais, in a letter to Rome, found fault on both sides. Hus, told of the result, remained bitter and fought against reconciliation on Hughes's terms.

To no avail. On February 22, 1859, McElroy arrived in New York with orders and guidelines from the general for resolving the dispute. On February 27, with Legouais and Murphy as companions, he went to Hughes's residence and the three of them literally got down on their knees before the archbishop of New York and apologized, on behalf of their Jesuit brothers, for their faults. They later presented Hughes with a written statement of their presumed offenses, all centered on statements Jesuits might or might not have made that were critical of Hughes. It was, of course, a humiliation, just as Hughes desired.

A few days later, Hughes showed up at St. John's for a lecture and stayed late for dinner with the Jesuits. Within the next few months, Hughes, confronted with evidence from lawyers, admitted that yes, the Jesuits did own Fordham. There is much irony in Hughes's concession; 140 years later, based on the fact that Hughes had founded St. John's with a mixed clergy and lay board of trustees, scholars would come to a very different conclusion.

Hughes solved the seminary turf problem by selling it to the Jesuits for $45,000. He promised to give them Xavier, but died before he could get around to it, leaving the donation to his successor, Bishop John McCloskey, St. John's first president.

Throughout the squabbles, Fordham had paid an additional price. Between 1856 and 1858, enrollment had dropped from 180 to 124. The battle had taken place beyond the binoculars of the press, but the falloff must have been due, in some degree, to grassroots bad feelings between the Jesuits and the diocese they had come to serve.

IV ⚊

As freshmen in the 1950s, we hadn't the vaguest idea of who Orestes A. Brownson was or what he represented. We would occasionally joke about it as we passed him on our way to and from the chapel on Sunday mornings. His huge green bronze head sits imposingly atop a granite pedestal; his back is to Collins Auditorium, the church's entrance is to his right, and his big face is looking ahead into the quadrangle court of the freshman dorm, Queen's Court.

To us, it was the all-purpose university heroic bust—the enormous head with flowing hair and the big beard. It could have been Charles Darwin, Karl Marx, or Leo Tolstoy; rather, we learned in time, he was our role model—America's first great Catholic intellectual.

Born in Vermont in 1803, Brownson moved from one religion to another as a young man; he was a Presbyterian, a Universalist minister, and, by 1830, a "freethinker." He became a charter member of the Transcendentalist Club and was simultaneously at home in two worlds—that of the most brilliant New England intelligentsia and that of the Boston working class, whose cause he had embraced as a social and religious reformer. He returned to the ministry because he saw religion as an instrument for social and economic reform, founded the *Boston Quarterly Review* in 1838, and published a socialist-like critique of American economic structures. In 1844, he established *Brownson's Quarterly Review,* which for twenty-five years delivered his opinions, with considerable impact, to an influential readership, and he joined the Catholic Church.

Thus American Catholicism had in its stable a formidable philosopher, apologist, journalist, and polemicist—what today we would call a public intellectual. But he had not stopped thinking for himself; he was the kind of upstart who inevitably makes American bishops nervous, unless they themselves are intellectuals who relish the free and unpredictable flow of ideas. Brownson's lifelong practice of thinking out loud in articles, letters, and lectures, his philosophy developing as he moved from one public issue to the next, also made him suspect. No school of thought could hold him for long, and his critics often attributed positions to him on the liberal-conservative spectrum that he did not hold, or at least not then.

Now, as a Catholic who held a variation of the doctrine that outside the church there is no salvation, he turned against his former associates in Unitarianism and transcendentalism to expose the inadequacy of their doctrines. In his insistence on the Catholic Church as the only valid source of salvation, he angered Protestants and worried those in the Catholic hierarchy trying to get along in an already hostile Protestant society. Most significant, he was an Americanizer, but not necessarily a precursor of the "Americanism heresy" condemned in the 1899 encyclical. To Brownson this meant that European immigrant Catholics should not cling to their national identities but should see their Catholicism as transcending a narrow national culture. Although he recognized the temporary need for immigrant priests to serve immigrant flocks, he did not want future

priests trained in American seminaries because they were often ruled
by the ethnic factions that already divided the church. Better they
should be educated in Rome: at least they would become cosmopolitan rather than stuck in their own Irish or German culture groups.

Throughout the rest of the nineteenth century, American
Catholicism was to be split between those who tried to preserve the faith
by reinforcing immigrant subcultures—Archbishop Hughes was
considered a leader of this group—and those who urged accommoda-
tion to American ways. When Brownson moved with his wife and
eight children from Boston to New York in 1855, expecting a more
freewheeling intellectual environment, he did not anticipate how he
would deal with John Hughes.

First, his argument that the American church should not be a
specifically Irish church offended the Irish. Second, as the Civil War
approached, the *Quarterly*'s position against slavery alienated him
from establishment Catholicism. Abolition was fundamentally a
Protestant crusade, and American Catholics were saddled with a
moral theology that condemned the slave trade, but not slavery as an
institution. American Catholics in the South, including the Jesuits
of the Maryland Province, owned or had owned slaves. Brownson,
antislavery and thoroughly democratic in outlook, was on the fringe
of the church.

Surely the Fordham Jesuits knew this when they chose Brownson
to receive Fordham's first honorary degree in 1850 and when they
invited him back in June 1856 to give the graduation address, with
Hughes sharing the platform. We don't have the text of what
Brownson said, but it was most likely a follow-up on recent articles in
which he had called for the separation of church and state and the
development of a native clergy. He had tapped into a rift within the
church: American priests were divided between those who saw
themselves as chaplains to a foreign colony in this country and those
who saw themselves as Americans and dreamed of converting
Americans to the faith.

Why had the Jesuits invited Brownson when they foresaw he
might offend Hughes? Perhaps they simply admired his brilliance and
wanted their handful of graduates to see the young American church
at its best. Perhaps, like today, when colleges give honorary degrees to

television news anchors and other celebrities, it was a bid for press coverage. Or perhaps the French Jesuits, knowing Brownson was perceived as anti-Irish, wanted to give him a platform. But the stage was set for trouble.

After Brownson's talk, Hughes turned to him privately and told him that, although he had not violated any church doctrines, Hughes could not agree with what he'd said; then, to the journalist's astonishment, Hughes, in his final remarks to the crowd, lambasted him with hostile and ironic comments. He could not allow Brownson's ideas to go uncontradicted, he said; he denied that America's laws were fair to Catholics, told the graduates that Catholic freedom existed only on paper, and exhorted the boys to prepare themselves for oppression and persecution. For Brownson, it was a public humiliation and, as he wrote to Hughes later, an abuse of Hughes's position as a bishop. Brownson had used his freedom as an American to express himself, and Hughes had crushed him with the weight of his authority "in a matter of simple opinion."

Actually, though he could not explain it to Brownson, Hughes too was a patriot who disapproved of national parishes. Although his strategy was to save the immigrant faith through a network of Catholic institutions that stressed the sacramental life and protected Catholic youth from the bad influences of Protestants, he did not envision American Catholicism as a string of disconnected Irish ghettos. With his propensity for combat, he simply reacted to Brownson as to one more adversary in his embattled world. Hughes later wrote to Brownson and apologized, insisting that he deeply admired Brownson and had intended no personal offense, but that day remained a small but significant symbolic moment in American Catholic history, posing questions that would keep coming back about Fordham's ambiguous and complicated relationship with American culture and ecclesiastical authority.

Although Hughes and Brownson regularly professed their respect for one another, the tension between them broke into the open again and again, in public print and in their encounters at Fordham, where Brownson apparently felt quite at home. Brownson had praised one of Fr. Auguste Thebaud's books in the *Review* and a St. John's philosophy professor, Fr. Charles Gresselin, S.J., whom

Brownson characterized as "really one of the most learned and accomplished theologians in the country," once wrote to Brownson that his *Review* "will pass to posterity among the few works that each century sends to the future and endless generations." He even volunteered his services as a proofreader. Gresselin, who moved to Boston College, remained Brownson's steady friend through a series of controversies, but was not afraid to contradict him when he thought he was mistaken.

While Brownson had strong opinions on everything, his views on Catholic higher education are at the heart of both his personality and his view of the church's future. Brownson's conviction that the development of Catholic colleges and universities was crucial to the American church's future sprang from what we might call his democratic elitism: the need to create an educated class that, through its sense of duty and responsibility, would raise a group of Catholic leaders above the masses and thus raise the level of Catholic culture. At the time, before the Civil War, both Catholics and Protestants were moving from a focus on their leaders to a more democratic outlook that still stressed piety and moral development over intellectual growth—a policy that, in Brownson's view, weakened the impact of Catholic institutions.

He wanted them to separate the colleges from the seminaries; raise their academic standards; restructure the classes with a clear separation between grammar (common) schools, high schools, colleges, and universities; downplay the "caring" atmosphere and make the boys more self-reliant and less shy and deceitful. He often defended Jesuit education, however, even though his four sons at Holy Cross in 1846, in their letters home, complained fiercely of mistreatment. William received such a bad beating that he almost lost the use of his arm, and a Jesuit philosophy professor accused John of heresy when he argued from reason rather than accept revelation.

It should be understood that, whatever his sons' complaints, and whatever his disappointment with their methods and policies, Brownson continued to love and defend the Jesuits. He really believed that Americans could have intellectual differences and remain friends. He even contemplated living at Fordham or Notre Dame in retirement.

In two words, Brownson believed Catholic universities should foster *free thought*. "We must give scope to the reason of the scholar, and not be afraid now and then of a little intellectual eccentricity. Better in our age sometimes to err, providing it is not from an heretical spirit or inclination , than never to think" (*Brownson's Quarterly Review,* July 1857). It would be a long time before Catholic higher education would describe its own goals in these terms.

A particularly provocative article in the *Brownson Quarterly Review,* "Dr. Arnold and Catholic Education" (July 1860), by Fr. W. J. Barry of St. Mary's Seminary in Cincinnati made Hughes furious. Catholic colleges are "failures," said Barry, because they are devoid of intellectual life. The students enter college with no love of learning and they "do not acquire a taste for it while there." The problem, argued Barry, is that the system was based on the old post-Reformation European—that is, Jesuit—curriculum, when it should have been based on the English. Americans think and speak, not like Italians and French, but like Anglo Saxons.

When Hughes arrived at the Fordham commencement on July 12, 1860, steaming over the article, he spied Brownson staring up at him from the audience. What was the famous man doing at a graduation when he was not part of the program? We can only conclude that St. John's graduations, in spite of the smallness of the graduating class, were somehow noteworthy events, and a Catholic writer with his ear to the ground would not want to miss one. Hughes was not to disappoint him. After congratulating the graduates, Hughes berated the writers who had been maligning Catholic education, then directed his words to the "great reviewer." Even if Brownson had not written the offensive article, he said, as editor he was responsible for it. The great universities of Europe, he said, based their greatness on their loyalty to their Catholic foundations.

Having put the silent Brownson in his place again, Hughes acknowledged that Brownson was a master of the English language and, amidst laughter and applause, urged the audience to subscribe to the *Review.* All this had no effect on Father Barry in Cincinnati, who fired off two more pieces critiquing Catholic higher education, including a version of the poem "Little Jack Horner," in which the church squats in the corner, congratulating itself on its fine schools.

With all this cantankerous feuding behind them, it is hard to fathom what the Fordham Jesuits had in mind when they again invited Brownson to be the commencement speaker in June 1861, particularly since they had been in a drawn-out squabble with Hughes over their property. Today, whatever the influence of faculty committees, these decisions are usually made by the president. Fr. Thebaud had just returned to the presidency in August and, man of the world that he was, he must have been particularly sensitive to the political situation. Fort Sumter had fallen on April 14, 1861, Fordham boys from both the North and South were on their way to war, and whatever the remoteness of the Bronx, this crisis could not be ignored.

Most likely, this is why Brownson was invited. Since Sumter, Brownson had gained renewed fame as a defender of the Union in his public lectures, and through his influence, both Protestants who remembered him as a New England preacher and New York Catholics were swinging toward the Union side.

Thebaud had lived and traveled in the South, and, while philosophically he knew slavery was immoral, he resented Harriet Beecher Stowe's portrayal of slave conditions in *Uncle Tom's Cabin*. At least, he wrote in his autobiography, Catholic slave owners treated their slaves with respect and their slaves were happy. Yet, though Thebaud was not an abolitionist, he was devoted to the Union cause. He favored the Emancipation Proclamation when it came, but he wished it had come when the church was prepared to bring the freed Negroes into Christianity.

Brownson, because he saw slavery in the Southern states as protected by law, was not an abolitionist, but he was profoundly antislavery on the basis of natural law. It was a crime against humanity, against the unity of the human race. He acknowledged that the black man was inferior to the white man, but that did not mean the blacks could be enslaved. Unfortunately, many Northern Catholics were proslavery, partly because they were Democrats, and partly because freed Negroes were competing for jobs in New York. The institutional church itself, expressed through statements of the bishops, condemned the slave trade but did not demand that slaves be freed. Hughes had traveled through the South several times and concluded that while slavery was an evil, it was "not an absolute and unmitigated evil." It brought Africans to civilization and, more importantly, to Christianity.

Brownson's address emphasized the moral obligation of his hearers to be loyal and patriotic in this hour of crisis. When Hughes came forward at the end, he suddenly launched into a fierce attack on the "club" of liberal intellectuals—those who wanted to Americanize the church—to which he wrongly thought that Brownson belonged. Brownson, shocked, stood up in his place to defend himself, but Hughes commanded him to sit down.

The event was a terrible debacle for all concerned. The Jesuits' first concern was to keep the story out of the newspapers, and they induced friendly reporters to cover it up. Then they whisked Hughes out of the commencement hall into a banquet, leaving their invited speaker standing all alone in the empty hall, ruthlessly frozen out, waiting for a train that would take him back to New York. According to Brownson's son, "Not one of them came near Brownson again."

Brownson never complained about his treatment; he even made excuses for the bad behavior of his hosts, although the excuses were, in effect, quite damning. He knew the fathers wanted to get control of the seminary building, St. John's Hall, that Hughes still owned, so of course they had to cater to him. A little later in the year, on a visit to Boston, when Brownson attempted to visit his friend and confessor Fr. Gresselin at Boston College, he was turned away at the door although the rector, Fr. Bapst, had originally invited him to stay there. Bapst rejected him most graciously, with tears in his eyes. Under the circumstances, Bapst had no choice, Brownson graciously acknowledged later. After all, he had just given a lecture before the Emancipation League in Boston, and the Jesuits had property in the South. If the Jesuits of Boston were to show hospitality to the antislavery Brownson, he concluded, perhaps Jefferson Davis would hear of it and charge the Southern Jesuits with hostility to the Confederacy.

Brownson was dismayed by a morality in which Jesuits could enjoy the blessings of democracy in the United States and yet not defend the Union. By their silence on the war, he felt, they had forfeited their right to teach young people.

Henry F. Brownson, Orestes' son and biographer, explains his father's ambivalent feelings toward the Society in *Latter Life: From*

1856–1876 (1900). He respected Jesuits as individuals, says Henry, but as a Society, with its emphasis on the centralization of authority, including the required teaching of one narrow interpretation of Aristotle, they were the enemies of reform and of robust, independent thinking. Jesuit education "so emasculates the soul, destroys or drives into hiding all mental activity, and causes strong and robust men to turn in wrath or disgust from the faith and piety confounded with the human machinery in vogue for sustaining them, and seek refuge in infidelity and indifference." In short, rigid Jesuit discipline, meant to protect faith, destroys it.

After Orestes Brownson died in 1876, one of the best-known men in America was quickly forgotten. In 1886, his remains were transferred from a Detroit cemetery to a crypt in the chapel at the University of Notre Dame. The same year, a committee of bishops and distinguished laymen attempted to raise money for a suitable memorial in New York. Contributions merely dribbled in, but by 1899 there was enough to commission a bronze bust, in its day the largest bust portrait in the United States, from the Boston sculptor Samuel J. Kitson.

It was 1910 before the New York City Parks Department consented to place it in Sherman Park at 104th Street on Riverside Drive, where it stood in obscurity until a gang of teenage vandals toppled it in 1937. Journalists were hard pressed to find historians who could explain who this famous fellow had been. Since no one cared, the city carted Brownson off to the municipal storage yard until, in 1941, Fordham President Fr. Robert I. Gannon, S.J., rescued him and set him up in the same spot where he had been both honored and insulted not quite a century before.

4.

Michael Nash Goes to War

Robert Gould Shaw returned to his family estate on Staten Island in the summer of 1856. The family had moved there some years before in order to be near his mother's eye specialist. A tutor, whom Shaw referred to as "the Crammer," was hired to prepare him for the Harvard entrance examination. With an exaggerated estimate of both his intelligence and the value of his free-wheeling European education, Shaw presumed he would pass easily and be ushered into either junior or sophomore year.

Robert's cramming was only one of the family's summer concerns. His father, who had been a Free-Soiler, had joined the new Republican Party. He had attended the party's first convention and helped nominate John Charles Fremont for president, and abolitionists were holding regular meetings at a neighbor's house that had become a regular haven for runaway slaves. Even the Crammer was part of the antislavery furor. A Harvard graduate who had also been educated by the transcendentalists at Brook Farm, he was destined to marry Shaw's younger sister and to become a general in the Civil War.

True to his prediction, Shaw did find the exam "very easy," but he was admitted only to freshman year. It was not long before his Harvard letters resembled, in some moments, those from Fordham.

He did not adapt quickly to the discipline and his grades were low, particularly in mathematics and history. "I hate Cambridge," he wrote, and thought about transferring to Columbia or New York University. But he held on and worked his way to the top half of his class of 1860, which he said the Harvard faculty had described as the "laziest class" they had seen in a long while. In spite of his small stature, of which he was keenly embarrassed, he played football for a while, then switched to rowing and boxing.

Shaw's love of the social life remained undiminished: he joined eight societies, played his violin with a musical group, and relished sitting around after a concert devouring ale, cheese, and crackers with the boys. Meanwhile, as before, he declined to let the political issue of the day—slavery—consciously dominate his attention the way it ruled the lives of his parents. As far as he was concerned, the Union should split; in that way slavery could be considered a purely Southern problem rather than a national disgrace.

Still uncertain of what he wanted to do with his life, although he had considered farming, Shaw left Harvard in 1859, moved into his old room on Staten Island, took a job in his uncle's mercantile business, dreamed of working in China—and quickly grew bored, depressed, and confused. When the election of Abraham Lincoln prompted Southern states to secede, he did what many young men in his social class did at that time: he joined the renowned, exclusive Seventh Regiment of the New York National Guard.

The surrender of Fort Sumter and Lincoln's subsequent call for troops to march to Washington inspired young urban aristocrats who saw this as an opportunity for their class to demonstrate its patriotism. The "Darling Seventh's" parade down Broadway on April 19, 1861, was a great moment in New York history, though an ironic one in view of how other New Yorkers would respond to the war. These young aristocrats had committed themselves for only thirty days when Lincoln had asked for ninety.

Marching along with Shaw that day was a young man with whom he had one important thing in common. If Robert had stayed at Fordham a few more years and attended the 1853 graduation, he would have been exhorted by the valedictorian, James R. O'Beirne, to honor his two great loves: America and Fordham.

Born in County Roscommon, Ireland, James came to America as a young boy with his parents and was handed over to the Jesuits. Starting his military career in the Seventh Regiment, he rose to become a brigadier general and Secretary of War Stanton's provost marshal as well as the pursuer of Lincoln's assassins.

Shaw recalled Fordham with bitterness, but O'Beirne remembered it with love. O'Beirne was one of the blustering big boys in the brutal boxing matches and football games who, having asserted their manliness, then staggered up to bed, gripping the bannisters in fatigue. His memories included his confessions to "dear, little Fr. Legouais"; the severe, unwrinkled, and immobile face of Mr. Michael Nash controlling the study hall with his ironlike stare; and the occasional appearances of the fat, eloquent Larkin, who one day thrilled the boys by bringing into their midst Thomas Francis Meagher, the exiled Irish patriot, who had escaped to New York after the British had banished him to Tasmania. The fiery Jesuit-educated Meagher stirred up in these New York boys all the woeful stories they had heard from their parents of Ireland's sufferings, and the spirit of resentment burned in their bosoms. Meagher too would join the army, command the famed Irish Brigade, and meet some of these same boys in the smoke of battle.

It is possible that Shaw shunned O'Beirne in the regiment because he was Irish. Shaw's wartime letters to his family do not speak well of the Irish troops, whom he distinguished from the "Americans." Irishmen in training to be sentinels, he wrote in a letter to his mother dated May 25, 1861, "seem sometimes utterly unable to learn or understand anything." Possibly this attitude was reciprocated.

But the attitude might also explain to some degree the mysterious silence in the few remaining archival documents, such as the minutes of the twice-monthly consultors' meetings during the war. The consultors consider a scheduled baseball game, two students who stayed overtime in Manhattan, and staging a philosophy discussion at Xavier, even as the rest of the country was enthralled with Fort Sumter, Vicksburg, Gettysburg, the New York Draft Riots, and Lincoln's assassination. Perhaps to Fordham's French-dominated faculty and Irish student body, the Civil War was not seen as their fight. Furthermore, close to 20 percent of Fordham's students were from the South, in addition to a large contingent being from Latin America. Perhaps Southern Catholic families who knew Jesuits from New Orleans and Kentucky, foreseeing the war, sent their sons to the Bronx for safety. Perhaps the fathers felt that the best way to deal with the greatest moral crisis in American history was not to deal with it at all. An incomplete list, published in the *Fordham Monthly* in 1902 of Fordham boys who served, includes thirty names, seven of them from the South. The list's compilers did not know Shaw's first name, nor did they know whether he was living or dead.

In *American Catholic* (1997), Charles R. Morris sums up scholarship on Catholic participation in the Civil War by describing two stereotypes. First, Irish Catholics were racist. Second, Irish Catholics were exceptionally patriotic and suffered a disproportionate share of the Union casualties. Evidence for the racism is in the Catholic paper the *Freeman's Journal,* whose editor, James McMaster, told a mass meeting that "when the President called upon them to go and carry on a war for the nigger, he would be d___d if he believed they would go." This was the kind of rhetoric that would feed the frenzy of the 1863 New York Draft Riots.

The evidence for exceptional patriotism doesn't hold up. Studies that Morris cites show that as a group, the Irish were the most underrepresented in the Union army. Nevertheless, their participation, whatever it was, and the myth that grew up around it have proved fundamental to the church's self-understanding of its place in American history. The stories that follow, based for the most part on documents in the Jesuit historical quarterly *Woodstock Letters* and in the *Fordham Monthly,* were written by Irish and French Catholics for one another and should be read in that light.

Writing his "Reminiscences" for the Fordham *Monthly* (June 1916) fifty years after the events described, General James R. O'Beirne, '53, A.M., LL.D., is still enraptured by the romantic glory of war. He writes also for an audience who is witnessing the slaughter of a generation of Europeans in World War I, which the United States is just months away from entering. Yet, however mysterious his glorification of battle may seem to today's readers—who know from history books and recent memory the human costs of the Civil War, the two world wars, and the Korean and Vietnam Wars—O'Beirne was nevertheless a genuine hero.

He was one of many Civil War–era recipients of the congressional medal and—with Rochester's Bishop McQuaid, the artist John LaFarge, and America's first cardinal, Cardinal McCloskey—was one of Fordham's most distinguished nineteenth-century alumni.

The Seventh Regiment disbanded soon after its arrival in Washington. Shaw attached himself to the Second Massachusetts Infantry, where he quickly became an officer, and O'Beirne joined the Thirty-seventh New York Regiment, known as "the Irish Rifles," and was off to fight with the Army of the Potomac in the Peninsular Campaign. This was Major General George B. McClellan's ultimately unsuccessful attempt in March–August 1862 to move against Richmond by taking his reduced army of 90,000 men—the other 38,000 held back to protect Washington—by boat down the Chesapeake Bay and overland westward through Virginia.

Making slow progress parallel to the Chickahominy River, they fought at Yorktown, Williamsburg, Fair Oaks, Mechanicsville, and Malvern Hill until, outmaneuvered by Robert E. Lee, who had taken command of the Confederate Army after Fair Oaks, McClellan retreated to Harrison's Landing in defeat. Between battles, Fordham boys and Jesuit chaplains, who had known one another as students and teachers from the 1850s crossed paths again and again.

Three St. John's students, the McMahon brothers—John E., James P., and Martin T.—all young lawyers, gave up their law practices to enter the service together. John, who had been a private secretary to Governor Seymour, was the first to die, brought down by disease in March 1863. His younger brother James fought in the Peninsular Campaign, survived Antietam, and as a twenty-six-year-old colonel, led his 164th Regiment into the Wilderness Campaign and the Battle of Cold Harbor in June 1864. There, during a hard fight at Charles City Crossroads, this tall and muscular Fordham comrade of O'Beirne, having been ordered to charge and take the rebel rifle pits, seized the colors that had fallen with their slain color-bearer. Waving the Stars and Stripes, he bore the Union flag to the summit and planted it on top of the enemy's fortifications, shouting back to his men, "Come on, boys; their works are ours. Here's your flag!"

He thus, of course, rendered himself a perfect target and paid the price for his conspicuous gallantry. One bullet split the sword raised above his head, a second shattered his right arm, and a third his left arm. He fell back into the ditch. When one of his fellow wounded offered help, he replied, "No, no, my man. I'm shot all to pieces. Save yourself." Offered whiskey, he declined, asking only to die in peace. His brother, General Martin T. McMahon, found his body riddled with eighteen holes.

During another battle, O'Beirne met a frightened Fordham boy in retreat. Louis (Edward) Binsse, "a mere, youthful, handsome lad," had fallen and clogged his rifle barrel with sand and was now too frightened to fire it. O'Beirne ordered him to quickly grab a rifle from one of the the wounded men nearby and start shooting at the enemy. Binsse obeyed. O'Beirne never saw him again but heard he had been wounded.

Throughout the campaign O'Beirne, even in the final seven days of fighting, never lost his sense of awe, his conviction that he was engaged in a splendid enterprise. As the army fell back on Harrison's Landing at Malvern Hill, he looked out over the magnificent plateau where the infantry, artillery, cavalry, skirmish line, and gunboats on the James River were simultaneously in plain view.

It was here that he heard that Fordham men in the Confederate army had been captured and were being held nearby. It was cold and raining, and ice formed on the trees and on the men's eyebrows and beards. So O'Beirne got some Irish stew and canteens of coffee and rode off in search of the prisoners. He found young Dillon from Georgia huddled under a tree with a group of shivering Confederates. O'Beirne jumped from his horse and cheerfully but carefully offered his old fellow student the coffee and stew.

Dillon gave him nothing but a black look and turned away as if O'Beirne were not even there. O'Beirne smothered his indignant rage and rode off toward the Irish brigade where, since it was Sunday, he hoped to attend Mass. His courteous visit to the prisoners had been a humiliating failure; his only consolation was that he had tried to practice the good manners he had been taught at Fordham. While he was with the Irish brigade, a shell came screeching in and landed in the mud at his feet. The rain and mud extinguished the fuse and young O'Beirne was not blown to bits. Otherwise, it had not been a good day.

O'Beirne earned his Medal of Honor at the battle of Fair Oaks, but his good luck did not carry him through the battle of Chancelorsville,

Robert E. Lee's most brilliant victory, where on May 2, 1863, Stonewall Jackson's cavalry reduced Joe Hooker's Union forces to in a wild rout. O'Beirne lay on the battlefield for three days—shot through the right lung, with a bullet hole in his leg and a shell wound to his head. Too wounded to fight again, he was made provost marshal of Washington, D.C., in 1864. That put him in the vicinity of, if not actually in, Ford's Theater on April 14, 1865, when John Wilkes Booth slipped into the theater, found Lincoln's box, put a bullet in the president's brain, and fled, leaping from the president's box to the stage.

It was O'Beirne's duty that night to seek out Vice President Andrew Johnson and lead him through the streets of Washington to the house where the president's corpse lay. He then joined the pursuit for the assassins, which was slow in getting started. It was April 17 before a cavalry unit galloped up to O'Beirne's headquarters and their captain asked, "Where must I go?"

O'Beirne replied, "How do I know?" and then, "Go, and don't return to Washington until you find Booth; but mind—don't harm a hair on his head." A number of groups took part in the poorly coordinated search, some keeping their information from the others with the hope of snagging the credit and the reward for the capture. O'Beirne later claimed that his party had been hot on the trail but had been called back at the last minute by a telegram from the War Department. In the investigation that followed, no copy of the telegram was ever found.

O'Beirne remained politically active for the rest of his life. He was editor of the *Washington Gazette* and a correspondent for the New York *Herald* during the Indian Wars. A lifelong Republican, he ran for office unsuccessfully several times, and devoted to Irish independence, he arranged for Charles Stewart Parnell to address the U.S. House of Representatives. Those who remember O'Beirne's frequent returns to the Fordham campus recall his "manly beauty . . . enhanced by a grandeur of soul."

II ✐

Peter Tissot arrived at Fordham from France as a twenty-three-year-old Jesuit philosophy student in 1846. His superiors put him to work as a procurator (buyer, bursar) and as a teacher of French, Spanish, and science. Students quickly learned both to dread and to admire him, partly because he was physically tough as well as lofty, refined, superior, and French "to the core." Sometimes his ascetic face, with its dark olive complexion, appeared humorless; at other times his eyes twinkled. At all times he carried his well-knit physique in such a way as to earn the admiration of adolescent boys. Sometimes he would tuck up his religious habit into his belt and charge into a football game, take over the ball, and outrun the boys who tried to bring him down. He was good at handball, too.

At heart, he was more a missionary than a teacher. When the call went out for chaplains to accompany the Northern troops into battle, Archbishop Hughes conveyed the request to Fordham's rector, Fr. Tellier, who offered Tissot the opportunity. Tissot volunteered in June 1861. He was thirty-eight.

He reported to the regiment to which O'Beirne belonged, the Irish Rifles, in which most of the 622 men were Catholic. Most had been born in Ireland, and the rest were from all over the East Coast; occupations included bakers, butchers, bricklayers, blacksmiths, carpenters, and cooks. Within a few weeks they were moved to Washington, where Tissot socialized with the Jesuits at Georgetown University and St. Aloysius Parish. By July 21, they were within earshot of the Battle of Bull Run, and in a decision that established his behavior for the rest of the war, Tissot headed for the front lines, determined to be wherever the men might need him.

Catholic chaplains in the 1860s were young men thrown into the military world without ten minutes of training on military mores or regulations. Then, as now, the chaplain was on the regimental commander's staff, often designated the "morale officer." He would offer religious services for the convenience of the officers and men, and earn their respect by being hardworking, understanding, human, and when necessary, brave.

A hundred and fifty years ago, a wartime chaplain saw his main obligation as hearing the confessions of Catholics about to die and baptizing non-Catholics into the true faith. He had to do this, he believed, or these men would go to hell and burn for all eternity. As antiquated as these ideas may seem to some today, in most of

America's wars Catholic chaplains risked their lives because they believed these ideas. This was before the revolution in sacramental theology that followed the decrees of the Second Vatican Council and before the theological notion of the "anonymous Christian," wherein even one who does not know Christ but who is open to the experience of God's love can achieve salvation.

Between January 1861 and March 1862, while General George B. McClellan strengthened his army by weeding out its weakest officers and drilling his troops in preparation for a major campaign, Tissot took care of his own regiment and traveled around the Washington and Alexandria area ministering to Catholic companies in ten other units. His method was to approach the officers and offer his services to their men, hear confessions, celebrate Mass, and give communion the following morning. Typical diary entries: "June 6th.—Baptized Capt. Johnson and Private Pelzer of my camp. 13th.—Preached at night on the Last Judgment, the whole regiment being present. My pulpit was a barrel. Heard confessions from 8 to 11 P.M."

He ministered to a soldier about to be hanged in the presence of several regiments for having either beaten or killed a woman in a drunken rage. When asked to offer services for a soldier who had committed suicide, Tissot had to decline, but he offered to speak to the men in place of a religious funeral. So the whole regiment was assembled, and Tissot mounted a box in their midst, though he does not record what he said.

Everywhere he went, he carried a small bell in his pocket that he would hand to the nearest soldier to ring to summon the men to prayer. Since the government did not issue large tents for church services, each chaplain struggled to find a proper place for Mass. The priests improvised—they put an altar on the back of a wagon or had the men build a makeshift chapel. Tissot turned his old personal tent into a small private chapel where he kept the Blessed Sacrament in a wooden tabernacle and kept a candle burning day and night. Sometimes he carried the Sacred Host around with him, but he felt embarrassed and anxious because so many of his duties had no reference to the Christ he bore with him.

Meanwhile, he was on the watch for Fordham alumni or friends—Captain Edward Binsse, Private Kenny, Major John

Devereux, General Martin McMahon, General O'Beirne, the legendary General Meagher, and Tissot's fellow Fordham Jesuit, Thomas Ouellet. Ouellet, also known as Willet, was a lithe little man, a severe martinet, known to publicly reprove officers who used profanity and to kick over the coffee cans of exhausted soldiers who sat outside eating their breakfast when they should have been attending Sunday Mass.

One Sunday, on February 2, 1862, Tissot's Mass attracted distinguished visitors: General Isaiah Bush Richardson and his wife. Richardson was a Vermonter who had fought in the Seminole War, the Mexican War, and on the frontier until 1855, when he resigned. He returned in 1861 and quickly won a reputation as a hard fighter and a brilliant leader. His men referred to him as "Fighting Dick" and "Greasy Dick." Tissot was very taken with Richardson and his young wife and was often a guest at their home. The wife was outspoken in her criticism of the church, but Tissot longed to make the general a Catholic.

When Richardson was slain at Antietam, the crestfallen Tissot was convinced that he would have become a Catholic if only a priest had gotten to him in time. Three years later, Mrs. Richardson wrote to Tissot that she herself had been baptized, her former defensiveness about religion being merely the devil's prompting, and that she now had the confidence of *knowing* what to believe, and yes, her husband, who loved Tissot's Mass, would have converted if he had not been so busy.

In March 1862, the Peninsular Campaign was under way, and Tissot accompanied the ten thousand men who sailed for Fort Monroe in ten steamboats, and he stayed with them on their march toward Yorktown. In May, as his men tramped through the rain and knee-deep mud on the way to the battle of Williamsburg, a young officer handed Tissot his money, over one hundred dollars, to send to his mother. The man had not been to confession for a long time and Tissot was compelled to warn him: "I have done my duty in regard to you. If anything happens to you—if you are killed and go to hell, you will have no one to blame but yourself."

"That is true," he replied. "You have done your duty; I take the whole blame on myself." The man passed on and was killed in the first minutes of the fight. But Tissot had given him absolution anyway, when the man wasn't looking, and clung to the hope that he may have been contrite and pardoned in time.

A month later, on the eve of the Battle of Fair Oaks (also called the Battle of Seven Pines), Tissot, riding his easygoing dark sorrel horse, caught up with James O'Beirne as he stood by the road with his men. O'Beirne had been neglecting the sacraments as well, and Tissot warned him that he might die in battle. The pious O'Beirne, holding Tissot's horse by the bridle, said with chagrin that he just couldn't find the time to confess.

"Yes," the priest replied. "You may do so now." Struck by the emotion of receiving a sacrament on the march, O'Beirne took off his cap and, his rifle swaying and sword jingling as they walked, poured out his sins.

The fight, which lasted all day, was a ferocious one. O'Beirne, wearing his colorful Zouave uniform with its bright jacket and broad pantaloons, stood in plain view and ordered his men to fire away, as he himself fired his sporting rifle fifty-three times at the enemy at close range. Somehow he felt invincible, partly because Tissot had given him an Immaculate Conception medal known as "the miraculous medal" and because he wore in his buttonhole a large bouquet of May flowers that he mailed back to his fiancée after the battle.

O'Beirne idolized Tissot and remembered him as a front-line priest, rushing about the battlefield administering the sacraments as shells exploded around him and bullets whizzed overhead. Tissot, on the other hand, says in his diary, amplified for publication in 1875, that he not only did not do that, but doubts that any chaplain flew from one wounded soldier to the next in the thick of the fight. If the chaplain exposes himself to fire and gets killed, he deprives the men of the sacraments that only he can bring. Rather, he would wait at the field hospital for the wounded to be carried in. "My experience has taught me that there is not much good to be done the day of the battle. . . . The place for the chaplain to do good is in the camp. If he does no good there, he had better stay at home."

On June 12, outside Richmond, Tissot fainted in the middle of a conversation. He said it was sunstroke, but he had been under a lot of stress. Two weeks before, his horse had been shot out from under him. The days were hot and the nights cold, and Tissot was worn down by sickness and depression. He sent for a fellow Jesuit, Fr. O'Hagan, who rode seven miles in the burning sun to the farm of a Dr. Carter to get

Tissot a bottle of fresh milk. By now McClellan's army was in retreat, and O'Hagan escorted the sick Tissot to Carter's farm with the hope that with shelter and care he could recover. But on June 30, the Confederates took the farm, made the Jesuits prisoners, and took them into the Confederate capital.

For seventeen days as "prisoners," the Jesuits had considerable freedom. They were welcome at the bishop's residence, where they socialized with other Northern priests and Confederate chaplains; bearing a cartload of bread, they visited the notorious Libby prison, a former tobacco warehouse, where over 1,000 Union officers were confined in eight rooms. In the sick bay, many lay stark naked on the bare floor, and the stench was so bad that the ailing Tissot had to rush from the room lest he faint.

Released in a prisoner exchange, Tissot returned to his regiment and his work, but desperate for a month's furlough, he sought out the division commander, General Philip Kearny himself. Because Kearny was famous for his foul mouth, Tissot approached him expecting to meet an enemy of the church. But the Jesuit found the general, a divorced man whose wife and daughter were Catholics, a "brave and generous soul," who sent for wine and cigars and entertained him with his romantic ideas about the Catholic Church, which he was convinced had the power and duty to stop the Civil War. Kearny granted a one-week furlough. Since only Secretary of War Edwin M. Stanton could grant a longer one, Tissot timidly confronted the gruff secretary in his War Department office. Stanton barked that he granted furloughs only on Monday and that this was Tuesday! But when Tissot uttered the word "prisoner," Stanton melted.

III ⟶

Michael Nash, sent to France to die of tuberculosis in 1856, did not die. Rather, he was rediagnosed by a better doctor, Emperor Louis Napoleon's private physician, who concluded that his lungs were fine; he had just been overworked. So he went on with his theological studies, was ordained in Germany on the Feast of St. Ignatius, July 31,

1860, and returned to the United States to be stationed at Frederick, Maryland, in September.

There, sick again, he says that he suffered more than he had all the preceding years of his life. Apparently, his Jesuit superiors were convinced that Nash was not too sick to work; in May 1861, they ordered him to join the Union army as a chaplain.

After an emotional visit to Archbishop Hughes, who embraced him warmly, Nash reported to his post on Staten Island in early June. The Sixth Regiment Infantry was known as "Wilson's Zouaves," named for their commander, Colonel William "Billy" Wilson. Zouaves—famous for their exotic uniforms, which consisted of red baggy pants, a dark blue vest, a blue sash, and a fez—were originally men's civilian drill teams modeled on the French army Zouaves, who were, in turn, inspired by the uniforms of Algerian tribesmen. When the Civil War began, they joined the army as groups and, in some instances, held onto their original uniforms.

The flamboyant Wilson, himself a Catholic though not well educated in the faith, was glad to have his own chaplain. He marched Nash out in front of his men, displayed him, and asked, "How do you like him?"

"What is his color?" the men replied, meaning his religion.

"He is a priest, a Roman Catholic priest," Wilson answered, and the men cheered.

Their parents were nearly all Catholics, but the boys had not been raised in the religion. They were a ragtag, poorly disciplined bunch, not interested in going to confession, but very devoted to having their fun in New York before heading to war. Meanwhile, when Protestant would-be chaplains showed up and argued for equal access to the troops, Wilson would stand them on a barrel and challenge them to preach. One, not knowing his audience, delivered a tirade against the Papists; the troops listened silently, then ran him out of camp.

In mid-June, ordered to board the S.S. *Vanderbilt*, which would carry them to the front, the troops rebelled, demanding two months back pay and a forty-eight-hour furlough. When Wilson saw that they were ready to shoot him rather than follow his orders, he negotiated a one-day leave from which the men returned "literally mad with liquor," fighting among themselves with knives, pistols, and bayonets. Many fell into New York Harbor and drowned, and during the first night at sea, five or six with the delirium tremens jumped overboard and were lost.

Their destination, revealed in sealed orders, was Fort Pickens on Santa Rosa, a forty-five-mile-long sandy island off Rebel-held Pensacola in the Gulf of Mexico. It was the only Union stronghold in the gulf, and the Sixth Regiment's job was to reinforce it and keep it away from General Braxton Bragg, who would menace the island with his bombardments and raids. During his eight months on Santa Rosa, Michael Nash wrote eleven long letters to Fr. Tellier at Fordham and to other friends, leaving us a brief but intense portrait of one long episode in his two years of military service.

At the sight of the enemy, the men's reluctance to go to confession evaporated, and Nash became a great favorite with the troops. At the end of the arduous three-day process of moving the equipment, the mules, and the men from ship to boat to shore, the Zouaves stripped off their uniforms down to their shorts and frolicked like porpoises in the surf, joyously turning their labor into a wild game. They competed to carry the priest's baggage ashore. They called the trunk with his vestments the "Catholic Church" and balanced it high above the swells. Finally, with a cheer, they lifted Michael himself in their muscular arms and bore him on their bare shoulders like a trophy through the waves to the beach. It was a rare moment of ecstasy.

The island itself did not welcome them. There were poisonous snakes, alligators, and mosquitoes, but because it was not the rainy season, little fresh water. While Tissot was able to offer Mass to his regiment at dawn every morning, as the Sixth Regiment's work schedule developed, Nash realized that the only convenient time to offer Mass was Sunday noon. When the time came for the first Sunday Mass, the sailors organized a choir. The tropical sun beat down on the assembly, and Nash was too exhausted to preach. He had not eaten well nor slept the night before, and the eucharistic fast required him to abstain from food and water from midnight on. His lungs had no power.

The rainy season came with the Fourth of July, turning daylight into darkness and hammering their tents with drops "like great stones."

At the sound of gunshots in the night, a little drummer boy—of whom several were from Fordham and Xavier—turned to Nash and said, "Father, I'm afraid! Hear my confession and I shan't be afraid to die." There was no attack, but Fort Pickens and the Southerners on shore exchanged cannon salutes. Because of the rain, there was no Mass. On July 8, one man died, not of gunshot but of typhoid.

As the months went by, Nash walked miles every day from camp to camp visiting the sick and making himself available to Catholics and Protestants alike. The zealous Wilson told him in a moment of irrational enthusiasm that he was so inspired by Nash's devotion that he would like to use his sword to make Catholicism the one true religion. Indeed, he forced Protestant officers from the fort who attended Mass to kneel down like himself.

In October, the Southern army launched a night raid in which Nash was momentarily captured by the raiders, only to escape during a fire that swept through the camp and surrounding trees. In a counterattack, the Union men drove the invaders through the wilderness toward the beach, leaving Nash surrounded by wounded Rebels who rejected his offers of prayers with exclamations like, "I'm an infidel," or "I'm a deist."

As the priest followed the tracks of the fleeing Confederates and their pursuers, the dead and wounded multiplied by the road. One Southern captain's face and ample chest were riddled with bullets, though there was no sign of pain on his face. A delicate, fair, blue-eyed youth with long curling hair grasped a terrible wound in his side. A mortally wounded Protestant corporal who had attended Nash's first island Mass called out to him for baptism. His canteen empty, Nash ran to the Gulf of Mexico, soaked his handkerchief, and dashed back to squeeze the saving waters of the sacrament onto the soldier's forehead. "Father, do not leave me," he pleaded.

"But there are at this moment many others stretched on the sand . . . as near death as you are," Nash replied.

"That is true," he said, "but they are Catholics, Father; they know how to die." His last wish was for Nash to find his family and help them overcome their prejudices against the church. Six years later, as Nash says in a footnote to his published letters, the boy's brother heard how he died and entered the Catholic Church.

By the time Nash caught up with the main forces, the Union men had cornered the fleeing Rebels at the end of the beach where they were trying to escape in the last remaining landing boat. When they refused to surrender, the Union captain ordered his men to fire into them at short range though they could fire not a shot in defense. Nash drew back in horror; the blood and gore of the helpless men had turned the Gulf of Mexico red. Though a Union victory, the night attack so demoralized the regiment with a realization of their vulnerability that Nash fell into another of his funks. "No missionary has ever been so isolated as I have been for the last six months," he wrote. To lift his spirits, he turned to Frederick Goggins, his Fordham drummer boy, who offered wisdom to be passed along to his classmates: "If a boy does not like college, let him become a soldier, and he will see the happiness of a life he does not know how to appreciate." In the midst of a severe hardship such as a night in the trenches, Freddy would turn to Nash and say, "How would the Fordham boys like this?"

IV ⌇

Back at Fordham, as far as we can tell, the boys carried on as if there were no war. To some degree, they followed the practice of another Catholic college, Notre Dame in South Bend, Indiana, founded in 1843, which may well have been the policy at other Northern schools. There both faculty and students were prohibited from taking sides in discussions of the war, and disputes that turned violent were severely punished.

In New York, August 1863, young Richard S. Treacy was told by his father that he was going to St. John's College in the Bronx, and Richard simply obeyed, it never having occurred to him that he should have been consulted.

It is possible that his father just wanted to get him out of Manhattan. Crowded into tenements in a city with the highest disease mortality rate and highest crime rate in the Western world, New York's Irish had recently exploded—angry at blacks for taking their jobs during strikes and at the Protestant middle class, who despised them. On July 11, as draft officers began drawing the names of New Yorkers to be conscripted, Irish men gathered and planned to retaliate. The city broke out in four days of riots, the worst in American history. One hundred five people died. Twenty-one were killed by the rioters and the rest by the police and militia, including many Irish Catholics called out to put down the riots. The crowds lynched six blacks and dragged one of the bodies through the streets. A mob of Irish women beat to death an Irish Catholic militia colonel who had fired on a mob.

Horace Greeley, editor of the *Tribune,* called upon Archbishop Hughes to ride out among "his people" and control them. In fact, some parish priests were heroically intervening to save lives. But Hughes was too old, too sick, and too humiliated by the behavior of "his people," who were confirming the worst that had been said about them, for him to act decisively. He sent out a notice inviting the people to come to his residence, where he would address them. But the five thousand who came were not the ones who had been burning the city to the ground. Sitting in a chair on his balcony, he went on for over an hour. His words were defensive and ineffectual—"I am an Irishman, too . . . and I am not a rioter." He died January 3, 1864.

With this experience behind him, Richard S. Treacy took the horse-drawn car at 26th and Madison Avenue to the train station at 42nd Street for the hour-and-a-half ride to Fordham, where he would stay for six years. A line of lordly elms guided him up to the Manor House, where the president was now Edward Doucet, S.J. (1863–65), Poe's old confidant. A cultured musician, he had grand plans for rebuilding the college; he bought a quarry and built a handsome stone gatehouse (now relocated to the center of the campus as the Honors Program House) just to see how the stone would look. But he did not improve the plumbing. Richard Treacy and his three hundred fellow students dragged themselves to the washrooms on cold winter mornings at 5:00 A.M., cracked the ice on the water pitchers, and poured the frigid water over their heads.

By the end of 1865, Doucet's health forced him to withdraw. He was replaced by Peter Tissot, an excellent man, but not blessed with the disposition that would allow him to enjoy a college presidency. He was a favorite with the students, especially the Northern boys, because of his war stories. But we are told that he was so unhappy that he sent a letter every day for four months to the superior general, asking to be removed.

V

In February 1863, Francis Shaw traveled to the Army of the Potomac's winter camp at Stafford Court House, Virginia, to personally deliver a letter to Robert Gould Shaw from John A. Andrew, the governor of Massachusetts, offering him the commission of colonel and commander of the fledgling Massachusetts Colored Regiment of volunteers. Robert Shaw agonized over the offer and, aware that he was going against what his parents had taught him, turned the governor down.

Then Shaw turned around and accepted. He wrote to his fiance, Annie Kneeland Haggerty, on February 8, 1863, that he thought of leaving the army, but that now he "had to prove that the negro can be a good soldier." He wanted to be a pioneer in proving this point. Then, having established that, he would now be obliged to see the war through. "At any rate, I feel convinced I shall never regret having taken this step," he wrote. He was ashamed that he had appeared cowardly in saying no. Shaw's biographer points out that prior to February, Shaw had never associated with blacks and still had prejudices against them. He referred to them as niggers and darkies and described black leaders he met as "surprisingly gentlemanlike and dignified." By March 17, he was very proud of his troops, the Fifty-fourth Massachusetts Regiment, and bragged about them to his mother.

In June, however, Shaw's black regiment participated in the pointless burning of the deserted town of Darien, Georgia. In a letter to Annie, now his wife, on June 9, 1863, a humiliated Shaw called this a "dirty piece of business." He considered facing court-martial by refusing to go on any more such expeditions, but in the end this embarrassment made Shaw all the more determined to prove his regiment's mettle.

So in the otherwise minor battle of the assault on Fort Wagner, which defended the entrance to Charleston Harbor, Shaw's regiment was assigned to lead the attack against the earthworks, and because the first wave in an assault was usually wiped out, the expected happened. In the same week as the New York Draft Riots, the Fifty-fourth lost nearly half its men and Shaw fell with a bullet in his heart. When the Union army asked for the return of Shaw's body, a Confederate office replied, "We have buried him with his niggers."

Peter Tissot died of cancer in 1875 at the age of fifty-two. Michael Nash lived on to work at Holy Cross and in Troy, New York, where he died of dyspepsia at seventy-one in 1895. James O'Beirne carried on until his death at seventy-seven on February 17, 1917. At the funeral Mass for O'Beirne at St. Thomas the Apostle Church in Manhattan, the Irish Rifles, the Seventh Regiment, and the Fordham Alumni Association paid tribute to the man who loved God, his country, and Fordham, but not necessarily in that order.

On April 6, two months later, in response to Germany's unrestricted submarine warfare, the United States declared war on Germany. General O'Beirne, had he been alive, would have volunteered, but neither he nor anyone else would ever call war romantic again.

5.

Jimmy Walsh Gets Started

Little Jimmy Walsh—thirteen years old, born the year the Civil War ended—had, then in his second semester at St. John's, never been flogged, but he had heard about those who had been. He wrote to his parents on March 4, 1879, in one of his very frequent but very short obligatory reports, that there had been quite a stir in the dorms the night before because they had had the first big floggings of the semester. Indeed, one of the boys who had been beaten was at that moment packing his bags and would go home tonight.

The chief flogger, he said, was none other than Fr. Raciot, vice president of the college. His method was to hit the boy's hands with a strap. If the boy refused to hold out his hands, he would pull the offender into his office and "give him a good cowhiding with a rawhide" and then make him again hold out his hands.

As might be expected, Jimmy's parents, Martin J. and Bridget Golden Walsh, of Archbald, Pennsylvania, wrote back and asked their son why someone might be flogged. They had a large brood of twelve children (six of whom lived to adult life) at various stages of their schooling and careers, and they had, in many senses of the word, an investment in Fordham. On August 11, 1878, Fr. William Gockeln, the president (1874–82), had written to Mr. Walsh and accepted his son James for a straight $300 a year, passing over some of the other fees that St. John's leveled consistently, with the understanding that Walsh Sr. would recruit more students from "your part of the country"—the Wilkes-Barre area—for St. John's. Let's keep this agreement, said Gockeln, "secret and private" among ourselves.

Well, the reason for the flogging was complex, and we can imagine that the parents would really have had to be there to understand. It seems that during night study time, between 8:00 and 9:00, when the classics students had the privilege of studying late while the others had to go to bed, the same Jesuit prefect had responsibility for discipline in the study hall on the first floor as well as in the dormitory upstairs. The boys in the dorm, some in cahoots with the boys downstairs, would make a lot of noise and upset him, and he'd have to run back and forth maintaining order in two places at once. To punish them, he canceled the privilege of night study.

This called for revenge. The boys upstairs created a little machine that, when dragged across the floor, simulated the noise of rats loose in the dorm. One perpetrator got caught. Furthermore, five boys stayed out late. Of course, they had to be "thrashed" and were.

Unlike his predecessor, Robert Gould Shaw, young Walsh talks of these rituals with awe rather than anger. Walsh was driven in part by the inspirational figure of his maternal grandmother, Peggy Kearney, who wrote to him from time to time and who is one of the reasons that, unlike his student contemporaries, Walsh could speak Gaelic. At sixteen, Peggy had made the ninety-three-day journey from Ireland in a ship the size of the *Mayflower*, during which time so many died that she was the only woman to survive and reach Quebec in 1826. She made her way to Pennsylvania, mostly on foot, where she married Martin Golden, a miner from County Mayo, and raised an enormous family, including her favorite, Jimmy. Her second daughter, Bridget, married Martin Walsh in 1864, and they opened a family store.

When the family store began to fail, the Walsh family moved the business from Archbald to Parsons, but left the oldest boy, Jimmy, behind with a large group of uncles and aunts who encouraged his precociousness. At six, he rejoined his family a "young man" extremely old for his years. The family business thrived, and the Walshes soon became known as one of the two wealthy families in the Wilkes-Barre area.

The Walsh boys were quite conscious of the differences between themselves and the other boys. The Walshes were students and their family made over $100 a month. The town boys, sons of Irish immigrant miners, would rather work in the mines—for as little as forty cents a day for the nine year olds to sixty dollars a month for the adult miners—than go to school. Together, they hung around in mixed-aged gangs as large as twenty and amused themselves by story swapping, swimming, smoking, rock fights, and exploring the mines that they were forbidden to enter. Most of the boys dropped out of school at twelve, and some of the boys as teenagers were on their way toward alcoholism.

Surely the contrast between his hometown and Rose Hill explains Jimmy's love of his new home at Fordham. He begins most of his letters, in loopy, preadolescent script, with the charming, "Dear Parents, I take my pen in hand." He asks about their health and assures them that his is just fine. Although, he says, for several weeks there's been something wrong with his eyes and the doctor has given him just the right thing for them. Later, there was something wrong with his side that required painkillers, and in November 1879, a dozen boys were laid low by chicken pox. For treatment, they went over to the infirmary, lodged for years in the old manor house just a few yards from his dormitory.

His younger sister Teresa was ill and, as the months went by, did not seem to improve, so his mother does not visit, though his father does. Jimmy Walsh has thrown himself into this new and marvelous life uncritically, uninhibited by homesickness or fear. By September 28, he reports with pride, he has already learned to conjugate a Greek verb, *tupto*, which he spells out for his parents in Greek script. For the future scientist, St. John's has a museum full of mineralogical specimens and some apparatus for physics and chemistry experiments. In the five-thousand-volume student library, he finds Jules Verne's *A Journey to the Moon*; in the study hall he sits quietly at his desk turning the pages of Sir Walter Scott and James Fenimore Cooper at the rate of almost a page a minute.

He offers no objections to the Jesuit-imposed daily schedule that meticulously breaks up the day into short periods concentrated on different tasks. He is up at 5:30, then has study hall, Mass, and breakfast, followed by class at 8:00. There are twenty minutes of recreation at 10:00, then study hall, dinner at 12:15, and more recreation at 12:45. Anyone who was a Jesuit in formation in the 1950s will recognize this schedule all too well.

Students were to be back in study hall at 2:00, followed by class, study hall, and then supper at 7:30. Bedtime was at 8:00 unless one had night study privileges. Those in the classics course went to bed at 9:00.

Meals often consisted of hoecakes, coffee, and bread for breakfast; hashed potatoes, beefsteak or "Fordham oysters" (some sort of prepared meat), applesauce, apples, and grapes for dinner; plus something light at 4:00 and supper at 7:30. Other evidence, from Jesuit diaries and from archaeological digs, indicates that because the Fordham farm had cattle and pigs, beef and pork were regularly on the menu. Shellfish, such as clams and oysters, appeared occasionally, but most often at celebrations. Indeed, James's younger brother Joe, who followed James to Fordham in 1884, wrote home on May 16, 1886, that a rector's feast served three kinds of meat and eight different desserts. For beverages, they drank soda—ginger ale and sarsaparilla, or "sass." The seniors were occasionally treated to beer, and, of course, the Jesuits in community drank wine, some of which came from the vineyards on their property next to the church, where the Jesuit graveyard is today.

The dining hall, then in the newly rebuilt brick wing of the Moat mansion, was a long, high-ceilinged rectangular room lit by windows overlooking the great lawn on the west and the second-division ball field, later Edwards Parade, on the east. The tablecloths were red at breakfast, white for dinner and supper, and white for all meals on feast days. In absolute silence, the students filed into the hall to places assigned so as to keep them segregated by age groups. Benches were placed on one side of each of the eight-man tables so that all students sat facing the front of the dining hall.

They stood not touching anything until grace was said, then sat down and ate in silence, listening to a fellow student read to them from a pulpit. The reader prepared in advance, determined to get the pronunciation right and avoid the embarrassment of having the prefect, who sat at a white-covered table at the north end of the room, call out a correction. When the meal was over, the prefect rang a bell and all stood, facing him. They answered the prayers, blessed themselves, and filed out with their arms folded, in silence.

For a family as cost-conscious as the Walshes, the long list of extra fees, such as a dollar a year for billiards and another dollar for baseball, was irritating. There was a fifty-cent charge to play football and other fees were charged for piano lessons and drawing. James loved music. He had played the piano at childhood concerts at home and wanted to play and sing at Fordham, but singing lessons cost sixty dollars a year. To his disappointment, the voice teacher told him his voice was in such a process of change that he should wait two years before lessons, but still, he should join the glee club.

Thursdays and Sundays were holidays, and other holidays were often proclaimed when not expected. The rector, or visiting dignitaries such as provincials or bishops, would declare holidays and earn the instant affection of a hundred or so adolescent boys. On Thursday mornings James and his chums loved to swim in the Harlem River, which was half a mile wide and salty when the tide was in. And there were a variety of other excursions: they would go "nutting," as Thoreau used to say, by collecting nuts from countryside trees, and on special permission days they would gather fruit from the Fordham orchards. Faculty could pick fruit on any day.

On other days the prefects would take them on long walks, some as far as twenty miles, to the Hudson on the west and Long Island Sound to the east.

Between 1867 and 1890, there was a chance they could catch sight of the crowds at the Belmont Stakes, the famous thoroughbred horse race that was run at the Jerome Park racetrack until it moved to the Morris Park racecourse east of the Bronx River to make way for the new Jerome Park Reservoir. There were special excursions such as a trip to Manhattan to see St. Patrick's Cathedral or to the great rolling hills of Woodlawn Cemetery. The cemetary was a long walk to the north on one of the highest elevations in the Bronx, from which they could see both the spot where Washington's army had encamped and the tomb of Admiral Farragut.

Young Joe on April 15, 1885, reported on his visit to the Jerome Park racetrack and to Woodlawn Cemetery, where he saw the "solid marble" tomb of J. Gould, "the grandest in the place." Unknown to Joe, however, Gould was still alive and not yet ready to claim his space.

A few days later, James, then a master's degree student and faculty member, got permission to take Joe to Barnum's Circus in Madison Square Garden, which was then still at Madison Square. He saw Tom Thumb and Jumbo the elephant, and he saw a blindfolded lady who crossed a tightrope on a bicycle, but otherwise he was not impressed. Nor, on a later trip, was he much moved by Brooklyn. "Brooklyn is not much," he reported on May 30, 1886. The short walk across the Brooklyn Bridge was long enough because his shoes were tight. Otherwise, he says, "I saw nothing else that I didn't see a hundred times before."

In the Fordham gymnasium, James could work out on two parallel bars or lift some dumbbells or swing some Indian clubs. In the reading room he could pore over several New York daily newspapers—including the *New York Herald,* which regularly covered Fordham commencements because James Gordon Bennett, the publisher, had sent his sons to St. John's. He could also read the *Freeman's Journal,* which was the Catholic paper that during Archbishop Hughes's regime had often criticized the Jesuits, the *Catholic World, Frank Leslie's Illustrated Magazine,* the *Boys' and Girls' Magazine,* and the *London News.* According to an October 1884 *Fordham Monthly,* "Every taste has been provided for and every caste of opinion, political or literary—to the exclusion (of course) of socialism, revolutionism and blood and thunderism—finds in some column or page its legitimate representation."

On Thanksgiving Day, James threw himself into a tournament that included handball, football, a wheelbarrow race, a potato-sack race, a running long jump, a running high jump, a standing long jump, a triple jump or "hop, step, and jump," a quarter-mile race, a one-mile race, a one-hundred-yard race, and a three-legged race. He played football, competed in the sack race, and either wheeled a barrow or was wheeled in the wheelbarrow race.

If we want to visualize James in these events, it helps to know that he later described himself as the "youngest, tallest, heaviest, and ugliest" member of his class. Whatever James's appearance and in spite of his later reputation as one of a handful of leading American Catholic intellectuals, he loved sports, and it is clear that the throwing of the boys into athletic competition on every level was simply an extension of the competitiveness that inspired the Jesuits' classroom teaching.

From the start, it was clear that James was quick to take a religious way of looking at the world. He joined the sodality for his age group, which had eighteen members, and he received permission from his confessor to go to communion every week, though the college rules required confession and communion only once a month. He enjoyed the obligatory annual retreat, with its four sermons a day, daily stations of the cross, nightly rosaries, and Benediction of the Blessed Sacrament at 9:30 before bed.

In a March 14, 1879, letter home, this thirteen year old makes a big point of explaining to his parents the popular misconception of the church's teaching on indulgences. He has learned, he says, that a certain number of days' indulgence granted for a prayer does not correspond to days of suffering in purgatory but to the days of public penance that a medieval penitent would have been sentenced to perform. The basic theme that will mark the rest of this young man's extraordinary life is taking root: the Roman Catholic Church is both true in its teaching and widely—sometimes deliberately—misunderstood. Young James will do his best in everything, and as he eventually gets a clearer idea of what he wants to do with his life, he will look for ways to straighten all this out.

II ⤙

Meanwhile, as America moves into the 1880s, the nation, New York City, the Bronx, Catholic higher education, and Fordham are going through a series of changes that will reshape the world into which James and his classmates will move.

Young Walsh was aware of one of Fordham's problems: the college was small. It is true that all American liberal-arts colleges were small during the nineteenth century, and most remained small until after World War I. But Fordham had been thinking big about the future. An architect's vision for the college, projected in 1864 by Fr. Doucet and resurrected in 1866 when the president, Fr. Moylan, imagined a future student body of six or seven hundred, depicts a five-winged, five-story, three-towered edifice that would have somewhat resembled Healy Hall, the main building of Georgetown's campus. By the time it was built in 1867 with granite from the college's quarry over by the Bronx River and designated as the first-division building, it was pared down to the east wing of today's Dealy Hall.

From 1849 to 1862, enrollment averaged 188. In 1863, 1865, and 1866, it was over 300. But for a number of reasons—the loss of Southern students, the poor American economy during the 1870s, and strong student resentment against the harshness of the still French-inspired system of discipline—enrollment fell sharply in the decade following the Civil War. In 1877, the year before James arrived, it plummeted to 166.

In 1868, three boys engineered a conspiracy in which thirty of them would go home for the Christmas holidays and transfer to Xavier during the break. Xavier had been growing in popularity to the point that it would enroll over 500 students and become the largest of the twenty-one Jesuit institutions in the United States and Canada by the end of the century. Part of its attraction had to be location, but it was also apparently more willing to adapt to the city of which it was a part, whereas Fordham clung to its rural seminary roots. Xavier was also a day school, less expensive and more accessible to the middle class.

The Fordham Jesuits reacted to the defection with their usual rigor. They expelled the ringleaders and, in 1870, considered sending censuring letters to the students and their parents to counteract what they termed the "lies and misrepresentations" spread about the school.

As a result of the defections, when James arrived, the greatest number of students were in the third division, aged ten to fourteen; then the second, those sixteen to eighteen; and finally the first, nineteen and over, which would be down to a handful by the time they graduated. Indeed, at the end of James's first year, nine students graduated. James's most vivid memory, forty years after his own graduation, was of the school's attempt to raise the total enrollment number to two hundred. A campaign was underway to win the "200th Boy." When the boy finally arrived in 1881, he was all the more exciting because he bore a distinguished name: he was Robert Emmett, son of a Walsh family friend and the grandnephew of the Irish patriot of the same name. Perhaps Martin Walsh had recruited him, and Fr. Gockeln's investment had paid off. Alas, it appears Emmett did not graduate.

As all this was going on, a series of small and not-so-small decisions inched the college into the late-nineteenth-century world. Some examples of these changes include napkins on the tables (1867), hot buns for the boarders in the afternoon (1868), chairs rather than benches in the refectory (1880), cups and saucers rather than bowls (1882), fire escapes (1883), and electric lights to replace gas (1889).

Moylan's successor as president, Fr. Joseph Shea, S.J., (1869–74), a Canadian remembered mainly for what his successors considered his misguided kindness, turned the whole seminary building and the fifth floor of the first division into a dormitory where the seniors, for the first time, could have private rooms. Fr. Gockeln, described as a six-foot-two-inch handsome Prussian and a born ruler of men, who spoke elegant French and Spanish, plus English without a German accent, immediately restored order and reversed the decisions of the lax and lovable Shea.

The next president, Fr. Patrick Francis Dealy, S.J., (1882–85) was a St. John's alumnus who had, at seventeen in 1846, gone right from St. John's into the Society and had his novitiate, regency, and tertianship there. It was he who finally broke with the French traditions and laid the groundwork for the modern Fordham. The Jesuits cannot claim that they always recognized this talent in their midst. According to custom, the rector/president would write a brief evaluation of each community member in the so-called second (or private) catalog; in 1853 the rector (probably Larkin) noted that Dealy's "ingenium," or intelligence and proficiency in literature, were only "mediocre," and his special talent was for teaching the younger boys. In those days, this was not a ringing endorsement.

Nevertheless, Patrick Dealy was a man of the world who, in his Jesuit course, had studied in Belgium, Austria, Montreal, France, and Rome and who had once, as leader of a pilgrimage to the Vatican, presented Pope Pius IX with an American flag. Dealy would be president for only three years, but the new America with which Fordham students would have to deal had been building at a furious pace and was waiting outside the gates to either embrace or devour its graduates.

In the four decades between the Civil War and the end of the Spanish-American War, the United States went through an industrial, economic, and cultural revolution that transformed its educational establishment as well. A new wave of immigrants—Germans, Swedes, Norwegians, Danes, Irish, Jews, Chinese, and French—flooded the cities, bringing both enormous human resources and a whole new breed of urban problems. New York had thirty thousand ships a year clogging the East River and Hudson River docks, and eleven thousand factories turning out furniture, clothing, and cigars. Newspapers such as the *Sun,* the *Herald,* the *Tribune,* and the *World* competed to tell the new population's story as New York became the financial and cultural hub of the country. This financial Mecca was home to the new millionaires who built magnificent mansions along Fifth and Madison Avenues as well as home to the "other half," the wretched Italian, Irish, and Chinese laborers, the newsboys and jobless gang members, the garment workers, penniless alcoholics, and criminal exploiters crammed into lower East Side tenements and slums.

Consider one immigrant to the new world who once came through Fordham's gate. On a hot August day in 1870, he made his wandering way to the Bronx and onto the Fordham campus. Twenty-one-year-old Jacob Riis, crushed by his beloved Elizabeth's refusal to marry him, had left Denmark in June to get a new start in a new world. As soon as he got off the boat, expecting to encounter wild Indians and buffalo, he spent half his $40 on a revolver for protection, stuck it in his belt, and walked up Broadway until a policeman gently advised him to put the gun away.

Unable to find work in the city, he joined a group of men on the way to Brady's Bend on the Allegheny River, where he worked as a carpenter and briefly as a coal miner. When France declared war on Germany, expecting Denmark to go to war as well, he was suddenly determined, in his patriotic enthusiasm, to work his way home and join the battle. He sold his clothes and tools and pawned his trunk and watch to pay for his train ticket back to New York. Penniless, he wandered the streets trying to enlist, but was rejected at the French and Danish consulates. On Third Avenue, filled with shame and rage, he trudged north, headed for the countryside, where he thought he might get farm work. Exhausted, he climbed into the back of a milk wagon where he fell asleep; in the morning the milkman found him and dumped him in the gutter. He stumbled upon the Bronx River, where he bathed, then he staggered through the Fordham gate.

He watched the boys, just a few years younger than himself, playing their sports on the great lawn that stretched up from the gate to the new first-division building and the manor house, and he soaked in the tranquility of the shade trees. Then one of the fathers, whom Riis later referred to as a "monk in a cowl, whose noble face I sometimes recall in my dreams," saw him, came over, and offered the starving young man something to eat. As a devout Lutheran who had never seen a "monk" before, Jacob sat in the refectory and devoured whatever the Jesuit set before him, half wondering whether, in return, he'd be asked to give up his Protestant religion or pay homage to the Blessed Virgin Mary. But like Edgar Allan Poe twenty years before, he was welcomed for whoever he was, and religion never came up. The father packed him some food for his next meal and sent him on his way.

His life improved. After several years as a carpenter, farmhand, hunter, trapper, and salesman, he became a lecturer, writer, and newspaper reporter and photographer. Elizabeth's fiance, an army officer, died, and now she was willing to marry Jacob. His exposes of slum conditions became the classic *How the Other Half Lives* (1890), and his friend Theodore Roosevelt, among others, referred to him as "the most useful citizen of New York."

III ~

Charles R. Morris describes this era in *American Catholic*. The Catholic population, he says, "tripled between 1860 and 1890, to more than 7 million, and Catholicism became the country's largest single religious denomination." Virulent anti-Catholicism took new forms, more likely in Michigan and Nebraska than in the urban centers of the 1840s and 1850s.

> The Church's ambiguous adapting to America had sufficed for
> the 1850s when it was only a fringe sect. But by the 1880s, it
> had grown so big, and so politically powerful, that attitudes

had to be clarified. The fundamental question was whether the church should recommence the process of assimilation to American institutions that had been rudely interrupted by the Irish immigration of the 1840s and 1850s, or continue down the separatist path blazed by John Hughes.

The American hierarchy was split between what was called the "Americanist" wing, led by the intense Midwestern patriot Archbishop John Ireland of St. Paul, Minnesota, and the conservatives led by Michael Corrigan, Archbishop of New York. Morris observes that if we could imagine Hughes, if he had not been a priest, as a U.S. senator, we could also see Ireland as "governor of Minnesota and a contender for a spot on a national ticket." The issues separating the two Catholic camps were those that already separated many Americans: the role of the newly formed labor unions, including the Knights of Labor, many of whom were working-class Catholics; the tensions between ethnic groups struggling for a share of the vast wealth available in this, the Gilded Age; and the debate over which practical policies would frame the new nation's intellectual life.

The modern university, modeled on the German system and with Johns Hopkins in Baltimore as the American leading example, with its emphasis on original research and its clear distinction between graduate and undergraduate courses, was just taking shape. The Catholic colleges, mostly Jesuit, were based on an earlier European model with a seven-year continuum of courses from grammar school through the M.A. The new American system, under pressure from state accrediting agencies, was forcing clear distinctions between high school, college, professional school, and graduate school.

One Catholic response to this, led by the liberal Americanists among the bishops, was the establishment in 1889 of the Catholic University of America as a high-level research institution that they hoped would offer an intellectual leaven to the 180 or so Catholic "colleges and universities" throughout the United States at the end of the century. *The Fordham Monthly* (November 1889) took notice. "So to day [sic], we cannot fail to regard the flinging open [of] the doors of our Catholic University as a public emphasis of the fact that the Church in the United States has emerged from her pioneer days and is on the eve of drawing to herself that fallen glory so long denied her."

Four years before, some time in February 1885, James had written to his parents that "the all absorbing topic" at Fordham was the proposed Catholic university and where it would be. At a dinner sponsored by Dealy's Catholic Club, the guest speaker, Monsignor Thomas J. Capel, who himself had failed in an attempt to establish a Catholic university in England, declared that Catholics were as yet neither intellectually nor financially ready to run a university; at this, Dealy, whose pet project had been to establish the Catholic university at Fordham, almost stormed out of the room.

James might not have known that the arguments against the bishops' proposal were mixed and many. Former St. John's seminarian, then Rochester bishop, Bernard McQuaid was convinced that Catholics would never support it financially. Fordham's former president Thebaud agreed and doubted that Catholics were ready for the highest level of graduate education. Although they did not go public with their reservations, Jesuits at Georgetown and Boston College and in New York worried about the impact this would have on their universities, while Dealy, with the backing of New York's Archbishop Corrigan, wanted the prize for Fordham.

Meanwhile, Dealy was taking a series of steps that would prepare Fordham for the next stage, when it would become a university and, in a hundred years, reach for "greatness." He would also introduce two institutions whose value, in the next century, would be questioned—football and ROTC.

While angling unsuccessfully for a decision that would have significantly changed Fordham's character, he threw himself into the political and cultural life of New York City. As part of a dream to develop prominent Catholic lay leaders, in 1871 he had organized the Xavier Union, known as the Catholic Club, a collection of business and professional men who would look for Catholic talent and be patrons of Catholic higher education. *The Monthly* (November 1882), which Dealy helped establish, reported that when Dealy first returned to his alma mater, every leaf of the grand old elms (planted by Fr. Thebaud in 1862) "whispered a thousand welcomes" and that over three hundred members of the Xavier Union, who had also petitioned the Jesuit general to allow Dealy to keep working with them, swarmed onto the campus on October 1 to congratulate their hero.

Dealy was also quick to call the carpenters to continue some construction projects. After the Civil War, the college buildings consisted mostly of St. John's Hall, the church, the original manor house that was used as an infirmary, and the 1838 Moat stone mansion, today's administration building with its various wings and appendages.

When Hughes bought the property in 1838, the main building was a square, three-story mansion just built by Dr. Horatio S. Moat, who had added one-story, classical wings north and south. To this, Hughes added several brick extensions that Thebaud, in his first term, expanded with other modifications. His successor followed the same pattern, so that by the late 1860s, the aerial view of the building resembled a big **E**, with a great hodgepodge of passageways, shacks, sheds, brick squares, and outbuildings tacked on.

There is scarcely a square foot of space on the Fordham campus today being used for its original purpose. The process—build a dorm, gut it for a lab, and make it a dorm again—began in the 1850s and has not abated. For example, the current administration building once housed a visitors' parlor and chapel on the first floor; on the second, science classrooms and a small library, and later, for over a hundred years, a Sodality Chapel; on the third, a dormitory for Jesuit brothers, with an astronomical observatory in the white octagonal cupola. The present two-story brick wings date from 1869, when they replaced the one-story wings of the original mansion. The southern end, to which a porch was added, has been the president's private residence and the infirmary. A particularly ugly three-story library wing stuck out from the center, from the door that now leads into the corridor next to the president's office.

Gradually, as the complex of connected buildings and wings was replaced by the monumental first-division building (now Dealy) in 1867, the science building (now Thebaud) in 1886, and the second division (now Hughes) in 1890, two principles continued to guide the constant makeshift redesigns: maintain separate dormitories for the three divisions to keep the age groups apart, and give each building a variety of functions.

For example, the second division of 1890, designed as a counterpart to the first division, was given a higher ceiling on the first floor to allow for a gym. It also had a billiard room, a reading room, washrooms, and a toilet. The second floor featured the vice president's office and a study hall with a slight slant in the floor, leading to a stage, to allow for theatrical presentations. The third floor consisted of eight large classrooms, each holding fifty boys. The entire fourth floor was a one-room dormitory that could be divided into two by a sliding door, and the fifth floor was a wardrobe. Hughes Hall was Fordham Prep until the 1970s, a dormitory in the 1980s, a faculty office building until 1996, and today, in a period of high enrollment, a residence hall again, with four students in every room.

Thomas J. A. Freeman, S.J., came to Fordham as a scholastic in 1872 with an engineering degree from the Columbia School of Mines. He got Fr. Shea to let him expand the science department and move it into the first floor and basement of St. John's, the former seminary building. He repaired some of the old instruments that had originally come from Kentucky and constructed his own heliostat, with a sixteen-by-thirty-inch mirror. Dealy helped him expand science even more.

Freeman also survived two explosions. In 1874, while generating hydrogen, he mixed it with oxygen. The blast broke all the glassware in the vicinity, momentarily paralyzed Freeman's hand, and ruined his clothes with sulfuric acid. In 1886, his assistant placed a cauldron of paraffin on the heater, the solder of the cauldron melted, and the paraffin caught fire. The flames scorched the opposite wall fifty feet away, destroyed the ceiling fresco, and melted the glass cases in the room.

Perhaps foreseeing that in the long run presidents are judged by the success of their athletic teams, Dealy boosted the baseball team and moved Fordham decisively into football.

The first official baseball game—the early version of the sport was known as rounders—had been played on November 3, 1859, and Fordham beat Xavier 33-17. The team, known as the Rose Hills, did well in the early 1880s, but of course not well enough to please the campus press. In October 1884, a *Monthly* editorial complained that although they had won many games the previous year, they had played badly with good luck. The following month, the lead editorial exhorted the boys to get behind the new football team, as "no game requires more agility and fleetness of foot, or more 'nerve' . . . no game brings into play all the powers of mind and body." The previous year, November 26, 1883,

Fordham had lost to Xavier 12-6. The editorial did not have its effect until the next year, but by the end of the decade, Fordham had established rivalries with Seton Hall, New York University, and unfortunately, Franklin and Marshall, which beat Fordham 56-0.

Taking advantage of an act of Congress that set up college instruction in military science and tactics, Dealy, in his last year, brought a cadet corps, and thus a little more excitement, to the Bronx. Between 1885 and 1890, Lieutenant Herbert G. Squires, who had served with the Seventh Cavalry in the Dakotas, built the cadet battalion to two hundred strong. Because his wife's family had a palatial estate at Irvington on the Hudson, each year Squires would march his men, in full uniform, to the estate for a picnic and a swim. When Squires returned to the Indian Wars in 1890, Lieutenant R. Edwards, one of the more colorful characters in Fordham's history, took his place.

A report dated May 20, 1890, by the army's inspector general, Colonel R. P. Hughes, was published in the *Monthly* (June 1, 1890). It gives an interesting overview of the school. Of 263 students, 187 were in military instruction. The Prep company of sixty students, all under fourteen years of age, showed particular zeal and pride. Fr. Scully, the president, had thoughts of getting horses for a cavalry troop, but Col. Hughes recommended against it. Col. Hughes was disturbed that Squires had been removed without being immediately replaced, especially since this was a growing college about to open a new building (Hughes Hall) that would double its capacity.

Col. Hughes had no reason to worry about the succession. Edwards, fresh out of West Point and thus only a few years older than the boys, was nevertheless a creature of awe. Over six feet tall, lean and straight with a sharp staccato voice, he always looked as if he were marching when everyone else walked. He was quick to whip the boys into shape: the manual of arms became as normative as the *Ratio Studiorum,* and faculty were given tokens of respect due ranking officers as students snapped to attention and saluted as they passed. Cadets held drill competitions for the honor of carrying the colors at the evening candlelight services during May in honor of the Blessed Virgin Mary; the cadets would line up, raise their muskets, and fire four volleys for the Queen of Heaven.

On parade, the battalion would march up and down the road in front of the administration building, under the elms, their heels clicking on the cobblestones as Edwards moved up and down the ranks, counting in step, inspecting the line, snapping, "Bully, boys, boys." "Steady on the left, Mr. Smith. Steady." "Bully, bully." He took his troops on the road, to the laying of the cornerstone at St. Joseph's Seminary at Dunwoodie in 1892 and the Columbus Day parade in Manhattan.

The boys loved him because he obviously loved them so much. He went to all their shows and activities and, though he was not a Catholic, joined them in prayer. Once at a football game, he started to rush from the sidelines onto the field to save a player he thought was being unfairly beaten up. They even admired him for his punishments. When a cadet committed a sufficiently grave offense (the record does not tell us what the offense was), he was court-martialed and reduced in rank—degraded, humiliated before his teenaged peers. Edwards, it is reported, would virtually weep with pride to see a young fellow accept a punishment manfully and show up in the ranks of a company he once commanded. There is a legendary case of a disgraced cadet who both kept a "manly attitude" during his degradation and who plunged into the Harlem River to save a fellow student from drowning. In response, Fr. Halpin, head prefect, with tears in his eyes and Edwards by his side, not only restored the heroic boy to rank but promoted him to a higher rank. The school rocked with cheers.

Edwards went on to serve in the Philippines and, as a general, to command the Twenty-sixth (Yankee) Division during World War I. When he died, he was buried in Arlington Cemetery on February 16, 1931.

Slowly, the Bronx was changing too. In 1868, Southern Boulevard was built, cutting off the main campus from its hills and quarry and the Bronx River. In 1874, the area west of the Bronx River was annexed by New York City, and in 1888, the city bought Fordham's thirty acres north of Southern Boulevard for $93,000 as part of the vast area to be Bronx Park. It was later divided and redesigned into the Bronx Zoo, the New York Botanical Gardens, Van Cortlandt Park, Crotona Park, and Pelham Bay Park, and Mosholu, Pelham, and the Bronx River Parkways.

For transportation, there was an old, unreliable horsecar line along Third Avenue to Fordham called the Huckleberry Line because the horse moved so slowly the passengers could get off and pick huckleberries along the route. But new forces were moving it out of the way.

The same year the city bought the Bronx Park land, the Third Avenue El reached 169th Street. It made it to 177th Street in 1891, to Fordham's gate in 1911, and to Gun Hill Road in 1920. This was the great stimulus to the population explosion in the Bronx. Homes and apartment buildings replaced farms, and three-quarters of the new population settled near the El route in the South Bronx. To the west, only a twelve-minute walk up the hill from the college, one of the great New York engineering feats of the turn of the century was underway. Conceived in 1870 and built between 1902 and 1909, the Grand Boulevard and Concourse, with eleven lanes and tree-lined dividers, stretched from 138th Street to the Mosholu Parkway, a few blocks from Fordham's Southern Boulevard gate. Lined with elegant apartment buildings—which featured large rooms and, in the 1920s, uniformed doormen—the Grand Boulevard and Concourse transformed the borough, luring wealthy citizens, mostly Jewish, from Manhattan to the Bronx. Archbishop Hughes's woodland retreat was about to be surrounded by a sprawling conglomeration of neighborhoods.

By 1907, the Broadway IRT arrived at Van Cortlandt Park. The New York Central and New Haven Railroads now linked a whole series of Bronx and Westchester County communities, such as Kingsbridge and University Heights, to Manhattan and cities farther north. Thanks to such developments in its infrastructure as roads, sewers, and buildings, the Bronx, which had only 17,079 inhabitants in 1855, had 200,507 just forty-five years later.

IV ⌐

This is the world into which Fr. Dealy's Fordham was moving. James Walsh mentions Dealy only a few times in his letters, but they must have been close, especially since James was chosen to deliver one of the student orations at his 1884 graduation. All of these, certainly to the delight of presiding Archbishop Corrigan, were on some aspect of conservatism. James's touched "conservatism in politics" and attacked progressivists who denied the importance of religion. This was consistent with the line of thought he had been developing since he first established himself as a polemicist.

Somehow James Walsh had to make his mark in this increasingly complex society, even though at a very young age he saw himself as separate from the life and culture of his contemporaries. His first contribution to the Fordham *Monthly,* October 1883, was an unsigned editorial, "Tendencies of the Age," which took issue with a *New York Herald* (October 7, 1883) editorial criticizing the church for not respecting liberty or keeping up with the progress of mankind. Mankind is not making progress, says the *Monthly* writer, when crime is up, church attendance is down, and "the very name Scientist has become almost synonymous with Atheist."

In the 1884 June/July/August *Monthly,* the summer of his graduation, young Walsh published a long essay, "The Recent Origin of the Human Race," refuting Darwinism, relying largely on scriptural evidence on the age of the human race. Moses is a trustworthy historian, he argues, so the human species cannot be more than 6,000 to 8,000 years old. Clearly there were two things James loved most in life: higher learning, particularly science, and religion. So James decided to stay one more year at Fordham, get a master's degree, and teach undergraduates—of whom his younger brother Joseph was now a member. Then he would join the Jesuits.

There were a few problems in his life that would make that goal problematic. Although he was very vigorous and loved sports, including baseball and football, for several years he had had problems with his health. In 1874, at the age of nine, he developed a very serious form of facial erysipelas, a disease then common in young and older people that makes the face break out in red blotches and a rash. Today it is cured by penicillin, but not in the 1870s. His case was so bad that a doctor who lived five miles away had to come and treat him daily, charging $7.00 a visit. To reduce the swelling and inflammation, the doctor made a series of incisions, leaving his face scarred for the rest of his life.

At college, in spring 1882, he developed osteomyelitis of the right humerus and his arm swelled to almost twice its normal size. The doctor made three long incisions from his shoulder to elbow, but had to leave the wound open to eventually allow a piece of gangrenous bone to work its way out. To hurry the process, each morning James used his shoe buttoner to scrape out the wound, until two months later, he could pull out the bone and let the wound heal. In 1907, when he was injured in a train accident, bruises on his spine proved to be tubercular, evidence that his 1882 condition may have been tubercular as well.

Like many young people, he also suffered from terrible acne on his face and back. On March 18, 1883, the seventeen-year-old boy writes to his father about dealing with the condition. A friend, Mr. Quin, presumably a medical student, has taken him to a medical school on 15th Street, where, stripped to the waist, the lad stands in an arena before fifty medical students as the doctor lectures about his various lumps, eruptions, whiteheads, and pimples. Apparently the diseased condition of his blood, since the erysipelas years before, had helped the acne take hold. But the doctor says he can cure this in six months, with a blue pill every three weeks and a powerful lotion of sulfate (zinc/2 and chloride/1). James asks his father's approval of the treatment, assuring him that only the medicine will cost anything. Evidently his willingness to be a spectacle for the class excused him from paying a doctor's fee.

In his last year of his regime, Dealy also introduced instruction in dancing, fencing, boxing, and horsemanship. He made plans for a swimming pool, but his term was up before it could be built. The Jesuit system of governance made it difficult for presidents to plan ahead. Since the president was also rector and since the rector has only a three-year term, with one possible renewal, Fordham presidents moved in and out before they could establish strong leadership.

Fr. Thomas J. Campbell (1885–88; second term, 1896–1900) put off the pool for forty years and let the other graces die as well. However, he was a vigorous thirty-seven year old who finished the science building and gave more legitimacy to the place of science in the curriculum. Traditionally, only the students who took Latin and Greek got the full A.B. degree, while those in the commercial curriculum received a certificate. Dealy, however, with his eye on the future, established a three-year program leading to a bachelor of science degree, and Campbell, with his eye on enrollment, stressed the science/English/commercial program.

His successor, Fr. John Scully (1888–91), a Brooklynite who had been dean of St. Peter's College in Jersey City, also retained the science program. He built the second-division building, and to the first-division building he added two wings, which were called the Faculty Building, of which the southern wing was a dining room and the northern wing a two-story chapel. On top, the first division put a little white dome and a towering, gilded cross visible from all the surrounding hills, which had their own cottages, churches, steeples, and elevated lines. This new cross was reputedly ten feet higher than the steeple on Trinity Church in lower Manhattan.

Scully's successor, Fr. Thomas J. Gannon (1891–96), swiftly abolished what he called the "demoralizing" commercial course, as a "Refuge of Idlers," but Campbell, in his second term, brought it back. Not that Campbell was an apostle of pure science. In 1897, in a speech at an alumni meeting, he told his listeners that the current trend in other universities to emphasize science to the neglect of the arts meant the "wreck of the universities and the deterioration" of their students. He assured them that "it is Catholic teaching alone that can elevate the human race from its degradation of ignorance and error." The same year, Fordham dropped the calculus requirement from the curriculum. No great university required calculus, they said, and unless he's going to be an engineer, the student's time is better spent on philosophy, literature, or history. Most freshmen today would agree.

The late-nineteenth-century Jesuits at Fordham and elsewhere were experiencing the first salvos of a battle that would heat up in the twentieth century, the fight for identity as expressed in a traditional curriculum. Ironically, while the Jesuits shifted back and forth in their commitment to any form of concentrated science education, the Fordham student who would, more than any other prominent Catholic in the first half of the twentieth century, dedicate his life to proving that Catholicism is a friend of science was studying to become a Jesuit.

According to a study by Fr. James P. Fagan published in *Woodstock Letters* in 1892, St. John's had graduated about 521 students; of those,

135, or over one-quarter, had entered the priesthood. A high percentage of these 135 students had been the best of the class—those who won medals, made retreats, were active in the sodality, and went regularly to communion. Of these, eighteen graduates and twenty-seven undergraduates were inspired by their teachers, who were nearly all Jesuits, to enter the Society of Jesus. For them—for men such as Patrick Dealy and James Walsh—the decision was not so much a bold move as a natural step down a path long pointed in that direction.

During the 1884–85 academic year, while working for his master's degree and teaching, James Walsh lived for three months at the St. Stanislaus Novitiate at Frederick, Maryland, but was back on campus at Easter. On August 15, however, the traditional day for novices to arrive, James was back at Frederick with a Fordham alumnus assigned as his "angel," or host, for the opening weeks. By December 20, he was already sending both spiritual and medical advice to his family. His parents are to tell Johnny Jordan, who has "had to leave St. Chas." (St. Charles Borromeo Seminary in Philadelphia) because of headaches and a bad stomach, to drink water and walk before breakfast, and take up ice skating, handball, baseball, and football. After all, says James, his own good health is due to exercise and a passionate love of sports. Joe, too, who has suffered nosebleeds, should exercise more and read less.

Furthermore, cautions the pious James, there are a few books in their father's bookcase, usually kept locked, that Joe should not read—not that he would "deliberately read a bad book," of course, but curiosity can easily lead one astray. He laments that the Wilkes-Barre Irish are indifferent to their religious obligation and that the present rising generation has attained so low a religious character. He will miss Christmas at home, but "then our good mother the Society takes care that joy shall not be wanting to her sons in holiday seasons."

V —

Meanwhile, back in the Bronx, a few other small and large events would, in time, gain larger significance. Between January 21 and 28, 1890, when the temperature was eighteen degrees Fahrenheit and the winds howling at sixty miles per hour, the bodies of the seventy-four Jesuits and students who had been buried in the original college cemetery on the other side of Southern Boulevard, plus the bodies of the four Jesuits who had been stored in the vault at St. Raymond's Cemetery since the city had acquired the Botanical Gardens property, were removed and reinterred in the new plot near the chapel, where they lie now. Two bodies could not be accounted for and remain mixed with the earth in the Botanical Gardens. The Jesuits continued to bury their men in the new spot until 1907.

On a spring day in 1891, white-bearded Henry Mitchell MacCracken, a Presbyterian minister and the chancellor of New York University, was enjoying a carriage ride with his sons along the orchards and fields of McCombs Dam Road in the Bronx, on the heights to the west of Fordham and overlooking the Harlem River. He was a visionary well tuned to what was happening—and what had to happen—in American universities, particularly in developing graduate education. Since other leading universities had followed the Johns Hopkins path, NYU had not kept pace. Furthermore, since the 1880s, NYU's Washington Square location had become a liability. The new immigrants, the nearby tenements, and the commercial development at Waverly Place and along West Fourth Street had robbed the neighborhood of anything like a college atmosphere. NYU needed fresh air and space for a science library, residence halls, and athletic fields. What better place to look than the Bronx?

That day he spotted a For Sale sign on the estate of H. M. T. Mali, an NYU alumnus and the consul general for Belgium. This was the place to which NYU would move its undergraduate campus, with Stanford White as their architect. NYU's presence in the Bronx would not last as long as Fordham's, but while it was to last, Fordham leaders would always have to ask themselves how they were like and unlike NYU.

That question certainly never came up on Wednesday morning, June 24, of that same year. A cool breeze tempered the summer heat, as thousands gathered under a cloudless sky beneath ancient elms decked with American flags to celebrate the St. John's College Golden Jubilee Commencement Day. Banners and coats of arms hung from the front of the administration building. A large tent was pitched on the great lawn sloping down toward the railroad. As a processional, Strasser's band from David's Island in Long Island Sound played "My Maryland." Archbishop Corrigan, with a train of acolytes in red and white, monsignori in purple, and Jesuits in black, processed along a path, flanked by cadets, to the altar to celebrate a pontifical military Mass at ten o'clock. Edwards had his battalion show their stuff, all leading up to the day's climactic moment. Then William Rudolf O'Donovan, a sculptor, handed Corrigan a cord that held up an American flag, blocking a tall object from public view. Corrigan gave the cord a sharp pull and the flag fell. The crowd broke into a glorious burst of applause as Archbishop Hughes stood before them in bronze.

And James Walsh? Whatever the wisdom of his advice on health, it did not seem to work for himself. He thrived while he was teaching back at Fordham, but in seminary studies at Woodstock, Maryland, the college that the Society had established in 1869 for all its philosophical and theological studies, he lost weight dramatically. At Fordham he had weighed 208 pounds; now, as a Jesuit, his weight fluctuated dramatically between 220 and 150 pounds. His eyesight, which had been a problem for him as a boy at Fordham, was also failing. In 1892, to James's shock, his religious superiors sent him home. He considered becoming a diocesan priest, but the bishop of Scranton said no.

To make his problems worse, his mother, who had set her dreams on her boy becoming a Jesuit priest, could not deal with his homecoming. For her, this was some kind of hometown humiliation, and it embarrassed her so much that she left Pennsylvania and moved for a while to the West Coast. Here, it seemed, was a potentially great churchman's career cut short.

6.

Becoming a University

One winter Saturday in 1999, I took three young women from my Books That Changed America course, in which we had been reading Jacob Riis's *How the Other Half Lives,* to visit the Lower East Side Tenement Museum, an old row house on Orchard Street with three apartments restored to resemble the crowded flats as they had been between 1860 and 1935. On the way back in the car, they asked me if Fordham had a school song; they had never heard one. Did Fordham have a school song? It has one of the greatest songs ever, I exclaimed, and I even sang it for them.

They would have done better to have been with little Ed Gilleran, a Fordham Prep student who went on to serve Fordham as an administrator for most of his life. On May 1, 1905, his parents took him to the Carnegie Lyceum, one of the recital halls in the old Carnegie Hall building, for an evening of music and drama performed by the Drama and Glee Club of Fordham University. The Dramatic Society put on a short farce and the Glee and Mandolin Club delivered their songs, featuring the tenor soloist William J. Fallon, '06, still a few years from becoming one of New York's most famous and controversial lawyers, known as the Great Mouthpiece.

Then another young man came forward and took up the baton to introduce a new song that he had written himself. He was a large, well-built fellow, a football player, with dark, deep-set eyes and prominent lips and nose. He looked into the faces of his colleagues, raised his hands and brought them back down, and they sang, "Hail, men of Fordham / hail. On to the fray. . . ."

The word *ram* had recently evolved from a slightly vulgar cheer the Fordham boys had chanted at the West Point football game: "One dam, two dams, three dams, Fordham." "Dam" was sanitized into "ram," and suddenly Fordham was identified with an animal, a mascot. The composer incorporated the new word into his fight song. As a musician, John Ignatius Coveney was largely self-taught, but he taught himself quickly and well. He played the piano and cornet best—indeed, he once played them both at the same time—but he also picked up the violin, cello, mandolin, and pipe organ, and could sit for hours in his room with his guitar. When a student brought him a violin-shaped, one-stringed instrument he had never seen before, he played that too, immediately. When he wasn't playing music, he played football, competed on the debate team, led cheers at the games, and wrote verse for *The Monthly,* which then, in his one disappointment, failed to name him editor in his senior year.

Every night in his Dealy Hall room, he said the rosary before midnight. Then, in the dark of the early morning he would suddenly awake with words and music in his head, and where the light from the lamppost cast itself on the wall of his room, he would jot down the words and music. The last line of his song was "We'll do or die." After graduation, Coveney survived in the highly competitive world of professional popular music long enough to write a fight song for the Boston Red Sox and somehow inspire the untrue legend that he had ghostwritten "By the Light of the Silvery Moon." Then in 1911, burned out by overwork, fever, and lack of sleep, he died.

In his own way, young Coveney in 1905 had done as much as several generations of Jesuits to give Fordham what any university needs to carry on—a unique spirit, an "identity."

The question raised about Fordham's history from the beginning—from its first years as a "semi-seminary" for Irish boys run by French Jesuits to its present status as a legally nonsectarian, three-campus collection of colleges in the "Jesuit tradition"—has always been identity. Not that *identity* was the buzzword of turn-of-the-century academic debates, nor that the college had what is now called a mission statement, which, in a more self-conscious age, spells out the idealistic wording of what the institution is trying to do.

Prior to the identity crises of the 1960s and 1970s, the identity, rather than a formula worked out in dialogue with the contemporary culture, was an inherited given, its operating principles spelled out in the three-hundred-year-old *Ratio Studiorum*'s rules for teaching and administering Jesuit schools. But in deciding how and where those rules would be applied, the early Fordham Jesuits seemed to have played their tune by ear, improvising, seizing opportunities to achieve their immediate goals, which goals themselves would mutate to match the opportunities.

Meanwhile, they seemed oblivious of, or indifferent to, some momentous events in American education until those events impinged on the fate of their schools. Since the 1890s, a reform movement had been realigning secular high school and collegiate education. In 1893, a group called the Committee of Ten was called into being by the National Education Association (NEA). Chaired by Charles W. Eliot, president of Harvard and famous advocate of the elective system which was anathema to many Jesuit educators, it issued a report that helped revolutionize American education. It expanded and loosened up the secondary curriculum and called for uniform college admission standards as well as a level of mastery to be achieved in each of several areas.

In 1895, another NEA group, the Committee on College Entrance Requirements, drew on professionals in various fields such as history, modern language, and mathematics to specify the standards for their own fields. This meant that "new" subjects such as history and geography, which Jesuit schools had taught as a tag-on to another subject or had offered for an extra fee, would one day encroach on sacred time set aside for Latin or Greek. In the Midwest, another voluntary agency, the North Central Association, attempted to codify just which qualities constituted a high school or college. It set quantitative college entrance requirements, such as requiring fifteen "unit courses" (a thirty-five week course, meeting four or five times a week, for forty-five minutes each period) for high school graduation. In 1906, the Carnegie Foundation for the Advancement of Teaching constituted itself as an accrediting agency by giving grants only to schools that met its standards.

In *Catholic Higher Education in America* (1972), Edward J. Power of Boston College makes the case that—much as we might be embarrassed to admit it today—American Catholic higher education in the nineteenth century had very little to do with Catholic respect for the intellectual life. He says that prior to 1850, three motives for founding colleges predominated: "to offer a preparatory or preliminary education for boys aspiring to the seminary; to create a center for missionary activities from which the good offices of religion might diffuse the message of the Church to unconverted people . . . ; and to conduct a Catholic house of study and discipline where boys and young men might live in a controlled environment and thus cultivate moral and religious virtue."

We have seen how closely the daily regime of the St. John's students resembled that of seminary novices and how thoroughly the controlled environment of study hall, dormitory life, and religious ritual determined the lifestyle, and thus the thought patterns, of the students. Meanwhile, seminarians with neither advanced degrees nor teaching experience were responsible for much of the classroom instruction, and the fathers, rather than focus exclusively on teaching, sallied forth to found parishes.

But the larger identity question was the same one facing the American Catholic Church: How does the community—whether the faith community of believers or the intellectual community of the university—remain truly Catholic in an ever-changing, American, democratic, and increasingly, secular culture? Recent events complicated this question for would-be Catholic intellectuals. The founders of the Catholic University of America, which opened its doors in 1889, were liberal accomodationists convinced that Catholics had to catch up, on the graduate-school level, with the latest learning in philosophy, biblical studies, and the natural sciences. But in 1899 and 1907, the popes issued documents—*Testem benevolentiae,* condemning a vague collection of ideas called "Americanism"; and *Pascendi dominici gregis,* against "Modernism"—that had their inevitable chilling effect on Catholic scholarship and free discussion. In *Pascendi,* Pope Pius X, to combat those modern ideas that he deemed dangerous, also called for a revival of Thomistic philosophy to offset these errors—thus lighting the spark of neo-Thomism, which, in various forms, became the centerpiece of Jesuit philosophical teaching until the 1960s.

In New York, however, on the pastoral level, while the reformers issued their reports, the church's response to this question of tension between the secular and sacred was both powerful and ambivalent. It combined patriotism and defiance. When Archbishop Hughes appeared before the New York City Common Council in 1840 to protest the educational policies of the common—he would say Protestant—school system, he began by swearing allegiance to the Bill of Rights; he then argued that a book that ridiculed Irish Catholics and was not a textbook did not belong on a public school library shelf. Perhaps Catholic education—both as the voice of an immigrant church and as the voice of a prophetic religion—was destined from the beginning to be in constant tension with the culture that enveloped it. But for the most part, Catholic colleges were founded, evolved, and grew in intellectual isolation from the rest of American higher education. They set their own standards, and even in the context of their own time, concludes Power, those standards were mediocre.

In the 1860 *Brownson's Quarterly Review* article that so upset Archbishop Hughes that he exploded at a Fordham commencement, W. J. Barry dared to say the obvious: that Catholic colleges were really high schools; that they were more concerned with promoting piety than with developing the intellect; and that their curriculum and teaching methods were more indicative of continental Europe than they were to the rhythm and values of American life.

In the 1880s and 1890s, Fordham made the first steps in moving from its French ethos into one more oriented toward the modern New York, which with the rapid urbanization of the Bronx, was coming up to the Fordham gates. Because of prompting by the New York State Board of Regents, between 1890 and the First World War Fordham clearly distinguished the high school from the college and then transformed the college into a university by launching a series of new schools, colleges, institutions, and programs. These included a medical school and law school (1905), an affiliation with the city-owned Fordham Hospital on Southern Boulevard (1907), a university press (1907), a seismograph in the basement of the administration building (1910), a School of Social Studies (1911) that evolved into a School of Sociology and Social Service (1916), a College of Pharmacy (1912), a Graduate School of Arts and Sciences and a teachers college (1916), a summer school (1917), and a journalism course that would launch the Fordham *Ram* (1918) and become the germ of a communications department that would send generations of Fordham men and women into the media.

The same year it became a university, Fordham gave up one of its most charming features—its farm. The space that now features Astroturfed sports fields and tennis courts once had rows of vegetables and a grazing area for thirty cows. Where the old gym now stands was then an apple orchard, and Bronx citizens riding north on the Third Avenue El could look out to the right and admire the hay crop harvested and stacked at summer's end.

Many of the new projects, it seems, were launched without a great deal of deliberation or philosophizing as to how each initiative flowed from the "identity" or "mission" of the school. The rector-president, who in 1893 answered only to the provincial and wielded close to absolute power over the all-Jesuit faculty, simply saw opportunities to expand the university's influence.

During these years, Fordham also established its firm presence in Manhattan with its new schools that would flower into the Lincoln Center Campus of the 1960s. Though the law school moved four times (Bronx campus, 42 Broadway, 20 Veset Street, 140 Nassau Street, and the Woolworth Building), the magnificent Woolworth Building (1913) in lower Manhattan right across from city hall, for years New York's most beautiful skyscraper, was "downtown Fordham." It housed, from 1916, the graduate school, the teachers' college, the School of Sociology and Social Service and, for twenty-eight years, the law school.

During these years, the student population would change significantly in two ways. First, it would grow gradually from 175 boarders and 70 day students in 1888 to 221 boarders and 321 day students in 1906. This shift from boarders to commuters came from the arrival of the Third Avenue El at Fordham's gate in 1900 and the connection of the First Avenue Subway with the elevated at 149th Street in 1904. Fordham would become a "day-hop" school and would not build another dormitory until it added the Robert's and Bishop's wings to St. John's Hall in 1940.

Second, by 1914, Fordham would boast a total of 1,700 students, 400 of whom were studying law. In 1915, Fordham granted almost twice as many law degrees (ninety-two) as undergraduate degrees (forty-eight). In 1907, Fordham had received a new charter renaming itself as Fordham University, with St. John's College officially retaining its original name for the time being, even though it had long been known as Fordham. By any measure, Fordham was still a small school, but its identity had been irrevocably transformed.

Today, of the twenty-eight Jesuit colleges and universities, only one, the College of the Holy Cross, is still purely a liberal-arts college. There are no business courses, no vocational programs, no master's degree programs—and it ranks as one of the best colleges in the United States. Colleges much smaller than Holy Cross, such as Wheeling and Rockhurst, have designated themselves "universities." In *The Dying of the Light* (1998), a historical survey of seventeen religiously affiliated institutions, James Burtchaell argues that the schools he has studied, including Fordham, by recklessly expanding schools and programs and accommodating their curriculums to secular markets and values, diluted their quality and compromised their religious identity. If this criticism is valid with regard to Fordham, the early-twentieth-century presidents took the fateful first steps.

Fr. Patrick Dealy is credited with moving Fordham away from French influence and more into the New York and American mainstream, but this move had been prepared by some earlier changes within the Jesuit Society itself. The 1869 founding of Woodstock College on the Patapsco River in the woods outside Baltimore gave American Jesuits a common school of philosophy and theology. This meant that the scholastics would no longer study abroad in France or Belgium, and the colleges, like Fordham, would not need to double as seminaries. Its publication, *Woodstock Letters* (1872), would be a bond of union carrying news of the goings-on in communities all over the country. In 1879, the Maryland and New York Provinces were joined, separating New York from the French-dominated New York–Canada Mission.

Thus, from 1880 on, the Jesuit teachers were more likely than their predecessors to consider where their students were coming from. Meanwhile, according to an 1885 study by the provincial, Robert Fulton, S.J., St. John's standards had slipped below those of the other province colleges, and the colleges as a group were not cooperating sufficiently in setting up common norms.

Xavier and St. John's vied between themselves to surpass the other in the classical courses and to make fewer concessions to the commercial course, but in 1889 they were challenged to face a new reality. The secretary of the state board of education decreed that standards formulated by the state board of regents applied to denominational as well as other secondary schools.

In 1895, the state board of appeals defined a "college" as a four-year school requiring four years of secondary education for admission. Since the Jesuit colleges had a seven-year program with students of various ages and since the curricula at Jesuit high schools did not correspond to those of the non-Catholic high schools, Jesuit students who applied to law and medical schools (medical schools at that time required only a high-school education) had found their applications contested. Even though Xavier demonstrated to a visiting committee from the board of regents whose members sat in on a Latin class in 1895 that its students were indeed capable of upper-level work, the handwriting was on the wall. Jesuits schools would have to conform lest they be publicly perceived as inferior.

The second and third generations of immigrant families were moving up socially and economically. They now had the resources to send their boys to better schools and were increasingly sending them to non-Catholic and secular colleges. Each year the enrollment crisis assumed more alarming proportions. A major symptom was the "small boy problem," with "little kids" numerically overwhelming the true college-age boys on campus.

An 1898–99 report of the United States commissioner of education showed that of fifty-nine Catholic colleges responding, only nineteen had one hundred or more undergraduates and seventeen had fifty or fewer. The same year, a study by a Notre Dame professor estimated that 1,500 Catholic students were at thirty-seven leading non-Catholic institutions, compared to 4,700 attending eighty Catholic schools, but only 973 of these were attending academically reputable Catholic schools. In 1907, it was estimated that 8,700 Catholics were attending secular institutions. Catholic educators had pleaded with the bishops to demand, as a matter of discipline, that Catholics attend Catholic colleges, but the bishops backed off. Some were more inclined to send chaplains to minister to their flocks on secular campuses than to force their young sheep into folds run by religious orders that bishops could not control.

Conservative Jesuits throughout the United States, in New York more than the Midwest, fought valiantly, sometimes bitterly, against compromise. They saw that raising standards also meant increased specialization, that teachers would have to learn one thing well rather than a little of everything, whereas Jesuit teachers had long enjoyed being known as brilliant generalists. When a Chicago Jesuit argued that specialization would make Jesuits real scholars, New York's Francis P. Donnelly, S.J., famous for his little textbooks that taught writing style by imitation, derided him for "obsequious truckling to half-baked theorists outside the Society who have no solid pedagogical principles." As historian Philip Gleason observes in *Contending with Modernity*, the Jesuit conservatives did not intend to defend mediocrity; they were defending traditional liberal-arts humanism; they correctly foresaw that modernization would undermine curricular coherence and increase the bureaucratization of higher education.

This is not to say that Jesuit schools had any future throwing themselves under the tank treads of change. The New York Jesuit schools began to adapt their program to the four-year/four-year scenario of the rest of the country. As Christa Klein demonstrates in her dissertation, *The Jesuit and Catholic Boyhood in Nineteenth-Century New York* (1976), the argument that the boys enjoyed a continuous education, which the intrusion of such other topics as the sciences would interrupt, was in actual practice a self-serving illusion. "The bulk of the entering students never completed the entire classical course of studies." At Xavier only 9.6 percent of the students completed the entire course; at Fordham, only 6.7 percent. Most students remained no longer than two years. Apparently parents and students in those days saw no necessary continuity in the seven-year course, or they wanted some Jesuit education but did not accept the Jesuits' traditional idea of how much was good for them.

II —

By 1905, by heeding both the state regulators and New York archbishop John Cardinal Farley, an original St. Joseph's Seminary graduate who wanted a well-coordinated system of education in his diocese, the Jesuits developed a new master plan. First, Fordham made a point of separating the youngest boys from the system. It turned down forty applicants under twelve and accepted only half its applicants from Latin America. In 1907, it designated St. John's Hall as a separate grammar school. The seventy-six boarders had their own dining room, featuring a full forty-five-minute served lunch with an emphasis on instruction in table manners. Second, Xavier, Fordham, and the newly opened (in 1900) Loyola School at 84th Street and Park Avenue, an exclusive prep school for the wealthiest families, would send their students to Fordham College in the Bronx. In time, Xavier, whose 16th Street neighborhood was becoming increasingly commercialized, was expected to move to a more residential area.

The years between 1890 and the First World War were also a time of subtler transformation in the college's internal culture. The ritual of building the school year around the church year continued, with good times marked by no less than fifty-four feasts, classified as first or second class depending on the whether three or two meats and four or three vegetables were served. After the feast, the fathers would retire to their coffee and liquors. At the Rector's Feast under the French, the lay faculty and senior students would join the fathers for wine; under their successors, the fathers would withdraw into their private recreation room.

The Minister's Diary of 1889–1900 gives us a few other odd insights into Fordham life and attitudes. The workmen were paid $9.00 a month and board—but "should not expect to be treated like the boys," so no dessert or preserves. Steam heat was turned on the first week in October and off in May. At the 1894 commencement, the reporters were made welcome with beer and cigars.

Enthusiasm for athletics, which picked up during Fr. Dealy's administration, increased, and the Jesuit teachers, consistent with the *Ratio*'s emphasis on "emulation," carried the spirit of competition that sports fired up into academic life. Football was hard to sustain because the boys were so small and because other schools were alarmed at the roughness and the number of injuries, but baseball became more popular than ever. In 1907, the world-famous journalist Richard Harding Davis, traveling in Africa, stopped to admire a French Jesuit mission in Wombali. The Jesuit, a big red-bearded man, asked Davis if he knew of Fordham, as Davis often passed near Fordham on the way to his Westchester estate. "Of course, I know it," Davis replied. "They have one of the best baseball nines near New York. They play the Giants every spring."

In other sports, a track team was initiated, and by 1916, there were eight new tennis courts and a tennis house. For a while, military drill and the atmosphere of discipline it effected complemented the healthy competitive climate.

Perhaps an early sign that some changes were under way was the decision to start selling cigarettes to the boys in 1892. A Jesuit brother opened the tobacco shop for the first few minutes of each division recreation, did his business quickly, and closed up. A concession indeed. There is evidence that the old disciplinary system was not working as well as the fathers had thought.

As the city grew closer, both in the new neighborhoods outside the gate and in the access to New York provided by the elevated line, the young men were even harder to control. The biggest offenses recorded in the Prefect's Diary, the Minister's Diary, the President's Diary, and the minutes of the consultors' meetings involved going to the city without permission, staying out all night, getting drunk, and fighting. The rector's notes from 1891 to 1896 contain accounts of forty-two violations serious enough to involve expulsion during years when there were only a few hundred students. Considering the small minority of the student body who were older boys, and that usually many more college boys break rules than get caught, this is evidence of strong resistance to Jesuit discipline.

Several of the boys had been caught frequenting whorehouses. In 1891, seven third-division boys revealed to their confessors that an English grammar teacher, who had graduated the year before but remained on as a faculty member, had come into their dormitory at night and molested them. Notes on other boys who were expelled indicate the attitude of the Jesuits toward their troublemakers: they were "undesirable," "suspicious characters," "effeminate," "self-willed," and "vulgar braggarts." Andrew Carnegie's nephew George, fifteen, a Protestant from Pittsburgh, is described as "a cigarette fiend, spoiled by his parents' indulgence."

One bright young man who tested the disciplinary code of the 1890s was James (Jamie) O'Neill, son of the actor James O'Neill and older brother of the playwright Eugene O'Neill. The father, famous for his long tour of America in *The Count of Monte Cristo,* was a loyal Catholic whose parents had hoped he would become a priest. Though he chose the stage, he made an effort to give his two sons some Catholic education. Eugene has documented the tragedies of their family life in *Long Day's Journey into Night* and *A Moon for the Misbegotten,* and biographers have tracked the careers of the children.

Jamie seems a particular case of a brilliant and creative young man who could not discipline himself well enough to succeed according to established norms, i.e., graduate from college. When he arrived at St. John's Prep in 1895 at the age of sixteen, he had already lived at Notre Dame as a young boy from 1885 to 1895 and spent a semester at Georgetown. He was a good student, wrote poetry at twelve, and impressed his peers with his sometimes irritating oratory. But the collapse of his father's career and the discovery of his mother's morphine addiction, combined with his mercurial temperament, made it hard for him to settle down.

He had, as one critic described him, great "phoenix" powers, and in many ways his performance during his three and a half years at Fordham was spectacular. He quickly jumped from the prep's second grammar to the college's freshman year and won prizes for three years in Greek, Latin, religion, English, and elocution. As an editor of the *Monthly,* he graced its pages with long poems studded with classical allusions, including an imitation of Pope's "Rape of the Lock" in heroic couplets and essays on Homer and contemporary theater. In his prize-winning essay on the state of American drama, he asks why the Golden Age is dead, why Shakespeare has been replaced by vaudeville. He concludes that the Jews who own the theaters are more interested in money than in art and thus feed the audience "only what will tickle their degenerate palates" (December 1898).

Ultimately his reckless sense of humor ruined his Fordham stay. As a senior he lived on Dealy five, called "Fifth Avenue," with twenty-five other seniors. He thought it might be fun to bet a friend that he could bring a prostitute from the Haymarket to campus, introduce her to the Jesuits as his sister, and sneak her up to his room.

For a while it worked. As brother Eugene recreates the scene in *A Moon for the Misbegotten,* students knew what was up and howled as Jamie and his girl, who wore black and "had eaten a pound of Sen-Sen to kill the gin on her breath," strolled among the elms with an unsuspecting Jesuit in tow.

Unfortunately for Jamie, the woman also had a sense of humor, or she forgot her part. At the last minute she reverted to character and blurted out, "Christ, Father, it's nice and quiet out here away from the damned Sixth Ave. El. I wish to hell I could stay here."

Jamie was expelled. The rest of his life, says a biographer, "was marked by a downward spiral of boozing, whoring, and prolonged periods of sponging off his parents." Nevertheless, stretching the truth, he bragged to Eugene, "Remember, my younger brother, that I graduated from Fordham University, that great edifice of learning. I was reading Aristotle, my boy, under compulsion necessarily, when you were playing marbles with yourself."

In April 1904, the consultors observed that so many students were staying out all night that the students obviously no longer considered it a serious offense. Should they expel them all? The same year, on December 21, perhaps rendered thoughtful by the Christmas season, the new president John J. Collins noted in his diary, "The only feature of discipline here which I strongly object to is the flogging. That has been both too frequent and too unreasonable." That the president, who was new to Fordham, was disturbed by this discovery, indicates that corporal punishment, though common in Catholic colleges, was not always condoned by thoughtful persons.

In February 1905, the consultors asked themselves whether they should abolish military drill. More than a hundred were already excused, and the regiment had poor discipline and poor leadership. They were also upset by the "obstinacy" of the seniors who stayed away from Mass and morning prayers. On April 20, 1906, another new president, Daniel J. Quinn, S.J., issued a directive that was to be read to all the students: Anyone who goes out at night without permission or stays out beyond the allowed time, 11:30, will be dismissed. In October 1910, the minister noted that two medical students had been in a fight in a pool hall on Pelham Avenue. Attempts to get the police to close the place had failed because the owner was "in" with the police. The saloon proprietor on the corner of Pelham Road and Third Avenue, however, had been successfully scared out of serving Fordham students at his bar.

III ⌐

To read, or reread, *The Thirteenth, Greatest of Centuries* (Catholic Summer School Press, 1907) today is to travel back between fifty and ninety years into three states of the Catholic mind, each a significant guide into three different aspects of the American church's attempt to define itself in its relationship to a changing American culture. The three minds are those of the American church, Fordham, and the author himself.

The keyword is *change.* To many pre–Vatican II Catholics, one of Catholicism's great attractions was that the world changed while the church did not. The church was, like Peter, the rock that bore the buffeting of time's storms but came through them with its doctrinal and moral integrity unbroken. Part of the intellectual underpinning of this point of view was the conviction that there had once been a time when Western civilization had achieved a cultural—theological, political, and artistic—unity that so embodied Christian principles that all reasonable persons could look at this era as a Golden Age, as historical evidence that the Catholic Church's teachings were valid for all times.

To some degree, perhaps, intellectual Catholicism's glorification of the Middle Ages can be seen as a part of the medievalist or the Romantic period in nineteenth-century literature, with Tennyson's "Idylls of the King," rewriting the Arthurian legends, and Charles Reade's *The Cloister and the Hearth* (1861), a great novel on the age of Erasmus, and later, the American historian Henry Adams's study *Mont-Saint-Michel and Chartres* (1913).

In another sense, backward-looking though it was, *The Thirteenth, Greatest of Centuries* was ahead of its times. The skeleton of its propositions would take on flesh in other forms during the Catholic Renaissance—the period between the two world wars—when, faced with the collapse of the secular values that had brought on World War I, Catholic intellectuals became convinced that the wisdom of Christian civilization offered principles on which a new world could be built. The Catholic philosophical revival would include scholars such as Jacques Maritain, Etienne Gilson, and Anton Pegis, and the popular radio preacher—and later TV phenomenon—Rev. Fulton J. Sheen, all of whom saw the revival of Thomistic philosophy as key to the church's long-term credibility.

The Thirteenth, Greatest of Centuries, basically a hymn of praise cataloguing the institutional accomplishments of the age, is not alone in noticing that the thirteenth century had been special. Its eleventh edition (1943) reprints passages from secular historians—Frederic Harrison, Macauley, Freeman, Fiske, and Henry Adams—as testimony to the century's greatness. Said Adams in *Mont-Saint-Michel and Chartres,* "The twelfth and thirteenth centuries were periods when men were at their strongest; never before or since have they shown equal energy in such varied directions or such intelligence in the direction of their energy."

Today, in general parlance, the word *medieval* is often used to express opprobrium, i.e., to represent ideas or values any secular, liberal, and enlightened rationalist, modernist, or postmodernist would reject, as in "the living conditions were medieval" or "medieval torture." On the other hand, Fordham's signature building since 1936 has been Keating Hall, with its great central clock tower emerging from the four Gothic turreted wings surrounding it, as if the whole building were a medieval fortress standing out against the modern world. Fordham's most beautiful modern building, the William Walsh Family Library, imitates Keating Hall's towers while rounding out its fortress corners, and the new residence, Millennium Hall, planted in the shadow of Keating, mimics Keating's Gothic character.

What did *The Thirteenth, Greatest of Centuries,* as a text, say to its readers between the 1900s and the 1960s? Let us work our way back.

The preface to the memorial edition (1943) by Fr. D. B. Zema, S.J., PhD., F. R. Hist. Sc., of the Fordham Graduate School of Arts and

Sciences, is one Jesuit's interpretation: "There is nothing that the modern world needs more desperately than to escape from itself. Like a drunken, delirious giant uttering gibberish about 'progress,' 'democracy,' 'science,' 'planning,' etc., the modern world is reeling in a bad dream, little aware of the precious heritage it has forsworn. In consequence, the twentieth has been a bad century."

The Renaissance, the Protestant Revolt, eighteenth-century rationalism, and nineteenth-century liberalism and nationalism had destroyed man's soul and turned him over to greedy commercialism, and the two centuries had reaped the harvest of barbarous war. Civilization was on the point of collapse. "If there are still thinking men," said Zema, they will see more light in this book on "the problem of postwar reconstruction than most other planning schemes that are rolling off the presses."

In the 1950s, *The Thirteenth, Greatest of Centuries* was prominent on the required reading lists in Fordham's introductory history courses taught by Jesuits. But intellectual fads die fast. In the 1960s at Shrub Oak, the seminary philosophy school in Westchester County affiliated with Fordham, the Jesuit scholastics were witnessing in their seminary courses the last gasps of the medievalism that the already-forgotton *Thirteenth* and the writings of the giants like Maritain and Gilson had come to represent.

To its original readers, this book was an illustrated personal tour through universities, cathedrals, technical schools, dramas, paintings, libraries, literary masterpieces, popular books, hospitals, and explorers and other great persons. Aquinas, St. Francis, Dante, St. Louis IX, and the medieval women saints were all represented with the intention of leaving the reader gasping with admiration for a better day. It also claims that medieval geniuses anticipated the findings of the modern sciences. St. Thomas Aquinas argues, for example, that man's resurrected body shares the same identity as the living person, just as the bodies of the young boy and the old man are the same person, even though the matter that composes it has completely changed. This, says the author, is a "marvelous anticipation of present-day physiology as well as a distinct contribution to Christian apologetics."

For personal reasons, the author is particularly concerned about the church's contribution to medicine. Pope Innocent III, he reminds us, was responsible for founding practically all the city hospitals in Europe. The church has been maligned by enemies who describe it as the foe of scientific progress; historians of medicine have charged, for example, that in 1300 Pope Boniface VIII forbade the practice of dissection. Not so. Boniface had merely forbidden the dismemberment and boiling of the corpses of dead crusaders who wanted their remains shipped back home from the Holy Land for burial.

The book touched on what might otherwise be considered odd questions because these questions were critical to the establishment of Fordham's medical school and because the author was James J. Walsh, M.D., Ph.D., Sc.D., Litt.D., LL.D., PeD., Knight of St. Gregory and Knight of Malta, as the 1943 edition identifies him.

Walsh had not allowed his forced exit from the Society of Jesus, his mother's shame over his "lost" vocation and clerical career, or rejection by the bishop of Scranton to defeat him. With his younger brother Joseph, he had gone to the University of Pennsylvania Medical School. Determined to get the best medical education available in his day during an era in which high standards for medical education had not yet been set, James and Joe traveled through Europe from 1895 to 1898, attaching themselves to the leading doctors in Paris, Rome, Berlin, and Vienna. James had learned French, German, Latin, and Greek at Fordham and Gaelic at home, and found Spanish and Italian easy to read because of his Latin background. He had also picked up some Russian, so he was ready to travel.

In Berlin, James put himself under the tutelage of Rudolf Virchow. This internationally renowned pathologist was also a historian and anthropologist who, like Walsh, refused to be swept along by the Darwinists and did not share the common late-nineteenth-century confidence in the inevitability of progress. A high point of their travels was an 1897 trip to Russia as correspondents for the New York *Medical Record,* which paid them $400 to report on the Twelfth International Medical Congress in Moscow. The brothers were surprised to find Russia much more scientifically advanced than they had expected. In an ironically infelicitous phrase that he would not use years later, Walsh wrote that Russian medicine was not "as medieval as we thought at first." Moving on to St. Petersburg, they followed up on James's interest in neurology by visiting Pavlov's laboratories and observing his experiments.

Back in Berlin, James had another chance to play the role of Catholic apologist. At the World Congress on Leprosy, one scientist suggested that leprosy was prevalent in northern South America because the church's abstinence rule required the population to eat more fish; according to one theory, this was a dietary basis for the disease. Walsh intervened: because of an indulgence granted Spain and shared by its colonies during the Moorish invasions, South Americans could eat meat at any time. Walsh found that evolutionists tended to blame heredity for leprosy, whereas the Middle Ages, correctly, saw it as a contagious disease.

The trip was having a profound effect on Walsh's career and thinking. On a personal level, he was gathering experiences, such as visiting cathedrals and hospitals, which he would work into his forthcoming books.

IV ⟋

On June 18, 1904, Fordham's president, John J. Collins, S.J. (1904–06), recorded in his diary that twelve physicians, all alumni of St. John's College, had joined the fathers in the community for dinner. They had come to be consulted on the wisdom of Fordham's opening a medical school in the fall. At the time, there were about 150 medical schools in the United States. Three days later, Collins announced he had decided to add one more, and a law school besides.

Alexis de Tocqueville noticed from the start the tendency of American lawyers to play leading roles in public life, so it was natural for Catholics to establish law schools as a route into the public mainstream. They were also one of the least expensive schools to set up. Notre Dame (1869), Georgetown (1870), and Catholic University (1895) led the way. Fordham started with 13 students and prospered immediately, with its first classes in a makeshift space in the newly opened theater building known only as College Hall. In 1907, there were 106 in rented space at 42 Broadway. By 1912, Fordham was bragging that 80 percent of its students passed the bar exam.

Establishing a medical school was another matter. To undertake so formidable a project at a few months notice by today's standards may seem reckless. But formal university-based medical education at the beginning of the century was still in its early stages. Until Johns Hopkins restricted admission to college graduates with a year of natural sciences in 1893, students could study medicine without having first acquired a college education. Only after Abraham Flexner's 1910 report for the Carnegie Foundation for Advancement of Teaching, which called for better laboratories, student access to hospital patients, and better teaching, did national standards cut down on the number of medical schools.

Jesuit colleges had been thinking of medical schools for some time. St. Louis University opened one in 1842. When Georgetown opened its medical department in 1849, there were virtually no admissions requirements other than the ability to pay the tuition. The faculty, most of whom were full-time physicians, were not interested in research. The course of studies consisted of a five-month program of lectures, some time in laboratories and dissecting rooms, an oral exam, a one-year apprenticeship, and a thesis. A graduate had to be twenty-one years old; most students had other occupations during the day and very few had any other college-level education. Creighton College opened a medical department in 1892, Marquette in 1907, Loyola of Chicago in 1910. Among the non-Jesuit schools, the Catholic University tried to negotiate a transfer of Georgetown's school to its jurisdiction in the 1890s, but the lay faculty, more than the Jesuits, refused to go along.

On Thursday, September 28, 1905, the Fordham School of Medicine opened with seven faculty, four of whom were physicians, and eight students, no building, and no endowment. Applicants needed one year of college work, including physics, inorganic chemistry, biology, and French or German. Because space in the old science building was not yet ready, the first classes met upstairs in the new College Hall, right across from the new law school. It was a disappointing start, but Collins was determined not to fail.

The forty-seven-year-old Kentucky-born Collins had come to the Fordham presidency short on experience but high on self-confidence and a willingness to make decisions. His first was to finish construction of College Hall, the immense, new Grecian-style classroom and theater building erected on the site of the demolished old original manor house. For a hundred years, friends of architecture and history would lament the thoughtless destruction of the oldest link with Fordham's past and its replacement with a towering, red brick hulk that clashed with the traditional granite of every building around it, particularly the chapel and St. John's Hall.

Next, Collins sold four acres of college swampland at the far Southern Boulevard end of the campus to the city of New York to build a municipal hospital. At the alumni dinner at Delmonico's in February 1905, the visionary Collins described a future Fordham University with not just medical and law schools but schools of engineering, pedagogy, and theology. He also exhorted the alumni to follow the example of Holy Cross College and to raise money for a new dormitory to be called Alumni Hall.

But it didn't happen. In 1906, Collins was already gone. The pope made him a bishop and appointed him administrator of Jamaica, in the West Indies, where he had been a missionary for eight years before coming to Fordham.

That year, Fr. Daniel J. Quinn (1906–11) appointed James Walsh acting dean of the Fordham medical school, where he also served as professor of medical history and nervous diseases. As a scholarly polemicist, Walsh did regular battle with anti-Catholic critics such as former president of Cornell University Andrew Dickson White, whose *A History of the Warfare of Science with Theology in Christendom* (1896) repeated the old charge that Catholic medical schools would never allow dissection. As an entrepreneur, Walsh helped establish Fordham University Press, which published most of his books; as a controversialist, he won the admiration of President Theodore Roosevelt, who entertained him with a White House lunch and delighted in picking Walsh's brain about the thirteenth century. Roosevelt read the book and many of Walsh's other works and praised him in print. The *Saturday Review* of London (February 8, 1908), less enthusiastic, called it a "dull, thoughtless, styleless volume." "It is difficult to imagine a reason why it should have been printed. . . . The matter is simply a mass of second-hand information, acquired but not assimilated." It sold 70,000 copies, but few readers today, familiar with contemporary standards of scholarship, would find it very satisfying.

As a dean, Walsh was a dynamic innovator. As a teacher, he would walk into class, pick out a student in the first minute, and throw him a sweeping question, such as, "Tell us about the brain." He added medical history to the requirements, introduced a course in physiological psychology, and to the displeasure of some faculty and the next president, put more emphasis on clinical experience than on attending lectures. Convinced that personal observation and experiment were the only real sources of knowledge, he sent his students to Fordham's neighbors, the Bronx New York Zoological Garden for lectures on comparative anatomy and the Bronx New York Botanical Gardens for classes on poisonous and diseased plants.

Early in 1911, he suggested to Fr. Quinn the establishment of a school of pharmacy that would require only one year of high school for admission. In the fall, only two recruits showed up and both dropped out immediately. With more careful planning and slightly higher standards, such as a high school diploma, the pharmacy school reopened the following year.

When Dr. Carl Jung, at the University of Zurich, received his letter from Walsh inviting him to deliver a series of lectures at Fordham in September 1912, Jung, at the turning point of his career, welcomed the invitation. He was fascinated by the United States and, in an earlier visit, had won the friendship of William James, whose psychology was developing along similar lines. Jung was also in the process of separating his ideas from those of Sigmund Freud, who had joined him on the previous American visit. Jung was interpreting Freud's sexual ideas symbolically rather than literally. This philosophical difference strained their personal friendship, and Jung's trip to New York would symbolize and deepen the distance beween them.

The *Kaiser Wilhelm II* delivered Jung to New York on September 18. He had plans to lecture in Chicago, Baltimore, and Washington, D.C., but the high point of the visit was the last two weeks of September, during which he delivered nine lectures to ninety psychiatrists and psychologists, plus a daily two-hour seminar for Walsh's extension course at Fordham. Jung was one of a team of a dozen international scholars whom the entrepreneurial dean had gathered on the Bronx campus that fall—a public event to demonstrate that Fordham medical school was worthy of serious attention. The date will go down in the history of science because, as Frank McLynn writes in *Carl Gustav Jung* (1997), "here Jung broke decisively with Freud" (200). He abandoned Freud's concept of libido and of infant sexuality, and Freud's broad tendency to interpret so much of human life in sexual terms. He developed his own theory, based on Adler, that the key to neurosis lies not in the past but in the present.

In the midst of the Fordham talks, Jung took time out to deliver a long interview to the *New York Times* (September 29, 1912) in which he analyzes the American psyche. The American man, he says, has not learned to love his wife. Rather, he pours his libido, his vital energy, into his business, gives his wife respect, hands the direction of the family over to his wife, and turns her into a mother figure. "You believe," he says, "that American marriages are the happiest in the world. I say they are the most tragic."

When, flushed with success, Jung returned to Europe, Freud wrote him a "welcome back" letter which began, "Dear Dr. Jung," rather than the earlier, "Dear Friend."

By 1912, Walsh had succeeded in winning Fordham a Class A ranking from the American Medical Association under the condition that a number of other reforms would be carried out. They had to open a clinic by October 1912, maintain a minimum of six full-time professors working full time for the school, and devote $20,000 a year, beyond tuition receipts, to improving teaching.

Walsh soon learned that the next president, Thomas J. McCluskey, S.J. (1911–15), although he signed a pledge to back Walsh's reforms, had no intention of doing so. In a decision that hurt him more than anything that had happened since he had left the Society in 1892, Walsh, in November 1912, joined by a group of faculty supporters, felt honor bound to resign as dean.

The following year, January 1, 1913, the new medical-school building—later called Old Chemistry, and now, as a residence hall, Finlay Hall—opened near the Bathgate Avenue entrance, allegedly for convenience in delivering corpses. It had two lecture halls, each with the capacity for two hundred students, there was to be a clinic on the first and second floors, and it had a working relationship with the newly opened Fordham Hospital, since the president of the hospital was also the school's new dean. Third-year students worked in the hospital's dispensary, which treated fifty thousand patients a year, and fourth-year students, in groups of five, served two month-long internships in medical and surgical wards, then moved on to other city hospitals. The following year, registration reached 315.

Briefly the school enjoyed, for its standards, a mini golden age. However, in spite of former dean Walsh's offer to help raise the money, and perhaps because of the war, the Fordham medical school was unable to attain the endowment needed to support a full-time faculty, and it closed its doors in 1921.

But James Walsh kept going. The New York *Telegram* (August 5, 1911) had called him "the busiest man in New York," an expert on nervous disorders but "an authority on ten or twelve other branches of human knowledge." James Gordon Bennett Jr., perhaps with some memories of his own brief stint as a St. John's student, named Walsh medical editor of the *Herald* in 1913. Pope Pius X had told Walsh in a private conversation in 1904 that he did not think much good came from controversial writing, but that if Saint Paul were alive today he would spread his good news through the printing press. The pope convinced Walsh to use whatever literary powers he had not for controversy but to spread the word about the faith.

He stayed in medical education as a lecturer and writer, and it was as a lecturer—in universities, high schools, parishes, and prisons—that he became best known, with his forty-five books and over five hundred articles as products of his talks. In 1930, an admiring freshman at St. Ambrose College in Davenport, Iowa, wrote to tell him of his fond but vague high school recollections of having heard him speak twice. All the boy retained was a "dim appreciation of a distinguished looking gentleman with a most pleasant platform voice and a startling likeness to G. K. Chesterton."

Until a few years before his death in 1942, Walsh lived with his wife, Julia Huelat Freed, whom he had married in 1915, in a beautiful home at 110 West 74th Street that he had bought when he began at Fordham. His daughter Moira was the film critic for *America* magazine for many years, and his son James graduated from Fordham in 1937.

V

Fr. Terence Shealy's career as a pioneer in the retreat movement was somewhat tangential to Fordham history, yet by sheer charism and leadership, when he touched Fordham, the impact was long lasting and profound. Born in County Cork, Ireland, in 1863, he was often the best of his peers in soccer, handball, and weight lifting at Sacred Heart College in Limerick. In debate, he excelled when the topic was something he really cared about. But his main gift seemed to be personal, an insight and compassion that led both fellow students and professors to come to him for advice and comfort. He didn't hesitate to break the college rules, such as leaving the campus without permission, if it was necessary to help a distraught friend. Though well versed in Greek, Latin, and Gaelic, his eloquence in English, the later source of his charm, took some time to develop.

Due partly to the influence of a visiting Fordham priest, he decided to join the Society of Jesus and came to America with the romantic vision of converting the vast expanses of this young nation to God's kingdom. As a scholastic, he taught at Fordham from 1890 to 1892, and returned in 1905 to organize the law school, where, though he had no legal training, he taught the required course in jurisprudence and lectured on medical ethics at the medical school. Asked how he could master the material that would qualify him to lecture on law, he replied, "I had to sweat blood to do it."

Shealy, like some of his nineteenth-century predecessors, seemed most happy when he was starting something new. Both *Harper's Weekly* (October 9, 1909) and the *New York Sun* (July 12, 1909) covered the opening of the retreat movement in which eighteen men, including non-Catholics, gathered at Fordham for a weekend of prayer and meditation based on the Spiritual Exercises of Saint Ignatius Loyola.

Though the Exercises went back to the sixteenth century and were originally administered by a Jesuit to an individual, the retreat movement, through which groups of laymen—workers, businessmen, professionals—went away to a special retreat house to listen to a director preach to them several times a day during days of monastic silence, had recently spread from France, Belgium, and Holland to the United States. Shealy led them through the traditional conferences on sin, the use of creatures, self-control, hell, and the kingdom. The vocabulary of manhood was dominant, the exhortations lush with military anecdotes. "We belong to a militant church and we must be up and doing," he said. "A great general was asked by a young officer what he should do to win distinction. He said, 'Try to get killed as often as you can.'"

Like so many of his Jesuit colleagues, Shealy mastered scholarly material well enough to teach it on an adult level to a variety of age groups and did so at Fordham, Holy Cross, Xavier, and Georgetown. His published Marymount sermons do not reveal the mind of a profoundly learned man, but of a direct and eloquent priest. Like other Catholic educators, he saw the faith as threatened by modern ideas. "What is the latest fancy of a fad-seeking world, a world ever ready to grasp any theory that will dull the voice of conscience: that man is descended from a beast."

His "expertise," as it developed, formed on social issues, but his ideas were not ahead of his time. "Women talk a great deal of their rights and very seldom of their duties," he said. Although Shealy taught that the church's social teachings emphasized the rights of the working man to achieve his full mental and moral growth, he feared the "tyranny of the lower classes . . . the autocracy of the gutter" more than he feared the tyranny of the ruling class. He predicted that Prohibition would bring on Bolshevism in America because it would encourage working men to defy the law. For him, "the revolt against authority" was the greatest evil that plagued the modern world.

The curriculum of the School of Social Studies, a series of free lectures offered in 1911 as an offshoot of the Retreat League at Fordham's law-school offices at 140 Nassau Street, centered on the dangers of socialism, then moved to Pope Leo XIII's *Rerum novarum*, on the rights of labor. The school grew, moved to Xavier, and in 1916 gave birth to the Fordham School of Sociology and Social Service, with the School of Social Studies as an affiliate and with Shealy as dean from 1916 to 1918.

VI ⚊

Fordham opened its teachers college in 1916 at a time when the New York public school system was going through a period of creative turmoil. The New York City Board of Education was still coping with the consequences of the 1898 merger of the five boroughs into

Greater New York. Most elementary school teachers came out of normal schools, two- or three-year institutions that emphasized practical skills rather than in-depth understanding of the material itself. Ambitious grade-school and high-school teachers quickly realized that to get ahead they would need bachelor's and master's degrees. Cardinal Farley, who had gone to Fordham and served as secretary to John Cardinal McCloskey, saw the importance of training Catholics professionally and encouraged Fordham's Manhattan ambitions. What we know today as the Graduate School of Education has evolved over eighty years, through numerous name changes, from what was originally called the Graduate School, which had the Department of Education and an undergraduate teachers college established in 1916. The Graduate School had a marvelously flexible statement of purpose, an invitation to a great cross section of New York professionals to let Fordham move them a few rungs up on the social ladder. The group of downtown schools included for a while an undergraduate liberal-arts school, the Manhattan division of St. John's College, which enabled students in the teachers college to cross register for St. John's courses offered downtown.

From 1916 on, all these exciting things happened in the Woolworth Building—New York's tallest and most beautiful skyscraper, right across from city hall and overlooking the Brooklyn Bridge, Newspaper Row, the old Five Points district, and the throbbing historic heart of old New York. Two consequences followed from this move. First, while Rose Hill was a male enclave, downtown women were getting Fordham degrees. When Fordham would step-by-step go coed in the 1960s and 1970s, it would be easier because for fifty years women had already been an undergraduate presence. Second, to those eighteen miles north on Rose Hill, this bustling new collection of enterprises at the transportation hub was a distant nephew, "downtown Fordham." But within two generations, the nephew would hear New York asking whether the "real" Fordham was at Rose Hill or in Manhattan.

7.

"We'll Do, or Die"

What most of today's Fordham students know about World War I they have picked up from an introductory American history course, assuming they take American history to fulfill the sophomore history requirement rather than taking Asian, ancient, medieval, or Latin American history. Or they learn about the war from reading Erich Maria Remarque's *All Quiet on the Western Front* in high school, with its descriptions of parts of blown-up bodies hanging from barbed wire fences and trees; or Wilfred Owen's poetry, with doomed youth coughing blood in gas attacks; or Ernest Hemingway's *A Farewell to Arms.* They are likely to read Hemingway as a love story, a tragic "relationship" between unlucky lovers, or an "antiwar" novel, not knowing how war correspondent Hemingway romanticized his own journalistic exploits in World War II. An earlier generation might have focused on the distinct character and resolution of World War I itself or the sense of betrayed idealism that helped coin the phrase "the lost generation."

As Fordham celebrated its seventy-fifth anniversary in 1916, the war that by then had been waging for two years in Europe forced its way to the forefront of student consciousness. In an odd story by H. McDonald Painton, '17, "The Apologia of an Assassin," in the *Fordham Monthly* (December 1916), an insane anarchist, Bohumil Spevaksh, a deranged student of Darwin, Kant, Spinoza, and Marx—who convinced him of the "absurdity of a future life"—comes to America in the first step of his plan to "by a purge of destruction, clean the world."

Convinced in a dream that Woodrow Wilson, a tool of the capitalists, has decided to enter the war, the anarchist gets a rifle and a window overlooking the president's parade route and, Oswald-style, kills him. Can we draw any conclusions about what ideas were in the Fordham air? That secular philosophers who deny the future life breed mad assassins? That Wilson may be in league with plutocrats who will make money on the war?

The next story, Matthew A. Taylor's "The Soul of a Soldier," is something else. A young French soldier, a priest who has been drafted right after ordination, sits in his trench, praying and thinking of his mother. After a German attack, the priest encounters a dying soldier who wants to confess a crime for which an innocent man is imprisoned. But a cloud of poison gas is about to envelop the trench, and the priest's gas mask is fifty yards away. Nevertheless he stays, writes the confession, pins it to the dying man's tunic, and absolves him as the "torturing fumes . . . tear his very throat and breast asunder."

When America entered the war in April 1917, the *Monthly* addressed President Wilson: "Command us. We are absolutely yours, for we hear in your voice the command of the Almighty."

In the long baccalaureate sermon at commencement in 1917, the Jesuit homilist attributes all the evils of the world—including birth control, abortion, oppression of the poor, and war—to the "popular trend away from belief in God and a life after death" in a "world running wild in a mad riot of the senses." The war, he says, is God's anger, his vengeance "unleashing the hounds of war" to "reap the bitter fruits of men's senseless sowing." Then he exhorts the graduates as if they were already troops about to do battle: "The voice of the past is rising from the graves of dead heroes . . . the word of God is singing in the ears of the nation and firing the hearts of the people to dare, and to do, and to die in glorious fulfillment of duty."

The young men responded in several ways. They enlisted in the famed New York regiment, the "Fighting Sixty-Ninth," which had a tradition of St. John's graduates. They joined the Fordham University Overseas Ambulance Corps, which had been established some months earlier to supplement the regular army's medical corps and was partially financed by alumni donations.

On Tuesday, May 29, 1917, Fordham friends filled a ballroom at the Waldorf-Astoria to give a grand send-off to the 127 men of the Ambulance Corps. As the men marched in formation into the banquet hall, the crowd stood and sang—the words taking on a meaning that John Ignatius Coveney had never foreseen: "Hail, men of Fordham, hail. On to the fray." . . . And finally, "We'll do—What'll we do? We'll do, or die." Between courses James P. Clark, '04, sang an adaptation of the "La Marseillaise," "March on, march on, brave Fordham boys; march on to victory."

In a speech accepting the flags from the color guard, H. McDonald Painton, who had written the mad-assassin story for the *Monthly*, responded that he and his friends had joined the corps not out of "spasmodic enthusiasm," but in the "spirit of humanity." Dr. James J. Walsh saw in their generosity evidence that the world was tired of individualism and moving toward idealism; then he told his audience of the war's enormous casualties—a million a month—but that the medical profession was returning eight out of ten to battle. Fordham's nineteenth-century hero, now Brigadier General Clarence R. Edwards, looked out from the dais and picked out the faces of his old cadets in the crowd, then warned—or reassured—the corps that they would not be behind the lines, but under fire "as many times as anything else carrying the American flag."

Last to speak was Fordham's president, Fr. Joseph A. Mulry, S.J. (1915–19). Early in his administration he had set up the School of Sociology and Social Science and the Graduate School in the Woolworth Building, but now he seemed to be making the war effort the major task of his administration. Rather than attempt a "masterpiece of logic and rhetoric and philosophy," he said, he would speak from the heart. His final thought, he said, was to urge them to look at the Goddess of Liberty as they sailed out of New York Harbor and remember that they were "going forth as Catholics who hear God's call in the call of your country, and who see God's face in the folds of the flag."

Charles A. Curtin was one of those 127 who sailed for France on the *Baltic* on August 23. He had come to Fordham in 1914 from the high school in Shenandoah, Pennsylvania. At Fordham, he ran track and played football for his class and joined the sodality. In midocean, there was excitement when a German U-boat hit the ship with a torpedo, but the damage wasn't much, and the *Baltic* continued on to England. Then over to Le Havre and a three-day train ride to Saint-Nazaire in the legendary "40 and 8s," box cars made to hold eight horses now crammed with forty men. There the Fordham men were divided and were attached to three French units for action. But it was not until March 1918 that they experienced the full magnitude of the war. Curtin's French Division moved to support the English front at Ville Quemont, near Saint-Quentin. For ten days the Germans pushed the English and French back toward the Oise River. The wounded flooded the hospitals, and Curtin and his comrades worked days and nights without food or rest to move the wounded to the rear as the Germans rushed onward. They stopped exhausted at Noyon.

As Curtin's ambulance pushed on through the carnage, he pulled troops aboard with wounds gaping, bleeding. There were nine wounded in a Ford built for four; two were on the fenders and two on the floor with their feet on the running boards. The "Tommy" next to him asked for a "fag." Curtin gave him a cigarette and asked about his wound.

"Oh, nothing much, only a ball," he replied, opening his tunic to reveal a hole in his chest where the bullet had gone in and come out the back. Before they reached the hospital, the man was dead, Curtin recalls, "with a cigarette in his fingers and a smile on his lips."

Back in the Bronx, those in ROTC trained at the army camp at Plattsburgh, New York, fifty in 1917 and sixty-one in 1918. Finally, those who stayed home participated in a four-month experiment called the Student Army Training Corps (S.A.T.C.), established by Congress to encourage men to finish college and get military training at the same time. Between the summer of 1918 and the armistice on November 11, 1918, bringing together students from Fordham, Brooklyn College, and St. Peter's College, the War Department occupied Rose Hill and set the curriculum, and the Jesuits adapted their philosophy and science courses to war aims and radio theory. The regular soldiers and sailors on campus joined the football team and helped Fordham beat NYU and Georgetown.

A delegation of religious dignitaries from France and Switzerland came over for the November 2 All Souls' Day outdoor military Mass, with six hundred uniformed military men in attendance at the academic assembly following as honorary degrees were conferred on two French bishops. Dr. Walsh stretched history a bit as he declared that 1918 was the one hundredth anniversary of the French Jesuits who were to found Fordham coming to America. After dinner, the French guests, many of whom had never seen a football game, watched Fordham play St. John's of Brooklyn. "It's a very wonderful game," observed His Lordship, the Right Reverend Eugene Julien, D.D., bishop of Arras, "but it shows the animal in man—doesn't it?"

By the time American troops arrived in France in June 1918, 1,520 Fordham alumni were in the armed services. Thirty-six of them gave their lives. One of the indirect casualties was Fr. Mulry, an effective orator, who had thrown all his physical and rhetorical energies into the war effort, giving patriotic speeches, conducting soldiers' missions and military masses at Fort Dix, longing to go to the front as a chaplain—Fordham sent five—to be with "his boys." In his sermons he castigated pacifists and conscientious objectors: "Go over there and take the trenches your brothers are holding for you. God wills it!" He left office early in 1919 and died in 1921.

A year after the war, the 1920 *Maroon,* the yearbook, gives a good idea of how Fordham saw itself as it made the transition from wartime to peace. All twenty-three professors were Jesuits, including ten scholastics. Of the sixty-four graduates, forty-three had gone to Jesuit high schools, twenty-seven to Fordham Prep. Nine were transfer students from other colleges, including four from St. Peter's College, which had closed its doors because of the war while some of its students were in the service. Six had interrupted college to serve overseas, three in the Ambulance Corps, one had spent three weeks as a German prisoner of war, and eighteen had home-front assignments like coast artillery or drill instructor.

If good things can be said to come out of wartime, one of Fordham's steps forward was its first weekly newspaper, the *Ram.* It was born of Fordham's first journalism course, offered as an experiment in the 1917–18 academic year. Since the course, meant to be practical and thorough, included every aspect of a newspaper's production, the lecturers were the executives, editors, and reporters of the *Brooklyn Eagle,* the Brooklyn *Standard-Union,* the Brooklyn *Times,* and the New York *World.* The course included a top-to-bottom tour of the *Eagle* plant, from the art department on the top floor to the presses in the basement rolling out the Sunday edition. Paul T. O'Keefe, the first editor, and his staff of twenty-three had originally planned to publish a mimeographed sheet to send to the Fordham men in France, but the journalism fever caught them, and beginning on February 7, 1918, they printed an eight-page edition each week through June. Most of the original staff went on to become lawyers.

The hero of the class was Frank Frisch, who should have graduated with the class of 1920, but dropped out in 1919 to sign with the New York Giants. Although he was small, only 165 pounds, at Rose Hill he also excelled at football, basketball, and track. He had left his class, but they still voted him "Done Most for Fordham." Known as the "Fordham Flash," he played for the Giants and the St. Louis Cardinals and was later a coach for the Cardinals. Frisch was famed as an infielder, fast baserunner, and colorful scrapper. In 1954, when he was a postgame TV commentator, he lamented, "Gone are the feuds, fines, profanity, and fun. This is an era of love and kisses." Among his loves were the petunias, magnolias, maples, and azalea bushes in his garden and his classical record collection, including his favorite pianist, Artur Schnabel. He died at seventy-four following a car accident in Delaware in 1973.

II ~

During the twenty years between Fordham's being drawn inexorably into World War I and the public collapse of its academic reputation in 1935, nothing very spectacular appeared to be happening, but a number of minor dramas were being played out that proved in the long run to be serious moments in the university's development.

The men who were presidents of Fordham were slotted into this position according to the usual Jesuit regulations. A rector, or religious superior who had proven himself as a teacher or an administrator in a seminary or college would be ordered down to Fordham, often still in his thirties—much younger than a man or woman becomes a president today. He would do his best to make his mark in two three-year terms before moving on to an administrative position somewhere else. To make his mark, he usually built buildings, which would last whether beautiful or ugly. Other than the mid-nineteenth-century appendages to the administration building and the farm buildings, and the unforgivable demolition of the original manor house to make room for Collins Hall, Fordham has allowed most original buildings, including some of their hideous renovations, to stand—to the glory and shame of the presidents responsible.

On a more significant level, however, the presidents of these years had to deal with three crucial issues.

1. The diversification and the expansion put in motion right before World War I continued. The Fordham University that had established a second campus in Manhattan set up satellite programs in the Bronx, Westchester County, and New Jersey.

2. Along with other universities, Fordham found its athletic program—for a while a "big-time" operation—on a roller-coaster ride of glittering success with a streak of winning seasons and eventual disappointment. The Jesuit administrators, continually admonished by specific directives from the Jesuit general in Rome not to grant athletic scholarships, appeared oblivious to the abuses under their noses.

3. The transition from the *Ratio Studiorum* high-school and college curriculum structure to that of a secular-styled university that conforms to the norms of what some Jesuits consider alien agencies—like Ivy League leadership and state accreditation boards—goes on.

The deeper question, however, is always what is happening in the classroom. One of the stars of these years was Francis Xavier Connolly. To many, he embodied Jesuit liberal educational values from the day he graduated from Xavier in 1926 to when he came to Fordham in the second semester of 1927 until he taught graduate courses on John Henry Newman in the mid-1960s. A handsome man with wavy blond hair, he joined the faculty in the 1930s; edited *Spirit,* the journal of the Catholic Poetry Society; created an influential anthology, *Literature, the Channel of Culture* (1948); and published a now-forgotten novel *Give Beauty Back* (1950) and some poems, many of which are more prayers than poems. He also taught generations of young men by example what a "Catholic intellectual" was supposed to be.

Writing in 1998, Richard Hurzeler, '57, remembers Connolly as "a Holy person." "He was a Man of God. There was something saintly about the man." He was humble enough to praise a student who manifested even ordinary wisdom. If a student had a personal problem, Connolly would drive miles to meet him and talk. Saying, "You haven't read the Bible?" to his honors class was a signal to pre–Vatican II students that the Bible did not belong exclusively to the clergy. When a frustrated Richard had to confront Connolly to discuss a mediocre paper, the professor expressed compassion, "It must be hard for you." The pupil, encouraged to be more revealing in his writing, wrote a better paper, extolling those who went to the ends of the earth in search of adventure. Connolly praised him, but added, "Can't one also find adventure in a life of sanctity?"

In the 1930s, Connolly believed the Catholic poet needed a cloistered atmosphere to protect him from antagonistic distractions. While some Catholic critics moved toward deeper engagement with non-Catholic writers, finding in Steinbeck and Hemingway and Joyce symbols and values that were compatible with Christian tradition, Connolly, as the selections in his anthology—heavy with John Henry Newman, G. K. Chesterton, Jacques Maritain, Gerard Manley Hopkins, and Thomas Merton—demonstrate, felt Catholics should turn inward to their own tradition.

As a Fordham student, Connolly's curriculum was overwhelmingly Latin, Greek, English, history, philosophy, ethics, and evidence of religion with two semesters of chemistry and physics and one of Spanish. In his history of Fordham in the 1941 centennial yearbook, *The Centurion,* he argues that one of its greatest presidents was Fr. George Pettit, S.J. (1900–04) because his record was one of "interior growth rather than spectacular public achievement." He gave academic scholarships to attract bright students, and his spirituality reached young faculty, "who began to feel that victory over Freshman Latin was a means of salvation." Above all, he resisted the Harvard-Yale-inspired trend toward the elective system, which abandoned the classics as the basis of the liberal arts. Freshmen students during Pettit's tenure, writes Connolly, read the "great books"—works by Cicero, Virgil, Livy, Tacitus, Hume, Plato, Sophocles, Thucydides, Spencer, Shakespeare, Milton, Newman, St. Augustine, and others—many in the original Greek and Latin.

This was a demanding program, structured around a Christian ideal and reinforced by strict student-life regulations, shared living experiences, and an esprit de corps that made college a "purposeful and joyous activity." Connolly's ghost surely howled when, in 1997, his old department dropped the required English course on Chaucer, Shakespeare, and Milton, partly because the faculty did not see it as a priority to teach it.

Yet critics of the traditional system may ask how thoroughly Plato or Livy were studied when students didn't all own their individual textbooks, and they may point out that rigorous adherence to a list of ancient Greeks and Romans in the first half of the twentieth century isolated Catholics from the main currents of secular, particularly scientific, thought. James J. Walsh, for example, who had attacked evolution as an undergraduate, accepted biological evolution without the Darwinian idea of progress in *A Catholic Looks at His Faith* and even points to the accomplishments of the then not-well-known Jesuit paleontologist Pierre Teilhard de Chardin as evidence that religion and science can be reconciled. It would be two generations, however, before science would replace the classics as the heart of Fordham's most challenging curriculum. And as late as the 1950s, progressive Jesuits would have to fight to get evolution a fair hearing in the classroom.

III ―

As each post-Pettit, post–World War I president left his buildings behind, the standard granite-faced image of the campus east of the administration building took shape. Fr. Edward P. Tivnan, S.J. (1919–24), a thirty-seven-year-old Bostonian with a Ph.D. in chemistry from Georgetown, was the man to close the medical school, but he made the first step in establishing a business school by opening a school of accountancy to prepare candidates for the certified public accountant exam in 1920. In 1926, Fordham added a two-year prelaw course between high school and law school. In a series of expansions under Tivnan's leadership, Fordham College went from 300 to 800 students, and the university from 1,800 to 5,000 students.

In 1921, the new dean of the Graduate School of Arts and Sciences replaced the old system in which one class teacher taught one section up to fourteen hours a week within a departmental system, to one in which, as today, he taught one subject in his area of expertise to several sections. Tivnan gave Fordham a new face toward the Bronx at the main Third Avenue gate with its memorial to the thirty-six men who died in the war, and with a new iron fence along Fordham Road with each stone pillar the gift of a class. In 1922, the editors of the *Sacred Heart Messenger* erected an imposing plant near the Bathgate Avenue entrance to house their printing presses and offices. After the magazine died, their building was renovated into a residence for Jesuit scholastics and is now an infirmary for retired Jesuits in their final years. A few months before leaving office in January 1924, Tivnan dedicated the new gym, one of the largest in the United States, with its 24,000 square feet of unobstructed playing space, spectators' gallery seating 1,100, and 70-foot-long swimming pool in the basement.

Tivnan's longest-lasting contribution, however, was his role in making science, particularly chemistry, a respected part of the curriculum. He had revitalized chemistry as a scholastic in 1908 by teaching Fordham's first real organic course. From the early years, Fordham had had nominal chemistry teachers, untrained scholastics who primed themselves to teach everything, but aside from Fr. Freeman's gallant efforts, chemistry had never been taken seriously. With the closing of the medical school, Tivnan, as president, moved part of the budget into establishing a new undergraduate and graduate chemistry department headed by Dr. Carl P. Sherwin of the medical school, with new quarters in the medical-school building. In 1920, the department awarded four master's degrees, and in 1921, its first doctorate.

Gradually, the department added more research scholars, including, in 1938, the world famous Dr. Friedrich F. Nord, former chief of research at the Kaiser Wilhelm Institute in Germany and founder and editor of several research periodicals. During the mid-1950s, the faculty attracted more research grants, and in the 1960s, talented young Jesuits in the Tivnan tradition came on board. Then, in 1970, the new chemistry building, Mulcahy Hall, with what the Fordham public-relations office apologetically termed its "starkly functional design," opened its six floors of classrooms, offices, and labs.

Tivnan's most charming legacy may be the 1924 seismic laboratory, built with stone quarried from a local subway excavation and created to house the instruments previously set up in the basement of the administration building where Tivnan had been in charge of them as a scholastic in 1910. Their new home was on the site of the present Loyola Hall. The laboratory was moved to the granite top of Rose Hill in 1927 and moved again in 1931 down to its present site just east of Freeman Hall to make way for Keating Hall.

When I passed the seismic laboratory a year ago, the door was flung open for the first time in years, as though it had been vandalized. I entered and peered down twenty-eight feet into cavernous darkness. In 1987, twelve years after the death at ninety-two of Fr. J. Joseph Lynch, S.J., a physicist who had run it for sixty years, the seismograph was being restored. In the tradition of many Jesuit scientists who found evidence for God's existence in the workings of the natural universe, Lynch made the Fordham seismic observatory the best known in New York as he recorded earthquakes in Latin America, caught murmurs of a German U-boat off the coast in World War II, and used seismic methods to search for St. Peter's Vatican tomb in 1951. Today it is both a museum, in that the original mechanical measuring instruments remain, and an active laboratory with computerized reading instruments. Students from the Bronx High School of Science come by to help, discovering, as physics professor Joseph Mancini said, a beautiful planet in their backyard.

Father William J. Duane, S.J. (1924–30), a fifty-seven-year-old New Yorker who graduated from Xavier in 1887, saw the law school registration soar to 1,484 by 1925 and the accounting course become the School of Business in 1927. The same year, he finished the new library that Tivnan had begun. It bears Duane's name and presently lies empty, waiting for its new incarnation as a visitors' center. Visitors will be told that the lovely Gothic gallery, with the light streaming through its stained-glass windows into what resembles a church or a medieval dining hall, once, like the gym, played a role as a Harvard building in the film *Love Story*.

Construction on Larkin Hall, the biology building, was begun in 1926. In 1930, Freeman Hall for physics opened, with its wide porch overlooking the parade ground just right for commencement exercises. Meanwhile, up went Loyola Hall with its nice large bedrooms for the Jesuit faculty (but still, consistent with 1930s Jesuit poverty, a common shower room and toilets down the hall). And in 1929, the 1844 chapel was doubled in size, and the transepts and the dome were added.

IV ⚊

With a historian's detachment, Edward J. Power writes that in the period between the wars when "football had its heyday in the Catholic colleges," an accident of history turned the spotlight of fame on Notre Dame. Other colleges, such as Fordham, Georgetown, and Detroit, followed the spotlight hoping that they too could rise to national prominence with a share of the football fame.

For a while they did. Football success rallied alumni who otherwise were indifferent to their school's academic reputation, and "finally, and at long last, it allowed Catholic colleges to rid themselves of the deep feelings of inferiority that had plagued them throughout most of the period of development." But, says Power, they failed to realize that football fame could not substitute for intellectual quality. "Catholic colleges lived too long with their sporting illusions and allowed the really important sides of their enterprise to mark time while they chased the rainbow of athletic fame." Then World War II drained off male enrollment, and the postwar generation of students had other things on their minds.

The golden era of Fordham football began in the mid-1920s, according to one chronicler, when one of the Jesuits spent a Saturday afternoon watching the Fordham team get kicked around. He walked all the way from the Polo Grounds, stormed into Fr. Duane's office, and convinced him to lend the Athletic Association $100,000 to turn the program around, with the loan to be paid back within three years.

Fordham's football history over the previous fifteen years had been a series of ups and downs, including several years with no team at all. In 1919, following advice from alumni who promised to assume full financial responsibility, direction and control of athletics shifted to something called the Fordham University Athletic Council. Three years later, Tivnan, who had not been paying attention, discovered that $32,327.05 in bills had piled up. NCAA rules were being disregarded; sixty-nine students—eleven in the college and thirty-nine in other schools—had athletic scholarships. During the year, twenty of these had left the school or had been expelled but continued to play on the team. Tivnan pulled back control, put a Jesuit in charge, and wrote to the president of the NCAA that he publicly favored quitting all intercollegiate athletics for ten years. His successors did not agree.

Fr. Aloysius J. Hogan (1930–36), a thirty-nine year old from Philadelphia with a Ph.D. in philosophy from Cambridge, arrived as Fordham's president when the enrollment was high (9,326, with 1,322 in the college) and there was no debt. He had bright ideas as to what the campus should look like: it should look like Cambridge. So he transformed the old parade ground/athletic field into the fenced-in quadrangle of Edwards Parade and, influenced by Gasson Hall at Boston College, drew up plans for the monumental Keating Hall, which the budget could not afford, but which would become the signature building of the campus.

Once the building was under way, Hogan's next dream was to install a statue of Christ, called *Christ the Teacher,* in the Keating foyer. The statue corresponded to his own idea of what Jesus would have looked like at eighteen, and he was sure it would inspire freshmen, who would identify with it immediately. He made this his personal project, studying Michelangelo's *David,* Rodin's *St. John the Baptist*, and Hoffman's popular portrayal of the child Jesus in the temple. As the chosen artist worked in his studio, Hogan dropped in and kibitzed, telling the artist to change this, modify that.

The finished model was shipped to Italy to be carved in white marble. It stands, a bit above eye level, on the wall of the Keating Rotunda today. It is thin, bland, stiff, and impersonal. Few seem to notice it, few of those know it is Jesus, and even fewer identity it with themselves.

In Hogan, Fordham had a member of that special species of priest-president who imagines that their sacred orders combined with the wisdom of office enable them to know more about sports than the coaches. At times, he took sports more seriously than he did academics. One Saturday when he realized it was too late to take a trolley and subway to Yankee Stadium for the Fordham–Oregon State game, he called his Brother chauffeur to get the car ready and then called the local police precinct for a motorcycle escort.

To the despair of the coaches, Hogan would review the games on Monday and give advice for the coming week. The baseball coach was Fordham legend Jack Coffey, who in fifty-five years as a student, coach, and graduate manager of athletics, is generally credited for giving Fordham a national athletic reputation. He was also a brilliant man, a master of Latin, Greek, and French, with a memory reputed to retain the names and birthdays of four thousand friends. That wasn't enough for Hogan. Once, after the team had lost a game 18-2, the exasperated priest told Coffey, "I help out as much as I can. But the exigencies of the job are endless, and I cannot be in two places at one time."

A few years before Hogan's arrival, according to the 1943 film *The Iron Major,* starring Pat O'Brien, up at a lesser known Jesuit university, Boston College, their very successful coach had determined that his age and health left him at most five more good years. To make money for his wife and nine children, he thought he should consider some of the offers from "big-time" schools.

Francis William Cavanaugh, born in Worcester, Massachusetts, in 1876, worked his way through Dartmouth by waiting tables. He played football so well that he left early to coach the University of Cincinnati. He graduated from Boston University Law School in 1903, but kept interrupting his law career for coaching jobs at high schools and colleges, including Dartmouth, making it clear that football was his first love after his love of family and country. In 1917, though he was over forty, too old for officers' training, he told his wife that he had to leave his new Holy Cross job and go to war. He enlisted in the field artillery, was promoted to lieutenant, and went over with the Twenty-sixth (Yankee) Division on September 2. A month later, as a captain commanding a battalion, he was hit by a shell during the Meuse-Argonne offensive.

Shortly before, he had written to his little son Davie that he had dreamed that he had fallen and that Davie had lifted him up. "You must always remember," he concluded, "that your father came into this war for the sake of all little children."

His head and face were badly damaged; he almost died and was in convalescence until September 1919. Entitled to a Purple Heart and a Silver Star, he declined to apply for either. At Boston College he coached and taught jurisprudence until he accepted Fordham's offer of $15,000 in 1926.

As a coach, "Cav" was famed as a creative innovator and as an exceptionally tough but inspiring leader. He was the first to put numbers on his players' jerseys and developed strategies to deceive opponents by placing his players so that a run or pass would never be obvious from the start. He emphasized fundamentals and calisthenics and utter fearlessness, and characterized the game as "75 percent fight." He began his locker-room orations in a whisper and—demanding that anyone not willing to lose an arm or leg get off the team—raised his voice to a thundering crescendo. Although it took him a few years to get rolling, he gave Fordham its first undefeated season in 1929, including a 26-0 defeat of NYU before a crowd of sixty thousand. They won every game but one in 1930 and 1931.

Tragically though, as a result of his war wounds his eyesight was rapidly deteriorating. As early as 1927 he had spent much of the season in the infirmary and sometimes he could not even see the players. In his last years, he was basically an inspirational figure on the bench who allowed the assistant coaches to run the games. In 1932, incapacitated, he was invited to resign; he died on July 29, 1933. Seven of his sons and daughters served in World War II.

To replace "Cav," Fordham reached out to Jim Crowley at Notre Dame. Jim was one of the "Four Horsemen." He had coached at the University of Georgia and Michigan State and was widely considered the most Rockne-like of Knute Rockne's pupils. His salary was $11,000. He brought with him as assistant coach young Frank Leahy, who later returned to coach Notre Dame. In Crowley's nine years at Fordham his record was fifty-six wins, thirteen losses, and seven ties, but his era is best remembered for the defensive line of 1935–37 known as the Seven Blocks of Granite. For three years, they held

Pittsburgh scoreless, though Pitt was then considered the country's most powerful offensive team, and even though one of the Pitt linemen again and again bashed Vince Lombardi in the mouth with his elbow, spilling Lombardi's blood and causing Lombardi to get stitches.

Like Rockne and Cavanaugh, Crowley had mastered the dramatic emotional locker-room pep talk, in which he would invoke both the millions of Americans listening to the game on the radio and his own dear gray-haired mother in her rocking chair in Wisconsin fingering her rosary for her son's team.

In 1934, three sophomore linemen—Vince Lombardi, from Brooklyn; Leo Paquin, from Brockton, Massachusetts; and Nathaniel Pierce, from Biddleford, Maine—moved into position. Four freshmen came on board—Al Babartsky, from Shenandoah, Pennsylvania; Alexander Franklin Wojciechowicz, of South River, New Jersey; Ed Franco, from Jersey City; and Johnny Druze, of Irvington, New Jersey. Because the term described the team over three seasons, the "Seven" were really twelve, later including Paul Berezney, Mike Kochel, Harry Jacunski, Jimmy Hayes, and Joe Bernard.

Lombardi as coach of the Green Bay Packers went on to become an American sports icon, the subject of several books, and a mesmerizing orator, most famous for his dictum that winning was the "only thing." Today anyone entering Fordham's Lombardi Center walks down a corridor with a huge photomural of the Seven Blocks on the left and the Hall of Fame and display cases crammed with trophies and Lombardi memorabilia on the right and in the lobby.

V

Vince Lombardi came from Brooklyn to Fordham with a football scholarship in 1933 after studying first at Cathedral, the diocesan minor seminary, when he was considering the priesthood, then at St. Francis High School.

While most of the 432 men in his class commuted by subway or carpool, the football players lived on Dealy Five or in St. John's Hall, dined on steaks at the training tables and hung out together in the Dealy poolroom.

Vince was basically a C and B student earning a B.S. degree in business. Kipling was the favorite poet of the class of '37; their favorite girls' college was Marymount; their favorite radio show, the feuding Jack Benny and Fred Allen; and their "spot" (bar) was Poe's Raven. Off the field and out of the classroom, Lombardi was active in the Parthenian Sodality for four years, but was mischievous and occasionally brutal. When the old Jesuit Brother Quinn, who didn't like athletes and would refer to them as "hogs on the way to the trough," turned Vince down for a dining-hall job, Vince bunched up with a group of his friends when leaving the dining hall and slammed a big piece of buttered bread on the old brother's bald head in retaliation. Sensitive to slights about being Italian, when a guy outside the men's room at a sorority dance referred to Vince as "the little Guinea," Vince knocked his teeth down his throat.

He was never the best or near-best player, and he did not always play first string; he got hurt a lot, sometimes seriously, but was a tough scrapper. Nicknamed Butch, he had a fierce blend of determination and animal vigor both on and off the field. Crowley drove the team especially hard on Wednesdays, when, screened from the press and student observers, he pushed the workouts into the evening. Lombardi reveled in the exercises, knowing he was part of one of the teams—along with Notre Dame and Navy—that drew the biggest crowds in the country.

Not everything was on the up-and-up. At the 1935 NYU game, two Fordham players concocted a story that they had been offered $1,000 bribes by gamblers to throw the game, just to tell the story in the locker room and fire up the Rams to a 21-0 victory. In the spring, the new president, Robert I. Gannon, S.J., who already had a reputation for sniffing at football as a distraction from the intellectual life, suspended Lombardi and another player for a bloody fistfight in the shower after the other fellow playfully called Vince a wop.

Somehow, everything turned around in the fall 1936 when the sportswriters, including Scotty Reston of the Associated Press, Damon Runyon, and Grantland Rice—who coined, "He [God] writes not that you won or lost / But how you played the game"—saw Fordham's winning streak as leading to the Rose Bowl. One night while the team was enjoying a double feature at the Loew's Paradise, the manager turned up the lights and invited an ovation for the Fordham boys. Runyon wrote a humorous piece about mascot Rameses VII, tired of being dragged around to games, thinking he'd be better off as chops with curry sauce.

The Pitt game, ending 0-0, inspired the Herald Tribune's Stanley Walker to ask whether "better or more savage football was played on any gridiron." Vince had been smashed in the jaw, requiring thirty stitches after the game, but Crowley sent him back in with a mouthful of blood. As Lombardi's biographer, David Maraniss, describes it in *When Pride Still Mattered,* "Here, for Lombardi, was the beautiful controlled violence of his game, holy war and bloody rite, refusing to yield, ignoring the body's fatigue. We do, or die."

This was the game that inspired Fordham publicist Timothy Cohane to remember a wirephoto cutline after the Holy Cross game in a 1930 New Haven *Journal-Courier.* It called the Fordham line "the Seven Blocks of Granite." Restated, it moved Fordham, for better or worse, into the world of sports myth.

After tying Purdue, the Rams' Rosebowl hopes hung on the NYU game. Playing sluggishly, they lost 7-6. Something was wrong. It turned out that four Fordham players had been sneaking over the New Jersey line on Sundays to earn a few dollars playing semipro ball under false names. Their teammates had known about it and covered for them.

In Maraniss's judgment, considering the context of Lombardi's whole career, the most important thing he took from Fordham was his Jesuit education, best represented by the required ethics course of Fr. Ignatius W. Cox, a well known polemicist, radio personality, opponent of birth control, and author of the text *Liberty, Its Use and Abuse.* As an inspirational speaker in later life, Lombardi still modeled his rhetoric on Cox's style. Says Maraniss, "From the Jesuits he acquired a larger perspective: duty, responsibility, and the exercise of free will were the basis of a philosophy that shaped the way he looked at himself and the world." Lombardi took a principle of St. Ignatius's, that "only those with free will could surrender it freely to achieve a higher ideal" and applied it to the Green Bay Packers.

Whatever his popularity, according to his family, Lombardi was basically a shy person, embarrassed by his induction into Fordham's Hall of Fame, because he, in his own judgment, had not been an outstanding player. His wife, Marie, recalls, "What Vince really wanted out of life was to be head coach at Fordham. He wanted to rebuild Fordham's football back to what it was in the days when he had been there."

VI ⸺

Perhaps with all the excitement it was easy to miss that the most important movement within Fordham and the Society of Jesus in general was their response to the intellectual currents building up in American higher education. We have seen one of the main themes of the Catholic Renaissance that followed World War I show up in some of the writing and public utterances of Fordham faculty and students even before the war.

Some Catholic scholars, like Fr. Moorhouse F. X. Millar, S.J., who was chair of Fordham's graduate department of political philosophy and social science between 1929 and 1953, argued that many elements of the American political system had their origins in the Middle Ages. Other theories, bolstered by Catholics' patriotic fervor during the war, emphasized the relationship between American and Catholic values.

The new Catholic lay-edited opinion magazine *Commonweal*, founded by Michael Williams, stated in its opening editorial (November 12, 1924) "that nothing can do so much for the betterment, the happiness, and the peace of the American people as the influence of the enduring and tested principles of Catholic Christianity." Furthermore, *Commonweal's* appearance coincided with the founding of a whole network of parallel Catholic institutions—such as the Catholic Historical Society, the Catholic Poetry Society, and the Catholic Book Club—and a movement called Catholic Action, which threw Catholic laypeople into the trenches of social reform by way of youth clubs and labor schools.

America, the Jesuit weekly, and *Commonweal* published a series of articles and editorials calling for a revival of Catholic scholarship. Due in part to the leadership of Fr. James A. Burns, C.S.C., president of Notre Dame and influential voice in the Catholic Education

Association, scholastic philosophy won priority over the classics and literary studies as the academic soul of liberal education. This would translate, usually, into five required courses, all taught in junior or senior years: some combination of philosophical psychology (free will, etc.), logic, metaphysics, the history of philosophy, and ethics. But the purpose of philosophy as an academic discipline was not so much the free rational search for truth as to provide a foundation for religion, a rational grounding of the faith, and a practical plan of life that would enable Catholic young people to make sound moral decisions as family members, businessmen, and civic leaders.

Contemporary observers who regret what they consider the "loss of Catholic identity" at Fordham and other Catholic universities tend to look for the source of the transformation in the 1960s and 1970s, a period of cultural and political turmoil that brought about a number of revolutions in American life. Yet the process of adaptation and professionalization really had its roots in the 1920s. Catholicism's militancy in the postwar years naturally brought it into conflict with secular values; at the same time, Catholic educational reformers saw that Catholic institutions had to either meet secular professional standards or fade into the margins of American life. On the one hand, a rising group of highly esteemed Catholic intellectuals in both America and Europe—including G. K. Chesterton, Hilaire Belloc, Karl Adam, Jacques Maritain, Christopher Dawson, Etienne Gilson, and Fordham's prolific historian and convert Ross Hoffman—offered a powerful apologetic for the validity of the Christian faith.

In *Restoration* (1935), Hoffman testifies that he owes a debt to Adam, Dawson, Maritain, Belloc, and Chesterton, and to Fordham's John P. Monahan, who received him into the church. *Restoration* is a refutation of skepticism and its revolt against the idea of God that has led man to fashion for himself "an anthropomorphic universe shrunken to a narrow compass of the senses." Hoffman had scorned religion as a youth, but devoted himself to socialism and liberal causes. Then a graduate course on the Middle Ages convinced him that "life had never been more thoroughly worth living than it was when Francis, Thomas, Innocent III, and Dante stalked the earth." Next he was drawn to the church's social-justice program, the encyclicals *Rerum novarum* of Leo XIII and *Quadragesimo anno* of Pius XI, and the church's plan for world peace. Finally, his reading and reason led him to God's existence and to the belief that the Father had revealed himself in the person of Jesus.

While many Catholic thinkers looked toward European Catholic culture for inspiration, another group, in the tradition of Orestes Brownson, dug into American soil to unearth an American-Catholic synthesis. Anyone who ever saw Robert C. Pollock, a young Fordham assistant professor in the 1930s, in action in the classroom, was swept up with his enthusiasm. While most Jesuits drew on Aquinas, Pollock turned to Emerson and William James, who built their systems on nature and experience. Though extremely influential in the classroom and at symposia, Pollock published only a few essays in *Thought,* where he reexpresses Catholic tradition in American terms. In a 1940 symposium on secularism, Ross Hoffman and Robert I. Gannon blamed the world's problems on the Protestant Reformation and John Dewey, while Pollock argued for an affirmation of nature. As historian William M. Halsey interprets their clash, "the most apparent contrast between Pollock and the others is his critical approach and the note of self-complacency characteristic of the rest of the symposium."

VII ⚊

Although brilliant individuals such as Hoffman and Pollock demonstrated Catholicism's intellectual riches, the educational reformers were far from satisfied with the church's progress. One sign that something was lacking was the decision of more ambitious Catholics to attend non-Catholic colleges. Although total enrollment in Jesuit colleges and universities doubled between 1920 and 1930, by 1940 an estimated 200,000 Catholics had chosen non-Catholic institutions. In 1931, Fordham's former president, Fr. Tivnan, echoing criticism offered by Orestes Brownson almost a century before, told a Jesuit meeting that students in Jesuit schools "have a reputation for lack of initiative when they graduate and go to other schools. They have been trained to depend too much on memory and too little on independent thought."

Aggravating their own situation, Catholic schools resisted the standards of accrediting agencies such as the American Council on

Education because Catholics lacked the endowment funds and research faculty to compete and because they resisted adapting their traditional curriculum to secular norms.

A small group of Jesuits struggled to move their schools in a different direction. Gradually, beginning with an informal meeting at Fordham during the Catholic Educational Association meeting in 1920, Jesuits formed an Inter-Province Committee on Studies (IPCS) to argue for various reforms: joining accrediting associations, creating stronger endowments, founding a Jesuit journal on education, and encouraging doctoral studies for Jesuit teachers. To make matters worse, while these Jesuits were working to adapt to the culture, the general in Rome, Vladimir Ledochowski, S.J., wrote to the American provincials on March 12, 1927, that the Vatican cardinal who was head of the Holy Office, Merry del Val, had complained that—because they had too many non-Catholic faculty and students, and because allegedly Jesuits did not have enough influence on policy or on students' spiritual lives—Jesuit colleges were not Catholic enough. Without saying how these guidelines were to be enforced, the general wanted limits on non-Catholic students and faculty and no non-Catholic deans.

Within a few years, however, Ledochowski, who probably had reservations about the Holy Office's accusations in the first place, became an advocate of reform. In 1930, he directed American Jesuits to learn from the procedures of the preeminent colleges and universities and to get Ph.D.'s, and most interesting, he urged Jesuits to eliminate petty rivalries, pool their resources, and cooperate with one another.

For the next forty years, Catholic educators would toy with the idea of creating a "great" national Jesuit university by concentrating Jesuit talent in, for example, Fordham, Georgetown, or Boston College, but for a lot of reasons, none of these schools was willing to diminish itself so one of the others might thrive. In 1934, a turning point in Jesuit educational reform, the general issued an instruction, established the Jesuit Educational Association (JEA), called on the schools to modernize and seek accreditation, and appointed a commissarius, Daniel O'Connell, S.J., of the Chicago Province, to implement his directives.

The commissarius's plan for Fordham, expressed in his report of February 24, 1935, had five points.

1. Move the graduate school from the Woolworth Building to the Bronx, build up its library, and add full-time professors.

2. Earn law-school accreditation from both the American Bar Association and the Association of American Law Schools.

3. Drop the pharmacy school.

4. Give the college an assistant dean and a new curriculum.

5. Put off moving the prep school for the time being

Fordham's soft spot was its graduate program, which similar to those at other Jesuit universities, had expanded wildly in the 1920s, but had not maintained quality control. A 1928 internal report to the NCEA showed that Fordham's record of awarding 325 master's and 108 doctoral degrees in five years was so beyond the number of degrees awarded by comparable Catholic institutions that we have to wonder what the degrees were worth, especially since four-fifths of the students were part time.

Fordham's president and other typical Fordham voices had been resisting these points for years. Francis X. Connolly's articulate, jovial mentor, George Bull, S.J., head of Fordham's graduate department of philosophy, argued in a classic 1932 address to the faculty, "The Function of the Catholic College," that "Catholicism is a culture, not merely a creed; an attitude, a whole complex of things taken for granted . . . and it is the business of Catholic education to impart that culture." He did not believe that the goal of graduate education was research. Catholic education had already answered the big questions about human existence; Catholic scholarship was not to search for "new" knowledge, but to contemplate more deeply the wisdom it had.

At the 1934 faculty convocation, Hogan told the faculty that he refused to be "stampeded" by the "purely extrinsic requirements of the so-called standardizing agencies." At the same convocation, Vince Lombardi's idol, Ignatius Cox, proclaimed, "I would say to the standardizing agencies: we are developing a type and a culture not your own, but still a type and a culture not inferior to yours, but to our minds infinitely superior."

In October 1933, Hogan had simply refused to fill out a questionnaire from the American Council on Education because he didn't like one of its norms, the number of books published by the faculty. As a result, Fordham did not make the ACE list of approved schools. Hogan was, however, concerned about AAU approval as a "University of Complex Organization" and did his best to make the case that problems at the graduate school—such as using high-school principals as graduate faculty members, a very high percentage of part-time students, and the distance of the library (at Rose Hill) from the graduate students—were being addressed.

The "Complex" category was for universities with graduate and other professional schools and at the time included three Catholic institutions: Catholic University, Marquette, and St. Louis University. The AAU warned Hogan in October 1933 that it was unwise to push for approval too soon, and the decision was postponed, but in November 1935 the bad news came.

Not only the graduate school had been dropped, but also the college, which had made the approved list for ten years. The college had been on the list since 1913, when the AAU adopted the existing roster of schools approved by the Carnegie Foundation for the Advancement of Teaching; it included Fordham, Georgetown, Boston College, and Holy Cross. Hogan protested that because the AAU committee had not considered the graduates of Fordham College, but rather only the graduates of the Manhattan Division and the teachers college, in evaluating how well Fordham graduates did in graduate schools, that criticism was unfair. His argument seemed to be, by implication, that the "real" Fordham graduate had not been judged.

The AAU's reasons were that Fordham graduates did not do well in other professional and graduate schools. The libraries both uptown and downtown were inadequate for either graduate or undergraduate use; on the Rose Hill campus reference books were locked in cases, and there was little evidence the library was used. Father Robert I. Gannon writes in his Fordham history *Up to the Present,* "It was one of the darkest single days in 125 years."

Most of the decision, however, apparently hinged on Fordham's attitude toward its libraries, a situation the AAU called "indefensible." Much of traditional Jesuit seminary and college education was not based on liberal access to books and wide reading, but on absorbing the lectures and notes of the professors, without access to contradictory points of view. In 1923, Richard Tierney, S.J., editor of *America* magazine, had complained to Jesuit superiors that articles submitted by Jesuits were often subpar because Jesuit writers didn't keep up on recent books in literature and philosophy. At least a generation would pass before Fordham overcame the intellectual inertia into which it had slipped. By the 1950s, Jesuits with doctorates from Harvard and the Sorbonne were joining the faculty, but change would come slowly: when the new Walsh Family Library opened in 1997, there were surely some in the crowd who longed for George Bull's lost "culture."

Birthplace and childhood home of John J. Hughes, archbishop of New York and founder of Fordham University. The cottage is located in the Ulster American Folk Park in Omagh, Northern Ireland. Standing in front of the cottage is Francis Canavan, S.J., professor of political science.

St. John's College in 1846.

Old St. John's Hall.

The Old Manor House, built c. 1690, was demolished in 1898.

The faculty of St. John's College, Fordham, 1859. Front row (l. to r.):
Fr. Tissot, Fr. Leguouais, Fr. O'Reilly, Fr. Schneider, Fr. Charaux.
Second row (l. to r.): Fr. Doucet, Fr. Daubresse, Fr. Fleck, Fr. Tellier,
Fr. Berthelet, Fr. Aubier, Fr. Graves.

The new Rose Hill Manor, built in 1836, as it appeared in 1860.

The student refectory, located in the Administration
Building from 1868–91.

The bust of Orestes Brownson in front
of the chapel and Queens Court, c. 1940,
with unidentified visitor.

Fordham class of 1875.

The baseball team in 1875.

The banjo, mandolin, and glee clubs, 1896.

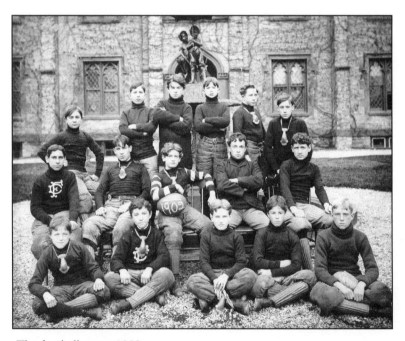

The football team, 1902.

Dealy Hall as it looked in 1902.

John Ignatius Coveney, composer of "The Fordham Ram."

The Seven Blocks of Granite, Vince Lombardi, front row, third from left.

President Franklin D. Roosevelt and Robert I. Gannon, S.J., as
FDR reviews the Fordham ROTC in 1940.

Laurence J. McGinley, S.J., breaking
ground for the Lincoln Center campus.

The Lincoln Center campus in an
artist's conception of how it will fit
into its proposed New York City site.

The Lincoln Center campus shortly after completion.

Aerial view of the Rose Hill campus in 1966.

Jesuit general Pedro Arrupe, S.J., celebrates
Mass in Fordham Chapel in 1966.

(l. to r.) Timothy Healy, S.J.; Leo McLaughlin, S.J.; Edward
A. Walsh; Michael Walsh, S.J., c. 1968.

Leo McLaughlin, S.J., and his successor, Michael Walsh, S.J.

Dr. Claire Hahn, professor of English, June 1974.

James Finlay, S.J., in the president's office.

Eileen Markey, with nephew Brendan Markey, at her graduation.

Joseph A. O'Hare, S.J., president.

8.

Gannon Takes Charge

In 1957, as young Jesuits at the novitiate at St. Andrew-on-Hudson, right next to Franklin D. Roosevelt's Hyde Park estate, many of us heard Fr. Robert I. Gannon's voice long before we ever saw his face. Gannon, former president of Fordham (1936–49), was one of our novice master's heroes, and one of Fr. Martin Neylon's ways of teaching virtue during the daily conference was to tell little anecdotes about the fathers he revered. Fr. Gannon, he said, as rector of the Regis High School and of the parish of St. Ignatius Loyola at Park Avenue and 83rd Street, would always join the community for coffee or recreation, mingling with his fellow Jesuits even though he was out night after night socializing with wealthy and prestigious people.

Then the master would play a tape of Gannon's latest speech, usually at the Jesuit Mission Dinner or the Friendly Sons of St. Patrick. His was a rich, plummy voice, with a clipped, cultivated English accent, similar to that of a few Jesuits who were not English but had somehow acquired the accent in the course of their educations. I'm afraid that I disliked him instantly. He was witty, yes, but his wit was often at the expense of ideas and persons I had admired all my life, such as Franklin Delano Roosevelt, our novitiate neighbor, whose grave I would visit on long walks. With the years, I am told by those who heard him, Gannon's after-dinner speeches became increasingly bitter as he turned his wit against the Kennedys and the younger generation of Jesuits, who were seen as agents of change.

Gannon was a Republican, a conservative, a traditionalist, and one of the more successful after-dinner speakers in New York. Perhaps it is understandable that in his political rhetorical excursions, he saw himself as matching wits not just with the most eloquent of American presidents but with a whole host of ideological opponents who stood between himself and the religious, educational, and political values to which he had dedicated his life.

In an address at the annual banquet of the State of New York Chamber of Commerce, November 14, 1940, he said:

> What, for example, is the prevailing philosophy of education in America today? . . . First, Exaggerated Experimentalism, second, Pragmatism, third, Socialism—and of the three the first is easily the most dangerous. For the whole tendency of this particular experimentalism is towards cutting off the past, ignoring the accumulated experience of the human race, starting anew, as if no one had lived before us. . . . What we need are things that are old, things that have stood the test of a hundred generations, things that are immutable.

His perennial villains were communists—beginning with the Spanish Civil War—and liberals. Liberals, he told the Friendly Sons of St. Patrick on March 16, 1940,

> are the greatest little slave drivers in the world. They are not as crude or as simple as the ward heelers with the big cigars. What they want is not so much our money as our children. They want our schools and colleges. They want the key positions in civil service. They want control of relief and all the social agencies, and they are getting what they want. Later, they hope, when they have the youth of the nation in their power, to eliminate all religions and all morality that does not conform to their peculiar ideology.

The antidote to liberalism, of course, would be the traditional virtues of the Irish, personified in his metaphorical Mrs. Kelly, who took in washing to support her lazy husband and large family and "kept her head unbowed amid sorrows that would have broken common clay."

It may seem incongruous, as Peter McDonough argues in *Men Astutely Trained: A History of the Jesuits in the American Century,* that the president of what was then one of America's most prestigious Catholic universities would consistently lace his utterances with anti-intellectualism, but Catholic colleges had consistently emphasized character formation over knowledge for its own sake. Gannon, however, was essentially a communicator. In McDonough's words, "He understood education to be one of the performing arts." He was, paradoxically, in the spirit of the Catholic Renaissance medievalists, imbued with nostalgia for a bygone era, but he had his finger sensitively enough to the wind to know that what Fordham needed when he took over as president in 1936 was a new image.

He had to redo Fordham not just on Rose Hill and in Manhattan but in the public mind as well. Once given authority, almost any educational administrator will, perhaps unconsciously, try to have his school bloom in those activities in which he himself does well. The would-be architect, uncomfortable with intellectual discourse, will build. It's no accident that among Gannon's legacies are an expanded theater program, a communications arts department, and a powerful FM radio station.

Gannon's vision for Fordham corresponded in many ways to his image of himself and an idealized view of his own Jesuit education. Ninth child of Frank S. Gannon, Jr., a second-generation Irishman and Staten Island railroad executive, and Marietta Burrows, an Episcopalian of English descent who became a Catholic the day before her marriage, young Robert received the best private education his family's prosperity allowed at Loyola School and Georgetown University. The father's promotions moved the family to Washington for six years, then back to New York, where in 1904 they settled in at 119 West 76th Street until Frank Gannon lost his job in the Panic of 1907. They moved to a simpler house on West End Avenue, and somehow the resources were there to keep the children in school.

In 1907, Robert, fourteen and still at Loyola, traveled to Europe with a friend, had a private audience with Pope Pius X, met the general of the Society of Jesus, who of course predicted the boy would be a Jesuit, and strolled through the gardens of the Tuileries. There his older friend pointed out a dignified old woman in black, seated on a bench feeding breadcrumbs to the birds. She was Empress Eugenie, wife of Napoleon III and empress of France from 1853 to 1871. There he also met an old soldier in a red shirt who had been with Garibaldi at Sorrento, and an Englishman who had fought with Chinese Gordon at Khartoum. As a college freshman he knew people, including his own parents, who remembered the Civil War, and a teacher who had dined on boiled ham with Daniel Webster.

When Robert attended Georgetown, the prep school and the college had a total of 120 students, nearly all of whom received the A.B. degree except for the handful who couldn't handle Latin and Greek and had to settle for the B.S. The university already featured a small medical school and a large law school. The curriculum and teaching were a reinforcement of the educational philosophy he had met at Loyola: a rigid list of required courses, with language, the classics, and philosophy the most important; the prelection, which previewed the next day's assignment; composition, which taught writing by imitating the style of a classical author; and emphasis on moral development.

Nevertheless, the academic atmosphere of old Georgetown was never very demanding, and Robert had plenty of time to enjoy the Washington social life, including White House receptions, sessions of Congress, the opera—with the portly President Taft applauding in ecstasy Tetrazzini's arias in *Mignon*—zipping across the surface of the Potomac as coxswain of the Georgetown crew, and hanging out on Old North porch smoking Fatimas and Melachrinos.

In the summer of his freshman year, Robert returned to Europe, where with two classmates he biked 1,540 miles from Naples to Paris, crossing the Alps at the Brenner Pass. Throughout his life, he would always be a man who had seen Old Europe, the world of 1870–1914, when he was young and impressionable; it is understandable that he might believe for the rest of his life that that was what the world should be like.

Gannon joined the Jesuits after graduation and returned to New York to teach at Fordham in 1919. Assigned as moderator of the drama club, he wrote his first book, *The One-Act Play,* a how-to manual for an activity that had long flourished as a staple in Jesuit education. After ordination in 1927, superiors sent him to Cambridge—which was then, he recalls, about half the size of Fordham—for an M.A. in English, though he would have preferred to have studied philosophy. His summers freed him to bike along the coast of Brittany and, in Italy, to learn how fascism was working at Perugia. The Italian experience convinced him above all that education should be independent of the state—independent of both government support and government control. He would have a chance to rethink this during World War II, when Fordham, down to a few hundred students, would desperately need a government-sponsored military training program in order to stay afloat.

By the time Gannon completed his final year of Jesuit training, called the tertianship, in 1929, he had received his first major challenge—he was to resurrect, as dean, Jersey City's St. Peter's College, which had closed during World War I, as a small liberal-arts institution. In 1930, the thirty-seven-year-old priest already had a fixed educational philosophy and clear ideas of what was wrong with American higher education in general.

According to his analysis, the new types of students entering college after World War I undermined the traditional liberal arts by demanding job-oriented courses. The rise of big-time college athletics, especially football with its athletic scholarships, brought men on campus who were unfit for college work and fostered an anti-intellectual atmosphere. The cafeteria-style elective system of Harvard's Charles Eliot abolished the traditional hierarchy of subjects in which classics ruled. Social and economic changes, such as the country-to-city population shift, mass production, radio advertising, expansion of credit, and unemployment, had weakened family stability and parental authority. The emphasis on science in Herbert Spencer's philosophy and in John Dewey's experimentalism, Dewey's rejection of absolute values, and his view of education as a series of ongoing experiences in which man learns to continually adapt to change made them enemies of the Gannon view of life.

With a typical stroke of classical imagination, Gannon decided that St. Peter's symbol would be the peacock, because, like the phoenix, it was to arise from its own ashes. He touted its downtown location, its nearness to public transportation, and its "Million-Dollar

Faculty," consisting of six Jesuits considered among the most talented of their peers. Its pre-1917 alumni were in prominent positions throughout the state, and the school was blessedly lacking in traditions—there was no entrenched faculty to gripe about Gannon's new ideas. This was to be a small, select liberal-arts college offering a four-year A.B. and a B.S. for premeds and science majors.

There were only a few hundred students, and their campus was little more than three rented floors of a downtown office building, some space in the old St. Peter's College (now St. Peter's Prep), and a gymnasium up Montgomery Street near the campus of today's St. Peter's College, but the students enjoyed the accessibility of their dynamic young dean and the enthusiasm of the six-man faculty. Ed McGlinchy, one of the first students, who later joined the Jesuits and taught philosophy at St. Peter's, remembers Fr. George Johnson, S.J., who made his English class write a poem a week. On Fridays, Johnson would read the best poems aloud to the class, holding back the best one for last. Sometimes the best was Ed's.

Within a year, however, Gannon was informed that his elitism cost much more money than the new St. Peter's could afford. So the resourceful new dean quickly founded Hudson College of Commerce and Finance, an evening program for an unlimited number of part-time students seeking, eventually, a B.S. in business administration. The profits from this very unselective enterprise would finance those getting the St. Peter's "real" Jesuit education. For the time being, the formula worked, and in 1936, Jesuit superiors were impressed enough with his record to name Gannon the twenty-fifth president of Fordham.

II ⚊

On first appearance, Fordham seemed a thriving enterprise, one of the largest Catholic educational institutions in the United States, with an enrollment of nearly 8,000 students, a faculty of 641, and property valued at $8,112,320. But it had big problems. The cost of the still-unfinished Keating Hall had gobbled up most of the university's financial resources, the flap over the firing of Major Cavanaugh in 1932 and other problems with "big" football still poisoned the air, and most important, the loss of accreditation had wounded the Jesuits' reputation nationwide.

Gannon, who as president, ex-officio chair of the board of trustees, and rector of the Jesuit community had virtually unlimited authority, gradually restructured the administration. Father Charles J. Deane, S.J., vice president of the university and dean of the college, became the secretary general, to administer problems that concerned more than one school, and in 1938 he named Anna H. King as dean of the School of Sociology and Social Service, the first woman to hold the rank of dean in any Jesuit University. He also created the positions of director of the summer school, director of placement, assistant dean for freshmen, and director of publicity.

On Gannon's first day on campus, Pat Kenealy, custodian of the athletic equipment, dragged the dazed new president into the gym and whisked him on a tour through the storerooms, pointing out the $46.50 football helmets and the sweaters, parkas, uniforms, and expensive training equipment, a warning that Gannon should not do anything rash about football as Fordham had too much already invested.

In his heart, Gannon was not a football fan. Asked about the Seven Blocks of Granite at alumni events, he would wince internally and secretly resent not being asked about the library, but his initial investigation convinced him that although Fordham did give scholarships strictly on athletic ability in violation of the Middle States Association, the Carnegie Foundation report, and the Jesuit general, and did go soft on athletes caught in disciplinary offenses, Fordham was no worse than other big-name teams. So he moved slowly on football, but quickly to regain accreditation. The college's status was reinstated within months, and the graduate school's within a few years.

First, as an opponent of "college for everyone," Gannon strengthened the college by cutting enrollment from 1,620 to 1,200, selecting fewer and better students, adding the freshman dean, and developing a guidance program. The college should not have more students than it could give personal attention and moral development. For an honors course, he segregated 10 percent of the class, gave them extra reading, and introduced a senior thesis. He designated Keating Hall the graduate-school building, moved the graduate school and its library to the Bronx, increased the library budget, and coordinated graduate and undergraduate faculties so that students at the college could take graduate courses. In 1938, he initiated a campaign to get Fordham a chapter of Phi Beta Kappa, a campaign that, partly because of Fordham's football scholarships, did not succeed until 1962.

Next, he turned his attention to the faculty, whom Gannon rated in 1936 as from "eminent to inadequate." Only a small percentage had Ph.D.'s; the overwhelming majority had received their degrees from Fordham or some similar Catholic institution; twenty-three had only a bachelor's degree. Gannon gave them three years for everyone to have at least an M.A., and by 1939 they did. In Europe, the rise of fascism and Nazism and the opening salvos of World War II drove outstanding refugee scholars, including Nobel Prize winners, to American shores; Fordham's catch was Victor Hess, who joined the physics department and stayed twenty-five years.

The historian Oscar Helecki came from the University of Warsaw, sociologist Nicholas Timashef from St. Petersburg, and Dietrich von Hildebrand from Germany. In 1938, the well-known European historian Ross Hoffman, who had been at NYU for twelve years, also joined the faculty. For a semester, Fordham also enjoyed the presence of the colorful polemicist-historian-apologist Hilaire Belloc, who made little effort to help his colleagues in the history department with routine chores, but who could shine at special events such as the Fordham-sponsored rally at Carnegie Hall backing the Franco side in the Spanish Civil War.

All of these men quickly boosted Fordham's reputation, and perhaps von Hildebrand's fame as an outstanding defender of traditional Catholic teaching proved most enduring. Born in Italy in 1889, he converted to Catholicism as a young man in 1914. A student of the phenomenologist Edmund Husserl, he received his doctorate in philosophy and became a professor at the University of Munich in 1924. When Hitler came to power in 1933, von Hildebrand, an anti-Nazi, fled first to Florence, then to Vienna, Toulouse, Spain, and finally Fordham in 1942. Before he retired in 1960, he wrote thirty books and over a hundred articles on philosophy and morality. He remained extraordinarily productive as an emeritus professor, particularly in defense of Catholic conservatives who, in the wake of Vatican II, sought to return to the church's traditional teachings. His *Trojan*

Horse in the City of God (1967) and his books on chastity and celibacy defended Pope Paul VI's encyclical *Humanae vitae* (1968), which repeated the church's condemnation of artificial birth control. He died in New Rochelle in 1977. According to von Hildebrand's spirituality, modeled on St. Francis of Assisi, man's vocation is not to change the world but to follow Christ.

Finally, at a time when only a third of Catholic colleges granted any tenure at all, Gannon, with the guidance of a seven-man committee, reformed the norms for salary, rank, promotion, and tenure, bringing them in line with the statutes of secular institutions. Under the old system, all these matters depended on the faculty member's reputation or bargaining power with the various deans, rendering laymen in particular very vulnerable in a complex clergy-dominated political system that they could hardly comprehend. Having granted some legal security, Gannon then raised salaries, so an assistant professor in 1937–38 could take home between $3,000 to $3,700 a year.

Although he courted the respect of secular peers, Gannon, above all a man of the church, drew a line on academic freedom. Historically, it would be another two decades before academic freedom would become a national issue and before some form of it would be more or less taken for granted at Catholic institutions. Gannon would apply his own version when faced with hiring a potentially controversial professor. In Gannon's view, each man had the right to teach the truth, the truth as the church sees it. A professor convinced that his personal version of the truth required him to criticize the church should look for work at a secular university.

Von Hildebrand had come to Fordham on the recommendation of the great French Thomist, Jacques Maritain. One day Maritain himself, who had already published several of the sixty books that would rank him as one of the greatest minds of the century, sat down in Gannon's office to discuss his own coming to Fordham as chair of the graduate philosophy program. He had brought with him quite a bit of political baggage.

In 1906, two years after their marriage, Maritain and his wife, Raïssa, a Russian Jew, influenced by the philosophy of Henri Bergson, had converted to Catholicism. After teaching at the Institut Catholique in Paris until 1939, Maritain, a staunch antifascist, was writing articles for *Commonweal* urging American Catholics to take the antifascist side in the early days of World War II. He had moved to New York in 1940 and was being courted by fellow Thomist scholar Etienne Gilson, who was trying to lure him to the Pontifical Institute of Medieval Studies at the University of Toronto, as well as by Notre Dame, the University of Chicago, and Princeton.

Maritain's political convictions sprang from his Catholic moral philosophy, and whatever university won him would have to deal not with an abstract metaphysician, but with a scholar trained in and with insights on science, art, economics, and foreign affairs, as well as philosophy and theology. Like the other leading French Catholic intellectuals—François Mauriac and Georges Bernanos—he was also a critic of the Franco side in the Spanish Civil War, and he had angered conservatives in both Paris and Rome. Gannon told an interviewer, Thomas E. Curley Jr. in the 1970s that Maritain, concerned about his academic freedom, said he was very opposed to Italy's Fascist government, then in negotiations with the Vatican. On political issues that were not in the content of Revelation, he wanted freedom to criticize the pope. Gannon refused.

So the greatest living Catholic philosopher made his wartime home in Greenwich Village, meeting with exiled French intellectuals and teaching and lecturing at a dozen universities, including once at Fordham in 1949. After the war, he served briefly as de Gaulle's ambassador to the Vatican and taught at Princeton until 1960. We can imagine that Gannon, a pro-Franco conservative who had welcomed the future Pope Pius XII to Fordham in 1936 and who had invested public-relations energy in good relations with the hierarchy, was avoiding political trouble. Ironically, in later life, Maritain in *The Peasant of the Garonne,* like von Hildebrand in *The Trojan Horse in the House of God,* identified most deeply with a pre–Vatican II vision of the church that Gannon appreciated and that was passing away.

III ⚊

To ease Fordham's financial crisis, Gannon raised tuition from $200 to $250 a term, won support from some foundations, and reluctant to incur debt for new buildings, received $100,000 from the widow of Patrick McGovern, who had built the New York subways. This gift was to build St. Mary's Hall, a dormitory for nuns on the grounds of the Ursuline sisters at Bedford Park, a few blocks from the campus. In another instance, at a private dinner party, Gannon's hostess wrote a check for $160,000, with $50,000 to follow, to pay for Bishop's and St. Robert's Halls, the two new matching wings attached to St. John's. Constituting the lovely Queen's Court, which opened in 1940, it had a real fireplace in its lounge, private showers, and a bowling alley in the basement.

Gannon's big project, the Fordham Centenary Fund appeal for $1,000,000, launched at an Alumni Day rally in 1940, achieved only 60 percent of its goal; 2,635 alumni contributed an average of $52 each, with a college average of $125. According to Gannon, Al Smith told him that "Catholics in this town are not interested in higher education. You have to show them a starving baby." Nevertheless, over his thirteen-year term, Gannon was a tireless and successful fund-raiser, often attending five dinners a week, entertaining his audiences with inspirational and witty attacks on communists and fascists and modern theories of education. He raised, by his own estimate, about $125,307.82 a year.

Giving his public-relations flair full flight, Gannon called national and international attention to Fordham by hosting a series of theatrical events, state visits, and conferences designed to portray this struggling Bronx corner of the "Catholic ghetto" as a stage on which future popes, reigning presidents, and a cross section of European diplomats were proud to appear. Already the steps of Keating were dubbed the "Terrace of the Presidents"; the names of visiting presidents from around the world would be embedded there.

As a young priest studying in Rome, Francis J. Spellman, later cardinal of New York and one of America's most politically influential churchmen, had won the friendship of both the wealthy Catholic philanthropist Mrs. (Duchess) Nicholas Brady, who had a home in Rome, and Cardinal Eugenio Pacelli, Vatican secretary of state, who recognized his talents by consecrating him auxiliary bishop of Boston in 1932. Spellman graduated from St. John's College in 1911, where he had played baseball and competed in dramatics and oratory. He joined the diocesan seminary rather than the Jesuits and after seven years in Boston was named archbishop of New York in 1939. Father Hogan was quick to give the young prelate an honorary degree, and Gannon's Fordham identified itself with Spellman as strongly as possible; indeed, Spellman's picture (always the same one) seems to have appeared in the *Ram* almost as often as it appeared in his diocesan paper, the *Catholic News*.

In the summer of 1936, when Pacelli let it be known that he would spend a long fall vacation at Mrs. Brady's Long Island estate, Inisfada, his quiet private visit was quickly turned into a Catholic media extravaganza. In the midst of a presidential election, cities, universities, and politicians vied for an afternoon—even a few minutes—of his itinerary, which would climax with a postelection lunch with the Roosevelts at Hyde Park. Having charmed three or four institutions a day and having seen America's wonders by directing his pilot to fly low over the Grand Canyon and Niagara Falls, Pacelli was ready to conclude his month-long tour of America at Fordham.

On Sunday afternoon, November 1, surrounded by dignitaries and celebrities, Pacelli received five hundred Fordham faculty on the Keating terrace. Then, with four newsreel cameras churning, he processed through a cheering crowd on Edwards Parade and mounted the steps to the gym, where he received an honorary degree. Gannon deliberately had an ROTC honor guard greet the future pope to demonstrate Fordham's opposition to pacifism. "For pacifism," he said in his remarks, "is to the true love of peace what prohibition is to temperance. It is the image of virtue distorted by heresy."

In May 1938, under the inspiration of Fr. Moorehouse F. X. Millar, Fordham invited all the nations of the Danube Valley to a conference on the future of that crucial region, only to have Hitler determine its future by moving into Austria. Fordham went ahead with the conference anyway. In September 1939, right after German troops had marched into Belgium, student delegates from all over Europe convened at Fordham for a week of prayer and intellectual discussion at the Pax Romana Congress. That same fall, Sarah Delano Roosevelt, the president's mother, came to help dedicate a plaque honoring her second cousin, James Roosevelt Bayley, Fordham's second president. The way was prepared for her son, a Fordham "alumnus," to make his return appearance.

IV ~

As Fordham approached its one hundredth year, if personal recollections, *Rams,* and yearbooks are reliable guides, the campus seems to have been a beautiful and fairly lively place. The minister of the Jesuit community, Alfred M. Rudtke, S.J., loved trees; indeed, he was inspired by the closing line of Joyce Kilmer's poem, "But only God can make a tree." In the early 1940s, he put in 1,800 beeches, birches, dogwood, elms, hawthorns, lindens, and oaks, including the second row of elms coming up from the main gate and replacing, in time, those elms that would perish from Dutch elm disease.

Gannon had announced that the centennial class, which would enter in 1937 and graduate in 1941, would be an exceptionally talented group. One of these students, Eugene (Gene) P. Rogers, has treasured his neatly transcribed notes from Fr. Theodore Farley, S.J.'s junior year epistemology, cosmology, ontology, and religion courses. Farley, who made every effort to be both understood and understanding, dictated the notes, pausing occasionally for questions. Every upperclassman had the equivalent of a major in philosophy, spending as much as three hours a day, five days a week, in the philosophy classroom. As with all required courses, the chances of its being taught dynamically and imaginatively to large groups were limited. Yet the average student seemed to appreciate the intellectual discipline of mastering a logical system of thought, including terminology such as *essence* and *existence, intrinsic* and *extrinsic end, real and logical being, being a se, ab alio, per se,* and *in alio.*

In religion class, Gene's first assignment was to write a seven-page outline proving to a non-Catholic who believes in God that he has an obligation to belong to the Catholic Church under pain of losing his soul. All the religion theses are arranged as syllogisms: "If Christ's words instituting the Eucharist are to be taken in their natural and obvious sense, they necessarily designate the real presence; but they are to be taken in their natural and obvious sense, therefore they designate the real presence." On to the Lenten regulations and Ember Days, then matrimony and impediments to marriage. The religion program was essentially basic catechism that a Catholic-school student would have learned a hundred times, but that a non-Catholic student might consider a challenge.

Both Gene and his friend John Clauss missed out on campus life because they spent half the day working at jobs in town. John was so poor that he ate lunch only once a week. He was grateful for the obligatory senior Oxford philosophy gowns because they hid the fact that he could not afford a change of clothes. John would not have graduated had not an administrator, Si Manning, picked up his tuition debt at the last minute.

For those who had time and money and could live on campus, there were literally dozens of clubs to join, including clubs for every state and borough, rifle and fencing teams, the Bollandists for historians, language clubs, the St. John Berchmans Society for Mass servers, sodalities, publications, orchestra and band, the debate team, and Mimes and Mummers. The glee club was in many ways the elite group, with their spiffy formal attire for the Town Hall Concert, their visiting concerts at women's colleges, and late-night songfests drinking beer at the Raven and the "G. A.":

> We meet again tonight boys in mirth and song.
> Let melody flow wherever we go.
> With hand in hand in friendship we carry on,
> And sorrow never know—ow-ow.

There were proms with big-name bands, the fall Harvester dance, the Sunday-afternoon tea dances at Marymount, and the football rallys with guest appearances by famous stars such as Dennis Day, Fred Waring, Mel Allen, and even Gene Autry. The minority interested in political and social issues gravitated toward the *Ram* staff, the debate clubs, and the sodalities. Students were very aware of Gannon's close friendship with Spellman and, for the most part, shared the "Catholic" pro-Franco position on the Spanish Civil War, the church's militant anticommunism, and what they saw as Gannon's "virulent anti-British" sentiments.

Not everyone loved the prewar Fordham. Gerard Flynn, now an emeritus university Spanish professor in Wisconsin, has self-published an autobiographical novel, *The Bronx Boy,* in which Fordham appears as the college, Rosadabrigid. In May, the sweet scents of honeysuckle and azaleas fill the air there and the great lawns sweep on all sides as students voluntarily cluster around the statue of the Blessed Virgin Mary and say the rosary. But religion is the worst-taught course and the philosophy professors, all priests, simply read from their texts. One who, says Flynn, personifies the school "was intolerant of ideas and people who delighted in them; he was an antihumanist teaching the pride of the humanities, who closed minds rather than open them."

V 〜

Meanwhile, some of the young president's troubles during his first three terms came from governance and relationships inside the Society of Jesus. Fr. Zacheus Maher, S.J., was then acting as the American authority of the Society during World War II, following the death of Fr. Ledochowski in 1942. From his headquarters in the Novitiate of St. Andrew-on-Hudson, Fr. Maher maintained the "old society," with its confining rules and customs dictated by Rome.

In 1943, Maher sent a *memorial,* a collection of letters based on his visitation of the American Assistancy, to all the houses. It totaled thirty-eight pages and included excerpts from the general's letters. Some of the topics covered were trivial, some dealt with broad policy such as athletics and coeducation and provided specific direction on practical matters such as vacations, table manners, alcohol consumption, college publications, and the training of young Jesuits. It gives a sense of how Rome sought to control the details of the daily lives of Jesuits and students alike.

Jesuits were not to attend professional sports events or listen to them on the radio. They could listen to the news only once a day, except during wartime, and after the war, they were to return to once a day. Jesuits should stop pretending that smoking was "good for their health" and give it up. The rector was not to have exclusive use of any car, and it should be a "poor man's car"; a Buick was a cause for scandal. Students might have six formal dances a year, and though there is no fixed number for informal dances, there should be fewer of them. If pictures of girls at dances are published in yearbooks, only those modestly dressed should appear, but it is better to have no dance pictures at all. Too many Jesuits attend too many dances and stay too late. Women are not to be employed as secretaries. Jesuits are not to attend public moving pictures. In posed yearbook pictures of basketball, swimming, track, and boxing teams, bodies are to be covered. Indeed, too much of what was in yearbooks, he said, was left to the students themselves, "who, swept along by the spirit of the age and judging as the world judges, often ape the performances of secular institutions."

Today the language and attitudes of Maher's letters may seem quaint. Yet he was fundamentally right in that in those early stages of the social and cultural change wrought by the media, the young, including Jesuits, were being quickly absorbed by the spirit of the age. Chances of Jesuits putting their fingers in the dike were slim.

In 1940, because Gannon had complained that running the university and overseeing the 120-man Jesuit community was too much, Maher separated the offices of rector and president, leaving Gannon with full power as president. He named Fr. J. Harding Fisher, S.J., as rector; under the Jesuit constitutions, this still made Gannon responsible for the university as well as being the religious superior of the community. It was all very awkward. Gannon had hoped for a separate superior with himself as rector, and Fisher, an experienced superior who had been a Fordham student from 1888 to 1895, was basically frozen out of any university role and asked to not attend any university functions. Fisher, who according to his biographers had the sympathy of the other Jesuits, bore the humiliation with tact and prayed for Gannon as he led the university through the war.

VI ⁓

Whatever the occasional shallowness of its intellectual endeavor, Fordham—and all of Catholic higher education in those years—had a problem it seldom discussed. There were no black faces in Fordham College and very few in any Catholic college or university. In January

1934, a very light-skinned black student named Hudson J. Oliver Jr., the son of a distinguished physician who was a Catholic convert and a highly respected New York teacher, graduated from Xavier and, along with his classmates, went up to Fordham to register.

At Xavier, Oliver had retained the rank of private throughout his four years; he had played class football and basketball, had run varsity track and cross country, and had been in the bugle corps. All the other members of class were admitted, but he was not and no reason was given. According to the Fordham registrar, the trustees had made the decision.

John LaFarge, S.J.—whose father, John LaFarge, one of America's best-known nineteenth-century artists, had gone to St. John's College in its earliest years—was the founder of the Catholic Interracial Council in 1934 and had been an editor of *America* since 1926. When he heard of Oliver's exclusion, he was furious. The trustees, he learned, had not been consulted, and Fordham's rector, Fr. Aloysius Hogan, was in LaFarge's judgment guilty of serious sin for his policy.

In his appeal to the New York provincial, Fr. Edward Phillips, S.J., LaFarge warned of the scandal this act of prejudice would cause and, contrary to his usually extremely cautious approach, threatened to expose Fordham in his writings. The provincial agreed to meet with Dr. and Mrs. Oliver, who were convinced that if their boy had to attend a secular university such as Columbia or City College, he would lose his faith. The boy told LaFarge, "I want a Catholic education *all the way through,* and none of that secular stuff." Reluctant to pressure Fordham, the provincial did pressure Fr. Dinneen, S.J., rector of St. Peter's College, which Gannon was just getting off the ground. Dinneen acquiesced, but he resented being forced to assume a duty that Fordham, a stronger institution, had shirked.

In a three-page memo to the Jesuit general, LaFarge laments that, although Fordham did accept Negroes in the graduate and law schools, both Hogan and the dean, Fr. Charles Deane, S.J., out of sheer bigotry were adamant against accepting Negroes. He frets about the scandal and the impact of this policy on Catholic interracialists most concerned about communist inroads in the Negro community. Without Catholic philosophy and moral training, he believes, Negroes will be all the more susceptible to communist propaganda.

In the scholastic logical method of raising and answering objections, LaFarge spelled out the situation. Would the students object to accepting Negro students? On the contrary, students would accept Negroes if the faculty did. Would too many come? No, only a few were qualified. Would they demand social equality? Might they cause embarrassment by coming to the prom? Not at all; they have no desire to mingle socially with whites, nor to meet white ladies. Wouldn't Fordham lose social status by admitting blacks? That should not matter if Fordham would do the right thing. Besides, no one would notice. In scholastic format: "If there were hundreds of Negroes at Fordham, *Concedo.* But one or two boys among hundreds, *Nego.*" LaFarge's lack of commitment to social equality, fundamental to personal relationships on a college campus, exemplifies both his famed caution and his lack of feeling for campus life. Lacking the temperament for a public protest, LaFarge concluded that there was nothing to do but pray and wait for a change in Fordham's administration.

On the grassroots level, through the sodalities and new associations, such as the National Federation of Catholic College Students, things were happening. Theologically, interracialists took inspiration from the doctrine of the Mystical Body of Christ, which emphasized the connectedness and interdependence of all Christians and, by extension, the human race. In 1936, in a welcoming address to the Catholic Interracial Council, which was holding its annual conference at Fordham, Gannon assured its members that "no student would ever be denied admittance to any department of the university because of race prejudice." Since Gannon had been dean of St. Peter's when young Oliver was foisted upon them, he must have known Oliver personally, and must have relished reversing a Fordham policy that had put St. Peter's on the spot.

The downtown schools had broken the color barrier years before. When Ruth Whitehead Whaley won the top academic prize, graduating from Fordham law school in 1924, the donor took the prize back at the last minute when he found out she was black. Dr. Willis Nathanial Huggins got his Ph.D. in education in 1932. But it would take the World War II years to get a black face in the Fordham College yearbook.

In February 1939, none other than Dr. Hudson J. Oliver addressed the sodality on racism, but we may conclude from the *Ram* report, he was too much a gentleman to mention that Fordham had refused to admit his son. Perhaps moved by the talk and by the vote of Manhattan College's 1938 senior class to establish a scholarship for a black student, the *Ram* editor, John M. Keavey, challenged his classmates in an editorial with the proposal that the profits from Senior Week be devoted to a similar scholarship for a Negro. The *Ram*'s logic was simply that racial integration was consistent with the Christian principles that Fordham preached. The senior class meeting, however, voted it down, one argument being that the Negro might want to bring a date to the prom.

Perhaps the Catholic activist most determined to embarrass Catholic educators into integrating their universities was Baroness Catherine de Hueck Doherty, a survivor of the Russian Revolution. Arriving in America as a penniless refugee and separated from her husband, she made a living as a waitress, then as a Chautauqua lecturer, enrapturing her small-town tent audiences with her glamorous life story. A convert to Catholicism, she embraced a life of poverty and began a spiritual movement similar in some ways to the Catholic Worker House founded by Dorothy Day. A vociferous advocate for the poor, the baroness established several institutions called Friendship Houses in Canada in the mid-1930s, then, on the invitation of Fr. LaFarge, set up a Friendship House as an interracial center in Harlem in 1938. Meanwhile, she made the rounds of the colleges and lectured to whoever would listen. In 1940, she conducted her own survey, one of several extant at that time, asking whether the colleges admitted Negroes.

A more extensive 1940 survey by Sister Maria Gratia, S.C., sent to 120 colleges outside the South to which 92 responded, showed that 38 colleges and universities had a total of 222 full-time Negro students. Forty-seven of the schools had or previously had Negroes; 59 were willing, but had no applicants; 20 had no policy; and 11 were committed to discrimination. The baroness's little November 1940 survey got some interesting responses: the College of Chestnut Hill said they had one Negro girl, who was doing well, but she did not attend dances or events where young men were in attendance; Albertus

Magnus, in New Haven, would accept one who met requirements, but not as a boarder.

The year before, on November 15, 1939, the baroness had addressed more than two hundred students in Keating's senior lecture hall. She urged her listeners to be united in their acceptance of Negroes and to save them from the "living hell"—meaning the terrible slums of Harlem—in which they lived. She had, she said, groups of boys all ready to enter Fordham, and if Fordham did not receive them, the communists would claim them as their own. Although the *Ram* report (November 17) mentions nothing extraordinary about the address, in her diary that night the baroness wrote that she "went too far" and "so am frightened."

The baroness did not say in her diary how she "went too far," but in her memoir, *Fragments of My Life* (1983), dictated from memory without notes or research and without giving dates, she describes what she calls a three-year effort to get the Fordham Jesuits to accept a Negro, sending them each year a new nominee who had a high-school average over 90 percent, was a daily communicant, and a star athlete, all to be turned away. So after ten minutes addressing her audience in protest against Fordham's policy, she dramatically stepped down and refused to go on, but the students "exploded," insisting that she continue. So she delivered a spellbinder on interracial justice that brought the students to their feet demanding that Negroes be admitted, while the Jesuits stared glumly from the gallery.

We can imagine the contents of the speech from her published essays. In the spirit of the muckraker Jacob Riis, she forced listeners to identify with slum dwellers by describing their plight in vivid, often sentimental, detail. Children are born with eager eyes, but "slowly, eagerness fades, limbs shrink, disease creeps in. Bad housing, bad food, lack of air and sunshine all take their toll."

Later, she recalls, the Jesuits invited her to dinner at a "swanky" restaurant, where twenty of them, including Gannon—"all quite slender and good-looking, dressed in their nice cassocks and belts"—tried to convince her that they could not accept Negroes because so many of their students came from the South. She replied bluntly that, according to her Bible, which she had brought with her, neither Jesus nor St. Ignatius would recognize their arguments. "I arose, bathed in perspiration. I have never gone through such a two-hour session in my life."

It's a good story, but marked with contradictions and confusion. The senior lecture hall in Keating has no gallery where the glum, disapproving Jesuits might have sat. Nor can Jesuits imagine twenty going to a dinner at a swanky restaurant in their "cassocks and belts," even in 1939. And for Gannon to oppose Negro undergraduates after swearing to the Catholic Interracial Council in 1936 that no qualified Negro would be excluded would make him a high-level hypocrite. Most likely, the baroness's memory confused and combined several other events.

An editorial in the December 7, 1939, *Ram,* three weeks after the baroness's talk, was called "Eclairs with a Baroness." It was probably written by the editor, Richard L. Breen, who was also a leading debater, and it describes an impromptu (perhaps imagined?) dinner between de Hueck, the editor, and the sports editor. At table, de Hueck challenges the student leaders, charging that the students, not the Jesuits, resist Negro enrollment. She appeals to the doctrine of the Mystical Body of Christ. The *Ram* editors are forced to simply confess the hypocrisy of their fellow students who claim to be Christian but shun black people, while Ivy League schools accept them. The editorial concludes with an ironic scene: "We rode downtown on the Third Avenue L through Harlem," feeling guilty, but not guilty enough to change.

The following year, November 1940, in response to the baroness's survey, the Fordham School of Education said they had eight Negroes registered, six undergraduates and two graduate students, and would like more; the Graduate School of Arts and Sciences had four. What was the basis for de Hueck's memory of Jesuits refusing Negroes because of their Southern constituency? Probably an encounter at Georgetown. According to her diaries, as late as April 1947, the baroness was lashing out at a sodality audience in Georgetown's Copley Lounge about Georgetown holding out as one of the few Catholic colleges still barring blacks.

A 1947 report in *Woodstock Letters* summed up the limited progress Jesuit high schools and colleges had made toward integration: twenty-six high schools could count but 20 Negroes in their total enrollment of 23,494, while twenty-one colleges (three not responding) had 436 Negroes out of 81,794 students. Saint Louis University, which had desegregated (in enrollment, but not socially) after much public controversy only two years before, had 150; Fordham had 102; Georgetown, none, although that school denied a policy of exclusion. Fordham's were spread among the eight schools, with most in education (20), social science (25), and adult education (20), and 6 in the College of Arts and Sciences.

Insofar as senior yearbook pictures are a reliable guide, it would appear that Matthew Ebenezer Adams, graduate of DeWitt Clinton High School, was Fordham's first enrolled Negro student. A premedical student, he entered, according to the World War II accelerated trimester schedule, in February 1943, then left to join the navy in June 1944. He returned in July 1946 and graduated in 1947.

Harcourt G. Harris, '48, also premedical, and Denis Glennon Baron, '48, an economics major from Fordham Prep, graduated the following year. Perhaps because he stayed at Fordham to teach economics in the 1950s, Baron, son of West Indian immigrants, was the best known of the first Fordham African Americans. Like many of his peers, he had interrupted his college stint in 1944 to join the Marine Corps, returning in 1946. Fluent in French and Vietnamese, he served the State Department in South Asia, France, and Africa. From 1969 to 1978, he was with the Mobil Oil Corporation, and in his last years he lectured in economics at the American University in Washington, D.C.

VII ⬝

When Roy Brown, '49, a Jamaican immigrant, arrived in February 1946, Fordham was still on the accelerated trimester system, in the first wave of the postwar G.I. Bill influx. About a half to a third of the students and some of the faculty were still in uniform. He had chosen Fordham because his stepfather's boss, a car washer on Manhattan's Upper West Side, had suggested it and because his parents wanted him to get a Catholic education.

He commuted from the desirable Edgecombe Avenue neighborhood in Harlem on the D train and fell in easily with the mature ex-GIs, and especially with the Irish Catholic boys, Dodger fans from Brooklyn. Philosophy was the campus's social glue, not because of its conceptual content, but because all eight hundred students were studying the same thing, giving everyone a common experience to talk about. Since of the three black men in his class, the other two were light-skinned, Roy was the "token Negro" on campus, but whereas a decade before students murmured that a Negro "wouldn't fit in at the prom," Roy's Brooklyn friends, with whom he played tennis and shot pool, went out of their way to make him feel at home in the cafeteria and at dances. Indeed, he never experienced any color bar until he applied to medical school. Neither a United States citizen nor a veteran, his best opportunity was in Zurich, Switzerland.

Over the years, what had become of young Hudson J. Oliver, whom Fordham had refused in 1934? In 1944, Fr. LaFarge, in a long letter to Zacheus Maher, turned a discussion about how best to oppose communism into a proposal that perhaps the American Jesuits should accept a Negro into their own Society. Ever cautious, he did not suggest that the whole Society should integrate, but just take one Jesuit school alumnus into the New York–Maryland Province. In fact, he had one in mind: "a young Negro who has made an excellent record both in studies and in conduct at St. Peter's College, Jersey City, son of a fine Catholic colored physician of that city and a good mother." In fact, the boy had already applied to the New York provincial and had been turned down "since there would be no place to use him in the New York Province."

He could be referring only to Oliver, but why does he refer to Oliver, admitted in 1934 as a St. Peter's College student, in 1944? It appears that LaFarge, whatever his good intentions, had not done his homework on his protégé. Young Oliver had failed seven courses at St. Peter's and had been dismissed twice. He left school in 1939, still lacking one course, without graduating. One official wrote of him that "in my thirteen years of experience I know no student who got the consideration Mr. Oliver received in St. Peter's of which he proved himself entirely unworthy." He would not be allowed another opportunity to receive his degree. But in 1946, after an absence of five years (perhaps he was in the service?), by intervention of the president, Fr. Vincent Hart, S.J., he got credit for a vertebrate-biology summer course not previously recorded, and graduated. Ten years later he considered a teaching career, but we don't know how it worked out.

Whatever Oliver's success or lack of it, his case was the catalyst that forced Fordham, St. Peter's, and the Society of Jesus to think more critically about their own racial policies. Father Maher did not order integration, but he sent a generalized letter around to all the provincials on May 3, 1945, saying that a Negro should not be excluded on the basis of his color, but that each province should consider how he might be "useful" to that province's work, and that one who might not appear "useful" in 1948 could become very useful in 1958, when he had finished his studies and the American racial climate might have changed.

Gannon, though by no means known as an agent of social change, was asked for a statement on racial discrimination in 1941, and issued one that combined his basic fairness, his awareness of the impending war, and his rhetorical flourish: "Discrimination, whether social or industrial, is always bloodless but cruel persecution. It is, besides, the perfect way to set brother against brother, the perfect way to ruin the morals of any country, even in times of peace. In times of national crisis, to deny our fellow citizens jobs that are suited to their abilities because of race, color, creed, or national extraction is criminally stupid."

9.

From *Oedipus* to Dachau

President Roosevelt's Monday, October 28, 1940, visit to Fordham is a day that will live in irony and ambiguity. According to Gannon's account, FDR's campaign manager, pressed by Republican candidate Wendell Willkie's surge in strength, called on him at the height of the fall campaign to request an honorary degree for the president of the United States. This was an odd request because FDR, as governor of New York, had already received an honorary LL.D. from Fordham in 1929. Gannon proposed in its stead a Roosevelt-Willkie debate on the steps of Keating Hall. When Roosevelt declined, Willkie asked for seats at the Fordham–St. Mary's game for Saturday, October 26, and Gannon naturally invited the Republican candidate to share the president's box. Alarmed, Fordham's Democratic alumni got on the phone, and FDR, as commander in chief of the armed forces, was invited to Rose Hill to review the 525-man ROTC coast-artillery unit, which had been elevated the year before to the status of a regiment.

This was, in fact, the climactic week of the campaign. A few months before, polls had shown FDR leading with 60 percent of the vote, but a series of events had forced the president, whose strategy had been not to formally campaign or even mention his opponent's name, to come out fighting.

The public mood had swung against any involvement in the war. John L. Lewis, president of the United Mine Workers, had delivered a vicious anti-Roosevelt speech, and Willkie, who had been calling FDR an isolationist and had accused him of not preparing America militarily, was now making wilder attacks on the "third term" issue, charging that "dictator" Roosevelt would install his wife, Eleanor, or one of his sons as president in 1944. Roosevelt's former friend Al Smith, grumbling that there were already too many dictators in the world, was supporting Willkie. To make matters worse, Joseph P. Kennedy, ambassador to Great Britain, returning to the United States on October 27, was rumored to be about to break with Roosevelt to back Willkie. With only a few weeks to go, FDR had announced that to "correct misrepresentations" by his critics, he would give five speeches. As he addressed each crowd he would add, to their delight, "I am an old campaigner and I love a good fight."

Gannon had mixed feelings about a Roosevelt visit. This was the eve of Fordham's centennial year, and FDR would be the first president of the United Sates to set foot on the campus. Gannon's anti-Roosevelt feelings were no secret; both Fordham historian Charles C. Tansill, later of Georgetown and the author of *Back Door to War* (1952), and Nebraska senator Edward R. Burke, member of the Senate Judiciary Committee, had written within the month to draw Gannon into a public role, to testify in the Senate in the "No Third Term" movement, but Gannon declined to go public as Fordham president. He told Tansill that "after the election I think every patriotic American should work for a single term of six years."

On Saturday, Willkie enjoyed a triumphant New York tour. He was thronged by enthusiastic crowds at the World's Fair, booed in Harlem, and both booed and cheered, though mostly cheered, at the Polo Grounds by 34,500 spectators at the Fordham–St. Mary's game that St. Mary's won 9-6, depriving Fordham of another undefeated season.

On Sunday, Italy invaded Greece. Roosevelt got hold of Kennedy and invited the ambassador and his wife to the White House for dinner that night. There, in the presence of Jimmy Byrnes and other guests he listened attentively to all of Kennedy's complaints, told him how much he admired all he had done, and secured his endorsement for the third term.

Monday morning, the presidential train arrived at Newark in the early morning. In Jersey City the president met with three hundred disabled children in wheelchairs and told them, "I know how it feels myself." From Bayonne he crossed to Staten Island, then took a boat to Brooklyn, crossed to Manhattan, and made his way north through overwhelming crowds. At Hunter College, President George N. Shuster, the highly respected Catholic intellectual, praised FDR's courage and sacrifice. Then the cavalcade crossed to Queens and to the Bronx, where the Grand Concourse was lined all the way with cheering throngs. As they turned off Fordham Road into the campus, the crowd broke through the police barrier and swarmed close to the car, now carrying Archbishop Spellman and Gannon, as it made its way through the gate, up the elm-lined path, through a crowd of ten thousand, and onto Edwards Parade, pulling up at the foot of the Keating Hall steps.

The press, students, and cheerleaders in heavy white sweaters with big Fs crowded around. As Gannon, clad in a biretta and long black cape, rose to take one of the microphones, FDR removed the misshapen brown fedora he had been wearing most of the day. Gannon's welcoming remarks, described by a student as "a slap in the face, but done nicely," were rhetorically clever enough to appear to praise the president of the United States without actually doing so. He did praise Roosevelt's mother, "the most charming of all the Roosevelts," who, when offered a glass of sherry in Gannon's office after having been drenched in the rain of the dedication ceremony a year before, replied, "For an awful moment I thought you were going to suggest a cup of tea."

Gannon also informed Roosevelt that while he was the first president to come to Fordham while in office, George Washington's visit during the Revolutionary War was commemorated by a huge boulder on the site. He described FDR as "one of the three or four most dynamic" personalities in the world and "the symbol of our generation." He told the assembled, "Today you stand before a man whose imprint is forever fixed on our national history. Our country has been reshaped in the last eight years and will never be just what it was before." One Gannon admirer wrote him the next day to say he was still chuckling over that last line.

Roosevelt's largely extemporaneous reply went for two minutes. He referred to Gannon as "my friend the rector" and himself as "an old alumnus of yours back for the first time in a great many years." On that cold afternoon he would welcome the sherry offered his mother, but had not time, and added that if invited to spend the night he hoped the rector would "not ask me to sleep on George Washington's Boulder."

Then he got serious. He did not mention it, but in spite of the excitement of campaigning, he had been on the phone a good part of the day conferring with the War Department and the White House on developments in Europe. The next day, though his advisers had urged him to put it off till after the election, he was determined to draw the first lottery number for the first peacetime conscription in history. Sixteen million men between the ages of twenty-one and thirty-five had registered, and tomorrow's process would determine the order of their induction for a year of military service.

Roosevelt called his review of the ROTC a "muster" because "it is an old word that goes back to the old colonial days in America when every able man had an obligation to serve his community and his country in case of attack." This was training, he said, "in the new faculties of warfare" to enable them to defend the lives of all the men, women, and children in America. The visit, lasting only a few minutes, was a jolt of realism to a student body more preoccupied with the upcoming Cotton Bowl game than with the world catastrophe that was about to sweep them up. As for the political import of the visit, one Democratic leader told the *New York Times,* "I feel better now about that business of last Saturday."

That night, though exhausted by what would be a fourteen-hour ordeal that brought him to the eyes of two million people, at 10:00 he delivered a rousing and witty speech for almost an hour to an overwhelming crowd of 22,000 in Madison Square Garden, with 30,000 gathered outside, bringing the crowd to its feet cheering and laughing. It was also the first political campaign speech to be televised, to 40,000 sets. Then at midnight he made his way to Pennsylvania Station, where his train waited to take him home.

II ⇝

Roosevelt's visit had, in ways that were yet to be understood, ushered in Fordham's Centennial Celebration. But the highlight, as planned, was to be the grand production of Sophocles' *Oedipus Tyrannus*, the first time in sixty years that this play had been given in the original Greek in the United States. Again, since university presidents tend to focus on the priorities in which they see themselves as talented, Gannon, who had published a one-act-play manual as a scholastic, had determined to make theater, long the heart of Jesuit education in Europe, a Fordham showpiece.

He had plans that year to refurbish Collins Auditorium, which had become a firetrap, by reducing the balcony and cutting seating from nine hundred to six hundred, building more changing rooms, and adding draperies to improve the acoustics. There would be a theater-in-the-round on the third floor for both classical and experimental productions. In Keating Hall, he would construct the Keating Little Theater with a sound and projection booth just right for experimental or student-written one-act plays, recitals, lectures, debates, and television. But for the present, for *Oedipus*'s sake, he was to milk Collins's facilities, with its wonderful center stage and two adjoining, slightly protruding side stages, for all they could offer.

The *Oedipus* production was the brainchild of a brilliant thirty-two-year-old Jesuit, William F. Lynch, S.J. A 1930 Fordham graduate, he was then in his regency, the teaching-training period in the course between philosophy and theology that had employed Jesuit seminarians at Fordham since 1846. Lynch, who had been writing articles on the relationship between theater and faith for some time, was a genius; he would eventually become editor of *Thought* magazine, an intellectual quarterly that Fordham took over from *America* magazine. He would become best known as author of *Christ and Apollo: The Dimensions of the Literary Imagination* (1960) and numerous other studies of the relationship between religious belief and aesthetic appreciation. He was also, in a way that only a few clerics can accomplish, well-connected at a relatively young age with talent in the New York arts community.

More important was the talent in his own classrooms. So when he proposed to his Fordham Greek classes that they should pro-duce the classics on stage in Greek, the students, many of whom had already had four years of Greek at Regis High School and two with Lynch at Fordham, took it in stride. In 1939–40, they put on several short plays in their original languages, but that was a warm-up for *Oedipus*. In October he pulled his stars, Robert T. Stewart, '42, who would play Oedipus, and Richard T. Burgi, '42, who would be both Teiresias and Jocasta, aside for drill. Stewart had five hundred lines to memorize.

What seemed to attract the outside talent was the scope of the enterprise. This had not been done in a long time, and it was hard to pass up the challenge. Virgil Thomson had recently returned from Paris to be named music critic for the *New York Herald Tribune*. He was beginning to establish a reputation as a composer with his opera based on Gertrude Stein's *Four Saints in Three Acts* (1934), one of whom was St. Ignatius Loyola. He also wrote the background music for documentary films such as *The Plow That Broke the Plains* (1936) and *The River* (1937). At this moment, Thomson was balancing his career as a journalist, a music critic who passed judgment on others' work, and his ambitions to be a conductor and composer.

That year for John Houseman's Columbia Workshop radio production of Euripides' *The Trojan Women,* in an idea never used before, he had composed a score that separated the scenes by sound effects and used music to help the listener distinguish one character from the other. Thus, he accompanied the three actresses with flute, clarinet, and English horn to distinguish their voices. When Cassandra mentions her child, Thomson introduced a tiny tune on a piccolo to "evoke the baby's presence."

Fordham's invitation was an opportunity to apply the same principles to choruses intoned in Greek. Since Thomson didn't know Greek, Lynch provided him with an interlinear translation of the chorus's part, with the Greek text scanned for cadences. Working phonetically, Thomson composed music for piano, drums, and wind instruments to support the text. As Thomson told the *Ram* (April 25, 1941), the music was not to supplement the action, but be a commentary on the action, "like the choir at a high Mass."

To choreograph the movements of the chorus, Lynch enlisted the young Erick Hawkins. Then about twenty-five, just a few years older than the Fordham boys, Hawkins had been trained by George Balanchine at the School of American Ballet and had recently joined

the Martha Graham Dance Company. He was soon to become
Martha Graham's best-known dance partner and later, husband. He
was to develop his own theory of a natural, free-flowing body movement that had the dancer become aware of the effort he should
expend without forcing it; we can imagine that he tried out his ideas
on the Collins stage.

Lawrence H. Reilly, '43, who played Creon, recalls that to the
young men, Hawkins came across as stiff at first, but soon he settled
in and his chorus was moving smoothly across the stage, singing
their choral odes. The sets were designed by William Riva, who
became a regular member of the theater faculty until the early
1950s, known to the students as husband of Maria Riva, Marlene
Dietrich's daughter.

On opening night, May 9, 1941, almost a thousand spectators,
including delegates from forty-five Eastern colleges, crowded into the
Collins space. In four performances, four thousand people young and
old heard and saw a cast of forty in a Sophocles tragedy as authentic
as the imagination of William Lynch could reconstruct. The fourth
performance was a benefit for Greek War Relief. Virgil Thomson
recalls being most impressed by Richard Burgi, who was only seventeen,
playing Jocasta with "a grand projection." Burgi later got a Ph.D. in
Russian at Columbia University and became founding director of
Fordham's Institute for Russian Studies, a professor at Princeton
University, and a constant presence at the Metropolitan Opera, where
he would encounter Thomson through the years.

Esther Basuk Smith, then a student at Theodore Roosevelt High
School across the street, was so poor that she had never seen a live
stage performance. This was her first. Fortunately she met a priest,
whose name she never knew, who explained it all to her, and she has
never forgotten that day.

III 〜

Seven months later, Lawrence H. Reilly and his friends were at the
football game at the Polo Grounds when word came over the loud-
speaker that the Japanese had attacked Pearl Harbor. His immediate

future was fairly clear: he was in ROTC, so he would be allowed to graduate in January 1943, then go into active duty within two weeks and receive his commission after officers' basic training. As in World War I, some would enlist immediately and others would be called up. Gannon issued a statement that Fordham would have no radical departure from its regular activity, but "carry on as normally and quietly as possible." However, plans were immediately set in motion for an accelerated degree that took three years with no summer vacation.

One student who had to adapt semiheroically to the new summerless schedule was Richard E. Priday, '43, a comuter from Bay Ridge, Brooklyn, whose family always moved to the remote Breezy Point, farther out on Long Island, during the summer. His usual commute from Bay Ridge to the Bronx ate up at least three hours a day as he struggled, studied, and slept on the subways. The new commute required him to walk to the bay at Breezy Point, get the Rockaway Point boat in to Brighton Beach, then take the BMT subway, change to the IND D train to the Bronx, and grab a cab for the race down Fordham Road to reach philosophy class before Fr. Charles Matthews could close the door and lock the latecomers out.

For Priday, the ferry ride was like an ocean voyage, and every interruption in the schedule a threat to his academic future; he could not afford to overcut philosophy. Then one foggy morning when he had no cuts left, a prominent lawyer on board dropped his briefcase into the water. He was on his way to court and that briefcase contained all the evidence for the case he had to present that morning. The ferry turned around and for what seemed an eternity circled the floating briefcase while a crew member tried again and again to hook it with a pole. The crushed Priday arrived at philosophy to find the door closed in his face. Somehow the kindly Fr. Matthews relented and let him in, but reminded him after class, "Don't think for a moment that I believed that cock-and-bull story about the lawyer's briefcase."

On March 6, 1942, the *Ram* had its first "casualty" when it lost its sports columnist, Bob Schmidlein, to aviation school. His farewell thoughts: "The United States is at war, and the frivolity and devil-may-care attitude that has pervaded over three years must disappear with the security and contentment that have already vanished with it. Sports and our life and liberty are threatened, and we must all make one decision to fight for their preservation."

In short, the effect of the war on Fordham's enrollment, as at other universities, was devastating, particularly because Fordham survived on tuition revenue rather than endowment. When FDR spoke on campus the day before the draft, total enrollment was 8,100; a year later it had lost 654 students, most of whom were part-time. Richard Priday remembers that in his class of 1943, just about everyone went right into the service immediately after graduation. It was a class that included two future university presidents—William J. McGill of Columbia and Robert J. Kibbee of City University—and the biographer of Andrew Jackson, Robert V. Remini, who taught history at Fordham and later at the University of Illinois at Chicago. In class, Priday recalls, Remini always raised his hand to ask a question right before the bell.

In the summer of 1943, two juniors left every day. By 1944, the 8,000 had dwindled to 3,086, 2,000 of whom were women, the rest 4Fs and boys under eighteen. By October 1944, there were only twenty-four in the Fordham College graduating class, the smallest since World War I. Nevertheless, Gannon told the *Ram* (February 24, 1944), "Come what might, we will not close any branch of the university, even if the classes have to be conducted in the outer office here."

In a brief transfusion between June 1943 and April 1944, the army established two units of the Army Specialized Training Program (ASTP) on campus to teach pre-engineering and language to about six hundred troops. This employed thirteen Jesuits and thirty-nine lay faculty as instructors; the impact was helpful, but brief. Presuming the university would survive, Gannon bought property. In 1943, when high rent drove Fordham out of the Woolworth Building, Fordham bought the 1899 Vincent Building, a fifteen-storey limestone building at 302 Broadway between Foley Square and city hall, for law, education, and business classes. Then it reorganized the School of Adult Education, later known as the School of General Studies, to attract students of every age, no matter what their background; it was a forerunner, in some ways, to the Fordham Lincoln Center College at Sixty.

IV ~

John Clauss, who had graduated as part of the sterling centennial class of 1941, was stationed in England as one of the many meteorologists on whose information General Dwight D. Eisenhower's decision to launch the invasion of Normandy hung. On June 4, Eisenhower, determined to proceed, scribbled out the first line of a radio message to his men that he would read to the world: "You are about to embark upon a Great Crusade." He also drafted a statement in which he would take responsibility for the mission's failure.

The previous morning, June 3, the LCTs (landing craft, tank) started moving out of the Dart River. On the transport *Thomas Jefferson,* in Company A of the 116th Regiment, the men, who now knew one another intimately, were relieved that after all the preparation this was at last the real thing. Pvt. George Roach, clinging to the religion that had brought him to Fordham Prep, was saying his rosary. The weather was getting worse, clouds hung low, and the troops could smell rain in the air. George knew that since Company A was to be in the first wave, "chances of our survival were very slim." The Channel drizzle changed to cold rain.

Omaha Beach, a crescent-shaped, ten-kilometer stretch of sand beneath tall, well-fortified cliffs, was the most critical and most heavily defended objective. The waters and beach were heavily mined and dozens of Rommel's machine guns and artillery had full view of the invaders. According to plan, George Roach would land with 40,000 men and 3,500 vehicles at Omaha on D day, but the plan didn't work. Because of wind, tides, and four-foot waves, only Roach's Company A came in where it was supposed to.

By the time they hit the beach, the men were soaked and seasick, and when the ramp of their Higgins boats (LCVP) came down, a hail of German machine gun bullets, artillery, and mortar fire hit them in the face. Of the 200-plus men in Company A, only a few dozen survived, and nearly all were wounded. Every member of the thirty-five-man assault team was killed immediately. Roach, who weighed only 125 pounds, was an assistant flame thrower carrying 100 pounds of equipment, including a five-gallon dram of flame-thrower fluid. He came down the ramp, his buddies dropping on every side, fell onto the sand, and started shooting at a house on the bluff.

Roach realized that except for one remaining live member of his assault team, Pvt. Gil Myrdoch, he was completely isolated. So, with Murdoch, who couldn't swim, and with both of them wounded, they went back into the water intending to let the tide bring them in at a safer spot. But the Channel tide rose quickly. They clung to a sunken tank, then struggled to swim in till plucked from the water by the coxswain of a landing craft.

By the time they caught up with Company A the next day, only eight men were ready for duty. When Brig. Gen. Norman "Dutch" Cota, who had from the start opposed a daylight landing, asked Roach what he wanted to do when the war was over, Roach replied, "I'd like to go to Fordham." He later wrote to his Prep swimming coach, telling him he had saved his life.

For John Manning, '41, Fordham had been an adventure, an escape from the world of 16th Street, where he grew up. He had studied Latin and Greek at Xavier on the same street, and at the larger Bronx campus, where he studied science, he enjoyed an English professor who drank too much but really knew how to take a play apart. He became a battalion commander in ROTC. As a young man, he already saw himself as an eyewitness to history. He had seen Lindbergh's triumphant return to New York in 1927; as a Xavier senior, on May 6, 1937, he had looked up to see the Hindenburg that had just passed over Fordham's Keating Hall a few minutes before on its last flight to Lakehurst in southern New Jersey. On October 28, 1940, he marched his regiment in review and gave the command, "Eyes right!" for the commander in chief. The next week, he voted for Willkie.

Commissioned in June 1941, Manning spent the early months of the war in the coast artillery, defending New York Harbor at Fort Totten. Since the Germans had no planes that could fly from Europe, bomb New York, and return, the battalion's principal adversary seemed to be Park Commissioner Robert Moses, who ordered their gun emplacements out of Central Park and Prospect Park and their convoys off the elevated highways and parkways.

Ordered overseas in July 1942, he set sail on the *Queen Elizabeth* on August 31. Confined belowdecks as they pulled out of New York

Harbor, he glimpsed through a porthole the Statue of Liberty with a blimp overhead as they passed out into the sea through a lane where a few months before he had seen a tanker, hit by a German U-boat, in flames.

Among the first troops stationed in England, John had to overcome his Fordham Irish prejudice against the British. He also underwent the first shock of many boys raised on "Thou shalt not commit adultery and shalt not even have impure thoughts" as he saw the camp followers, the ten-year-old boy at the gate selling his sister, the line of men at the fence, and the girls on their knees to accommodate them. Then there was a different challenge to his faith. After a tour of an old country church, the Anglican priest invited John and his friend to kneel and pray. Pray with a Protestant? If it was wrong, he could be forgiven in confession. They prayed for their safety and the safety of their companions in their great undertaking against the Germans. They drove silently back to camp, convinced that that moment was the strongest prayer they had ever experienced.

On November 1, 1942, the battalion sailed for French West Africa, spent the winter in Oran, then moved to Tunisia in February 1943 and to Algiers in April. Here his Battery D, Sixty-second AAA Battalion, saw its first action and shot down one plane. One night, enchanted by a movie vision of the Algiers Casbah, the young lieutenants made their way through its filthy streets to the famous bordello known as the Sphinx. The Fordham men had come to observe—two undressed fat women on a bed in the center of a large room demonstrating sex acts—but not to stay. Downtown, they found a theater next to the elegant Hotel Elette, where Josephine Baker starred. To this day John can still hear her singing "Two Loves Have I" as she kicked her long white-clad legs over her head.

In the invasion of Sicily of July 1943, Manning came face-to-face for the first time with the battlefield dead. A mile from the beach, the rotting, maggot-ridden corpse of an Italian soldier killed a day or so before lay roasting in the sun, the horrendous stench polluting the air all around. They buried him in a shallow grave and marked it with the bayonet on his rifle and his helmet atop on the rifle's butt.

In Sicily, an officer's life was occasionally pleasant—there were USO shows with Bob Hope and Jack Benny, beach swimming, and churches to visit—but it was more often depressing. An officer's basic tasks are to keep equipment ready for action and his men fed, out of trouble, and free of VD. One GI fell in love with the madame of the local whorehouse, moved in with her, caught meningitis, and died; another slipped out to meet a whore and, crawling through the fence to get back, was shot in the head. A British Spitfire pilot flew too close to the American guns and was shot down with half his head blown off. In Italy, preparing to invade Southern France, Manning and some of his men visited the Vatican; in a long room overlooking St. Peter's Square, Pope Pius XII was carried in on his chair, he descended and walked down the aisle shaking hands.

In France, the Sixty-second AAA Battalion operated with the Thirty-fourth AAA Brigade and adapted its versatile 40 mm gun to a field artillery role. When Marseilles fell on a beautiful day, Manning's convoy made its way through the sun-drenched countryside, the scent of its blooming flowers in the air. A beautiful young girl, a wine bottle in her hand and her long bare legs flashing beneath her skirts, came loping like a deer from her home down to the road.

In late November, as the advance guard of the Seventh Army headed toward the Rhine, the Sixty-second Battalion moved into Strasbourg, only to be ordered by Eisenhower, who feared a Battle of the Bulge–like trap, to retreat in January—and then, following a plea from de Gaulle, to take the city again. Through an extremely wet and cold January and February, American and German forces fought for the Rhine. Then, on March 27, 1945, Manning's C Battery of the Sixty-second Battalion, now fortified with new weapons—the quad 50s (four 50-caliber machine guns mounted on a rotating turret)—crossed the Rhine and turned southeast as German resistance melted away.

Outside a village, seventy Germans, who he had expected to fight, came forward with their hands in the air. One officer startled Manning by appearing from behind to surrender to him personally. Manning spun around with his pistol in his hand and saw a man his age wearing the uniform and skull insignia of the hated S.S. Overcome with rage, he pushed the pistol into the captive's stomach and pulled the trigger. Fortunately, the safety was on, but Manning wrote later, "It is fifty-four years since that day and I can still see the look in his face as he realized I had meant to kill him. . . . I would recognize him tomorrow if I met him on the street. But had that pistol gone off, I don't think the sight of his backbone crossing the street would have fazed me."

Those emotions were reinforced by what he saw a month later. Manning had bought a camera in Sicily and become a skilled photographer. A few miles from their quarters at the quiet town of Schwapmunchen, in the last days of April 1945, Manning and some of his men made their way to a camp at a town called Kautering, one of a series of subcamps to Dachau, which had operated from May 1944 until that very month. There, the bodies of five hundred men who had been workers in an underground aircraft factory had just been unearthed. Rows and rows of corpses lined the road from the gate. Manning took pictures. In the photos, now in the Fordham archives, the corpses lie in piles or spread out on rocky dirt. Some are blackened as if burnt; others are pale, white, bald, with mouths open, naked or half dressed with prison pants pulled down, skin taut over skeletons, arms folded across bare chests, huge pelvises jutting out, legs spread or curled up.

Years later, Manning photographed Douglas MacArthur, presidents, popes, and the Republican National Convention. He worked twenty years for the Army and Air Force Exchange Service, and he made a Jesuit tour of Europe and served Mass in one of the rooms of St. Ignatius Loyola in Spain. He remains convinced that the world is no better or worse than it was two hundred years ago.

V ~

In the last months of the war, the *Ram* published in small print a series of long newsletters put together by Fr. Lawrence Atherton, S.J., and Fr. Farley, which consisted of items collected from Fordham men around the world and then mailed to everyone on their list. In a typical letter (March 23, 1945), Farley asks for prayers and reports on answered prayers: Jim O'Connell, x '45, reported missing in January, was reported found, a prisoner of war, while his family was in the last days of its novena rosary. Dick Mulcahy, '43, crashed into another plane over

Yugoslavia; two bailed out, but we don't know which two. So pray for Dick. Mike Suozni, x '45, says there are other Fordham men with him on Iwo Jima, but doesn't mention their names. It looks as if there might be a football team next year, if they can find a coach.

When FDR died, the *Ram* editorial (April 27, 1945) went back to Gannon's 1940 welcome and adopted its rhetoric without the irony. For them, FDR really was the symbol of their generation. His loss was an "act of God . . . a God who takes away from earth a leader who by passing into the next world becomes mightier and greater and more flawless; a leader who now deprived of any human weakness and limitations and free from criticism becomes a symbol and an example for future generations."

In 1946, to celebrate the centenary of the charter by which the State of New York incorporated St. John's College in 1846, President Harry S. Truman received an honorary doctor of laws on Keating Terrace, now known as the Terrace of the Presidents. He paused to ring the Victory Bell on the steps of the gym.

With the influx of ex-GIs such as George Roach, registration rose to 13,200 by 1949. These waves of mature young men, financed by the Serviceman's Readjustment Act (known as the "G.I. Bill," 1944), saved Fordham financially, yet Gannon remained an opponent of higher education for the masses. President Truman's Commission on Higher Education viewed advanced education as a necessary step in the development of democracy and proposed building bigger institutions to provide this opportunity for all those who wanted it. Gannon saw this as an expression of the same John Dewey philosophy he had opposed for years and scorned the plan as a "fraud." "A third of the so-called students," he said, "are in the way, cluttering up the place and interfering with other people's education."

Fordham College accepted eight hundred freshmen "under pressure" for 1947–48, but Gannon hoped to whittle them down to 450. Meanwhile, he increased the boarding population from 130 to 740 in 1936, making it more representative of the country by giving scholarships to the best students in Jesuit high schools and attracting foreign students to make Fordham more cosmopolitan. To house Jesuits in their studies, in 1946 he put up Spellman Hall, a red-brick three-story residence behind Keating. Meanwhile, a Bronx campus division of the business school opened in Reidy Hall, a temporary building behind the gym, with a freshman class of 360 in 1947.

Insofar as George Roach was typical of the postwar generation, he started in January '46, took summer courses, hung out with his own age group at neighborhood bars, such as Harry's Hub on Fordham Road, and carried on their philosophy debates over Harry's free lunch. Though he was only twenty-one, he felt older, and his group said no to the "college type."

A faculty star of the time was Louis Budenz, former editor of the communist *Daily Worker,* and now a convert to Catholicism. He was an associate professor of economics and an occasional witness before congressional investigating committees. In 1948, Vince Lombardi was back on campus as an assistant coach of the new freshman football team living on the fifth floor of Dealy Hall, where he put his freshmen to bed, checked to make sure they hadn't brought in beer, then sat up and drank a few with Fr. Timothy Healy, S.J., who had been sent to Fordham for several reasons, including to work at the radio station.

George's favorite teachers were Gabe Liegey and F. X. Connolly in English, although Connolly was devoted to Evelyn Waugh while George leaned toward Graham Greene. He remembers an image in *The Heart of the Matter* of sunlight shining on a dirty pool of water in the gutter. This, to Roach, was God's light that shines on everyone, even on those in the gutter. After graduation he ran into Connolly on a train, and his old teacher offered to recommend him for a graduate degree in English, but George didn't follow up; he went into sales. After thirty years of drinking too much at night, he entered a twelve-step program and now, in retirement, runs a halfway house for homeless ex-prisoners and makes an annual directed retreat at St. Ignatius Retreat House on Long Island.

Surely, for many, the late 1940s were a difficult transitional period, depending how one felt about the "old days" before the war. For faculty who had been to war, these were creative months. Connolly, for example, had played handball with Bill Lynch in 1941, joined the navy in 1943, and returned in 1947 to edit his anthology, *Literature, the Channel of Culture.* Edgar L. Kloten, a drama professor who had been in the Coast Guard for four years, was now reviving the theater program with a production of *Saint in a Hurry,* a life of St. Francis Xavier.

The fact that veterans were not as committed to extracurricular activities as younger students was understandable, but Fr. Farley didn't see it that way. A *Ram* (April 16, 1946) interviewer, Len Baker, respected the priest who had spent twenty years at Fordham, enlarged the glee club, and baptized star football players, but he was struck to find the otherwise cheerful priest letting off steam about the lack of spirit: "There's no question about it—the college spirit is not the same today as it was before the war. The boys have lost that old spirit. Many of them want to be paid for working on extracurricular activities."

VI ⌁

Now, three major tasks faced Gannon. The one he considered the most important development of his term of office was establishing the Department of Communication Arts, including the FM radio station WFUV and the theater; the one far from his heart was bringing back football. Finally, he wanted to dedicate an appropriate memorial to Fordham's war dead.

From the beginning, the communications program, originally conceived as a separate college and referred to as a school of public opinion, was an ambitious project, but one made possible by a grant from the Michael P. Grace Trust of $20,000, with the promise of a continuing annual contribution of $10,000. The program had two main characteristics. First, it was to be both theoretical—relying heavily on the Jesuit curriculum's requirements in philosophy, theology, languages, and the humanities—and practical, with the students trained in journalism, radio, and theater skills by leading professionals. Film students with Fordham language training, for example, would be expected to understand foreign films without reading subtitles.

Second, it was apostolic, in that it aimed at raising the level of ethics in the mass media (though that term was not yet current) with a transfusion of ethically trained young Fordham men into the bloodstream of American radio, journalism, film, and theater. At the beginning, journalism and radio were to be for undergraduates and theater and cinema for graduate students, but in the early years the program's status was often in flux and occasionally in crisis. For a while, one wing of the enterprise, theater, flew close to the sun. For the next six years, they produced seven shows a year, many of them original creations, and Fordham became a sort of off-Broadway center.

Gannon had high hopes for the new FM radio station, WFUV (Fordham University's Voice), particularly because, as he told the Grace Trust, he had heard that "left-wing organizations and communists" were moving into the expanding commercial FM field. WFUV, with its one-hundred-foot tower, would be a missionary venture, getting Catholicism, adult education, and Fordham to a population of 11.5 million. It would also give every student in the radio division of the department practical experience with every job in the station before graduation. A typical week's programming (8:30 A.M.–10:00 P.M.) would consist of recorded music; student drama; book, play, and film reviews; live music (student vocalists with piano); religion (Sunday Mass, "Know Your Saints," interviews with missionaries, prayer); and live sports.

The new head of the journalism program, Fr. Alfred J. Barrett, S.J., proposed afternoon classes for college students and evening noncredit courses for graduates; most of the teachers would be Jesuits and professional journalists, and there would also be guest lecturers such as Fr. LaFarge and Henry Luce. Barrett advocated strong editorial and financial control of the student publications, the *Monthly* and the *Ram.* He ran a popular summer writing workshop and was frequently photographed, a handsome sight with his gray hair and black Jesuit habit, reading poetry outdoors under a tree. He would read either Edgar Allan Poe's work or his own, from his book, *Mint by Night,* with students sitting at his feet gazing at him with admiration.

Installed first in journalism and later as department chair, Barrett was one of those few American Jesuits who, through his many talents, enhanced the reputation of the whole Society. Born in Flushing, the oldest of nine children, six of whom entered the religious life, he was a poet, a skilled watercolorist, a journalist, a playwright, and a pastor. During World War II, he was an army chaplain from 1943 to 1946 in Texas, England, and at the University of Paris. But he was not born to be an administrator, and his program was headed for a storm.

On October 28, 1946, Mrs. Anna Helmers sat down and, begging that she not seem to offend, wrote the president of Fordham a polite, even adoring, letter in which she praised him as a public speaker. "I love the way you say the word *world*," she said, but she also dared to offer one implied criticism. She had just sat through the tragedy of the Fordham vs. Merchant Marine Academy game at Kings Point; the Fordham boys had tried so hard but hadn't done very well. She was sure they would do better, if only Fr. Gannon would go to the games and offer "spiritual help."

Football was back on a very modest scale and that's where Gannon wanted to keep it. Yes, they had made a profit of $48,464.89 in the Seven Blocks 1936–37 season. But public attention was shifting to professional football, and profits were going down steadily in spite of a boost in the Cotton Bowl (1941) and Sugar Bowl (1942) toward the end. Intercollegiate sports were suspended for the war, and in 1943, Coach Jim Crowley joined the navy.

After the war, however, the alumni and the New York sportswriters pressed hard for a return to the old days of glory; Gannon said he would go along if the alumni could raise $50,000 a year for three years, and that ended that. His own plan was for a modest 20,000–30,000-seat stadium with a cinder track on campus with a lot of home games for students, alumni, and friends.

Unfortunately, at the communion breakfast of the Fordham University Club of New Jersey on October 19, 1947, at the Robert Treat Hotel in Newark, Gannon, somehow unaware of the reporters in the room, let his witty rhetoric run ahead of his prudence on the football question. Clearly the sniping of the alumni, some anonymous letters, and the sportswriters had gotten to him, and he was saying what he really thought. Having a "top team," he said, according to the *New York Times* (October 20, 1947) didn't do Fordham any good. He would settle for a "first-class team, just below the high-power class." "We are not interested," he said, "in providing business for the gambling fraternity. We are not interested in catering to the subway circuit as a whole. We are interested in staging contests for our students, the alumni, friends, and those on the subway who cross themselves." He called the managers of the Polo Grounds, where Fordham had played, "extortionists," and the sportswriters the "tyrants of tyrants."

This was an invitation to the sportswriters to pile on again. Since there are a lot of people in New York who ride subways but who don't use the sign of the cross, Fordham's president seemed to be writing off people—such as Protestants, Jews, and those with no religion—who might otherwise be friends of the school. It was not a good time, but Gannon had the comfort two months later of Fordham alumnus Arthur Daley, in the *New York Times* (December 15, 1947), reconsidering the issue and concluding that Gannon had been right all along. The college presidents, said Daley, could purify college sports overnight if they wished, and here was one "who has been pursuing a sound policy all along, receiving only criticism for his efforts, not that that would deter him one iota."

The war memorial was to be a renovation of the old St. John's Church into a new University Church dedicated to the 229 World War II alumni who gave their lives. Relatives and classmates of the war dead, plus the undergraduates, raised $220,000, and the names of some of the deceased mark the large wood-carved stations of the cross along the chapel walls. Francis Spellman, now cardinal, presided at the dedication on December 8, 1949.

But one of the long-term casualties was to be Gannon himself. After 1946, when Spellman invited him to accompany him to Rome for the consistory naming Spellman a cardinal, Gannon increased his speaking schedule, embroidering his addresses all over the East Coast with reflections on what he had seen of postwar Europe, where, he was convinced, the world looked to the pope and to the cardinals as the only force that could save civilization. Whether or not the speaking engagements were wise, it is easy to understand Gannon's pouring his energies into the lecture circuit while the football controversy was grinding him down, and exhausting himself in the process.

In 1948, he had been reappointed for an unprecedented fifth three-year term, but the New York provincial, Fr. John McMahon, S.J., must have noticed his physical decline at the memorial dedication. A month later, a stunned fifty-five-year-old Gannon received notice that he was to leave the presidency in February 1949 and become superior of the Mount Manresa Retreat House in Staten Island. It is unusual to remove a university president in the middle of a year, but neutral observers such as the *New York Times* could attribute the suddenness of the change to the mysterious workings of Jesuit obedience. "Few educators in this generation," said the *Times* editorial

(January 3, 1949), " have so happily combined the virtues of intellectual brilliancy, urbanity, and wit."

In two critical ways Gannon had saved Fordham: he had regained accreditation, and he had kept it going during the studentless years of the war. He had also sustained his private vision of a small, elite college, as he did at St. Peter's College, while financing the university with funds from general-education enrollment and government programs. He was lucky that the Catholic intellectual culture of the 1930s and 1940s received his rhetoric with some warmth. But the changes in the church brought on by the Second Vatican Council during the 1960s and in the Society of Jesus by a series of general congregations aimed at bringing the Society in line with the advanced theology of the council left him confused. His speeches and conversations were increasingly laced with regret and strong words about a culture in which he no longer felt at home.

10.

Lou Mitchell Meets
G. Gordon Liddy

When J. Harding Fisher was a student at Fordham in the early 1890s, the president was Fr. Thomas Gannon, a man with none of the oratorical gifts of his famous successor, but with his own dry view of the world, which he delivered annually to his boys after the reading of grades before vacation: "Boys! Go straight home! Your parents are awaiting you! There are dangers lurking in the city! Go straight home!"

Of course, the boys did not go straight home. They made their rounds of the alehouses and sang their songs; some got into trouble, and some of those got expelled. But the early Gannon was doing what most Jesuit presidents did in the broad sense, since they saw themselves not just as professors but as pastors and "fathers": they drew the line between the values of the world, which were outside the Third Avenue gate, and those of the enclosed community on Rose Hill.

But the march of history, including two world wars, the flood of the more worldly wise veterans onto the campus, the commitment to studying the mass media—which tend to overwhelm those who would cling to traditional values—and the astounding development of the Bronx, all had a way of slipping through the fence separating Fordham from the outside world.

Politically, the icons of the 1950s were Dwight D. Eisenhower, whom Fordham men supported over Adlai Stevenson two to one; the Red-hunting senator Joe McCarthy, whom friends fought over daily in the cafeteria; and General Douglas MacArthur, who had promised to "fade away," but who waited in the Waldorf-Astoria Towers for the right moment to return. We watched the 1952 Nixon "Checkers" speech on TV in the Ramskeller, the new snack bar that replaced the bowling alleys in Bishop's Hall basement. On Wednesday afternoons, we donned our ROTC uniforms and paraded around the campus, past the newly opened Martyrs' Court with its modern eight-man suites and common rooms, along much the same route the cadet corps marched in the 1890s, hoping the Korean War would end before we were called in.

The 1950s were also the last years in which the Catholic Church projected a strong, some say dominating, image over American culture. Stars such as Bing Crosby, Spencer Tracy, and Pat O'Brien played tough but charming priests; Msgr. Fulton J. Sheen's *Life Is Worth Living,* with its total audience of thirty million, beat Milton Berle's TV ratings; and combative "waterfront priests," such as Jesuit fathers Dennis Comey in Philadelphia and John Corridan in New York took on the mob and inspired *On the Waterfront.*

At midcentury, however, the social forces put in motion by the 1900 arrival of the Third Avenue El at Fordham's gate—such as the new mass transportation, the apartment-building boom, and both middle-class and the immigrant population booms—were coming to a head, and the first signs of what would become the Bronx's downward spiral began to appear.

In 1904, the First Avenue Subway connected to the Third Avenue El at 149th Street in the Bronx, creating the Hub, a new business center with theaters, and in 1928, an Alexander's Department Store. In the 1928 film *The Jazz Singer,* Al Jolson jubilantly tells his mother, "Mama dahlin', if I'm a success in this show, we're going to move up to the Bronx," as if this were the fulfillment of a dream. Indeed, for ambitious middle-class Jews, Irish, and Italians determined to escape the overcrowded tenements of Manhattan's East Side, a move to the Bronx was exactly that. With its network of six beautiful parks and its splendid four-and-a-half-mile Grand Boulevard and Concourse stretching from 161st Street to Van Cortlandt Park; with its luxurious five-story art-deco apartment buildings, its tree-lined separate traffic lanes for pedestrians, autos, cyclists, and horse carriages, and the magnificent Loew's Paradise movie theater (1929), where clouds floated across the star-studded ceiling, it had definite attractions.

In 1922, ground was broken at 161st Street for the Concourse Plaza Hotel, a luxury apartment hotel that would long be a symbol of Bronx gracious living and political power. Colonel Jacob Ruppert, the brewer and owner of the New York Yankees, decided to move his baseball team out of Manhattan's Polo Grounds and started work on Yankee Stadium. The same year, a tall, good-looking young man with straight black hair and well-tailored suits, a graduate of Fordham College and Fordham Law School, was elected Bronx County sheriff and leader of the Bronx Democratic Party. Edward J. "Boss" Flynn reorganized the party structure and built his power of loyalty, patronage, and jobs. He was also a man of ideas, a reader, always alert for ways to use the power of government to better people's lives, as well as an unashamed master of "machine" politics.

Flynn, son of Irish immigrants and youngest of five children, grew up in a Bronx that still retained its rural, small-town atmosphere. In a sense, his political education began at Fordham, where he followed his brother Fred and where they sat up discussing the problems of the world in late-night bull sessions. When he joined that world, he was, he says, "not a very wise and social-conscious young zealot." He was an early backer of Roosevelt for both governor and president, however, and he became FDR's behind-the-scenes adviser and friend, and a powerful influence within the New Deal.

Flynn's years of influence coincided with the Bronx's golden age, made possible by a combination of circumstances, such as the healthy economy of the war and postwar years, the public-transportation system that rushed the three out of five Bronx inhabitants who worked in Manhattan to and from their jobs, the relatively stable civic virtues of the ethnic, largely secular Jewish population, and the steady population growth that peaked at 1.5 million in 1950. The Concourse Plaza thrived—a symbol of the good life, frequented by politicians, sports stars, and visiting college teams playing Fordham—and the Bronx promoted itself as "the Nation's Sixth City."

During the depression, Flynn used his Washington clout and his appointment as administrator of public works for New York, New Jersey, and Pennsylvania to build up the Bronx: Orchard Beach; parks, pools, and playgrounds; improvements in the Botanical Gardens and Bronx Zoo; a campus for Hunter College; the Bronx County Building at 161st Street and Grand Concourse; the post office at 149th Street and Grand Concourse; extensions of the IND subway; and the Triborough Bridge. Meanwhile, the Bronx renamed itself the "Borough of Universities."

However, all this improved infrastructure could not withstand the new wave of migration that hit New York during and after World War II—poor, uneducated blacks who were escaping both the indignity of Southern segregation and the mechanization of the cotton farms, and poverty-stricken, largely illiterate Puerto Ricans, who flew into New York at the rate of twenty thousand a day at the cost of a thirty-dollar airline ticket.

The blacks went to Harlem. With its population in flux, the area declined, with the crime, alcoholism, drugs, gang violence, and family breakups that historically distinguish every slum. When the Puerto Ricans could no longer be contained in Spanish Harlem, they began streaming over into the South Bronx; there were over sixty thousand of them by 1950. Neither group came with job skills, and many of the cultural values that gave Puerto Ricans some stability on the island, such as family loyalty, could not survive the new pressures of big-city life. In too many instances, a "macho" black or Puerto Rican male would father a string of children from a series of women and move on without assuming any responsibility. The mothers joined the welfare rolls and moved their families into public housing.

In 1950, the Puerto Rican population was concentrated in the southwest, in Mott Haven and Melrose; by 1970, 26 percent of the Bronx population would be Hispanic. The face, language, and noise level of the old Bronx neighborhoods changed dramatically. Bodegas replaced Jewish groceries, and the new immigrants, to escape overcrowded apartments, moved their social life into the street, blaring music from their windows at all hours of the night.

One other man, even more than Ed Flynn, changed the face of the Bronx as well as of Fordham. On July 3, 1970, Terence Cardinal

Cooke, Fordham president Michael P. Walsh, S.J., and Nelson Rockefeller unveiled a monument on the plaza of the Fordham Lincoln Center campus. It was a bronze bas-relief on a marble foundation that read, "ROBERT MOSES, MASTER BUILDER, FRIEND OF FORDHAM." Without Moses, Fordham would not have had a campus at Lincoln Center, but in the judgment of some urban historians, without Moses, Fordham would have had a more livable Bronx.

Moses's building projects of forty years, as parks commissioner and head of the Triborough Bridge and Tunnel Authority, welded New York together and gave a share in the good life to millions. He established a network of highways, parkways, and seven bridges that encircle Manhattan and link the five boroughs with New England and the farthest reaches of Long Island, and he developed hundreds of playgrounds, swimming pools, and beaches. At the same time, by making automobiles, highways, and quick access to the suburban good life the center of his city-planning vision, he facilitated the middle-class abandonment of the central city and Bronx neighborhoods as the population shifted to Queens and Long Island. His critics say that he destroyed established, healthy, ethnic neighborhoods by displacing their populations—in the Bronx and at Lincoln Center—as he rammed his highways and projects through and over their homes.

In his monumental and highly critical biography of Moses, *The Power Broker* (1974), Robert Caro focuses on the construction of the Cross-Bronx Expressway, with its destruction of an East Tremont neighborhood fifteen blocks south of Fordham Road, as typical of Moses's most socially damaging projects. Whether it should be there or not, the Cross-Bronx is always a shock as the ugliest highway in the world. Gouged out of granite known as Fordham gneiss, this seven-mile scar on the urban landscape connects the George Washington Bridge with New England (Route 95), and Queens Whitestone with the Throgs Neck Bridge. For fifteen years, from planning in 1945 to completion in 1960, with efficiency in moving traffic his sole criterion, Moses blasted, dug, and churned his way through or under the Grand Concourse, subway lines, bridges, Els, and neighborhoods.

In one mile of an East Tremont integrated Jewish neighborhood just north of Crotona Park, he knocked down fifty-four apartment buildings and displaced thousands of inhabitants rather than alter his route by a few blocks. In a way that anyone with experience can verify, Caro describes the impact of the unbearable traffic noise on the surrounding quality of life. "So the sound of the Cross-Bronx Expressway at rush hour is a roar, punctuated by the snarl and grind of shifting gears and the snort and growl of acceleration, and, of course, the sudden, loud harsh backfires—and all this sound, magnified by the underpass and the high brick walls that line the sides of the expressway cut, comes out of that cut and over the neighborhood as if out of a gigantic echo chamber."

The kind of "urban planning" that contributed to the decline of the Bronx and the central city was typical of that operative in most major cities after World War II. As Moses did, so other "urban renewers" also ran beltways around cities and freeways into their hearts, knocked down old housing that had been designated as "slums," and replaced them with sterile high-rise projects and apartments. A later generation would restore old townhouses rather than demolish them.

But centering on Moses passes over evidence that the population drop near the Cross-Bronx was similar to the drop in other parts of the borough and in Brooklyn, which had no comparable expressway. Other factors contributed to the decline. In 1955, the Third Avenue El ceased to connect the Bronx to Manhattan. Fordham suffered from the historical fact that the old Bronx housing constructed west of the Bronx River and south of Fordham had been all high-density apartments, with narrow streets and no room for the backyard, lawns, trees, porches, single homes, or parking that became the basic stuff of the American Dream. But a bike ride east along Pelham Parkway reveals a number of low-density, single-home neighborhoods that are not quite suburban, but are more livable than the South Bronx.

Furthermore, since it opened, the George Washington Bridge had been like a gun firing heavy traffic into the Bronx. That traffic had to go somewhere. The expressway had been on the drawing board since the regional plan of 1929; if it or something like it had not been built, a lot of those trucks would be on Rt. 1, also known as Fordham Road.

Today, as Fordham students, at home on two campuses, take the Ramvan from Rose Hill to Lincoln Center, they move through the worst and best of Moses's worlds, as the shuttle maneuvers the evening traffic rush down the Bronx River Parkway (which Moses did not build) onto the Cross-Bronx Expressway, south onto the West Side Highway to Lincoln Center (all three of which he did build). In the 1970s, Moses, now old and deaf but still formidable, came to the Rose Hill campus and sat down for an hour of conversation with a group of students, a good number of whom had read Caro's 1,200-page tome. One student, wanting Moses's autograph, spontaneously asked him to sign Caro's book.

II ⌐

Lou Mitchell remembered the day in 1948 when his brother brought him up from Harlem to the Bronx on a gentle autumn afternoon—a day, perhaps because of the excitement, strong in sounds and smells. In the trees outside Dealy Hall, where he checked in at the dean of men's office and trudged up three flights of stairs to his long, high-ceilinged dorm room, two blue jays quarreled with a catbird and a kingbird chased a hawk.

The dining hall and kitchen were directly below, and odors of both cooking and garbage wafted up to the windows and mixed with the standard dorm smells of unwashed socks, cigarette butts, and soot from the traffic on Fordham Road. In the hallways he heard showers dripping, toilets flushing, suitcases snapping open and shut, and fellow students griping about the lack of closet space, or confessing, only a few minutes into their new lives, that they were homesick already.

His brother gone, Lou sat alone in his darkness.

George Zimmerman, who lived across the hall, came in to say hello. He had seen immediately that Lou was blind, so he quipped that Lou was better off that he could not see him. Lou soon heard from others that George was essentially a good-looking man; he concluded, as George remained a lifelong friend, that George had "a more profound beauty than any exterior accident of color, proportion, and balance could provide."

Lou, a mixed-race son of Willa Spaulding and Ulysses S. Mitchell, who moved from North Carolina to Harlem in the 1930s, came to Fordham from the New York Institute for the Education of the Blind. Victim of a hereditary disease, retinitis pigmentosa, his eyesight had begun to deteriorate when he was a young boy. Through his adolescence and college, the condition followed its course to the point that he was almost totally blind when he arrived at Rose Hill. He was relatively short and frail, though not always thin, with a large, round head that he held at a tilt, giving the impression that his eyes were trying to focus on some shape or light off-stage, but it seems that Lou was about as blind as one could be.

It was part of Lou Mitchell's passion to deny—if not his blind-ness—the idea that, as a man who was both black and blind, he could not throw himself into every part of Fordham life as wildly as anyone in his class. At the New York School for the Blind, although one of his teachers had told him he would never amount to anything, he was determined to discover what he did well. The music program gave him a foundation in Bach, Beethoven, and Brahms, and also freed him and his fellow students to soar off into jazz. At the piano he discovered that he could play by ear. For fun, he loved to cross his hands over, the left hand playing the right-hand parts.

Meanwhile, Lou, whose father had died, had caught the attention of Monsignor John Quinn, pastor of St. Francis Xavier Church in the Bronx. He brought Lou, who had not been born a Catholic, into the church, arranged for his protege to be tutored in Latin and Greek, and steered him toward Fordham. In the 1940s, neither America nor the American Church had clearly declared itself on where black people fit in the plan of salvation, and Quinn, in his own way, was making a statement.

To a degree, Lou, though he had no money, was well fixed. He had a New York State scholarship for two years, with tutors and read-ers paid for by state funds assigned to him, and a recording device, when it worked, to record classes. He had access to a Braille library, recorded books, and other aids from the Xavier Society for the Blind, assigned counselors and volunteer readers among his friends, and a device for taking class notes in Braille, though certain Jesuits objected to the noise he made punching in the Braille symbols. Also, almost daily, he took the subway down to the Lighthouse, the New York Association for the Blind on East 59th Street, to use their resources.

So, insofar as he could pull it off, in the public image Lou was not considered a blind man. He began by mastering—or trying to master— the Fordham campus on his own. At night, he prowled and plunged around, bumping into trees and into signs that had been moved from the spot where they were the night before, getting the lay of the land. One night he stumbled into a row of obstacles that turned out to be the tombstones in the Jesuit graveyard. He huddled between the rows, embarrassed, until the security patrol had passed. As the months went by, he also figured out the subway system, and in later years he also traveled frequently to Vermont, Washington, and Europe.

In class, though he took Braille notes, he relied most heavily on his memory and on the friends who read to him. This array of readers was his own special encounter with a cross section of his peers, and among his friends, who soon were legion, a reading session would be a happy occasion of real intellectual discourse. Sometimes even his professors were pleased to take time to read to Lou. One was the young Andrew Myers, who would become both a nationally respected authority on Washington Irving and one of Fordham's most beloved professors until his death in 1998. It became clear that Fordham teachers saw in this blind, physically unprepossessing young black Harlem man something of themselves, and they embraced him as if he were a young bird they could help to fly.

Meanwhile, Lou went around as though he could see as well as anyone. In the rare times that he failed to fit in, he sometimes interpreted his rejection as a double prejudice against one who was both black and blind. He auditioned for the glee club, for example, listened to the other three contestants sing, and was told, in spite of his musical background, that he "did not fit their needs at this time." So he joined the band and developed an affection for its curmudgeonly moderator, Fr. Harold Mulqueen, S.J., who had come to Fordham when it had a grammar school, had graduated from the college in 1914, had returned as band moderator, and had been there ever since.

Reportedly, Mulqueen was still loved by men whom he had disciplined in the dorm with his paddle years before. Lou played the glockenspiel, parading up and down the field in a maroon and white uniform at one losing football game after another. Since Lou was so well educated by the time he arrived at Fordham, he spent a lot of time coaching fellow students in Greek, Latin, Spanish, English, French, and history, or simply in how to organize material for class. Occasionally, however, he had to put up with teachers who, he surmised, did not want a blind black boy in class, such as a social-science professor who told him, wrongly, that there was no way he could pass, and a Jesuit who spoke in class of kikes, spics, and niggers—and apologized later.

More typical was Fr. Joseph Donceel, S.J., a quiet, shy philosopher from Belgium who taught the required senior course in philosophical psychology and who, for good reason, was voted favorite teacher year after year. Donceel was that rare combination of the productive intellectual who also had the time and humility to treat his students as friends. A small man with a large, round head and prominent eyes, Donceel, after being ordained in 1938, came from Belgium in 1939 with doctorates in psychology and philosophy. Though he had intended to come only for Jesuit tertianship, he was cut off by Hitler's conquest of Belgium, so he stayed to teach at Loyola College in Baltimore, then moved to Fordham in 1944. Belgian authorities had tried to get Donceel to return by way of England, where he could be drafted, and he had tried to enlist in the U.S. Army as a chaplain, but Belgium would not allow it.

Fond of sports such as soccer, cycling, hiking, tennis, and swimming as a young man, Donceel impressed 1940s students with his vigor, intellectual enthusiasm, and gentle humor. Students in the 1950s also saw this quiet little man as a pioneer in his public struggle with church authorities to teach the theory of evolution in class. Jesuit censors, reportedly at the instigation of Ignatius Cox, had not allowed Donceel to include the chapter on evolution in his textbook, so he brought J. Franklin Ewing, the Harvard-trained anthropologist and friend of the French Jesuit paleontologist Pierre Teilhard de Chardin, into class as a guest lecturer. The rotund Ewing often involved students in his summer archeological digs for the bones of the Jesuits martyred by Indians at Auriesville, New York. To the awe of the seniors, Ewing brought along his basket of fossils to Donceel's class, including the skull of "Egbert," unearthed in Lebanon. As he spread them out on the desk, Ewing left no doubt that, yes, one could be a Catholic and believe in evolution at the same time.

Lou, as sensitive to voice inflection as sighted people are to facial expression, also saw Donceel as a man who disciplined his passions; he was thrilled with the priest's ethical courage and humility. Donceel hated racism. "If I were a bishop," he told Lou, "I would excommunicate all bigots, Louis. Hatred and segregation are immoral. They are violations of God's fatherhood and the brotherhood of man." Yet when the priest came to Lou's room to hear his confession, he would say, "Let's talk, Lou. This is not your confession alone. I need forgiveness too."

In spite of a few bad encounters during his six years in the college and graduate school, Lou, an English major, was generally enthralled by the Fordham faculty. Fr. Joe Landy, S.J., Monsignor Quinn's nephew, lived on Lou's floor. Francis X. Connolly was another favorite, as was Gabriel Liegey, who came to Fordham as a student in 1922 and sent many of his own fifteen children to Fordham too. Dietrich von Hildebrand taught him the philosophy of love and the philosophy of St. Augustine. Dr. Robert Pollock, with his colleague Fr. Robert Roth, S.J., was an eloquent interpreter and advocate for John Dewey, whom Gannon had seen as enemy number one. James McCabe, who read poetry aloud with a rich, mellow baritone, introduced Lou to the "real" John Milton, whose sonnet on his blindness provided Lou with a spiritual motif that would stay with him all his life.

For Lou, as for all his friends, Friday night was the time to hit the Webster Avenue bars. For him, as for most, beer was an instrument for conviviality: the guy who in class or the dorm corridor seemed indifferent or dull, at the Raven or the Web became a potential lifelong friend. As a beer drinker, Lou did not have long staying power and would sometimes nod off in the booth; at other times he was almost up to dancing in the streets and would link arms with a friend to guide both home. One night, at a place called O'Brien's, a brawl broke out between two girlfriends of the bartender, and in seconds it involved the whole establishment. Lou had to be rescued from a hail of flying bottles and shattered glass.

Lou was elected vice president of the senior class. One of the best-known people on campus, he moved socially among a wide variety of college students, graduate students, faculty, and administrators. His companions ranged from the warm and loving Joe Coviello, who helped him to understand and express his feelings and to overcome the early training that said don't touch, to the hulking Arthur Cushing Hickey, first-string tackle who burst into Lou's room, sat on him to proclaim his physical superiority, and mixed up Lou's socks so he would be embarrassed by wearing the wrong colors the next day. Lou mixed well with student leaders such as classmate Bob Beusse and Jack Loughran, '54, and Jack's talented circle in Martyrs' Court. Meanwhile, Lou composed the music and wrote the lyrics for a half-dozen class shows and accompanied them on the piano. In 1952, a typical senior show, *Rams Away,* satirized philosophy class, ROTC, and WFUV.

Despite all this success, and to a degree perhaps unnoticed by his friends, Lou was very sensitive to any perceived slight because of his race. At the failed glee club tryout, he had heard the voices of his competitors and was not convinced that they were better. One friend who had invited Lou to Boston to meet his family had to withdraw the invitation when his mother balked. Another friend invited him home in a tone of voice that signaled to Lou that he was supposed to refuse.

As a sophomore, Lou invited Rosa Almara, a Puerto Rican girl from 102nd Street in Harlem, to the sophomore dance. Rosa, thrilled with the invitation to a big uptown university, appeared radiant in a gown of willow blue Peau de Soie that her mother had sewn. She wept for joy as the taxi conveyed them in reverent silence to the Bronx. The band played "Smoke Gets in Your Eyes" as Rosa led Lou to a lonely table in the corner of the gym. No one invited them to join a group.

When the band played Latin numbers such as "Besame Mucho" and "Jealousy," Lou and Rosa held the center of the floor and danced with joyous abandon, conscious that eyes were on them. Back at their table, a sophomore came over to act friendly and said all the wrong things: "You two can really dance. They say most of your colored people can really go at it anyway. So good to meet you, Rose. That gown really matches your complexion. Oh don't let my date hear me; she would be jealous. She's Italian and that's even a little rough on us."

Another boy came by, slapped Lou on the back, and added, "How did you manage to pick this one, Lou? She's quite different. She's kind of pretty. I'll bet she doesn't go to Manhattanville or Marymount. They don't have her kind at those schools. It's good to have a mixed dance for a change." In the ladies' room, girls asked Rosa how could she date a blind man and why she did not stick with her own kind.

Tired and hurt, Lou and Rosa left the dance and took a cab back to Harlem, again in silence. Later Rosa married a butcher and moved to Cuba; her mother was murdered while selling a mantilla on the New York City streets. When the time came for the senior prom, Lou went alone.

In 1954, a friend, Bill Carlson, convinced Lou to visit an eye specialist, who found his case "interesting," but not only offered no hope but cautioned him that since his condition was hereditary he should not have children. It was an emotionally difficult period. When some friends tried to create a fund for his financial support, he was profoundly offended and upset; his teaching stint at the School for the Blind, where he was given a class of retarded children, was a failure, and because he had finished his graduate studies, Fordham authorities signaled that it was time for him to leave the campus, but he was turned down twenty-five times in a summer apartment hunt. When he applied for the diocesan priesthood, in fulfillment of Monsignor Quinn's original hopes and acting on dreams fed by years of prayer and serving Mass, he was told no.

So Lou moved back to Harlem and began a Ph.D. in English at Columbia. There he won the friendship of Mark Van Doren, who recommended a better program at NYU when he retired. Lou began teaching literature at Scranton University in 1961 and finished his Ph.D. in 1967. Meanwhile, he traveled around the United States and Europe, and taught some courses in Spain. He called friends from the airport when he returned, visited their families for a few weeks, and played the piano for them, delighting their children.

Lou taught in Scranton for the rest of his career, writing regularly for newsletters and magazines and receiving awards from African American, civil-rights, and theater organizations through 1988. In 1982, he received the Educator of the Year Award at the 128th annual Fordham College Dinner. He told the assembly that whatever he had achieved had been through a "prodigious amount of help" and by learning how to "step aside from help as politely as possible." The main lesson he had learned, however, was about love, "that only too much love is love enough." To be an image of God, he said, is to love as God loves—"for others, not for oneself."

III ~

One of the four stars of the "WFUV-SJ" skit in *Rams Away* and an admirer of Lou Mitchell was a five-foot-nine-inch, wiry, self-confident young student politician named G. Gordon Liddy, who would go on to a career in law, the military, government, and broadcasting. Liddy always knew when Lou was in class because he could hear him clicking, taking notes on his Braille machine.

Gordon's father, Sylvester, a wealthy and prominent lawyer from North Caldwell, New Jersey, had graduated from Fordham in 1924. At Fordham, Sylvester had run varsity track, been president of the dramatic club, served as associate editor of the *Ram,* the *Monthly,* and the *Maroon,* and won the best-actor award. Graduating from Fordham law school, he had joined a firm with an international reputation.

Gordon, who as a freshman lived on the fifth floor of Dealy Hall, joined the cross-country team until he had to stop because of an enlarged heart. In student politics, he joined the Republican Club, which made him one of the minority in the prevailing political climate. He ran for office, was elected to the student government and the boarder council for years, and won an award for drafting a new student-government constitution. On the staff of WFUV, he wrote and performed in biblical dramatizations.

Gordon's favorite teacher was the young Robert Remini, who looked liked Andrew Jackson—thin as a rail with a long, hawklike face. At the time, Remini was one of a strong group of lay faculty that included historian Sam Telfair, Erwin Geissman and Robert Brown in English, and James R. Brown in political science. These teachers were known for their comparative liberalism, their role in the American Studies movement, and their warm hospitality to students. Remini, who used to act out Jackson's duels in class, achieved greater eminence than his peers as a published scholar.

In his autobiography, *Will,* Liddy describes his early life in Hoboken as a determined struggle to overcome a number of profound fears by subjecting himself to a series of painful tests and conquering them through willpower. Some fears were religiously inspired. The nuns at SS. Peter and Paul School, for example, told the story of the little boy who made a sloppy sign of the cross and awoke the next morning to find his arm "withered, twisted, and paralyzed for life." To Liddy, being made in "God's image" meant being like God by conquering fear. He conditioned himself by accepting head blows from his German fencing instructor without flinching, by leaping from one city rooftop to the next, by standing under the *Hindenburg* as it roared overhead, and by eating a rat that he had killed and roasted.

As a small child, Liddy fell under the influence of the family's eighteen-year-old German maid who saw Adolph Hitler as Germany's savior and thrilled young Gordon by playing the "Horst Wessel Song" and Hitler's speeches on the radio. At the same time, Gordon was mesmerized by Roosevelt's eloquence, which created a struggle for his young mind. His father, an anti-Nazi, eventually fired the maid and educated his son on the meaning of anti-Semitism, but some of his childhood fascination may have lingered. Joe Coviello remembers Gordon stopping by his dorm room and talking about "what a great guy Hitler was." Since Joe was a World War II navy veteran, Gordon may have chosen the wrong audience for his ideas.

Gordon considered Fordham a "feast for the mind and a challenge to the spirit," and he appreciated that Jesuits had "absolute control" and were known as the "shock troops of the Catholic Church," so well organized that Heinrich Himmler had used them as a model for his black-uniformed SS. Gordon's favorite class was logic.

After his ROTC military service, graduation from Fordham law school, and release from prison after serving time for his role in the Watergate affair, Liddy returned to Fordham as a guest speaker on "Government: Perception vs. Reality" in 1981, 1985, and 1991. He told the capacity crowds who packed the gym, "The Jesuits taught me how to think. They did not teach me what to think. I am not their fault."

Liddy loved Fordham enough to send three sons there in the 1980s. Jim, '84, a water-polo and swimming star, joined the Navy Seals. Raymond, '86, transferred from St. Louis University after visiting his brother Tom, '86, and meeting Tom's friend Gerry Reedy, S.J., the very accessible Fordham College dean and later academic vice president who lived in Walsh residence hall. In 1984, when Tom was an R.A. in Walsh, he and Jim chased and nabbed a knife-wielding intruder who had gotten access to the hall and tried to rape a resident. When Pax Christi demonstrated against the Reagan administration's policies in Central America by protesting the campus appearance of Caspar Weinberger, Tom took the microphone and spoke for Reagan's policies. For his junior year, encouraged by economics professor Edward Dowling, S.J., he studied in Indonesia. Then Tom joined the Marines and later returned to the Fordham Law School.

IV ~

If it helps a university president to look like a president, Laurence J. McGinley, S.J. (1949–63), was singularly blessed. Of medium height, with glasses and graying hair, he exuded dignity, spoke slowly with a rich, warm baritone, and when shaking hands, held his visitors' hands for what seemed a long time as he looked them in the eye, convincing his guests that he took them very seriously indeed.

McGinley graduated from Xavier High School in 1922, was ordained in 1935, studied Scripture at the Gregorian University and the Biblical Institute in Rome, worked briefly at the Vatican Radio, and taught at Woodstock College from 1942 to 1949. As a Scripture scholar, he was one of the first Catholics to write sympathetically about form criticism, an approach to the Gospels not merely as a strict historical record of the events covered but also as a reflection of the life and issues of the community that had preserved the tradition.

McGinley had a way of addressing his audience as "Members of the Fordham Family" that projected authentic paternal warmth. Though McGinley may have read Rev. Zach Maher's admonition seven years previous against a rector's having a personal car, students saw him glide by in a sleek black limo and concluded that he lived the lifestyle that a president deserved. Instead of living in Loyola Hall, he had an apartment at the south end of the second floor of the administration building, where his sunporch looked out over Duane Library and the elm-lined path. Since the old title of rector still made him father and superior of the Jesuit community, custom required that he preside over evening meals, most of which were taken in silence. The rest of the Jesuits, not permitted to leave until the rector finished, would sometimes fidget nervously, having already folded their napkins as the slow-eating McGinley moved methodically toward coffee and dessert.

As McGinley assumed power on February 2, 1949, he issued a statement that summed up where he thought Catholic education stood.

> With all the challenges from without and the reexamination of pedagogical tools in the light of changing needs, one thing is constant—the importance in time and eternity of the individual student. For him alone we build buildings, stock our libraries, plan courses, and engage the most brilliant teachers. The minute education forgets that all these exist for the student, that they are means to an end and not an end in themselves, it loses its ability to educate.

Faithful to this commitment to the individual, he signed every single diploma with a fountain pen as two Jesuit scholastics, his assistants, collected the signed sheepskins, waited a few minutes for the ink to dry, and put them in order for the graduation ceremony.

Occasionally, too, McGinley would give signs that he shared his predecessor's conservative worldview, wherein Catholic education stands as a bulwark against secular, liberal values. In remarks that caused some stir at the October 1, 1952, Mass of the Holy Spirit, he warned students that the dangers of their time were not just the banners of communism, fascism, or militarism, but "the colorless banner of those pale men who have no values, the Liberals in education, in the U.N., in the journals, and in the diplomatic service—the Liberals for whom no good thing exists in heaven or upon earth that can transcend themselves . . . the pale men without values, the unhappy Liberals, desperately unhappy—and desperately dangerous."

The prime reforming force of the 1950s was the college dean Thurston Noble Davis, S.J., another Xavier graduate who also had a Ph.D. from Harvard. He was a disciple of classics scholar Werner Jaeger and was in the forefront of the Society of Jesus' move to inject Jesuits with the best possible secular graduate degrees into the

Jesuit-university bloodstream. Joseph R. Frese, S.J., for example, was a Harvard Ph.D. colonial historian, a disciple of Samuel Elliot Morison and the elder Arthur Schlesinger. Joseph P. Fitzpatrick, S.J. was the sociologist who would reach out to the Puerto Ricans of the Bronx; he was trained by Harvard's Oscar Handlin, a Jew who taught Fitzpatrick what it meant to be Irish. Leo McLaughlin, S.J., and J. Quentin Lauer, S.J., were from the University of Paris. These men were part of the answer to the perception that Catholic university education was second rate.

They also had a profound, perhaps unforeseen, internal effect on Fordham. In the philosophy department, the official doctrine was Thomism, as understood by Jacques Maritain and Etienne Gilson. Lauer, however, was a Hegelian, and Donceel, influenced by Louvain's Pierre Scheuer and Joseph Marechal and the German Jesuit Karl Rahner, taught what became known as transcendental Thomism. Most important, these new professors, including Roth and Pollock, brought the idea that the university is not a seminary. For Donceel this meant that ideas could be taught, but never "imposed." Fordham was still pulling away from its 1841 seminary roots.

As these men were establishing themselves at Fordham, the American Church's most influential historian, Msgr. John Tracy Ellis of Catholic University, was completing an article for Fordham's *Thought* magazine (30, Autumn 1955) that would spell out Fordham's—and all of Catholic higher education's—problem in brutal detail. "American Catholics and the Intellectual Life" began with Denis W. Brogan's observation that "in no Western society is the intellectual prestige of Catholicism lower than in the country where, in such respects as wealth, numbers, and strength of organization, it is so powerful." To a degree, Catholicism's low intellectual standing was due to anti-Catholic prejudice and the church's mid-nineteenth-century priority of sustaining immigrant faith in a hostile city, but ultimately, he argued, Catholics were responsible for their low academic status.

Leaders such as John Lancaster Spalding, bishop of Peoria; John Ireland, bishop of St. Paul; and Orestes Brownson had spoken out, but Catholics had not listened. John LaFarge, the artist father of the Jesuit interracialist who had gone to St. John's but moved to Mount

Saint Mary's College in Emmitsburg for his senior year, had read Herodotus, Plautus, Catullus, Dryden, Molière, and Hugo as a boy and passed that reading enthusiasm to his son, who read Boswell's *Life of Johnson* twice while still a child. This was atypical, however; most Catholic families cared more about material goods than books.

Bluntly stated, Catholic ecclesiastical leaders, because of the shortcomings in their own educations, did not appreciate the value of the intellectual vocation. Catholic universities, rather than concentrate on an area in which they could be expert, such as the revival of scholastic philosophy, pursued financially lucrative programs such as engineering, business administration, nursing, and the like. Finally, they had overemphasized moral development and neglected the intellectual virtues. Obviously Fordham readers of *Thought* had to ask how much these accusations applied to them.

Thurston Davis, like McGinley, was a formidable personal presence, with straight black hair, a deep voice, and careful diction that had served him well when he played Hamlet at Xavier. His aristocratic manner both awed and amused students. Peers remember that he was paternal even as a high-school student. One day he called the honors program into his office, invited them to sit around on the floor, and asked the bewildered group, "Well, boys, what's on your minds?" as if the boys had called the meeting. The class mimics would imitate his "spontaneously" joining students at a cafeteria table—as if he were King Saint Louis IX of France receiving his subjects under a tree—and groping for something ordinary to say.

But he had a very clear idea of what he wanted to accomplish as dean. In his first address to freshmen, he exhorted them to "plunge in," and he set about creating an atmosphere into which they could plunge. Davis was an educational idealist, in the sense that he tried to make practical decisions on the basis of an imagined world. He had published an article, "Blueprint for a College," in the *Jesuit Educational Quarterly* (October 1943) in which an all-Jesuit faculty of seven priests and two scholastics would teach an elite student body of one hundred males the classics, philosophy, history, science, and religion to prepare them for leadership in journalism, creative writing, theater, radio, social work, labor unions, politics, and teaching. Keeping contact with their alumni, the Jesuits would mold a cadre of lay Catholic activists in the "cultural professions" to do battle against the secular forces that would otherwise dominate public opinion in the second half of the century.

Obviously, Davis could not limit Fordham College to a hundred elite men, but he moved boldly to improve academic standards. He started an honors program and a junior year abroad with his old Xavier friend Joe Frese in charge. He removed ineffective teachers, including Jesuits, from the classroom, instituted three-hour final exams, which were administered in the gymnasium, combined graduate and undergraduate faculties, and required faculty to assign "outside readings" of books beyond the textbooks and class notes. As with Walsh's *Thirteenth Greatest of Centuries* or Hilaire Belloc's *The Road to Rome,* the readings typically reinforced the romantic ideal of European Catholicism, but students like Lou Mitchell and his circle were delighted with a dean who believed Catholics had to read.

To reinforce the international dimension of his vision, Davis founded the Institute of Contemporary Russian Studies in the summer of 1950. Richard Burgi, on loan from Yale for a year, was the program's first director. The institute foresaw that the Cold War could not last forever. Fordham wanted to be in a position, in the words of Burgi's successor, J. Franklin Ewing, "to supply Russia and the people of the USSR with the best cultural and, above all, spiritual aid that we can. This meant training men who understood the Russian people." They started with one hundred students.

V ⟶

We are just the start of
The spectacle we're part of.
We hope you're gonna like our show.
Other numbers follow,
Till then we holler,
Hello, hello, hello.

We don't have to tell you,
We don't have to sell you,

The beauties in our grand tableau.
Some of them are beauties,
And all are cuties,
And all of them say Hello.

We hope you like our show.
Hello, hello, hello.
A great, big fat hellooooo.

It was the opening of the May 1952 *Mimes Night,* a hello that turned out to be a good-bye.

The 1951–52 season was in many ways one of the Fordham Theater's most memorable. Along with the usual class shows and the annual Jesuit One-Act Play Festival, the Collins stage saw lavish productions of Gogol's *The Inspector General* and Kaufman and Hart's *The Man Who Came to Dinner,* while the upstairs theater-in-the-round presented James Barry's *Hotel Universe* and Dryden's *All for Love.*

Alfred Barrett, S.J., now chair of the communications department, was hitting his creative stride. The Spanish-made film, *Loyola, the Soldier Saint,* opens and closes with Fordham scenes, including one of Barrett lecturing students in the Keating Blue Chapel on the life of St. Ignatius Loyola. It had its debut at the Holiday Theater on Broadway and 47th Street in April 1952. Celebrities such as Maria Riva appeared, the Fordham band played, the Pershing Rifle drill team did its tricks, and WINS broadcast the event. The *Ram* published a positive review by a naval chaplain, but today's audience would consider it, apart from the Barrett sequences, unwatchable. Barrett's own lyrical drama climaxed the season. Called *Once upon a Midnight,* it was based on the life of Edgar Allan Poe and had original organ music and ballet sequences depicting the struggle between Good and Evil, with Evil represented by the Raven.

Barrett's original epic passion play, *Oh, My People,* starring football player Andrew Romeo as Jesus, was in the works. Set during Christ's agony in the Garden of Olives, the plot flashes back and forth through time to depict modern sins, such as the execution of Jesuit Padre Miguel Pro during the persecutions of the Mexican Revolution in 1927, for which Christ suffers. The play would have a long life, directed by John Leonard, S.J., and performed for twelve years in various locales, including a crowd of sixty thousand at the Polo Grounds in 1955, always with a star athlete in the lead to stress the "manly" image of Jesus.

But theater people, by the nature of theater as an art form, can be perceived as "trouble." Sometimes unconventional, their creativity can be a source of tension between themselves and their institutional sponsors, especially when the sponsor is a conservative Catholic university. In 1942, in the wake of the *Oedipus* triumph, Gannon had complaints on his desk that "Collins Auditorium is getting a bad reputation for irregularities." Girls were in and out of the building frequently. A male college student and a girl described as "one of the women who hang around Fordham" remained in the control room long after lights were extinguished in the auditorium. Two dozen liquor bottles were found in the scenery room, perhaps as props from a show. These complaints seem to have been a foretaste of 1951–52.

The May 1952 *Mimes Night* featured one slightly risqué song about a couple who had bought an electric blanket and now no longer needed to sleep together to stay warm, and concluded with a comic ballet in which a line of chorus boys threw around a short, rotund, and vulgar ballerina played by a comic favorite, Sonny Lockman. It went over so well that there was talk about putting it on the popular TV show *The Ted Mack Amateur Hour,* but the students were informed that Thurston Davis had vetoed the idea as "not representative of Fordham." Meanwhile, cast parties at the Decatur Bar generated stories that would not be "representative of Fordham" either.

In the eyes of the administration, however, and particularly for the tough-minded academic vice president Edwin Quain, S.J., the main problem in both the theater and communications departments was academic integrity. Was it possible for a Catholic university to have an academically sound graduate theater program when the students were really not motivated to study theater as a liberal art—that is, as literature, history, philosophy, and ethics—but only to perform in shows and promote their careers? Casts were often dominated by players only loosely connected with Fordham; a *Monthly* writer characterized them as "professionals," as "devotees of 'the *theatah,*'" as evidence of the "liberalism" against which Fr. McGinley had recently warned.

No one was more aware of the personnel problems than Barrett, who wrote to McGinley that the theater was hopelessly polarized between Barrett and the clique of faculty and students surrounding director Edgar Kloten. They had driven out a succession of Jesuit chairs since 1946 and were now spreading calumnies concerning Barrett's friendship with his secretary, who sometimes worked late in the office. Those who knew Barrett knew the stories were not true, but the scandalmongers had done their damage. Barrett suggested that both he and Kloten be removed.

Quain's analysis to McGinley was withering. In Quain's perhaps overharsh judgment, Barrett did not have "the type of mind" for an academic situation, had "no respect for facts," and talked "altogether too loosely." Kloten, in spite of his "pious guff," should "have nothing to do with an academic program." His courses had no clear content, he wanted to give academic credit for acting in plays, he wanted nonmatriculated students in his productions, and worst of all, he thought communications students who flunked their courses should stay on as actors if they had "talent and adaptability." Flunking students out, Kloten said, "lessens student morale."

The solution was to terminate all theater faculty. Barrett was to teach religion in the business school. Leo McLaughlin became department chair. Journalism teacher and *Ram* adviser Ed Walsh was named to the endowed chair of Patterson Professor of Journalism, and his friend Vaughn Deering, who had a distinguished career as a Shakespearean actor and drama coach, was retained as a voice and diction teacher and as a director of plays.

The cast of the May *Mimes Night* returned in September 1952 to find the Mimes and Mummers still alive as a student club but the Fordham Theater, with its big productions, dead "for a year." The Mimes had enough life to give new freshman Alan Alda a start, but theater as an academic enterprise never returned. With Leonard as moderator until 1968, the students in the Mimes ran their own shows, selecting plays themselves. In the 1970s, determined to maintain their independence, they deflected a Jesuit assigned to moderate or direct them. For six years, Leonard resurrected a "professional" off-Broadway summer theater, but students complained that the professionals got the star parts.

In 1952, Quain received confirmation of his decision to close the theater in a conversation with McLaughlin, Philip Scharper, an English teacher and moderator of the *Monthly,* and Walter Kerr, former director of the Catholic University Theater who was also the *Commonweal* theater critic and then critic for the New York *Herald Tribune.* Kerr agreed that academic theater was virtually impossible at a Catholic institution; professionals didn't want academic training.

During rehearsals for *O My People,* which he kept going after leaving the communications department, it became obvious to his coworkers that Barrett was not well. Often he would temporarily black out, then insist on going on. Few knew that, because of a cataract, he was losing sight in one eye. Toward the end he kept saying yes to anyone who asked him to preach, lecture, or write. A physical exam declared him in good health, but on the way home from giving a retreat for priests in Morristown, New Jersey, Alfred Barrett died of a heart attack on November 9, 1955. He was forty-nine.

A fellow Jesuit wrote in his obituary that Barrett was

> the sort of man whom an impartial observer would unhesitat-
> ingly declare born for glory or disaster. . . . He attracted people
> not merely because he was personable and even handsome,
> but because he really liked people, because he was friendly,
> honest, and a man of good will. He was unreserved, almost
> to the point of naivete, but he was highly intelligent, he was
> a good judge of character, and he possessed a healthy and
> unfailing sense of humor.

Barrett was not a great poet, but he wrote some memorable lines, such as this conclusion to "Loss of Faith":

> There is between our dreaming and our seeing
> One pulsing continuity of being.
> Ah, when the life of glory we achieve
> Why grieve?
> We only lose our having to believe!

In 1966, Leo McLaughlin—who had moved rapidly from chair of the communications department to Fordham College dean, to dean and then president of St. Peter's College, then to president of

Fordham University—called Leonard in and told him he wanted him to drop the Passion play. Leonard asked why; it didn't cost that much, it raised money for the missions, and it got lots of publicity for Fordham in the New York press.

"That's just the problem," McLaughlin replied. "It looks like too much Catholic propaganda associated with the university." Leonard wasn't bitter; he knew the play was old and out of date and would have to be rewritten if it kept going. But the decision was a telling example of how a new Fordham was trying to reposition itself in the public mind.

11.

Football Loses, Courtney Wins

The theater is both the largest and smallest of worlds, and what may have stunned a corner of the Rose Hill campus was but a blip on the screen in the daily lives of young men and women who, often holding down full-time jobs, commuted to Fordham's downtown schools at 302 Broadway.

Margaret Garvey, growing up in Brooklyn in the 1930s to the 1950s, read biographies of Jesuit saints and attended the Summer School of Catholic Action directed by Fr. Daniel Lord at Fordham in 1940 and 1941. She left Brooklyn at 7:00 A.M. and, by trolley and subway, made class in Keating Hall by 8:45. There she spent the day in small group discussions with delegates from all over the country, returning to Brooklyn at 4:00 P.M.

In 1948, a secretary at a branch of Wall Street Bank, Garvey took the advice of a priest who urged her to go to college, so, in days when the subways were surely safe, she worked full time and commuted to the Fordham School of Education for six years of night and Saturday courses, not to become a teacher, but for her own enrichment. Her classmates included a policeman, a corrections officer, a Jesuit's mother, and some Franciscan brothers, one of whom became president of St. Francis College. She still remembers finishing the last page of the last blue book of her poetry course in 1954, putting a period at the end of her essay, heaving a sigh, and taking the subway home for the last time.

In a career pattern that proved typical of many women in the church, the next year Garvey entered the convent and got master's degrees in both psychology and counseling at other universities. She then left the convent and returned to the Wall Street Bank in 1975, married a high-school teacher named Larry Mangan in 1979, and retired in 1990.

While Garvey was working, commuting, and studying, many of her School of Education friends were loosening up the all-male social atmosphere of the Bronx—including competing for the Miss Fordham crown. In football season, six to ten finalists, selected by a committee, appeared on the front page of the *Ram* and balloting got under way. In 1953, for example, the winner was Pat Shalvey, a five-foot-seven hazel-eyed brunette. President of her Perry Como fan club, daughter of a fire captain, with a brother in Fordham Prep, Shalvey had lived in the Highbridge section of the Bronx all her life. On the day of the big Football Weekend rally, a motorcade bore her down Fordham Road to the gym as she waved to the crowds from her convertible. She appeared on stage with Rameses XVI, latest of a long line of real rams who, for the time being, had survived kidnapping or slaughter by Fordham's enemies. She was crowned at the Victory Dance, which to the committee's disappointment, drew only two hundred couples. But Shalvey's judgment on the honor was clear: "It's the most wonderful thing that ever happened to me."

If there were too few couples at the dance, it was certainly the fault of the young men who were too lazy or too shy to stop into Keating Hall to meet the new social directress, Mrs. Aletta Lamm. Mrs. Lamm, who had grown up in Saxony as Aletta Baroness von Gundlach, a war bride who had married an American army major in Holland, was determined that every Fordham man could meet the right woman. She staged Sunday-afternoon tea dances in La Lande Lounge in Martyrs' Court, taught ballroom dancing, kept an extensive card file of young women, whom she categorized as "pretty," "vivacious," "good sport," etc., arranged meetings between the boy and girl at her

Pelham Parkway home, encouraged the boy to meet the girl's parents to check return-home times, and invited dates from out of town to stay overnight at her house.

Fordham dances featured society orchestras such as Lester Lanin (1951) and singers such as Ann Crowley, star of *Paint Your Wagon* (1952). In one beautifully chaotic moment at a freshman dance on April 1953, a big car pulled up in front of the gym late at night, the doors flew open, and Jimmy Durante, followed by his entourage of singer-dancer Eddie Jackson, drummer Jules Buffano, and other hangers-on, burst out of the car like twenty circus clowns pouring out of a Volkswagen. They swept up the steps, through the doors, and onto the bandstand. Durante took over the piano, threw the sheet music into the air, heaved the piano top to Buffano, and played and sang "Inka Dinka Doo." Eddie Jackson, strutting in his top hat and tux, sang "Bill Bailey, Won't You Please Come Home." Then, pandemonium having been established, they were gone.

II ⤙

The new Junior Year in Paris program, as conceived by Fr. Frese, gave what they hoped were carefully selected students a lot of freedom. I was one of the second group to go to France. We enrolled as *auditeur libre* in philosophy at the Institute Catholique and in major courses at the Sorbonne. We did not have to take exams in French, but rather wrote papers that we sent to Fordham, which gave us credit for a year.

As a result, I, for one, stopped going to philosophy classes, attached myself to Fr. J. Quentin Lauer, who was finishing his doctorate on the phenomenologist Edmund Husserl, and just read and read. Lauer, a big gravel-voiced man who looked more like a truck driver than a philosopher, surprised me by saying right off that Thomas Aquinas was "not the only philosopher." So I read lots of John Dewey and Poe and about forty other books and wrote foreign-correspondent articles for the *Ram*.

Most of us lived with French families, while I, who had lived in Toulouse with the lovable Baures family—a general, madame, and three daughters near my own age—when in Paris, stayed in a student residence, College Stanislaus, on Rue de Rennes a few blocks from Boulevard Montparnasse. On the boulevard we congregated in the famous cafes Le Dome and Le Select, hoping that Hemingway, who had just survived an African plane crash, would come by when he was in town.

We did most of the same things all students abroad do—the Louvre, the Moulin Rouge, Folies-Bergère, Fiesole, bullfights, and Venice—and met and fell for wonderful young women from Smith College, Sweetbriar, and New Rochelle.

I also did a pilgrimage on foot to Chartres, spent two weeks in the St. Andre Benedictine monastery in Bruges, and went on a jackal hunt with French hosts in Tunisia over the Christmas holidays. My friend Bill Flynn and I participated in a political discussion group called Conference Ollivain, where Bill, whose French was very good, spoke on "Are the French the Valets of the Americans?" We spent animated evenings talking with international figures such as Robert Schuman, a father of the European Union; Pierre Mendès-France, the premier who both urged the French to drink milk and extricated France from Vietnam; and the great Catholic novelist François Mauriac, a vivacious, wiry man with a raspy voice that came from the back of his throat.

Several of us were also swindled out of a few hundred dollars each by a little old blind man—a seventy-plus "professor" named Pierre Poulin whom we met outside the Sorbonne. He won us over by giving us French lessons and impromptu lectures on opera and art as we sat in sidewalk cafes, and he smoked his Gauloise, dropping ashes he did not see all over his coat.

We gave him money to buy the tickets for a tour of Italy that he personally was to conduct. How the blind man would lead us through the Uffizi Gallery we did not ask, and the tour, of course, never happened. Informed that he was a swindler, we confronted him. It was tough. He told us more lies to put off paying us back. He said that he was writing a history of the French Revolution and the printer had cut his thumb and bled on the manuscript, and that he would pay us this afternoon if I would lend him subway fare to get to the bank. I did. He didn't. We loved him and pitied him, not just because he was old and poor and blind, but because he taught us well—and he might have loved us, too. We told the police, who obviously thought we were fools. They went through the motions of arresting him, but they let him disappear. The last time I ever saw him, he said, "I'm not a bad man; I've just done bad things."

III

The low turnout at the 1952 Football Weekend could easily be interpreted as a symptom of a deeper malaise, which often hits colleges in the way that mononucleosis or the flu do, called "low school spirit." Twenty years of Fordham spirit had been associated with the rise and fall of football, and now Fr. McGinley, who had moved decisively on the "theater problem," was inching toward a decision on football.

During the 1950s, the student press was as close to being a house organ as an administration could hope. The *Ram* had reported the death of the theater without much fuss, and the *Monthly*'s article, which had been shown to Fr. Quain before publication, supported his point of view. The faculty advisers read all copy and occasionally suggested that writers consult administrators for advice. The editorial cartoons were often inspirational religious tableaus wherein a young man carried the cross down the road of life, avoiding Satan lurking behind a tree; editorials endorsed Catholic Press Month, the annual retreat, sacrificing for Lent, and the privilege of donating money for Jesuit Missions or to build the new Jesuit seminary at Shrub Oak.

Since football's return after the war, faculty and students had viewed it with a mixture of affection and indifference, while alumni and New York sportswriters mustered more emotion. Some of those most concerned with Fordham's academic standing considered football a distraction. Professor Sam Telfair, the colorful historian admired for his dynamic lecturing style and his mastery of battles, names, and dates scrawled on the blackboard, was a favorite among football players who could sleep through most of his class but wake up for a lively digression. "They study, all of them," he drawled. "It doesn't help, but they study." He gave one team captain a grade of 6 (out of 100) and in no way would raise it to 60.

The fall of 1952, however, was an emotional time for the program. Coach Ed Danowski, who had played under the "Iron Major," starred with the New York Giants, and coached Fordham for six seasons, had been signed in 1951 for another three-year term. Assistant coach Vince Lombardi, who would have liked the job, had left in 1949 for West Point. In his public utterances, McGinley's support for football was firm but qualified. He was proud that twenty-seven members of the team had averages over 80 and promised to keep football "as long as our alumni and student body will take the trouble to cross the Triborough Bridge to Randall's Island."

In August, the team captain and previous year's most valuable player, Jack Hyatt, was stricken with a nearly fatal attack of polio and rushed in an iron lung to the Sister Kenny Institute. There he received the last rites, and hundreds of friends prayed for his recovery; the crisis passed and he began to improve.

Four weeks later, the Thursday night pre–Holy Cross game rally was planned as a spectacular tribute to Hyatt. The crowd of 1,500 rocked with cheers and songs. Robert Alda, father of Alan and known as the star of *Guys and Dolls,* sang "Walking My Baby Back Home," and Anne Bancroft, who appeared in *Don't Bother to Knock,* gave an inspirational talk. Hyatt's friends praised him; then, as the crowd fell silent, they played a tape-recorded message from Jack. A moment later, the master of ceremonies stepped forward and peered down the center aisle toward the gym door. There, walking unaided down the aisle was Jack Hyatt himself! He could walk. He was here. The crowd cheered so long and loud that no one could hear the speeches presenting Jack with an award.

A few weeks later, spirit had slumped again. The rally for the Quantico Marines game drew only seventy-five students, and the Randall's Island stands were empty. The *Ram,* under editor Jack Freeman, addressed the problem with a series of thoughtful editorials. School spirit for other activities—the Mimes and Mummers, publications, politics—was very high, but this didn't carry over to football. A letter writer, Robert Moroney, suggested that Fordham lacked spirit because it lacked "the essentials that create spirit—a common purpose, shared ideals, a humble attempt to attain an intellectual life." Until those qualities were attained, he said, reviving football was like "animating a corpse" (November 14, 1952).

In a special extra edition, printed in quick response to a *Journal American* story that football might be dropped, the *Ram* editorials began to shift responsibility from apathetic students to "hypocritical athletic policies" and the administration's "overall lack of interest" (December 17, 1952). In the last issue of the year, when the editors had taken copy to the printers, Freeman realized that he still had eight inches to fill on the editorial page. With no moderator on hand to check the text, Jack sat at a typewriter and wrote:

"Why do you kick that dog?"

"Because it's mad."

"How do you know?"

"Wouldn't you be mad if I kicked you?"

and twenty-eight more lines arguing, in effect, that the administration was responsible for the team's failure by not giving it enough support. The rest of the tone was mild, but from the administration's point of view, Freeman had gone too far (December 19, 1952).

Today Jack (Jacob) Freeman is a freelance writer who covered Martin Luther King for the Montgomery *Advertiser,* edited copy for the *New York Post,* and wrote for Tom Brokaw's *NBC Nightly News.* But he is known in *Ram* lore as the first editor to be removed. Or perhaps he was the editor who began the system of changing the editor every semester rather than every year.

The administration gave football two more years. With four wins and five losses in the 1953 season and a losing 1954 season, Danowski resigned. Interest switched to other sports such as basketball and track in which Ed Conlin and Tom Courtney, even in their junior year, were breaking records. On December 14, McGinley, as a courtesy, sent a confidential letter to Cardinal Spellman enclosing the next day's news release that football was finished. The "deficit has been and would be for the predictable future, about $100,000 annually. We simply haven't the money any more." In his public statement, he concluded that "at long last, our head must rule our heart." The *Ram* editorial concluded, "Let us accept it and get on with our education, redoubling our support for the remaining sports which represent us" (December 16, 1954).

IV ⸺

While parts of the Fordham family were feuding over football, others were deeply disturbed each day—at lunch, in the dorms, and in class—about something else that was happening to America, and to American Catholics in particular. Gordon Liddy saw the campus as more Democratic than Republican. Another view would describe Fordham students as overwhelmingly conservative, but with a more liberal leadership cadre that would often seize the initiative on public issues. Many of them were in the National Federation of Catholic College Students or the National Student Association. They were involved with the Association of Catholic Trade Unionists and the sodality, and some visited the Catholic Worker House.

In national politics, because the church hierarchy was militantly anticommunist and because Senator Joseph McCarthy, a Republican from Wisconsin, was known to be a Catholic and to have begun his anticommunist crusade at the suggestion of a Georgetown Jesuit, Catholics were widely perceived as supporting McCarthy, whom civil libertarians saw as an opportunist and a dangerous demagogue. Some Catholic intellectuals, however, were powerful McCarthy critics.

Commonweal's opposition to McCarthy had been outspoken for some time. Father Robert Hartnett, S.J., editor of *America* magazine, was convinced that McCarthy's tactics were a threat to the Constitution and to civil liberties, and attacked McCarthy beginning in 1952. By 1954, the uproar about him from laypeople and from fellow Jesuits was so vicious that the Jesuit general, Fr. John Baptist Janssens, silenced *America* on that topic. In Fordham's Loyola Hall, McCarthy was generally a forbidden topic of conversation because it made people so angry. When Hartnett, worn out, left *America* in 1954, Thurston Davis was sent downtown to replace him and Leo McLaughlin moved from the communications department to the dean's office.

McCarthy's influence was fading in 1954 following the excesses of the Army-McCarthy hearings and the Edward R. Murrow *See It Now* special exposing his tactics, but Fordham student activists were still disturbed that the words "Catholic" and "McCarthy" were associated in the public mind.

So the same issue of the *Ram* that reported football's demise also featured a letter to the editor that the writers also sent to the *New York Times* and the *Brooklyn Tablet,* signed by 101 seniors and protesting against the "identification of Catholicism with the cause of Senator Joseph R. McCarthy." The letter had been written so that both McCarthy critics and supporters could sign it, and some of both did. It respected the right of Catholics to support McCarthy, but rejected the notion that "faith is any way increased" by that support.

The result was as if the Fordham 101 had desecrated a shrine. For weeks the *Tablet* filled its letters pages with assaults on the Fordham students, including personal attacks on the student "intellectuals" who were so stupid about the threat of communism. As the angry replies piled up, the original letter writers sat up in the *Ram* office with Ed Walsh and Leo McLaughlin, anxious to fight back, but the administration thought it best to let the conflict pass.

IV

Today Rupert Wentworth, a retired chemistry teacher from Indiana University in Bloomington, writes chemistry textbooks full time. In his spare time, joined by fifteen friends, he makes sandwiches and serves them, along with chips, fruit, and milk, to poor, homeless, and jobless people—people who a few decades ago would have been institutionalized but who are now fed by volunteers.

This is not something that Wentworth learned at Fordham, but something he does in imitation of Christ. He switched from Fordham Catholicism to Methodism around the time of his second marriage, though he holds no bitterness toward the obligatory faith that was part of his life at St. Peter's High School in New Brunswick, New Jersey, or on Rose Hill. Like many of his friends, he did resent the mandatory daily morning Mass and was creative in getting out of it without getting caught, but he liked Benediction and can still sing *O Salutaris Hostia* in his head.

He lived with seven lively friends in Martyrs' Court, one of whom, Carl Candels, had a regular job as an extra at the old Metropolitan Opera. Whenever Carl couldn't make it, he found a friend to take his place, so any number of Fordham men today can tell their families that, yes, they stood on the stage of the Met holding a banner in the last act of *Meistersinger* as the curtain went up and they gazed out into the Golden Horseshoe, and the "Prize Song" began. Rupert and his roommate were the only students who liked the horrible veal cutlets served in the dining room, so they would collect as many as forty at a time and store them on their windowsill. To their annoyance, one of the resident Jesuits who had a passkey for the fire doors connecting the buildings and suites would cut through their apartment just when the boys were cursing and swearing, and when they sat around with their shirts off, the Jesuit would admonish them to put their shirts on lest they scandalize those walking by outside.

Though successful as a science major, Rupert recalls little of whatever he might have absorbed in philosophy or anything else; as he describes it, he "majored in New Rochelle." He also ran track.

His roommate was a very pleasant fellow runner named Tom Courtney from Livingston, New Jersey, six foot two and 185 pounds, described variously as "handsome" and "husky," with a high forehead, close-cropped blond hair, square jaw, and toothy smile. While most runners are slender and wiry, Tom was broad-shouldered and muscular. One afternoon when Tom annoyed the students on the floor below him by bouncing a ball on the floor, a huge football player came roaring up to put him in his place. Their altercation was over in a minute, and Football lost. Rupert was dedicated enough to the sport, but Tom was absolutely driven; although he once described his three main interests in life as "oil painting, reading, and girls," nothing was to get between Tom and his running.

From a family where his father and four brothers were all athletes, Tom played baseball and basketball at the Caldwell, New Jersey, high school, but gave them up to run. With a record of twenty wins and two losses, he took first place in the half mile at the New Jersey State Championship and accepted a track scholarship to Fordham. His personal events were the 880, the 1,000, and the half mile, and in 1954—with Terry Foley, Frank Tarsney, and Bill Perschetty—he was the anchor man of the Fabulous Four two-mile relay team, with thirteen straight wins. Although Tom didn't win everything—he had a pattern of losing on indoor banked tracks while breaking records on the flat surface—in junior year, coach Art O'Connor, who himself had run for Fordham, began mentioning the word Olympics to his star. For the next year and a half his training became both grueling and methodical as he kept a daily log of everything he did.

After graduation, O'Connor took Tom on an international barnstorming tour, losing a few races and breaking records at others in Los Angeles, Denver, Belgium, Finland, and Prague. At Tampere, Finland, Tom accidentally lost a race in which he was well in the lead by finishing on the oval because the officials neglected to tell him the finish was on the straightaway. The official winner insisted that Tom accept the trophy but he absolutely refused—and won a gold-spoon sportsmanship award in its place. Now he had two things on his mind: his military obligation and the Melbourne, Australia, Olympics of November 1956.

The army gave Tom time to train, and on Sunday, November 25, when Tom took his place on the starting line for the 800-meter race, eyes were on him as a favorite. Years before, three other Fordham men had gotten into the Olympics, but Tom was the first with even a foretaste of victory.

Quickly Tom took the lead. He had been preoccupied with passing Arnie Sowell, who had beat him in Los Angeles and Denver, but suddenly, with only thirty yards to go, Britain's Derek Johnson snuck through on the inside and pulled ahead of Tom. Already exhausted, Tom called on some inner strength and surged ahead, beating Derek by a single stride. The time, an Olympic record, was 1:47.7. Tom said later that God had helped him do it. He was so wrung out, however, that it was an hour after the race before he had the energy to come out and accept the victory. A few days later, he won a second gold medal as a member of the 1,600-meter relay team.

Two weeks later, Fordham assembled the Fordham band, the Livingston High School band, the ROTC, and the student body at Poe Park on the Grand Concourse, put Tom Courtney, in his white Olympic sports jacket and straw hat, in an orange Cadillac convertible, and paraded down Fordham Road, through the gate, and up to the gym, where Fr. McGinley gave him another trophy. Then there was a big dinner that night at Mama Leone's restaurant, an alumni cocktail party on Saturday, and an appearance on the *Ed Sullivan Show* on Sunday night.

VI ⟿

While Rupert and Tom were running, some other students were making smaller names for themselves in other ways. Ed Conlin, six foot five, toted up records that made him the most outstanding basketball player ever at Fordham: 242 out of 563 field goals, 191 of 242 free throws, an average of 25 points per game, and a total of 1,886 points in four years.

John Catoir, a business-school student, came to WFUV for the same reasons that had inspired Fr. Gannon to start the station. He had seen Fr. James G. Keller—the Maryknoll priest who popularized the slogan "Better to light a candle than curse the darkness" was founder of the Christophers and author of *You Can Change the World*—in short films, and John was convinced that if he could get into radio and TV he could make them a tremendous instrument for good.

He also ran track and made some high-jump records as a freshman. At WFUV he was announcer for the daily news broadcast in which his classmate Charles Woods (who changed his name to Charles Osgood when he found out that CBS already had a Charles Woods) read the news in a voice that was already authoritative and deep. Every day after class, John took the subway down to WNBC, where he worked as a page until midnight. In time, the idealistic John got the feeling that NBC might not be the best fit for him, so he joined the priesthood, took over the Christophers, and directed them for eighteen years.

A humor magazine, *The Thorn of Rose Hill,* flourished for about a year in 1955–56 and then withered. The *Monthly* editors fought among themselves, displeased their Jesuit moderator, and lost their jobs, and the magazine faded in and out. It reappeared in a new incarnation as *The Halcyon* in May 1956. In 1954, a freshman section had stuffed the lock of their classroom so that the professor couldn't get in, and class had to be called off. The section's class representative was brought to trial before the student court and was, of course, speedily acquitted. Peter Marinelli, '55, celebrated this moment of Fordham history by satirizing the student government in a three-part epic poem modeled on Pope's *The Rape of the Lock*. The *Halcyon* published the full text of this poem as well as a story, "The Baby," by Alan Alda, in which a young married couple who have not had a child struggle to communicate about the wife's announced pregnancy, accomplished without the husband's consent.

Don DeLillo grew up a few blocks south of Fordham at 182nd Street and Adams Place, where Arthur Avenue cuts south from Fordham Road through the heart of the Belmont section, the Bronx's own "Little Italy." He went to Cardinal Hayes High School and to Fordham, where he majored in communication arts. Like most of the Fordham students who wanted to go anywhere with their writing, DeLillo fell into Ed Walsh's orbit in Robert's basement and did a term paper for him pouring out his goals as a writer. Walsh kept it on his shelf to show to other young writers years after DeLillo's novels had made him famous.

In February 1957, DeLillo saw the Jackson Pollock exhibit at the Museum of Modern Art and, a little puzzled by the experience, decided in a *Ram* column (February 28, 1957) that Pollock must be a "representation of a contemporary trend . . . an artistic wilderness scrawled in shapeless perspective and chaotic design." The young critic was too sensible to attack something he didn't understand and too honest to pretend he understood something when he didn't. He concluded that Pollock had received the "homage which comes to those who vary from the norm, regardless of the quality of their achievement."

Dean Leo McLaughlin's attempts to create an atmosphere of excellence were showing results. Fordham College beat Syracuse University on the last radio broadcast of *College Quiz Bowl* in 1955, and McLaughlin took the team to Luchow's for dinner. He instituted an old Oxford tradition of an Encaenia, an honors ceremony prior to graduation, with a witty Lord of the Manor speech and a proclamation in Latin, and he founded the Fordham Club, a collection of the twenty to thirty "most outstanding" seniors, who would serve as advisers to the dean.

Fordham's first Rhodes Scholar, Brian Daley, '61, practiced this emphasis on doing things well. He had come to Fordham from St. Peter's Prep, joined the honors program, was accompanist for the glee club, and prayed with the sodality. Though a classics major, he assisted economist Fr. William Hogan, S.J., known as "The Steel Priest," on research for his two-volume history of the steel industry. At his final Rhodes interview, the *Ram* tells us, an imaginative committee member asked Daley to defend the debating proposition:

"Resolved, that Columbus went too far." Brian "treaded water violently for a few minutes," then responded that Columbus "was obviously a hot-headed Latin from the Mediterranean, totally lacking in the virtues of classic English moderation. Had Columbus veered west instead of going too far south, he would have landed in South Carolina. There would have been no Spanish-American War and America would have remained neutral during the Second World War."

Later, Daley told the *Ram,* "I don't intend to hide behind books all my life. I hope to do a good deal of writing, and possibly enter politics or industry in later life" (January 12, 1961). Wrong. He became a patristics scholar and a Jesuit, and taught at Weston Theological Seminary and Notre Dame. But Brian had one more thing to accomplish before leaving for Oxford. On May 11, the combined glee clubs of Fordham and New Rochelle performed Mozart's *Requiem* in Carnegie Hall. For director James Welsh, it was the first time a Catholic College in the east had done anything this difficult; it was a "step forward for Catholic colleges." For Brian, it was a landmark: "Now we have become a major organization." Many at Fordham felt the same way about his Rhodes.

VII ⤺

If Fr. Gannon felt that his greatest contribution to Fordham was WFUV, McGinley also saw clearly what he would be remembered as having done. His vision was consistent with that of the 1840s Jesuits who were not satisfied to limit their influence to the Bronx. In McGinley's years, Manhattan had become the center of the world. It housed the United Nations headquarters, hosted World Fairs, endured the Robert Moses–engineered building boom, and exercised leadership in culture and the arts, and McGinley itched to make his own impact on the scene.

In March 1958, McGinley wrote to a foundation president, "February 28, 1958, will probably prove to be the most significant date in Fordham University's modern history." It was the day Mayor Robert Wagner signed the deeds transferring the title of 320,230 square feet, the two blocks between 60th and 62nd Streets from

Columbus to Amsterdam Avenues, to Fordham at a cost of $2,241,610. The space was immediately north of St. Paul's Church, the parish of the Paulist Fathers, and south of four blocks destined to become the Lincoln Center of the Performing Arts. It would include, as its centerpiece, the new Metropolitan Opera House as well as the New York Philharmonic Orchestra, the New York State Theater, a repertory theater, and the Juilliard School of Music. As the plan evolved, it would also embrace a high school of the performing arts, a public school, a bandshell, underground parking, and 4,400 apartments—4,000 of which were luxury apartments.

At a Biltmore Hotel luncheon on January 20, 1959, McGinley unveiled Fordham's three-stage plan for its $25,000,000 project. First would be the law school and its library, to be completed in 1960; second, the Schools of Business, Education, Sociology and Social Service, and General Studies, to be finished by 1962; and finally, a student union, more classrooms and libraries, and an elaborate bell tower.

Factors over the next few years, including public opposition and a shortage of funds, would force continual redesign of the plans and make those deadlines a fiction. The bell tower never did appear, for example, but McGinley never wavered. The New York *Herald Tribune*'s editorial (January 21, 1959) could almost have been written by him: "The proximity of a university to a center devoted to such arts as the theater, the opera, and the symphony is no accident, for each of these in its own way contributes to the mainstream of enlightenment that flows through and gives meaning to human history."

In 1955, McGinley's need for a new downtown campus coincided with some other events. The property at 302 Broadway was scheduled for the wrecker's ball, the occupants of the doomed old Metropolitan Opera House on 39th Street needed a new location, the philharmonic had to leave Carnegie Hall, and Robert Moses had a vision for a "reborn West Side, marching north from Columbus Circle."

Tipped off about Moses's plan by Fordham alumni, McGinley, who knew Moses because Moses had known McGinley's father, sat down with his friend. When McGinley checked with Cardinal Spellman for approval, the cardinal exclaimed, "This is the greatest thing that has happened to Fordham since my predecessor, Archbishop Hughes, built the university up at Rose Hill."

The instrument would be the Housing Act of 1949, which enabled a city to condemn substandard dwellings—then known as slums—and acquire the property. The city would then offer the property for sale at public auction at a minimal price for an institution that serves the public good such as a university or opera. The federal and city governments would then make up the difference between the price the civic sponsor pays for the land and the value of the property demolished. The Lincoln Square project forced out eight hundred businesses and seven thousand low-income families; Fordham was responsible for demolishing the homes and relocating the families removed from its own property.

The project and Fordham's participation in it faced at least two kinds of opposition. One was personified by a lawyer, Harris L. Present, chair of the New York Council on Housing Relocation Practices, with the support of Protestants and Other Americans United for the Separation of Church and State (POAU). Present sued to block Fordham's role on the grounds that state funds were being used to support a religious institution. His suit moved through a series of courts, including the United States Supreme Court, until August 1958, when it was definitively turned down. Fordham won the case but lost precious fund-raising and construction time.

To McGinley, Present was an irritant who had seized the church-state issue as a club because he opposed the concept of urban renewal. One day McGinley met Present at court and asked him privately what he would do with his time when he ultimately lost. Present replied, "Spend more time with my daughter."

The other opposition was both more theoretical and more personal. One man's slum is another man's home. The area to be bulldozed was known as old San Juan Hill, because a number of its residents were veterans of the Spanish-American War, and it included the landmark 1887 12th Regiment Armory. To Moses, it was simply a slum, and the *New York Daily News* (March 3, 1959) described it as "once the toughest neighborhood in town, a spawning ground for violence and crime . . . a rat-infested, garbage-littered area of rotting tenements and decaying brownstones." It had once teemed with commerce, but was today "an area of desolation, where boarded-up brownstones stare blindly at the walls crashing down around them." Ironically, some of the old brownstones there had been built by Lawrence McCabe, McGinley's grandfather.

Moses was confident of his working partnership with the Catholic Church in New York and of his good relations with Cardinal Spellman, who owned much of the property where Moses would want to place a highway, a bridge, or a housing project. Presuming that all Catholics should therefore be "on board" for Lincoln Center, Moses was irked whenever a priest raised a question about his policies or his methods. In February 1958, Chicago Msgr. John J. Egan, a highly respected pastor and activist and executive director of Cardinal Stritch's Committee on Community Conservation, attended a high-level workshop in East Lansing, Michigan, on urban renewal, was alarmed by what he learned, and sent a strong but carefully reasoned article to Thurston Davis, editor of *America* magazine.

With only a passing reference to the high cost of the apartments scheduled for the "renewed" Lincoln Center property, Egan spelled out the dangers to lower-class Catholic neighborhoods and parishes where urban-renewal projects quickly ram in a superhighway, wipe out historic streets, force out corner groceries—making the housewife drive five miles to a "convenient" supermarket for a loaf of bread—and dislocate the poor without a thought for their welfare. These decisions, he says, are made by faceless technocrats with no understanding of the human beings whose lives they disrupt. "No churchman, of whatever faith," he says, "be he pastor or bishop, can look with equanimity at this destruction of healthy social cells."

America accepted the article for publication; then Davis, a prudent, cautious editor whose predecessor had been silenced on the McCarthy issue and who was not naturally disposed toward controversy, sent the galleys of the article to Robert Moses.

There is a story about Moses to the effect that he had received an honorary doctorate in humane letters, but had never written a humane letter in his life. Although Egan never mentioned Moses by name, Moses took the article as a personal attack. In Moses's reply, Davis was reminded that Moses had cordial relations with "your church and your own Order." Moses told Davis to consult Spellman and McGinley, and characterized Egan's piece as "so bitter, dogmatic, so biased, so factually wrong in many instances, and so reminiscent of the sensational press that I am astonished at your printing it."

Moses sent copies of the letter to McGinley and a banker friend, and McGinley did what Moses expected: he called Davis and had him kill the article. Read today by an urban historian, Egan's observations are conventional wisdom, a fair warning of the harm urban renewal can do, but Fordham was behind schedule in building and fund-raising and bought into Moses's attitude that no criticism should be allowed to slow them down.

Meanwhile, Fordham had to remove the people who lived on its two blocks and project both the appearance and the reality of humane concern. Tenants with relocation problems who called McGinley's office or wrote with complaints received letters from Michael Sheahan, McGinley's secretary, or Fr. William J. Mulcahy, S.J., his treasurer. The *New York Post* ran a story (October 21, 1959) on three people, Mr. and Mrs. Milton Lacks and Katherine O'Neill, the last remaining tenants of the sixty-six families who had lived on the corner of 60th and Columbus. The proposed alternatives, they said, cost twice as much, or lacked elevators, or were half the size of their present homes.

According to the final report (November 30, 1959) of Braislin, Porter & Wheelock, the firm engaged by Lincoln Center to undertake the relocations, 1,158 families had inhabited the Fordham area. Of these, 60 percent had relocated themselves and received a $275–$500 bonus for doing so; 24 percent had homes found by Fordham's real-estate agents; 10 percent were relocated by New York City; and 6 percent fended for themselves in unknown ways. Of the 2,805 families and commercial tenants on the entire Lincoln Square site, only three were actually evicted.

Now all McGinley and his staff had to do was raise the money and get it built.

VIII ⚊

The Lincoln Center for the Performing Arts Board, headed by John Rockefeller, honored McGinley by sticking with Fordham during the church-state legal battle, allowed Fordham to use the term

Lincoln Center in its title, and granted him the key to the old armory as a memento.

The full symbolic importance of Fordham's new presence at Lincoln Center would evolve over the next forty years, as building plans evolved and the relationship—sometimes tense—between the Rose Hill and Lincoln Center campuses forced both campuses to redefine their identities. This was particularly true in the mid-1990s when the uptown and downtown colleges combined their faculties and 95 percent of their curriculum, and what was historically *the* Fordham, Fordham College, had to rename itself Fordham College at Rose Hill because there was now another Fordham College at Lincoln Center, which was both its partner and its rival.

In 1960, the new downtown presence marked "Fordham's fuller emergence in the greater community about it . . . and the recognition by that greater community of Fordham's contributions," as *Ram* columnist Kevin Sheridan put it (May 5, 1960). In other words, it was now impossible for the president to say, as he had said sixty years before, "Boys! Go straight home. There are dangers lurking in the city." From now on the boys—and the girls—were in the city, and they were at home there.

Finally, that same spring, Fordham moved into the larger world in another important way. On the afternoon of February 1, 1960, in Greensboro, North Carolina, five black students from the local North Carolina A&T College walked into the Woolworth's department store, sat down at the counter, and demanded to be served. Woolworth's took money from both white and black customers but did not serve blacks at the lunch counter. The next day, twenty-four more black students joined in. Within two weeks, there were fifty-four sit-ins in fifteen cities in the South. Word spread north, and Fordham's chapter of the Catholic Interracial Council decided to move their tactics beyond prayer and discussion groups. On March 30, twenty-one students assembled in front of the Campus Center at 11:45 A.M., and their president, Hugh Carr, gave them their instructions: "Remember, don't be boisterous. Don't crowd the sidewalk or prevent anyone from entering the store. All we want to do is protest."

Carrying their signs—FORDHAM INTERRACIAL CLUB PROTESTS WOOLWORTH'S POLICIES TOWARD NEGROES—they marched solemnly up Fordham Road to Woolworth's and picketed the store for an hour, calling attention to the fact that Woolworth's was part of a chain that refused to serve blacks in the South and that therefore the Northern branches and their patrons shared in the responsibility for this injustice. Bronx citizens gathered around and talked. A black workman said, "Maybe this will help us." Other Fordham students laughed and called the demonstration "ridiculous." And the campus had something new to talk about for days. The *Ram* editorial came right to the point: "We applaud this small but determined group who publicly expressed their union with and sympathy for southern sit-in strikers. It was the first public gesture of this kind by Fordham students" (March 31, 1960).

The 1960s had arrived at Rose Hill, and nothing would ever be the same.

12.

Jesuits and Women

One summer afternoon in 1998, I biked from Mitchell Farm, Fordham's Jesuit villa house in Mahopac, Westchester County, to the little town of Shrub Oak about a half-hour south of Mahopac. There I pedaled laboriously to the top of a steep country road called Stony Street, where a vast four-winged Colonial rose-brick structure sprawled across the horizon. It was a building that could have been a public school, a corporate headquarters, a factory, or a prison.

I had been here before. I felt like Charles Ryder, the narrator of Evelyn Waugh's *Brideshead Revisited,* who came upon Brideshead Castle at the end of World War II after not seeing it in twenty years, except that Charles's memories of Brideshead, for all their pain, included days of joy and love.

The large boxy edifice before me now was a branch of Phoenix House, a drug-rehabilitation program headquartered on Manhattan's upper West Side. Before that, it was a fundamentalist Bible school, and before that, Loyola Seminary College of Arts and Letters. When I graduated from Fordham as an ROTC student in 1955, I joined the Sixty-second AAA Battalion (AW) in Mannheim, Germany, where John Manning had left it at the end of World War II. In 1957, I joined the Jesuit novitiate at St. Andrew-on-Hudson, then moved to Shrub Oak for philosophy in 1959. Both the novitiate and Shrub Oak were branches of Fordham at that time.

A fellow Jesuit has said that he once tried to revisit Shrub Oak, but halfway up the hill he got sick to his stomach and had to turn back.

Planning for Shrub Oak had begun as far back as 1945. In the early 1950s, the American Catholic Church was so prosperous in both cultural influence and vocations that the Jesuit New York and Maryland Provinces were clearly unable to accommodate both the three years of philosophy and the three of theology at old Woodstock College in the hills outside of Baltimore. They were convinced that they needed a new seminary, a philosophate, in New York, and one with a huge chapel and a large sanctuary so that in years ahead, as more and more men became priests, they could be ordained there too. The New York architects of Voorhees, Walker, Smith, and Smith studied Woodstock to prepare plans for its counterpart in the north, and Jesuit fund-raisers reached out to their most generous benefactors, including the students in their schools, for the money. They achieved their goal of $5 million by 1954.

From the beginning, the most difficult question was where the new seminary should be located. One school of thought, on a European model, says that priests should be trained near the people, in the big city and on a university campus, where they can have contact with people with secular minds. The other tradition, on the original, more American Fordham model, isolates young men in the country, remote from distractions to study and from some occasions of sin. Regardless of this tradition, however, the St. Louis and New Orleans Provinces had placed their philosophates at St. Louis University and at Spring Hill College in Mobile.

In 1945, as part of the broader province consultation, Fr. Laurence McGinley polled his faculty colleagues at Woodstock for their opinions as to where the new school should be located. The various proposed sites included St. Andrew-on-Hudson, the Brady mansion at Inisfada, the campus of the new LeMoyne College at Syracuse, and the retreat house at Monroe. The strong majority of the Woodstock faculty favored Fordham, however, with the student residence either a short walk from the campus or on the campus by the Southern Boulevard gate, landscaped with trees to set it apart. Their arguments were all academic and intellectual: they felt there would be heightened stimulation for faculty and students alike, as well as competition, increased self-confidence, special lectures, and access to New York libraries.

As McGinley summarized their arguments, "It seems to be the modern way for intellectual progress." The fathers caution that only faculty who "will not succumb to the attractions of city life" should teach scholastics. The minority argue for healthy country air and tranquility and warn that lay teachers, because of "doctrine and attitude," should not teach scholastics. They fear a loss of vocations. What about discipline? What if someone goes to a movie? He would be punished, as at St. Louis and Spring Hill, by being sent back to the novitiate. Perhaps Fordham would object to having its name so closely associated in the public mind with a seminary, as with Seton Hall or Catholic University. On the other hand, those schools always were seminaries; Notre Dame, Harvard, and Yale all have seminaries or divinity schools without loss of prestige.

I rode my bike up to the front door but did not go in. The chapel, I was told, was now used for meetings. Below, on what had once been a parking lot, some girls watched a group of boys play an aggressive game of basketball. Around back, the cottage to which the fathers used to retire for drinks and special faculty dinners was still there, but the tennis courts were overgrown, and the pool had long ago been drained. In the graveyard, I read the headstones but hardly recognized a name.

On the long, flat lawn behind the south wing, I pulled up and watched a game of touch football. Within minutes some of the players gathered around me. Who was I? Had I actually lived here? Had I been on drugs? Were the men in the graveyard students who had died in college? I pointed out the window to my room, the last on the top, or fourth, floor from which on a clear day I could see the Empire State Building. When they finish their program here, these young people say they will get jobs or go to college. The father of one works at Fordham. They like it here; we did not.

On December 27, 1945, fifty-one Jesuits—all the superiors of the New York Province, plus periti (advisers) from New England and

Maryland—met at Xavier High School, not to decide the question, but to advise the provincial, Fr. Francis A. "Butch" McQuade, S.J., on his decision. The allowed method was not to vote, but to talk all day, reflect, and later fill out a questionnaire about the progress of the meeting. What was your position before the discussion began? What did the consensus seem to be? Did you change your mind? And so forth.

To read the signed ballots is to get a *Rashomon* insight into the province mind. Several report that Fordham was "eliminated," one that Fordham "carried the day." In spite of the Woodstock memo, the anti-Fordham—or really, antiurban—forces were stronger. Again and again, fears surfaced that Fordham lacked privacy and recreational space, that the city was a threat to religious discipline, and that there were the temptations of movies, shows, a flood of visitors, and the families and friends of the men to whose houses they would flee. The talk was so antiurban that one father noted, "I found myself resenting the idea that our scholastics could not live in the city."

McGinley himself was "undecided" about the Fordham campus, but wanted a place near New York. Of the two Fordham delegates, J. Harding Fisher was strongly opposed; he didn't want Fordham to look like a seminary, and he thought the scholastics would be weighed down by term papers from other faculty and neglect philosophy. Only Robert I. Gannon, boldly backing Fordham, talked tough. "It would be better," he said, "to drop a few foolish philosophers who don't know how to behave in the big city than to remain in intellectual mediocrity."

In the following months, after examining twenty sites, in correspondence with Cardinal Spellman, who was initially reluctant to have another religious institution in Westchester, McQuade decided on what he considered the best of both worlds, a secluded country spot "conducive to quiet religious life, intellectual training, and physical health," an hour from Fordham, for $155,000. The following fall, Fr. Quain appointed fifteen Shrub Oak Jesuits to the Fordham faculty.

We were supposed to like it. The rolling countryside was beautiful. In addition to the pool, there was a lake at the bottom of the hill for ice skating, and we found a hidden quarry in the woods where we could swim. There was a theater in which to put on our own shows, such as *The Mikado* and *Command Decision,* and we watched movies, most of them, prophetically, about sinking ships, such as *The Wreck of the Mary Deare* and *A Night to Remember,* set aboard the *Titanic.*

There were opportunities to bus down to Fordham for occasional lectures or courses. The library was good, and the faculty and staff were, for the most part, kind and professional. A few were brilliant scholars, and some seminars, such as one on James Joyce, and some lectures on the history of ideas are fondly remembered. In other ways, the gap between the professors and students, though all belonged to the same religious order, was as wide as the Grand Canyon.

In an article on the school's opening in *Woodstock Letters* (February 1958), historian Francis X. Curran, S.J., wrote, "The new Loyola Seminary is an enduring memorial to the generosity of our friends and benefactors, and to the wisdom and planning of our Fathers." But it would be gone by 1970. The planners can be faulted for ignoring the wisdom in McGinley's survey, but perhaps there is no way they could have foreseen the phenomenon of the 1960s and the generational revolt that swept the world, even behind seminary walls.

Those who went through Shrub Oak give several reasons as to why their experience was so bad. For some, it was the physical and emotional isolation of 136 twenty-five-year-old males stuck on a Westchester hill, subjected to many of the same rules of surveillance as St. John's College boys in dormitories a hundred years before, while their contemporaries were dating, marrying, working on doctorates, or volunteering for the 1960 Kennedy campaign. Meanwhile, lights were to be out at 11:00 P.M., and an assigned scholastic patrolled the floor, made notes, and reported those with lights on to the authorities. Some blame the architects for the building's coldness, for the long, straight, sterile corridors, and for the suffocating uniformity of the same bed, yellow desk, bookcase, typewriter table, and vinyl chair in every room.

For those with any intellectual imagination, the problem was, as one said, "the lies," meaning the irrelevant philosophy. Dated textbook Thomism was delivered from mimeographed notes, in thesis form, refuting adversaries the class had not read. Lectures and oral final exams were conducted in Latin in a way that tested memory and linguistic agility more than the comprehension of philosophy.

Furthermore, the final oral determined whether a man went "up" or "down." Assignment to the "long course" meant that he was considered capable of higher studies and leadership. If he was sent to the "short course," it was assumed that he would "do good work anyway." One of the more frustrating experiences was in the history of philosophy course. The professor lectured from his chaotic notes, of which every student had a mimeographed copy, but gave a final exam based entirely on his past fill-in-the-blanks exams, which the class was forced to memorize. Students never got to read the philosophers themselves, but only those notes and old tests. A typical question was, "Plato's _____ were _____." A legendary scholastic scribbled in, "Plato's balls were blue."

For several years, the pattern of relatively minor incidents of insubordination restricted itself to scholastics who stole liquor or steaks from the fathers' supply or from the kitchen for their own parties and picnics. One group, caught having a party at a cabin in the woods, was punished by a *culpa,* a public reprimand requiring them to kneel on the dining-room floor and recite their fault. The father minister who would scan the chapel at evening litanies from the choir loft to catch those who were absent, found that the full-length sacristy mirror before which he preened in his vestments had been stolen and stashed in the chapel tower.

The Jesuit general, following an exhortation by Pope Pius XII, had forbidden young Jesuits to smoke, but of course they did— secretly and alone or with a friend who could be trusted—"violating poverty" by accepting cigarettes or cigarette money from home. Since TV was permitted only by exception, such as for watching a Fulton J. Sheen talk on the negativity of modern literature, we watched the Kennedy-Nixon debates secretly on a monitor in the physics lab.

By 1968, the rebellion had become more overt. Scholastics, by coincidence sharing independent attitudes with fellow young Jesuits in France and Spain, refused to take exams. Rural isolation had failed to seal off Jesuit seminarians from the revolutionary spirit, the rejection of authority that seemed remote from the goals and ideals of this generation throughout the world. How radical a turning point this was in the Society's history can only be seen a decade later when its membership decline could be visualized on the charts. In the mid-1960s, word would spread each night as to who had left that day. Of 139 scholastics at Shrub Oak in 1961, a third are still Jesuits. Of the 136 in 1968, there are less than a fourth.

In the summer of 1969, the scholastics moved from Shrub Oak to Murray-Weigel Hall, formerly a residence for Jesuit graduate students, on the Fordham campus. Ironically, the country air had exacerbated the very problems that the site was supposed to avoid, and the young men still ended up at Fordham, as the prudent heads had so feared twenty-five years before. Six of the faculty, who already had status as Fordham faculty members, joined the Fordham Jesuits at Loyola Faber Hall.

One, Fr. Vincent Potter, S.J., later became academic vice president at Fordham; Edward Brande, S.J., in mathematics, became a president of the faculty senate and later was academic vice president at St. Peter's College; and Gerald McCool, S.J., achieved a reputation as one of America's leading Thomists. Fr. Robert Johann, S.J., the former *America* magazine philosophical columnist who wrote about the philosophy of love and had better rapport with Shrub Oak scholastics than some, left the Jesuits and married, but remained at Fordham until he retired.

The influx of Jesuits, both students and teachers, helped to reemphasize the centrality of Jesuit presence and Jesuit philosophy in Fordham's culture, particularly since several Jesuits went into administration. Others established continuity in a variety of other ways. Among those teaching the scholastics were Fr. Joseph Dolan, who had been a student of Ignatius Cox in 1939 and returned to Fordham in 1960. Another teacher, Fr. Robert O'Connell, was a Holy Cross ROTC graduate who had done destroyer duty in World War II. He got his doctorate at the Sorbonne, came to Fordham in 1962, and earned a reputation for scholarship on St. Augustine.

Father George McMahon, who taught briefly at Shrub Oak, became a long-time dean of the college, an administrative vice president, and a chaplain at Lincoln Center. Through his many friendships, he was one of those "Mr. Fordham's" who knit generations together. Father Roth, the expert on Dewey, underlined the department's strength in American philosophy and succeeded McMahon as dean.

Father James Loughran came in 1970 as McMahon's freshman dean, lived in B house and Martyrs' Court, finished his Ph.D. at Fordham, and joined the philosophy department. He also organized a half-court basketball tournament for his friends, called the LIT (Loughran Invitational), in which McMahon played, followed by beer and sandwiches at B house. In 1979, he succeeded Roth as dean and later became president of Loyola Marymount, acting president of St. Mary's at Emmitsburg and at Brooklyn College, Fordham academic vice president, and president of St. Peter's College.

With all that experience behind him, Loughran became known for a few fairly provocative opinions. He thought that Fordham had made a mistake in continuing big-time athletics and was doomed to failure because it could never compete big time. At a time when so many complained that there were not enough Jesuits, he thought the Jesuits should start a new college in Arizona; in the 1970s, Fordham had too many Jesuits, and they were getting in one another's way.

The Murray-Weigel scholastics both did and did not enter fully into the life of the campus. One, Tom Curran, became an editor and columnist for the *Ram,* and later left, married, and became a prominent newspaper editor at *Newsday* and the Newark *Star-Ledger.* Another, Mark Aita, was in charge of a freshman residence hall, Queens Court, went to medical school, and ran a parish and medical clinic in a poor neighborhood in Camden, New Jersey. Some plunged into the liturgical life or into social activism on and off campus. Some stayed home. The internal problems that plagued them in the country did not disappear. A few of the more creative scholastics produced a short film about the ghost of Shrub Oak haunting Murray-Weigel Hall.

II

When Fr. McGinley, "the Intimate Leader," as the *Ram* called him, stepped down in 1963, Fr. Vincent T. O'Keefe, S.J., his tall, friendly, red-haired executive vice president, who had a special gift for remembering names and faces, was the natural successor. Born in Union City, New Jersey, O'Keefe taught at Regis High School, studied at Louvain and Münster, and earned his doctorate in theology at the Gregorian in Rome. Like McGinley, he had taught theology at Woodstock since 1954 before coming to Fordham as academic vice president in 1960. When he called his mother to tell her he was being moved to Fordham, she asked, "What did you do?"

First on the list of things to do was implementing results of the massive self-study begun in 1958 by academic vice president Edward F. Clark, S.J., in preparation for the ten-year Middle States Association evaluation. Written by Francis J. Donohue, recent president of St. Mary of the Plains College in Kansas, this eight-volume report was an exhaustive analysis of Fordham's status and a proposed vision for its future, focusing on a few special topics for the Middle States team's consideration. Fordham also had questions about itself, such as whether its administration should be centralized or decentralized, what its total enrollment should be; and what would be the best areas for the graduate program to concentrate on.

A profile of the university in 1962, when its total enrollment was 8,951, lists ten units: Fordham College (1,836 full-time, 114 part-time); Graduate School of Arts and Sciences (1,304); School of Business (714 in Manhattan, 638 in the Bronx); College of Pharmacy (312 men, 40 women); School of Adult Education (724 full-time undergraduates, 81 full-time graduates); School of Law (649 men, 24 women); School of Sociology and Social Service (99 men, 120 women); School of General Studies (508 men, 635 women); School of Philosophy and Letters (96 Jesuits); and Fordham Prep (831). St. Andrew's was not listed.

The report recommended greater integration of faculty through university-wide departments. It recommended a "new" four-year coeducational college to provide the liberal arts courses, uptown and downtown, for the three professional schools of business, education, and pharmacy. It noticed that the graduate students were overwhelmingly New York Catholics, with more than a third of them priests and religious, and that almost half of the Ph.D. students were not taking courses but still plodding along on their dissertations. In short, there were too many ABDs.

Significantly, the report observed that Fordham's comparatively slow enrollment gain over 1958–61 (2.67 percent, as compared to St.

John's 33.12 percent and Boston College's 16.4 percent) was due to its "failure to build up an accurate public image." Fordham's image was that of Fordham College with a law school and a graduate school tacked on, a "man's college for men," even though only the college and the seminaries were all male.

According to the study, a composite Professor Fordham, pasted together from the 293 full-time faculty, would be an elderly Catholic New York man (90 percent were male), married with 2.7 children, living in Westchester, not active in civic affairs, probably with a Ph.D. (only 52 percent had Ph.D.'s), and not producing scholarly books or articles.

In a blunt memo reflecting on the *Faculty Characteristics Study,* Donohue described the academic inbreeding, except among Jesuits, as "difficult to believe" and, in business, education, and law, as "a positive disgrace." There were too few women, except in social service, which had too many. These were mostly unmarried women without a Catholic education, who were thus unable to transmit "our beliefs and principles" or "to advise others how to live." Only seven faculty (one in Fordham College), including part-timers, were divorced or separated, but three were teaching clinical psychology and guidance. Donohue thought Fordham should find teachers in those areas who were themselves "successful in meeting life's problems." On scholarship, he observed, the basic problem was the "very high proportion of full-time faculty who produced nothing at all."

A composite Mister Fordham of 1961, based on a university-wide survey of 428 seniors and compared with a National Opinion Resource Center national sampling, was a single white male planning to marry that summer, with a part-time job, from a family earning less than $7,500 a year in which the parents had not graduated from high school. A self-described political liberal, his goal was to get "a basic education and appreciation of ideas." He would select a job that let him "help others or be useful to society," but he did not want to "live and work in the world of ideas." He would like further study, especially if his parents were poorly educated, but not now. Pharmacy and business students were more likely to rank "making a lot of money" as a major goal.

The March 1963 Middle States reply to the self-study expressed confidence in Fordham's "present eminence" and "future distinction," and answered some of Fordham's questions with more questions of its own. Above all, Fordham should develop the habit of "thinking like a true university, rather than as a federation of schools," and develop a faculty senate in which faculty could participate as members of a *university* faculty. It favored a new coeducational college and added that Fordham College should not be allowed to "become an enclave." It asked whether pharmacy should continue as it was and whether there should be a liberal-arts college in Manhattan. It suggested that each department rigorously examine its graduate offerings.

III

"First Thomas More Coed Accepted," the *Ram* announced (November 13, 1963). The previous spring, the New York *Journal-American* (March 26, 1963) had written, "Real live American beauties are set to blossom on Fordham University Rose Hill Campus—but there is many a male student who would prefer that the transformation be nipped in the bud."

The admissions office had decided to put its best face forward—in this instance a "blond, attractive" one—to project an image of success for the new college opening with two hundred young women, then called coeds, the following fall. In the prefeminist vocabulary that dominated all the discussions of women on Rose Hill in the early years, the "first girl," Joan Ann Poroski, was a "five-foot, eight-inch beauty" with green eyes, from Maria Regina High School in Hartsdale, where she scored in the 99th percentile in the National Merit exam and won prizes at the science fair. She played the piano, sang, wrote short stories, and when she heard that Rameses XIX had died, wanted to donate a new one until she heard that a live ram cost $2,000.

By June, the last girl accepted was as strong as the first. Ingrid Liepene, from Walton High School in the Bronx, was a "pert young coed" ranking tenth in a class of 766 who swam and spent her spare time "helping others." In her Fordham class the average SATs were 640 verbal and 596 math.

Behind the scenes, the opponents of Thomas More joked that it was the "3-D school" of "Dames, Dopes, and Dollars." But Anne T. O'Keefe, the admissions officer responsible for making the first

Thomas More class one that would defeat the critics and who herself had been a 1960 Miss Fordham semifinalist, had a clear idea of the class she wanted.

For one thing, there would be no nuns. They would "put a damper" on things and make the school look "like a convent." She would accept married women and allow girls to marry while students. Personally, O'Keefe was not opposed to women working after marriage, but she was "absolutely opposed to working mothers." Those interviewed so far, she told the *Ram* (October 3, 1963), were "exceptionally good looking." Beauty would not be a factor in admission, "but neatness, poise, and personality" would definitely count.

There would be no mixed classes. Presumably this was because women needed a different, more supportive atmosphere, because they wanted to establish a separate identity and because, for other reasons, the administration wanted to keep men and women separate.

O'Keefe's original plan had been to start the self-study's "new" college, called Campion for Jesuit martyr Edmund Campion after whom an Oxford College had also been named, as coeducational. But the Fordham College Jesuits dug in their heels. At the time, only one fourth of the traditionally male Catholic colleges had admitted women at all. The decisive voice was that of Fr. Frese, O'Keefe's successor as academic vice president. He wanted a high-standards women's college named for Thomas More, martyr-hero of Robert Bolt's popular play *A Man for All Seasons* and a strong advocate of education for women. Frese even wrote to Carmelite nuns in Georgia, his home state, to have them pray that the college would be named Thomas More.

The first dean was Fr. John Donohue, S.J., a professor in the School of Education with a Yale Ph.D. who had written three books on Jesuit education. Donohue later quipped that he was selected because they wanted to assure New York Catholics that the school was respectable and he looked like Cardinal Spellman. As assistant dean, they recruited Yale Ph.D. Patricia Plante and, as dean of students, Jean Murphy, who later wrote a dissertation on the Thomas More curriculum. Everything was ready to go; the first class was being recruited, and the newspaper articles had appeared, when suddenly one torpedo—a Jesuit one—almost sank the whole ship.

Those were still the days when *everything* a Jesuit school did needed approval from Rome. Fr. John McGinty, the New York provincial, called O'Keefe in and told him he had gone too far. In various ways, he had exceeded the strict permissions he had received when Thomas More was first approved. O'Keefe sensed immediately that anti–Thomas More Jesuits had "gotten to him," made an end run, and convinced the provincial to kill the school, and indeed, McGinty told O'Keefe to call the whole thing off. O'Keefe replied that if McGinty canceled Thomas More, he would have to find a new president for Fordham.

When Susan Barrera first saw Fordham, she was a sophomore at Mary Louis Academy, in Jamaica, Queens, at a sodality summer workshop on Robert's Rules of Order. Her father, who had come from Ecuador to attend St. John's University, and her mother, from Holland, had met in Queens and eloped. Susan fell in love with the campus, and when she heard about Thomas More, she knew immediately where she wanted to go.

Because she had advanced-placement credits in Spanish, her schedule would occasionally make her the only girl in a room of forty-nine men. She was excited by the open intellectual atmosphere and the freedom to question after the stifling atmosphere of high school, but wary about challenging the teacher in an all-male classroom. Early on, she needed the protection of the Thomas More structure and found a role model in Patricia Plante, without whom the 413 young women in her class could easily have disappeared.

Susan had heard that some Jesuits didn't want women there, and the grumpy Fr. William Grimaldi, S.J., a classics professor in charge of their honors program, told her that he was one of them. Yet she saw him as a "softy" beneath the gruff exterior, and he later confessed that the arrival of women was the best thing that ever happened to Fordham.

By the mid-1960s, Fordham's token 1960 participation in the Woolworth's picketing had assumed new dimensions. *Ram* space that a decade before had gone to football and social life now went to urban riots, the civil-rights movement, why there were not more Jesuit grads in the Peace Corps, the Mexico Project, which sent Fordham students to Mexico for the summer to build houses for the poor, and questions about ROTC and Vietnam.

In the summer of 1964, six male students descended for three months on Napola (pop. 800), a town eight miles north of Mexico City, that had the luxury of cold running water but no phone or telegraph. They built an elaborate latrine for themselves with a sliding chair over a long ditch that, considering their diarrhea, was well used, and they constructed a "model home"—one with pigs and chickens penned up to keep them out of the house, with windows and floors, and a raised, dirt-free hearth—which the peasants could imitate to improve their own homes.

The following year, Susan joined twenty men and women who flew to San Antonio and endured a twenty-two-hour bus ride to Mexico City. There, in the bus station, they followed the signs for Potrero and rode another bus ten hours into the night. Something was wrong. Potrero was not supposed to be that far. The bus deposited them at a desolate crossroad where only the light from a poolroom shattered the darkness of the street. Alas, Susan, who spoke Spanish, learned that this was Potrero, but not *their* Potrero, so they went back another hundred miles into the night. Once established, the boys built homes and the girls taught English, did vaccinations, washed clothes in the river, distributed garments, and walked miles into the country, toting a plastic anatomical doll with removable organs, to teach the women hygiene.

Back on campus, Susan gave herself over to her honors program thesis on the "Courtly Love Tradition in Dante and Shakespeare." Meanwhile, love came her way. In her first history class, assigned to an all-male classroom, she retreated to the back of the room to be as invisible as she could. Since there weren't enough seats, one of the forty-nine men, John Fay, had to stand against the wall behind her. John looked over her shoulder, read her name and address on her notebook, and called her up.

When Irma Jaffe first saw the campus, she was a curator at the Whitney Museum of American Art, a scholar and an authority on John Trumbull and Joseph Stella. Invited, in a Thomas More initiative, to teach art history, she wasn't sure she wanted to leave a wonderful position at a great museum for the academic life in which she had no experience. But the campus was so beautiful, so exotic with those Jesuits strolling around in black habits that it was like being back in the Middle Ages. Within a short time, joined by musicologist and choral director James Kurtz, she had established a fine-arts department. It was small at first. She was not, as her critics whispered, an empire builder, and she knew she could not demand too much of girls whose parents said, "What are you doing that for? How's that going to get you a job?" when told they were taking an art history course.

In general, the Thomas More women developed a strong bond among themselves, forging a distinct identity that endured for years. Of course, there were some complaints. Their only housing the first year was the Susan Devin residence for working women at 198th Street and Grand Concourse, with its tiny rooms, 7:00 P.M. weeknight curfew, and complaints from the older residents if they typed their papers loudly. On campus, there weren't enough ladies' rooms, and they weren't allowed in the swimming pool because the boys in those days swam nude. In February 1965, the girls offended the Fordham boys by sponsoring a mixer with Manhattan. Fordham boys griped that 75 percent of the TMC girls were from local Catholic high schools and went home to their parents every day. Nor, according to the male cheerleaders, did "Ramelettes" have what it took to really whip up spirit at the football game.

The arrival of women coincided with football's return, this time as a club team through student-government initiative, evidence that a campus, which a decade before had "lacked spirit," was coming alive. As other evidence: on November 6, 1964, 2,800 students packed the gym to hear Robert F. Kennedy, who was running for United States Senate. When John Kennedy was assassinated two weeks later, the *Ram* (November 24) wrote: "John Kennedy lifted the hearts of older people and made them feel younger. He appealed to the younger generation to meet the challenge of the modern world. His magnetism turned into inspiration for those who learned to admire him." On Ash Wednesday, Fr. Donald Moore, S.J., celebrated the first "Hootenanny Mass," adding Negro spirituals to the liturgy, which was still in Latin and Vatican II had yet to transform.

When the administration decided in 1972 that Thomas More had served its purpose and sought to merge it with Fordham College, its loyal alumnae fought hard. They argued that the needs of women were different enough to require separate structures to support them, that Thomas More's higher academic standards, made possible by their selectivity, would be watered down, and that in extracurricular activities and leadership opportunities, women would be swallowed up in a male world.

In a six-page single-spaced letter to the trustees, Barbara Stolz, '69, vice president of the Thomas More Alumnae Association, was forced to disagree with her dear friend and mentor, James C. Finlay, S.J., who since teaching her political science a decade before had risen to the presidency. When she was a student, in tears in his office on a bad day, he had told her to stop feeling down on herself, to stop "over-achieving"—reaching always for A-plus—and get involved helping other people. When she was thinking of law school, Finlay told her, "Don't do it. If you go to law school it will bring out the dark side of your personality. It will ruin you." Now she was telling Finlay: Don't do it.

At the November 28, 1972, meeting of the Rose Hill Campus Council, an administration-faculty-student body entity created in 1970, Finlay argued that the budget couldn't handle separate schools and that the separate college still caused public confusion as to whether or not Fordham was truly coeducational. Furthermore, an administration survey showed that the women students themselves were no longer attached to Thomas More's identity. There was no clear faculty consensus, although a faculty senate subcommittee of five voted three to two to retain the school. After long debate, the council tied 21 to 21.

The "first coed," Joan Ann Poroski, left at the end of her first year. Barbara Stoltz got a Ph.D. in the politics of criminal justice at Brandeis. Patricia Plante left Thomas More in 1968 and married a Jesuit. Susan Barrera married John Fay the year after graduation. John got his Ph.D. in biology and works with the Fish and Wildlife Bureau, Endangered Species; Susan, with an Ph.D. in American literature from George Washington University, teaches at Marymount University in Arlington, Virginia. Her class published a commemorative booklet with pictures and a poem that begins:

> How is it that we,
> Young, naive, girls at seventeen,
> Battered the walls of time and tradition,

Scaling mountains of men?
Did we walk quietly through the third avenue gate,
Or climb, perhaps, through a friendly open window?
Did we blow in with the wind one autumn day,
Lie softly on the soil, and suddenly, bloom?

Like Shrub Oak, Thomas More College lasted little more than a decade and then was absorbed into the larger institution where it had belonged in the first place. Unlike Shrub Oak, Thomas More radically transformed Fordham College, first by forcing Fordham men—faculty and students alike—to rethink the role of women in Catholic education and in their own lives.

No one foresaw then that within twenty years the old glee club would be blended into a male-female chorus and that, backed by federal legislation, women's sports would have parity with men's, that women would be playing rugby, that the 1999 *Ram* masthead would list twenty-two women and six men, and that in many Jesuit colleges women would outnumber men 60 to 40 percent.

Second, as a fresh institution willing to experiment, it enriched the Fordham curriculum with the fine-arts department, its own honors program, and its emphasis on values. One of its less-noticed but most significant impacts was that it gave Jesuits, who most of their lives had lived in all-male worlds, a chance to develop lasting friendships with women faculty and younger women.

In 1995, the Jesuit 34th general congregation issued a statement on the "Situation of Women in the Church and Civil Society" that admitted the pattern of discrimination against women in the church and urged Jesuits to "listen carefully and courageously to the experience of women." By that time, women were much more active in campus ministry liturgy than men. Yet the Vatican had forbidden the discussion of the possibility of women priests. There is no survey answering the question of how many Jesuits would like to see women ordained. But certainly welcoming both Shrub Oak and women to Fordham dramatically transformed Jesuits' image of the church.

13.

Leo

Sometime during the 1969–70 academic year, Leo McLaughlin, who had lost the Fordham presidency in December 1968, and taken the position of chancellor, came up to me in the Loyola Hall recreation room during drinks before dinner with some personal news. "I'm telling you this because it's something you might want to do yourself someday. I'm leaving Fordham to go to Johnson C. Smith, a black college in North Carolina. I'm going to run a new experimental program to teach writing with the help of video. It sounds like an exciting idea."

It struck me as typical Leo, as he was fascinated by the media and their possibilities. He would want to do something for social justice, such as help black people. And he was restless, and this was a new venture. He was also a terribly wounded man. A high percentage of the men in that very room were convinced that he had "sold out" *their* university. They had played a major part in driving him from office, and it must have been excruciating for him to live with them.

In recent memory, Fordham deans have had generally good reputations for being personal friends with students. Depending on their talents and the restrictions of the legal drinking age, various deans have played basketball and tennis, run marathons, led long walks, cooked dinners, downed beers in local pubs, or just sat up late in residence-hall bull sessions with young men and women. When the students who knew him well speak of him today, Leo McLaughlin is always "Leo." What struck us most was his mix of exceptional intelligence, lively imagination, and human warmth. He was tall and lean, with dark, brush-cut hair flecked with gray, alert eyes, and an ever-so-slight lisp that some thought he had acquired at the Sorbonne in Paris by mastering French pronunciation so well. The word *love* came naturally to him, though not so often as to water down its meaning.

For those who had known him as dean, the 1965 news that Jesuit superiors had suddenly yanked him out of the presidency at St. Peter's College to replace Fr. O'Keefe, who had just been elected assistant to Fr. Pedro Arrupe, the Jesuit general in Rome, seemed to promise a Fordham golden age. He had the kind of openness the 1960s required and the spirit to ride the winds of change without being blown away.

II ⚊

In *The Anxious Years: America in the Vietnam-Watergate Era* (1984), Kim McQuaid, like many historians, names 1968 as the year that "things fell apart." It was the year of Robert F. Kennedy's and Martin Luther King's assassinations, the Tet offensive, the "police riot" at the Democratic National Convention in Chicago, and the flowering of the New Journalism, that hybrid literary form that came into vogue because nonfiction and fiction writers alike needed both techniques to do justice to those mysterious and tragic days.

McQuaid lists phenomena that startled some educators as well as others who saw their world crumbling. "Alarming mixtures of hallucinogenic drugs, cannabis, crime, premarital sex, coddling of offenders, uppity kids, foul language, and irreverent and possibly dangerous Black Power advocates sporting Afros, biker glasses, berets, and black leather jackets appeared to millions of the normally faithful to add up to a compelling argument for the immediate restoration of traditional values and behavior."

Within the church and universities, six events were setting the stage on which McLaughlin's pledge in his inaugural address of October 18, 1965, that "Fordham will pay any price, break any mold, in order to achieve her function as a university," would become a battle cry.

First, Catholic intellectuals were facing issues of mediocrity raised by documents such as John Tracy Ellis's 1955 *Thought* article and Fordham's self-study. Among the Jesuits, the decision to send men for Ph.D.'s to leading Catholic and secular universities was bearing fruit, and Fordham's Loyola Hall community of 128 men, one of the largest in the country, was strong in scholars, particularly in philosophy and theology.

Second, the younger Jesuits, still in studies but aware of the new era's opportunities and challenges, began asking what was the best apostolic use of the Society's limited resources. Perhaps traditional institutions such as Fordham were too big and "too institutional" to respond quickly to 1960s issues such as urban poverty and world peace. Perhaps they were too impersonal, too "like a hotel" to meet the emotional needs of a generation already accustomed to shared prayer, a moral theology that justified contraception, and the free-wheeling liturgical experimentation that had taken place at Woodstock College while Vatican II was still in progress. In the Fordham Jesuit community, Loyola Hall was known as the Kremlin and sometimes acted as though it were a separate province; it did not enjoy a reputation for hospitality among the early 1960s. Jesuit summer-school students who lived in sweltering dormitories and were discouraged from crossing the Kremlin's threshold.

A high-level, three-day conference on higher education took place at Woodstock College in October 1964. There were thirty-five invited participants, including several presidents, and the conference was followed by a symposium in *Woodstock Letters* in 1965 which gives a time-capsule glimpse into the heady-wine thinking of those years.

Since there were 820,000 Catholics on secular campuses and only 390,000 on Catholic campuses, should not the Society shift its manpower to Newman Clubs, to individual faculty appointments at Ivy League schools, or into new small Catholic colleges on secular campuses? Since there was no Catholic equivalent of Harvard, should not Jesuits pick one or two of their twenty-eight colleges and make them university centers, moving teams of their best scholars to those schools where they could deal with the world's problems in profound scholarly depth? But which of the twenty-eight would offer its "best" to a rival in Washington or the Bronx? A Georgetown speaker argued that even Georgetown lacked enough Jesuits to prefect dorms and teach philosophy and theology. But Fr. Michael Walsh, S.J., president of Boston College, said large numbers didn't matter; one good influential *scholarly* Jesuit in each department and a few key Jesuit administrators were enough to establish Jesuit identity. Others agonized over the hypothetical identity crisis of the "hyphenated priest," the intellectual torn between his prayerful, priestly character and the all-consuming demands of scientific research. If there could be "worker-priests," what work was compatible with holy orders? Could a priest be a garbage collector?

Third, the Vatican Council issued a decree on religious liberty that Catholic priests, nuns, scholars, and students quickly applied to themselves. The brilliant, young Swiss theologian Hans Küng, author of *The Council, Reform and Reunion* (1962), triumphantly toured American universities delivering a message of freedom that Americans were ready to hear: "A Christian never has to accept a dogma of the Church if it would be against his conscience." In practice, this became freedom of dissent on questions of sexual morality, permission to leave the religious life and marry, and license to become, in a word, an autonomous agent. In a way, *autonomy* became the 1960s' two-edged magic word, so apparently ennobling to the individual who made it flesh, yet threatening to the authority who saw the individual as subject to itself.

Fourth, some church authorities made matters worse by abusing their power. In 1963, the Catholic University of America banned four progressive theologians from speaking on the campus, and in 1965, St John's University terminated thirty-one professors in the middle of the semester to preserve St. John's religious character. Hardly a year went by without several stories of priests or nuns being punished for challenging church bosses on a social or religious issue; cleverly, radical student protesters would goad authorities, including university administrators, into forcefully cracking down—thus, in a propaganda victory, exposing the "fascist" strain at the institution's heart.

Fifth, the leading Catholic universities decided they would compete for excellence on the same terms as secular schools. In July

1967, a group of twenty-six presidents and other intellectuals, including three men from Fordham and two bishops, met for three days at Notre Dame's villa house in Land O'Lakes, Wisconsin, where they produced a six-page manifesto, "The Nature of the Contemporary Catholic University." This was part of an ongoing attempt to harmonize university goals with the Vatican II document "The Church in the Modern World."

The main theme of this statement is clear in the first paragraph. To achieve excellence and be a university in the "full modern sense," the Catholic university "must have a true autonomy and academic freedom in the face of authority of whatever kind." At the same time, Catholicism must be "perceptively present and effectively operative." Other themes emerged, such as that theology, the principal means of this presence, should be in interdisciplinary dialogue with modern culture; that the university is the "critical, reflective intelligence of the Church"; that research should focus on problems of "great human urgency"; that students should learn to serve society by working in the inner city for civil rights and for peace; that students and faculty, in "warm personal dialogue," should experiment with the liturgy and "new forms of Christian living"; and that all members of the university community should participate in university decisions. "Autonomy," "freedom," "service," "dialogue," "experiment"—the whole zeitgeist of the 1960s was there.

Finally, and for some institutions traumatically, virtually every leading Catholic university restructured its governance so that it no longer "belonged" to the religious order that founded it, but instead to the representatives of the constituency it served and that supported it now, as represented by its newly formed lay-dominated board of trustees. To be eligible for state financial aid, particularly in New York State, schools redesigned their curricula in a "nonsectarian," though not necessarily "secular," mode so that, for example, no student would be required to study Catholicism, but could opt for world religions or the Koran.

Most significant in the long run was that the religious communities were legally incorporated separately from the university. In practice this meant that trustees, not the Jesuit provincial, appointed and fired the president, and that academic departments, dominated by laypersons, decided whether or not to hire, promote, tenure, or fire a Jesuit. Jesuit salaries went to the Jesuit community for its own maintenance, and Jesuits might or might not return some of the surplus as a gift to the school. To some Jesuits, this was a new level of personal responsibility, a new opportunity to share the same risks, insecurity, and challenges as lay colleagues. To others, it was a devastating blow, a loss of power, a "sellout."

Appropriately, McLaughlin's ascendancy coincided with Fordham's 125th anniversary, and the convocation address of April 5, 1966, by Fr. Pedro Arrupe, general of the Society of Jesus, could be read as an endorsement of McLaughlin's vision. Drawing on the language of Vatican II's "The Church in the Modern World," he said that the church must not just scrutinize the "signs of the times" and interpret them in "the light of the Gospel," but reinterpret the Gospel—see the "changing face of Christ"—in the light of history. The church, he said, has learned from the American experience to affirm religious liberty and human dignity. He called on Fordham to promote dialogue with believers and unbelievers, to respect the findings of science as compatible with faith, and to protect freedom in the search for truth.

III

When Peter Fornatale grew up a few blocks south of Fordham on 188th Street, there were seven three-family houses there, their apartments all inhabited by Italian extended families like his own. His father was the ice man who delivered big blocks of ice to the iceboxes of apartments since they did not get refrigerators till 1963 and to the chemistry labs and cafeterias of the university. When he was a boy, the blinking red light on top of the WFUV tower was the focal point of Peter's dreamworld; more than anything, he wanted to be part of the action in that radio station.

He arrived in 1963, in time to experience and even prod the rapid transformation of Fordham's popular and intellectual culture during the O'Keefe-McLaughlin years. He was the only male in a math course for Thomas More women, and the women treated him like a king, even doing his homework from time to time, but his heart was in the radio station. He was also dazzled by the Keating Little Theater with its projection booth, where he discovered *Citizen Kane* for the first time. John Culkin, a creative Jesuit who was a disciple and interpreter of the Canadian philosopher of the media Marshall McLuhan, hired Pete for a 1965 summer workshop.

At the time, WFUV music programming was a standard mix of opera, classical, polka parties, swing, and a "cheerful earful" of top forty and old hits. Finally in control of his own two-hour Saturday-afternoon "Campus Caravan," Pete began moving the WFUV sound from the era of the Kingston Trio, the Clancy Brothers, and Peter, Paul, and Mary to the Beach Boys, Simon and Garfunkel, and Arlo Guthrie. College stations were beginning to see themselves as creative, paving the way for commercial FM stations, treating each record, not as a separate entity, but as connected to other songs by theme, sound, and tonal elements. They also used the music, whether "The Ballad of the Green Berets" or Arlo Guthrie's protest against the draft, "Alice's Restaurant," to express the politics of the generation. It was too bad for Pete that he had to graduate in 1967 and move on to a thirty-year career as a disc jockey on WNEW-FM and K-Rock and miss the chance to take the Fordham course with Marshall McLuhan.

In a sense, the McLuhan professorship was a fitting symbol of McLaughlin's administration; it highlighted the communications department and projected an image of Fordham as a bold, forward-looking university. Since McLuhan was a convert to Catholicism, it represented Catholic education's respect for science, consistent with Arrupe's exhortation, and its "reading the signs of the times." Then, because McLuhan's position, the $100,000 Albert Schweitzer Chair in the Humanities, had originally been state-funded, it forced the issue of whether or not Catholic identity was a liability, since that identity had cut Fordham off from state support. And since McLuhan's teaching turned out to be only a mixed success, McLaughlin critics could check this off as another of Leo's not-so-good ideas.

By 1967, McLuhan was the director of the University of Toronto's Center for Culture and Technology. He was known as the author of *The Gutenberg Galaxy: The Making of Typographic Man* (1962) and the best-selling *Understanding Media: The Extensions of Man* (1964), and was a media star in his own right, a lecture-circuit personality and subject of an NBC-TV special. His thought resists summary, and his lack of clarity opened him to ridicule, but some of *Understanding Media*'s ideas are that as a medium is an extension of a human being, so a computer is an extension of the nervous system; that "the medium is the message," in that the telegraph, for example, contains printed words that contain speech; and that media are "hot" or "cool," depending on how intensively they engage our senses. Radio, print, and movies are hot, whereas telephone, speech, and television are cool. Culkin explains "the medium is the message" by looking at parts of the proposition from four perspectives—the medium itself, the message content, its impact on the receiver, and its relation to society. These terms are now standard in introductory communications theory textbooks.

Culkin, who had known McLuhan since 1963, convinced the fifty-five-year-old star and his team, including his son, Eric, to accept the chair and move his family, bringing two daughters and a son along to a beautiful home in Bronxville for the year. Suddenly, the New York attorney general Louis Lefkowitz decreed that Fordham, under the nineteenth-century Blaine amendment to the state constitution forbidding direct or indirect aid to any religious institution, was ineligible for the Schweitzer Chair, but Fordham honored its commitment with its own funds.

Fittingly, the same *Ram* (January 6, 1967) that announced McLuhan's appointment reported that, at the invitation of theology chair Christopher Mooney, S.J., a Protestant minister, thirty-year-old Lutheran Robert L. Wilken, had joined the theology department. A new coeducational commuter college would also open in September 1968 at Lincoln Center. The dean, Arthur A. Clarke, S.J., said its faculty would include "outstanding educators," would be "geared to New York City," and would emphasize the humanities, social sciences, and fine arts. Word spread that the program was conceived as "an honors program for the masses." The *Ram* editorial praised Mooney for recruiting Wilken and, noting a report that Woodstock College was leaving the woods of Maryland for either Yale or Fordham, urged Mooney to snag Woodstock too. All the news suggested that Leo was coming on strong.

McLaughlin's imaginative showpieces in his reach for greatness included the McLuhan appointment, a three-three program that enabled Fordham Prep students to complete both high school and college in six years, the new college at Lincoln Center, and another new experimental college at Rose Hill. The first of these would have an ambiguous start.

During the spring semester, students geared up for McLuhan's arrival. The *Ram* (March 3, 1967) reviewed his latest book, *The Medium Is the Message,* and ambitious juniors and sophomores filled out applications and lined up for interviews with Culkin for the forty spots in McLuhan's yearlong special seminar. Culkin assured them that McLuhan was a "genius" and "a threat to organized traditional ways of thinking," but assured them they would be "coworkers," not "an empty bucket into which you pour knowledge."

On the morning of McLuhan's first lecture class in September, 178 students and a large contingent of journalists sat scribbling away in the Campus Center ballroom as the man variously described as "genius," "oracle," and "carnival pitchman" arrived. He was wearing a summer suit and desert boots, and said things such as, "A funny man is a man with a grievance," "We do everything we can to hide from the present," and "In the electric age there is no more nature."

But McLuhan had a secret. He was a very sick man. For eight years he had suffered dizzy spells and blackouts that had been diagnosed earlier as a mild form of epilepsy, but which now were getting worse. In October, he blacked out in front of his class and could not continue his lecture.

McLuhan didn't want to admit he was ill, but Culkin confronted him and convinced him to enter Columbia-Presbyterian Hospital for three tests. After two of them, they knew he had a brain tumor that should be removed, having been discovered just in time, but typically, McLuhan resisted an operation. He continued to teach, but the illness had worn him down and the spells kept coming back. Finally, under pressure from his wife and Culkin, he agreed to an operation. With over two hundred calls from the media clogging the switchboard on the Saturday morning after Thanksgiving, three teams of neurosurgeons began their work at 8:00 A.M. and did not emerge until 5:00 Sunday morning to declare the surgery a success.

In the weeks that followed McLuhan was in terrible pain and had lost five years of memory; his wife had to help him with names. At one stage, the doctors wondered whether he should be sent to an asylum, but as soon as he got home to Bronxville in mid-December, he went right to work and by January he was back in the classroom. Nevertheless, a recovery that was expected to take three months was not complete for three years.

IV ⌐

If the McLuhan experience raised the question of legal Catholic identity, social changes were chipping away at other behavioral restrictions that traditionally had shored up a Catholic-school atmosphere. In May 1966, coats and ties were no longer required in the Campus Center, and the following September, the Ramskeller started selling beer. In January 1967, on a trial basis, all dress-code rules were suspended. In February, in response to student petitions, Dr. Martin Meade, vice president for student affairs, granted permission for liquor in the residence halls, but drew the line against female visitors in the rooms because it could lead to fornication. He would not, he told the *Ram* (February 3, 1967) "let a guy and a girl go into a bedroom with a bottle of scotch, close the door, and not come out for twelve hours." The *Ram* editorial called his logic "ludicrous."

A political scientist from Duke, an expert on Edmund Burke, and a former associate editor of *America,* Francis Canavan, S.J., is a tough-minded conservative with no hesitation to let anyone know where he stands. He was popular with bright students who wanted to go to law school. They would bunch around him when Martyrs' Court, A house, held its annual faculty receptions and would prod him on political issues, reveling in his sharp answers and caustic wit. In 1967, he was convinced that McLaughlin was paying too high a price for so-called greatness.

Using 1966–67 *Ram* articles, editorials, and columns as ammunition, Canavan published an article, "To Make a University Great," in *America* (July 15, 1967) in which he quotes and ridicules the faulty thinking of student writers who had demanded liquor and girls in their rooms. One columnist had said, for example, "Of course there will be fornication if parietal hours are granted, there is now and always will be. More to the point: Are students going to allow the university to decide matters of personal conscience for them? If anyone, then perhaps if we're bad they'll go to hell for us, too—if there is a hell."

Canavan noted the increase in vandalism—students defecating in washing machines, for example—the desire for less theology, the petition from 175 Thomas More girls for contraceptive information, and the administration's plan to give sex education that would indeed include discussion of contraception.

Canavan's point was that, for these Fordham spokesmen, student "freedom" came down to sex, liquor, and anticlericalism. More significantly, however, his polemic was a public shot across Leo McLaughlin's bow from a leader of a group within the Jesuit community, a signal that at least some in the Kremlin didn't like what was going on. McLaughlin was aware of their opposition. He told a *New York Times Magazine* writer, Thomas Fleming, a Fordham alumnus, (December 10, 1967), "I'd be foolish not to admit it. I feel sorry for them. Nothing in their previous training has prepared them to face a future as totally uncertain as the one we are confronting here at Fordham and elsewhere."

A few on the *America* staff had tried to dissuade Thurston Davis from publishing Canavan's attack, but Davis stuck with it and soon published several replies (August 12, 1967), some of which raked Canavan over the coals. One reader said that Canavan had convinced him to not send his daughter to Fordham. But Robert R. Meury, '64, made his reply a voice from his generation. He wrote, "I and other discontented students with whom I raised hell were sons of the absurdity, aridity, legalism, and pharisaism into which the Mystical Body of Christ has evolved."

He put current student negative attitudes in the context of the long background of the clerically enforced curfews and bed checks that had gone before. When he himself needed simple assurances of truth and love, he said, he was "subjected to countless recapitulations of the Trinity, discipline, the Assumption, temporal punishment, serious matter, infallibility, etc. I found myself beginning to regurgitate my entire upbringing." Meury was glad "a new administration has already begun to turn the old girl inside out."

V ~

But "turning the old girl inside out" was not supposed to wipe out the university. That September, McLaughlin used the Mass of the Holy Spirit to announce that "Fordham was faced with the greatest crisis in its long history of crises." The previous year's deficit was $500,000, and this year's would be around $1 million, with most of the deficit spending attributable to the "greatness" program. At the same time, Fordham was committed to a $62 million building program, over five to eight years, which included Lincoln Center, the new chemistry building, and renovation of Collins, the library, and Larkin Hall.

Although he had forty thousand alumni, only 17 percent contributed anything at all. Obviously, either too few really loved the school, or Fordham's fund-raising efforts had been totally inept. Fordham had to survive on tuition, its $14 million endowment that would soon be spent to get through the crisis, and government aid—now in jeopardy because the McLuhan case had raised the possibility that with the broad interpretation of the law, even state regents scholarships might be lost.

According to Robert Kidera, vice president for university relations and development, if all state aid was lost, Fordham faced three choices: (1) close the university, (2) make it totally nonsectarian without any religious affiliation, or (3) turn it over to the state. "There's no doubt we're losing a lot of money," he said, but "I'm convinced that unless we're great there's no use surviving" (*Ram,* October 3, 1967).

There's an unattributed anecdote wherein Leo explains his attitude toward money in terms of his early life. His father was a lawyer who was still practicing at ninety. "My father lost two or three fortunes," he said. "I never knew whether we would be vacationing on the Riviera or selling apples on the street." To Leo, life was risk, and there were worse things than bankruptcy. To him, the idea that Fordham would go out of business was not the end of the world. Better no Fordham than a mediocre one.

By April 1968, in what came to be called the "Holy Thursday" crisis, the estimated deficit for 1968–69 was $3,719,264. The atmosphere had generated rumors, reported in the *Ram* (April 26, 1968), that Fordham would sell the Lincoln Center campus to Columbia and that the Bronx Fordham would be sold to the state and called Rose Hill State. Already University Relations documents were playing down Fordham's connection to the church. A report of the Select Committee on the Future of Private and Independent Higher Education in New York State, under McGeorge Bundy, while it advocated getting around the Blaine amendment to help private universities, criticized Fordham for poor planning, that is, for upgrading faculty and facilities without regard for the budget. For example, one centerpiece of greatness was increasing faculty salaries to move Fordham into the highest ranks; full professors were getting $22,000, but Fordham had no money to pay more.

To deal with the Bundy report—to become eligible for state funds—the trustees brought in Prof. Walter Gellhorn of Columbia University to answer the question, "What must Fordham University do to achieve parity before the law with nonsectarian private universities?"

VI ⌐

What was the status of the other experimental programs? They were in the ring, trading punches and warding off blows. Ideally, in the three-three program, a prep student who started in eighth grade could look forward to a doctorate by the time he was twenty-one. In 1968, in its second year, a hundred prep students, working under the theory that in the traditional four-four system a lot of time is wasted, were squeezing four years into three by means of summer study, group discussions, and individual work, and they were planning for language training in Europe.

Father Robert Keck, S.J., former principal of McQuaid High School in Rochester and director of the program, was very conscious that this kind of program required not just that students move faster but that they approach learning in a different way. The new teaching methods included contract learning, whereby the student and teacher drew up a contract as to what was to be accomplished, and portfolio evaluation. Both methods demanded a lot of personal time from the teacher that the planners had not allowed for. At any rate, when McLaughlin left in December 1968, the three-three plan fizzled.

In the early version of the greatness dream, Bronx Fordham was to become the national university, while the new Lincoln Center College of Liberal Arts was for bright New Yorkers with no plans for graduate school who wanted a broad liberal-arts education rather than a heavy science curriculum. It was also, consistent with the self-study proposal for a new college, to provide the basic courses for the downtown colleges of business and education. It was to be relevant, with every student having a social-action project involving them with the poor, and it was to be ecumenical, with an introduction to world religions rather than a required theology course. It also bought into one of the flimsiest popular 1960s experiments: to take pressure off, there were no numerical grades, just high pass, pass, and fail.

Rather than traditional departments, it offered three broad divisions: social studies, under the world-famous anthropologist Margaret Mead; humanities, with a Great Books approach, under Prof. Harry Levy, former vice chancellor of City University of New York; and the arts, under historian Livingston Biddle. All these would somehow be coordinated for a freshman class of 300, of whom, if plans worked, one third each would be black, Hispanic, and white.

Not everything worked. The new fourteen-story classroom building, the Leon Lowenstein Center, wasn't ready for the first September 1968 class, so students crammed into law-school rooms until February 1969. The *Ram* (September 10, 1968) asked whether the new school was a "fly-by-night moneymaker, invented in the heat of the financial crisis." The school, of course, had been planned years before, but it's possible that if it had been ready on time its income might have alleviated the university's budget crisis that semester.

What about those minority students who were to make up two-thirds of the first class? Sociologist Fr. Andrew Greeley, at Fordham to run a discussion on his new book, *The Changing Catholic College* (1967), passed the word that a young Chicago priest, Daniel Mallette, had irritated Cardinal Cody by picketing a segregated swimming pool in an apartment complex owned by Loyola University of Chicago and might welcome a new job. Father Clarke brought him on to recruit and counsel blacks for the first class. Mallette brought six from Chicago and, with the financial help of $70,000 in stocks begged from United Parcel Service and a big Higher Education Opportunity grant, rounded up seventy more.

On his own in the city, Mallette lived for a while at St. Thomas the Apostle parish in Harlem and for a time as a resident faculty member in Martyrs' Court, G house. For a year, he also doubled as a cab driver, cruising the streets of Manhattan on weekends for the excitement, education, and extra income, until some informer, scandalized at the idea of a cab-driving priest, turned him in. Calling him on the carpet, Cody demanded, "How would I explain it if you were shot?"

The biggest Lincoln Center problem, however, was that no provision had been made for the 302 Broadway faculty of the business school and the School of Education, who were supposed to be melded into the new college. They understandably expected to teach what they had always known, and the new people, with a different divisional structure, were geared to their unique experimental program.

In January 1969, Paul Reiss was named first the dean of Lincoln Center, replacing Fr. Clarke, and later academic vice president of the university. He was a sociologist whom Fr. Joseph Fitzpatrick had brought in from Marquette to develop a new required course for introducing all freshmen to social problems. He forced the abandonment of the new curriculum and told both faculties they had to learn to work together. The experiment was over, but a new college with traditional departments was on its feet. He added an evening program for students of any age called EXCEL, which attracted more students than the day program. As vice president for both campuses, once order had been established, he had to deal gradually with Rose Hill faculty who saw the Bronx as the "real" Fordham and the downtown faculty as second rate.

VII ⟶

The last pillar of the "greatness" temple was established at a lunch between Leo McLaughlin and Elizabeth Sewell in September 1965.

Sewell was a small, delicate, radiant, ravenlike poet with a dream of her own. Born in India of English parents and educated at Cambridge, she was the author of nine books. She was an intellectual who had so integrated literature and her life that neither time nor continents could separate her from her fellow poets and their work.

In America, she taught at seven colleges, at each she gathered around her junior faculty and graduate students who shared dreams, especially about founding a new kind of college, a *polis,* that would change the whole face of education. What better home for the *polis* than Fordham? They would all live, students and faculty together, in an old apartment house on 191st Street right across from the campus. They would call it Bensalem College for the island academy in Francis Bacon's poem *The New Atlantis.*

It was the 1960s idea of college as Camelot or as Eden, the fresh start in the Garden before anyone had sinned, as if hundreds of years of inhibiting traditions could be wiped away, leaving only freedom in its place.

The nine founders began their planning in August 1966. The first community of six teachers and thirty students, carefully selected on the basis of essays and interviews (one of which lasted three hours), gathered from around the country in July 1967. The plan was to do general education for six months, study the concept of revolution for five days, then draw up seminar topics and book lists as the basis for the in-depth study, guided by a faculty mentor, to be pursued according to each person's enthusiasms.

There were to be no requirements and no grades, only portfolios— which could consist of papers, a diary, a box of postcards, drawings, or tapes—and the student's self-evaluation. Students who worked with McLuhan tended to shy away from written records of what they did. A Pakistani poet, however, sold the group on one requirement; they should break out of the confines of Western thought and learn Urdu, to symbolize the community's transcendent unity in a quasi-sacramental way, although that unity was quickly shattered.

The first class, having been told that they were free, had other ideas. In the first week they proclaimed "revolution" and ceremoniously tore up their schedules. From then on, all decisions were made by consensus, meaning that one ornery holdout could paralyze the group on any issue, such as regulating noise, organizing a seminar, removing a disruptive person, or selecting next year's incoming class. With no authority, the group split into factions, with those into "learning" pitted against those into "living," and from there into "freaks," "fascists," blacks, and women's liberationists. A group that ran a little day school moved into the school; another group moved to City Island with a faculty member's family. For the one-third who were self-motivated and who developed strong ties with teachers both at Bensalem and the larger university, the three years were a golden opportunity well used.

For others it was a living hell, a *Lord of the Flies* tribe loose in the Bronx. When black membership rose to 30 percent, more of the conflicts centered on race. In the summer of 1971, two Bensalem black students were involved in a knife fight with neighborhood Italians, and a Bensalem white girl was arrested in a holdup with a black boy she had met on a Bensalem project. A student died in a plunge from a window.

As an experimental college, it was studied often by visiting educators and journalists from *Esquire, Look,* and *Saturday Review,* who usually concluded that something exciting was going on, but that whatever it was, it lacked structure. By 1971, the experiment had died for three reasons: the faculty had abdicated their responsibility to evaluate students, substituting a vague idea of "personal growth" for intellectual accomplishment; Elizabeth Sewell was a visionary but not an administrator; and as the original Bensalem was on an island, so was this one, and it was emotionally and academically isolated from the university of which it should have been a part.

The Rose Hill Campus Council voted 25-17-2 to put the program to sleep with the pragmatic sadness of a cowboy shooting his own wounded horse. On the graffiti-messed walls of its house a student, mimicking the opening line of *Love Story,* scrawled, "What do you say about a six-year-old college that dies?" Another answered, "A lot of people in this place live their entire lives with the illusion that they are free."

VIII ⚊

Unfortunately for the McLaughlin administration in the tumultuous year of 1968, they could not pick their times for crises.

Collectively, Fordham students were not accustomed to protests or demonstrations, and only a minority seemed to care about the larger world. In 1965, the *Ram* writer Mary Ann Roman (February 25) interviewed Fordham students on the turmoil at the University of California at Berkeley, where Mario Savio and his Free Speech Movement conducted a mass sit-in that led to the arrest of eight hundred students. She concluded that academic freedom protests were unlikely at Fordham, mainly because "nobody gives a damn."

Civil rights, on the other hand, did stir some souls. In response to police brutality in Selma, Alabama, seventy-five students and faculty joined a protest march in Harlem on Sunday, March 14, and on Tuesday, a thousand joined a rally in front of the gym to hear Fr. Philip Hurley, S.J., moderator of the LaFarge Society, charge that many groups marching in the St. Patrick's Day parade excluded blacks. They cheered Fr. Herbert Rogers, S.J., adviser to the Liberal Club, who denounced the long silence that had been "interpreted as an approval of oppression." Five juniors, joined by Fr. Rogers and James R. Kelly, S.J. (who later left the Jesuits and became a Fordham sociology professor), left to join Martin Luther King's Selma march.

The following summer, the body of Christopher O'Sullivan, '58, who had passed up a scholarship elsewhere to enroll in Fordham's ROTC, came home from Vietnam. Within the next year, interest in the war slowly mounted. In late February, the newly formed Student Peace Union picketed the ROTC review on Edwards Parade. The following year, the issues seemed to be liquor, women in bedrooms, and the absence of coats and ties in class, but in April 1967, the Ad Hoc Committee of Fordham University Students Against the War, inspired again by Fr. Rogers, recruited over a hundred students to join the Spring Mobilization to End the War in Vietnam rally in Central Park. A group of students and Jesuits, including a scholastic, passed out antidraft fliers to students at Roosevelt High School across the street.

By November, there were strong feelings about the draft. Although a June 30, 1967, executive order granted 2-S status, a draft deferment, to all full-time undergraduate students in good standing, the draft and military recruitment became contentious issues. In November 1967, following an October interference with navy recruiters, the Students for a Democratic Society (SDS) threatened to block air force recruiters and sit in at the president's office. McLaughlin threatened to expel them, and his executive president, Timothy Healy, S.J., sent individual letters to four faculty, threatening to fire them if they participated.

And so it went, with six hundred attending a campuswide "Think-In" to discuss the war in December 1967. Faculty involvement increased. The SDS, led by Ivo Banac, later a history professor at Yale, extended its issues from Vietnam to "the destruction of United States imperialism" and advocated for its replacement by "an industrial democracy," a system in which workers would control production. Emboldened by relatively successful protests against recruiters, Banac turned the SDS's energies citywide, opposing a Transit Authority subway-fare increase and a Fordham tuition hike. Anyone who questioned Banac's patriotism would get a formulaic reply: "Patriotism is the last refuge of a scoundrel. Our loyalty is to the people."

IX ⤝

The first two weeks of December could be called the "Fourteen Days That Shook the World," or at least the two little worlds of Rose Hill and Fordham's turf at Lincoln Center. Virtually every day students demonstrated, sat in, slept in, or broke in somewhere—at Lincoln Center, the Campus Center, or the Administration Building. They began with a manifesto, highlighted by the same-day announcement that the new liberal-arts college at the Lincoln Center experimental program was being scuttled and by the invasion of Martin Meade's office by angry blacks, both of which generated a series of confrontations that left Fordham in shambles for the Christmas break.

By December 1968, a new broadly based student-faculty group called the Coalition for a Restructured University was formed, which included the SDS, the Society for Afro-American Advancement at Fordham (SAAAF), and other groups. It issued a manifesto signed by fifty-three students and faculty, addressing a full list of campus controversies. They wanted full implementation of the Gellhorn Report, which was just being circulated, black courses and teachers, student participation in the curriculum, the end of dorm restrictions, a university senate that would include students, student and faculty trustees, and an end to the university's complicity in the government's "murderous intervention in the Third World."

In December, fifty members began a sleep-in and hunger strike in the Campus Center, and seventeen members of SAAAF burst into Martin Meade's office, shoved a desk against his door, and held him for two and a half hours, demanding that he sign a statement "repudiating" a recent government rule allowing universities to deny financial aid to students who participated in campus disturbances.

In SAAAF's view, this rule discriminated against black and poor people. As a matter of fact, the rule had been government policy for some time and had nothing to do with race. Critics of the SAAAF felt that they had seized the atmosphere of excitement generated by the manifesto to dramatize their demands. By the following Monday, these included use of Keating Hall for neighborhood meetings, money for an off-campus storefront, an institute of black studies, a 20 percent black student body, and pass-fail grading for black students.

When he was finally released from his office, saying he had not been held against his will, Meade did some more work, had dinner with his assistant dean and student representatives, and attended the basketball game in the gym. He finally closed shop at 11:30 P.M. and left for his Harrington Park, New Jersey, home. The next morning he awoke before 5:00 in terrible pain and was rushed to the Englewood hospital at 5:30. He had a heart attack and was listed in critical condition. Many blamed the demonstrators who had held him in his office.

The following Monday afternoon, a hundred members of the coalition and SAAAF pressed their demands, telling McLaughlin to "get to it" and present his answers to them by 6:00 P.M. While McLaughlin, missing their deadline, worked with Dan Mallette on a response, the demonstrators chanted, "Let us in," and pushed against the glass doors. Taking orders from SDS's Banac, some crawled in a basement window and others got through an unlocked door, but the invaders were not disruptive. Some, they said, just wanted to keep warm. When a *Ram* reporter tape-recorded Banac giving directions to his troops and its editorial (December 10, 1968) criticized him for leading an "outright attack" on the building, Banac wrote that the *Ram* was racist and that black people were going to be free, "as Malcolm put it, 'by any means necessary.'" The editors, he said, could shove their tapes "up their tight asses" (December 12, 1968).

X

On Friday, December 6, after the 12:30 Mass for the recovery of Marty Meade, the churchgoers streamed over to the Campus Center for a public forum with Walter Gellhorn, professor of Columbia Law School. With his colleague R. Kent Greenwalt, Gelhorn had been commissioned to report to Fordham's trustees precisely what a church-related university must do to gain legal acceptance as "a completely independent institution of higher learning."

McLaughlin had been enthusiastic about establishing a real lay board of trustees since Paul Reinert, S.J., president of St. Louis University, had raised the issue with other Jesuit presidents in May 1967. The Schweitzer Chair case, coupled with the possibility of state aid called "Bundy Money," made a "new identity" as a nonsectarian institution a priority. Based on the recommendations of the Select Committee on Aid to Private Higher Education and chaired by the Ford Foundation's McGeorge Bundy, these funds would be granted based on the number of degrees conferred each year.

The report, released in October 17, 1968, created a sensation. The New York press covered it, the *Ram* presented a full text of its sixteen recommendations, and for the following months the whole community talked of nothing else, other than racism, tuition hikes, the budget crisis, and Vietnam.

In the middle of all this, Timothy Healy, one of the main architects of the new identity and a McLaughlin alter ego, left.

The burly, gregarious Healy had lived on Dealy Five as a scholastic in 1947 with the freshman football team and assistant coach Vince Lombardi. He had watched Lombardi be squeezed out by alumni who saw him as a threat to coach Ed Donowski. Larry McGinley had brought Healy back in 1955, ostensibly to run the radio station, but really to rein in the dissident College Alumni Association, which was interested only in reviving football, by creating a broad federation of all the schools. He lived in D house in Martyrs' Court and attracted students such as Brian Daley and John Kirby—and the following year, a student named Winston Churchill—whom he prepped for Rhodes scholarships and who won.

Healy left long enough to get an Oxford graduate degree in English, then joined McLaughlin as a vice president in his greatness project. The previous year he had published a pseudonymous article in *America,* called "Georgeham, 1984," arguing that clerical control of a university impeded its progress. One of his first decisions was to close the School of Pharmacy, convinced as he was that it was mediocre and would not win reaccreditation. Healy helped select Gellhorn, who spent six weeks researching the project on campus, including interviews and sitting in on classes, and shared a drink with him in the office. He saw Gellhorn as a Fordham friend and implemented many of his suggestions before Gellhorn wrote the report.

Healy left in order to start a school in Harlem, but he became vice chancellor for academic affairs of City University of New York, a pioneer in their controversial open admissions program. He then became president of Georgetown, where he put Daley, Kirby, and Churchill on the board of trustees, and eventually, he was director of the New York City Public Library.

Whatever the reasons, Healy's departure left Fordham without the central figure in the Gellhorn process who would have been most adept at explaining it to the public; today the report represents one of the least understood moments in Fordham history. Father Quain, head of the Fordham University Press, refused to publish the text as not up to his scholarly standards, but the authors found another publisher and Healy wrote the introduction.

The Sectarian College and the Public Purse (1970) is a 212-page, gracefully written case study crammed with footnote references to the leading authorities on Catholic education, including Andrew Greeley, John Donohue, David Reisman, and Christopher Jenks. There is even a long citation of Charles Whalen, S.J.'s negative judgment on the report in *America* (November 16, 1969). In Whalen's view, which he still holds today, the Gellhorn report was emphatically not the solution to Fordham's problem; its recommendations would have made Fordham another Columbia, but not a first-rate Catholic university.

As to the critical question of who owned Fordham, Gellhorn, citing the research of Francis X. Curran,. S.J., determined that the Jesuits had never owned Fordham. Rather, since it was incorporated by Archbishop Hughes in 1846 with nine non-Jesuit trustees, it belonged to the trustees. Later, when the trustees were all Jesuits—and, the joke went, had to be rounded up in ambulances to have a meeting—the Jesuits still didn't own it. In the 1960s, this was consistent with the thesis of Catholic University canonist Rev. John McGrath and one that the other Jesuit presidents also embraced, that historically, educational and health institutions did not become ecclesial property, but were "owned" by their corporations and held in trust for the public.

Gellhorn's portrait is sympathetic and respectful of the religious atmosphere he describes; he was aware that most of the changes in ambiance and discipline—priests wearing ties, only a few of the classes beginning with prayer, few pious statues in sight, the *Ram*'s being uncensored, students being truly free to challenge church attitudes on sex and religious doctrine—had developed independent of his visit.

The Jesuit community was separately incorporated in early October and laypersons of varying religious backgrounds were already prominent in the administration. Plans to restructure the trustees, merging the nine Jesuits with the lay advisory board, were under way. Shrub Oak was already closing.

Altogether, Gellhorn listed sixteen steps that would shade the university's "personality" so that it would not be seen as "denominational" or "sectarian."

Although to this day some strongly believe that Fordham "sold its soul" by implementing the Gellhorn report, for the most part the plan was not implemented. Leo McLaughlin was the last president chosen by the Jesuit provincial, and Mitchell Farm was transferred to the Jesuits. However, the prep was separately incorporated but not moved off the campus, the church was not sold to the Jesuits but remained the University Chapel, Fordham did not sever its ties with other Catholic institutions, and there was no attempt to broaden the interests of the university press.

Today, alumni still get hot under the collar deploring "the day the crucifixes came down," but that's not what Gellhorn called for. He tentatively suggested that if Fordham attracted a more non-Catholic and non-Christian student body, "institutional stress on a single religious symbol should be ended." Gellhorn's personal suggestion to Healy was, "In all the buildings where there are crucifixes, leave them. If you build a new one don't put them in. But it doesn't really matter one way or the other."

A memo was prepared by Robert Kidera for Fr. Michael Walsh, S.J., as to what actions had been taken on each item in Gellhorn's report. It reads, "As for symbols, the university feels no need to remove those that already exist. . . . Because Fordham was founded under Catholic auspices, it is to be expected that these reminders of the historical fact will be found on campus." On the manuscript, either Walsh or Kidera edited out the phrase "nor to erect any additional ones on its grounds or its buildings," noting Gellhorn's agreement.

XII ~

At the October 1968 faculty convocation, McLaughlin tried to place Fordham's turmoil within the context of changes in the church and the "financial bind" affecting all private universities in the country. He disclosed that the previous year's anticipated deficit of $2,300,000 had been reduced to $1,975,103.36, and gifts and pledges for 1967–68 totaled $9,094,029, including an anonymous gift of $2,500,000.

The bad news, however, was that the enrollment income for 1968–69 had fallen short, projecting a current deficit of $1,046,000. The way out, in the short term, was to cut spending, raise tuition, and hire no new faculty; in the long run, they could hope for increased income from Lincoln Center and for state and federal aid. The Gellhorn report, he belatedly reminded his audience, called for them to change "some characteristics," not to "change our character."

Within a few weeks, McLaughlin's fortunes were slipping toward doom. Normally, Jesuits hate community meetings, preferring to watch TV or stroll around Edwards Parade after dinner, but now, with issues such as separate incorporation and the Gellhorn report to discuss, they packed the Loyola recreation room and displayed the rhetoric they had polished twenty years before. One quipped that "asking a secular Jew to make a judgment on a

Catholic university was like asking Eichmann to write a history of Israel." Their deepest feeling was one of having lost control—financially, administratively, and spiritually—of something that had been *theirs*. Some lay faculty shared the same feelings.

Healy, in an interview years later, characterized McLaughlin's enemies as "a small group of noisy Jesuits . . . unenlightened and ridden by slogans." Canavan estimated the critics as probably over half the community; they, who correctly perceived that if you give away the power to hire, you give away the institution. There were many liberal Jesuits who shared McLaughlin's vision, even though they might not have expressed it in Healy's terms of "dragging Fordham kicking and screaming into the twentieth century." The following spring, an appointed house committee drew up a statement on Fordham for a province meeting that echoed the Land O'Lakes themes, but conservatives are more likely than liberals to speak with one voice, while each liberal has a vision of his or her own.

Because the big meetings were unwieldy, a select group of house consultors and elected council members met with McLaughlin and some of the Jesuit trustees at a special session at Mitchell Farm. Canavan remembers it as one of the more painful experiences of his life, because it hurt to see Leo, with whom he did not agree, subjected to such biting criticism. One especially volatile father exclaimed, "Leo, you have led us down the path to destruction." Leo didn't answer back and didn't try to explain; he just sat there and took it.

James Hennesey, S.J., was the superior who had been writing regular reports on the situation to Andrew Varga, S.J., one of Arrupe's assistants and a former Fordham philosophy professor. That Thanksgiving evening, Hennesey received a cable summoning him immediately to Rome. There, at a meeting with Arrupe, Varga, and Michael Walsh, president of the trustees, Hennesey was instructed to tell McLaughlin to resign. Back home, he waited a week, then delivered the message. McLaughlin replied, "Tell him I'll do it, and I'll never tell anyone why."

Shortly afterward, a group of Jesuit and lay trustees met secretly at the Sheraton Hotel at LaGuardia Airport. Walsh, renowned for his political instincts, put the situation simply:

"If a president has lost his constituency, he can't be president."

"Then who will be president?" asked lay trustee Joseph Kaiser. Walsh replied, "I'll sacrifice myself."

Edmund Ryan, S.J., and Victor Yanitelli, S.J., former Fordham vice president for student affairs and now president of St. Peter's College, were delegated to take Leo out to dinner and tell him.

When their car pulled up to the Loyola porch, Leo greeted them, "I know why you're here. Let's go get a good drink and enjoy ourselves."

The official resignation took place at a meeting at *America* magazine on December 14, with the announcement following on December 18. This means that all through the exhausting ordeal of the December demonstrations, the building occupations and Meade's attack, McLaughlin knew that his presidency and his dreams for Fordham were over.

In 1989, Tim Healy, on his way to the directorship of the New York Public Library, gave his own evaluation of these years. "I still regard the loss of Leo McLaughlin as a deadly blow to the university, but I suspect that is not a popular opinion, nor a very general one. It's fascinating that the people who shot him down profited largely from absolutely everything he had done. Here was a man who unfortunately thought ahead of his time, and in those days at Fordham that was an unforgivable sin."

After he left Fordham, Leo saw few of his old friends. An alumnus who visited him at Johnson C. Smith found him distracted and perhaps embarrassed by the visit. He left the Jesuits and married a younger woman, a longtime friend of his family, and moved to New Jersey to teach at Ramapo College of New Jersey. He suffered a series of strokes that impaired his speech over the years, but he returned to Fordham once during the sesquicentennial celebration to appear in solemn academic regalia with the other living ex-presidents. His health deteriorated and his wife died. Alone and with no one to care for him, he was invited by the provincial, Fr. Joseph Parkes, to live at the Murray-Weigel Hall Jesuit infirmary.

I stopped in to see him at Christmas 1995. He looked the same, but there was no telling what was going on inside. We had not seen each other in almost twenty-five years, and I have no idea whether he remembered me or not, but he was very animated and bustled around the room talking unintelligibly, as though in tongues, explaining some new idea.

When he died, I was out of town and didn't learn about the funeral in the University Church until I returned. Some of my alumni friends who came in for the Mass took the presence of so many Jesuit concelebrants at the altar as a sign that wounds had healed. One told me he was never more proud of Fordham than on that day.

14.

The War at Home

"I am a Fordham graduate, class of 1962, and I am proud of it. I am also an American. Of this too I am very proud." In October 1965, Lt. Daniel F. Garde sat in his officers' quarters near Saigon and worked on an unusual letter home. He had heard that college students had been demonstrating against American policy in Vietnam and was appalled. He did not know whether any Fordham students had been involved; he was confident that they would be above this kind of "pseudo-intellectual activity," but just in case, he was sending a long missive to the *Ram* (October 20, 1965) to warn his fellow Fordham men about what was really at stake in this war.

Everything in Garde's education at Brooklyn Prep and Fordham had prepared him for this moment, both as to risking his life and as to explaining his reasons for doing so to his generation. His European-history professor, Jeremiah O'Sullivan, had himself been a paratrooper in World War II and by his example had given his classes a set of values by which they might live. His military enthusiasm made keen by drilling with the Pershing Rifles, Dan arrived at Fort Bragg with his regular-army commission just in time for jump school, became a paratrooper, and was sent right to Vietnam as an adviser to a Vietnamese ranger battalion, which he led on search-and-clear operations.

If the so-called peace demonstrators had read Lenin, Mao-Tse-Tung, Vo Nguyen Gap, and Truang Chin, he wrote, they would know that the word *peace* is not in the communist dictionary. Communism is "like a great strong fire which is spreading all over the world . . . kept alive by terror and violence." He had seen eight Vietnamese children forced to watch as communists tortured their parents to death. A mother of three young girls, aged three, five, and eight, and wife of a Vietnam defector, was awakened by a grenade exploding in her home, only to find her daughters blown into fifteen indistinguishable pieces.

The student demonstrator, he says, is basically selfish; he sits on his "soft, fat duff" enjoying the benefits his ancestors have fought for and unwilling to sacrifice for his own children, the next generation.

He tells his readers that he would like to hear from them. Many do write; they are very appreciative and thank him for helping them to rethink their position.

"I am looking to you both as my President and my Commander in Chief to give me some valid reason why I and other young men in our country should risk our lives in a war we do not understand." In June 1965, Private First Class Armin Merkle was at home in Thornwood, New York, on a family-farewell leave from Fort Riley, Kansas, and he was writing a letter to Lyndon B. Johnson, president of the United States. Twenty-seven years old, he had been thinking this through for years, but now his conscience had been forced by his unit's orders to report to the Pacific theater of operations. He tells the president that he "cannot contemplate being involved in a battle situation when I have no philosophical or moral reason for being there."

At first, Armin and Fordham were not a perfect fit. Armin's parents were German immigrants, and his grandfather, a mayor, had been jailed by the Nazis. Fordham students were conservative Irish Catholics who cheered for William F. Buckley when he debated Catholic Worker socialist Michael Harrington on campus. Most Jesuits were of the same mind; when Armin told Ignatius Cox that he wanted to study abroad, Cox told him that Europe was a hellhole of vice and that he should stay home and marry a nice girl. But Armin did meet teachers who opened him up to the world, such as sociologist John Martin, anthropologist J. Franklin Ewing, and the cerebral Quentin

Lauer, who told his classes that to get an A they had to teach him something he didn't know. Above all, the intellectual humanist Joseph P. Fitzpatrick inspired him to do volunteer work with Hispanic children and helped him to get a job as a social worker. A retreat with Fr. Daniel Berrigan, S.J., was a turning point for Armin as Berrigan, unlike other retreat masters who concentrated on the evils of sex and alcohol, convinced Armin that he could make a difference in the world.

With a double major in sociology and German, during his senior year Armin lived with his sister on Washington Heights overlooking the Hudson River. He biked to class up and down Fordham Road, with his philosophy robe flying in the wind. After graduation, rejecting Cox's admonition, he enrolled in a master's program in history at the University of Munich, hoping that he would also avoid the draft. He left the program in 1963 at the age of twenty-five, however, and his draft board had not forgotten him. Ten days after his letter to President Johnson, Armin received a reply from Lt. Gen. J. L. Richardson, who assured him he was helping to stop communism and "upholding the freedoms enjoyed by our country today." The letter arrived just as Armin was disembarking from his troop ship in Cam Rahn Bay.

The outfit, a 105 mm howitzer battery of the Seventh Artillery Battalion, had a horrible first week. Huddled in foxholes with no sleep, they lost six men to sniper fire, largely due to inexperience. Merkle served on a forward-observer team, then moved out with the infantry on their search-and-destroy missions. He saw a lot of things of which he, as an American, was ashamed. Advisers stood by while South Vietnamese troops tortured their prisoners. One young prisoner was bleeding to death, but the interrogator refused him medical aid unless he talked, and he died. A young Vietnamese boy wandered into their perimeter and was shot dead. The troops slung his corpse across the front of their jeep and took pictures as if they were hunters who had just bagged a deer. Merkle complained to the lieutenant, who replied, "Sometimes, Merkle, you just have to look the other way."

Merkle did not look the other way. When he got out of the service, he toured the Far East and Europe, then joined the Veterans Against the War in Vietnam, speaking and debating at every chance he got. He earned an M.A. in history and taught high school in Pleasantville, New York; in 1997, he joined a group of forty-five American and Vietnamese veterans, former foes, both able-bodied and disabled, on a reconciliation bike ride the whole length of Vietnam. The next year he returned to a Fordham history classroom to show a documentary film of the trip.

II ⌒

When Mike Walsh took over Fordham in January 1969, it looked as if his major challenge was to restore fiscal solvency. As it turned out, in his first year and a half, the major emotional drain became "the war at home."

As a priest and a Jesuit, Walsh could not be silent on the moral issues the war raised. As a university president, he could not allow protests to reduce the campus to chaos. New York Jesuits might refer to him, with admiration, as a "Boston politician," but his staff, such as Academic Vice President Paul Reiss, saw him as a hard-driving, efficient administrator who piled the work on, always very gently, with requests such as "Do you think that maybe you might . . . get this report to me *today?*"

Walsh also dealt differently with the rector of the Jesuit community. Whereas Jim Hennesey had been a frequent visitor in McLaughlin's office in the Administration Building for freewheeling discussions, Walsh controlled his meetings with Hennesey by dropping in on him. Walsh lived in a spartan, virtually empty room in Loyola-Faber Hall. In the social hour before dinner or later at night in the snack room, he would smoke away, holding a cigarette in front of his face as he mumbled inaudible confidences to his Jesuit colleagues, leaving them convinced that he had shared some secret with them but with no idea what he had said.

By academic training, Walsh was a biologist; but he had no hobbies, no interests other than the maneuvers, the planning, and the challenges of the job. As one friend put it, "All Mike needs to be happy is a pack of cigarettes and a lighter that works." In his first faculty convocation, he surprised some who probably expected him to talk about the budget by making it clear he wanted more faculty research. His belief that all the Society needed was one *scholarly* Jesuit in each department was not yet widely known. While the community liked him, he did not hesitate to contradict those he thought were wrong. When a Jesuit at lunch complained that a younger priest who did not usually wear the collar put one on in order to visit radicals who had been thrown in jail, Walsh replied that he wanted more like that younger Jesuit and appointed him to deliver the homily at the Christmas midnight Mass.

The work of straightening out the finances had begun under McLaughlin, who had the faculty budget committee reexamine every line, paring the budget by almost 20 percent. Now, since most of McLaughlin's staff had left for other jobs, Walsh had to build his own team.

He started by naming Joseph Cammarosano, a conservative, tough-minded economist, as executive vice president. Cammarosano had experience as chair of the faculty budget committee and had been on the faculty senate from the very beginning, with a reputation as a loyal troubleshooter. Backing him up was Felix Larkin. A friend of every president since Gannon, Larkin was the chair of W. R. Grace and Company, as well as of the lay-dominated board of trustees. Larkin came to the campus every Saturday for six months to help institute a sophisticated budget system similar to W. R. Grace's.

At budget negotiations, Walsh and Cammarosano would play good cop–bad cop. Joe, laying down the decree that there would be no more electric typewriters and not a nickel for social spending, would take the hard line: sorry, the money just isn't there. Walsh, conciliatory, would come up with something. When I told Walsh I wanted to start a new *Commonweal*-like student opinion magazine called *Point,* Walsh gave me $500. With the help of $1 million of Bundy aid in 1970, the team turned the financial situation around in two years, moving from a $2 million deficit in 1968 to a $2 million surplus in 1970.

Paul Reiss was the troubleshooting dean at Lincoln Center in August 1969, when Arthur Brown, the academic vice president, resigned, and Walsh, in his nice way to which no one said no, asked Reiss to be acting vice president and keep the deanship too. Both Cammarosano and Reiss were devout Catholics utterly devoted to Fordham. Cammarosano was a dynamic teacher and preferred the classroom to administration; Reiss was the kind of man who, had Fordham been ready for a lay president, would have fit that position well.

The Walsh years also brought to maturity a quiet revolution that had begun under O'Keefe. The lay faculty, who a generation before had been looked upon as assistants to the Jesuits, were emerging not only into partnership with the Jesuits but also, both collectively and as individuals, into major roles as university leaders. As the university moved through the 1969–70 academic year from one crisis to the next, nothing was decided, as it might have been years before, by the president simply telling people what to do. When Walsh made a decision, he usually knew that he had a faculty consensus or a formal vote of the faculty senate to back him up.

O'Keefe started the process with his friendly, easygoing personality, remembering names and noticing people on campus. The Jesuit community also opened up a bit and experimented with a program of systematically inviting large groups of faculty to dinner. While O'Keefe was away at the Jesuit general congregation in Rome, Joe Frese, as academic vice president and acting president, removed long-time departmental chairs and brought in a new generation, who took advantage of their direct access to the president by initiating some initiatives toward structural reforms.

Reiss, a sociology chair, had faculty elect the next chair rather than let the dean make the appointment. Roger Wines, as history chair, reduced the teaching load from four courses per semester to three. George McMahon, S.J., college dean, reformed the curriculum with the faculty's cooperation, installing a four-four plan, with four four-credit courses per semester. Ideally, though the student would be taking one less course per semester, the courses were supposed to be much more demanding, with more books, papers, research projects, and library time assigned, leading to deeper, less superficial education. Some teachers did beef up their courses; some taught the same old surveys.

III —

The events of November 1969 had been in the making since the previous spring. In April, an SDS-led demonstration had forced army, navy, and marine recruiters out of the old chemistry building. A week later, the demonstrators occupied the south wing of the Administration Building; they sat down, filling the corridor leading to Walsh's office. Novelist Norman Mailer was on campus with Jimmy Breslin, campaigning to become mayor and city council president of New York City. Mailer pushed his way inside, stood on a desk, told the students he was on their side, and left. Later that night, 150 boarders marched on the building with the intent of throwing the invaders out, but security guards turned them back. Walsh, backed by a faculty majority, got a court injunction to remove them.

On October 15, 7,500 students and Bronx residents climaxed the daylong Vietnam Moratorium against the War with a candlelight ceremony on Edwards Parade. The event had featured speeches by Senators Charles Goodel and Jacob Javitts, Mayor John Lindsay, Allard Lowenstein, and David Halberstam. Walsh, who had begun the day with a Mass for peace, joined seventy-six other college presidents in a statement charging that "our military engagement now stands as a denial of so much that is best in our society." During the day, students and faculty, including Quentin Lauer, who also knelt on the steps of Cardinal Cooke's New York residence to protest the cardinal's silence on the war, stood on the Grand Concourse and solemnly intoned the names of the Vietnam War dead.

On Wednesday afternoon, November 12, about seventy students stood on the steps of Keating Hall getting revved up for their next move. A large crowd blocking the building had aborted their takeover of the ROTC offices in Belmont (Faculty Memorial Hall) a few hours before. They had said at an open meeting a week before that they were going to take the Administration Building. For some reason, however, as they streamed down the Keating steps and across Edwards Parade, crashed through the old mansion's glass doors and through the wooden doors into Walsh's office, they came as a surprise. Walsh, Cammarosano, and Meade had been meeting inside.

"Get out of here," the invaders said, and the administrators withdrew to the north wing while the demonstrators barricaded themselves in the secretarial pool and corridor of the south wing.

For the next seven hours, crowds of both sympathizers and anti-SDS students surrounded the old building, some coming and going through side windows. The New York City police mixed incognito with the crowd and waited in uniform outside the gates to be called in. Walsh's advisory committee met in the north wing, going through the formal procedures established the year before; the occupiers in the south wing debated whether they should leave peacefully or wait for the police to drive them out.

Three student leaders from Walsh's advisory committee crawled in a window to inform the demonstrators that the committee had voted 6-5 to call in the police if the security guards failed to expel them, adding that, of course, the five students had voted to let them stay overnight.

At 7:30 P.M., Meade announced over his megaphone that those who left now would be charged with illegal entry in a university court; those who remained would have to face the police. Eight came out. He repeated his warnings at 8:30 and 9:30. The IBI (security) guards put their shoulders to the wing's wooden doors. The students inside threw water on them and fought them with sticks. Paul Reiss watched a guard wedge an iron bar between the door and the frame between the hallway and the president's office and told himself this was terrible. He wondered what had happened to American higher education if it had come to this.

At the sight of an injured guard, Meade called the police and ordered, "Nobody gets out. Seal the building." Knowing that the police were on the way, students poured out the windows, grappled and fought with guards who tried to arrest them, and turned a security vehicle upside down. When six students were arrested, demonstrators yelled, "Off the pigs," and demanded that charges be dropped.

As the *Ram* editorialized, "The inability of the Fordham University community to reason together and accept the decisions that will better serve those interests is incomprehensible" (November 13, 1969).

In the months that followed, groups offered various reasons as to why charges against the arrested students should be dropped. It was suggested, for example, that the administration had escalated the violence by sending the guards to break down the door; nonradical participants didn't realize the seriousness of their acts; Walsh, as a Jesuit priest, should show mercy. Black students charged that it was a racist plot of the guards to pick on a black participant, and they threatened reprisals if his charges were not dropped (*Ram*, November 12, 1969). Three weeks later, reflecting on these events, Walsh told the *Ram* (December 21, 1969) that he had two regrets: He wished that he had sent a few more people in to talk to the protesters, but he had been talked out of it; he also thought he should have called the police earlier and not used the guards.

It was Wednesday, March 11, before the arrested students, now known as the Fordham Five, finally came to trial at the Bronx County Courthouse on the charge of criminal trespass. They dismissed their attorney, Lou Steele. They were determined to defend themselves and to make it a political trial, shifting the issue from trespassing to the immorality of the Vietnam War and ROTC.

The prosecutor was Bronx district attorney Burton Roberts, a widely respected, hardworking prosecutor also known for his theatrical style, quivering voice, and ruddy face when he got excited. With two hundred spectators already in the room, the defendants asked that the doors be opened so more could come in. When Roberts answered, "No one outside wants to hear you," the spectators chanted, "Bullshit, bullshit."

As the trial progressed, the defendants relished the opportunity to cross-examine the administrators on the stand, from Meade to Walsh, as to how they had made their decisions on November 12. Pressed as to why he had evicted the protesters, Walsh replied simply, "They didn't belong there." All five were convicted on April 9 and received suspended sentences in May.

IV ⟿

While the trial was going on, another controversy was simmering. It was very different in that it had nothing to do with American foreign policy, but in the long run, it was crucial to Fordham because it raised deeper academic issues—about what good teaching is, about the fairness of faculty evaluation by students and faculty peers, and about the role the larger community should have in faculty decisions.

It concerned a tenure case. The English department had denied tenure to Prof. Ronald Friedland, a young, bearded, provocative teacher who had a way of getting students excited about literature. Friedland had not published much in the way of scholarly articles, though he had written a novel about teaching called *Bringing It All Back Home,* and he was generous in directing honors theses and in giving student tutorials. A visitor to the English department on almost any afternoon would discover a line of students outside Friedland's office, waiting for his advice. Not everyone loved him. Some found his criticisms sarcastic, biting, and arrogant, but others, particularly United Student Government vice president Robert Reger, did not care that much about scholarly articles if the teacher taught well.

To Reger, a tall, dignified, smart, buttoned-down young man without a radical pencil in his book bag, the tenure decision constituted a case of injustice to one man. On a larger scale, however, it was a test case as to how much say students should have in departmental decisions. On March 16, four hundred students filed into the English department and presented a petition with 850 signatures and 248 personal letters demanding a reversal of the Friedland denial. Students also submitted a petition of 200 signatures for Dr. Anne Trensky, wife of Russian professor Paul Trensky, whose contract had not been renewed. Prof. Joseph Grennan, English chair, responded by announcing a public meeting in the ballroom and a session between tenured faculty and six students to talk things out. But he canceled the open meeting at faculty request, and at the small meeting the faculty, according to a participant, "just nodded."

Throughout these steps, Reger was undergoing a turning point in his life. Essentially a conservative person accustomed to trusting authority, he found as he went from one authority to the next that no one could offer a satisfactory answer to his question: Why had Friedland been denied tenure? He had already gained assurances from Friedland that there were no skeletons in his closet. He was told that the "real reason" was that Friedland was teaching an evening course at Lehman College, but Reger already knew that many faculty were teaching part-time at other schools without Fordham's objecting. Maybe Friedland's being a Jew in a predominantly Catholic department was a factor, but no evidence supported that theory.

Reger decided to do the one thing that gets administrators' attention—take a building. At 11:00 Sunday night, April 12, Reger wore his hallmark three-piece suit and striped tie, as he and 250 followers peacefully broke a window in the president's office and filed into the Administration Building. Remembering the mess the SDS had left in November, Reger ordered his troops, "Don't take anything, don't break anything. Don't give them the opportunity to say it was cleaned out by students."

For Reger, the central issue was Friedland's tenure. According to Friedland, his own tenure didn't matter. He told the *Ram* (April 14, 1970) that the issue was the students' voice in decisions that affected their education. He went on to attack unnamed colleagues in the department as liars and hypocrites whose "contempt for the students" was a "result of self-contempt." This theme returned later at a general faculty meeting when a senior department member stood up and, having asked Friedland's permission to explain why he had not been granted tenure, laid out the norms and the department's needs, and added that Friedland had shown contempt for the department. This meant, in context, his disdain for their scholarship, those erudite research essays that protocol demands, but that, allegedly, no one reads.

The building occupation lasted for two days. The four hundred students now involved posted an Under New Management sign on the door, informed Walsh that he had been "fired," and took over the switchboard, answering the phone with, "Liberated Fordham." A caller asking for Fr. Cammarosano was told, "Dr. Who? I'm sorry, he no longer works here."

New York TV networks showed up to interview the totally non-violent Reger, who came across as a polite but steel-spined Wall Street lawyer. Since the issue was tenure and because the occupying students were not radicals but the true leadership of the students, from SDS to YAF (Young Americans for Freedom), Walsh knew that this situation could not be handled in the same way as the November battle. He offered a committee of three students, three faculty chosen by the faculty senate executive committee, and one administrator, appointed by himself, to review the case.

That evening Reger presented Walsh's proposal to a general meeting that went for hours in Walsh's own office, now the headquarters of the occupying army. Somehow the office held an estimated two hundred people, including the SDS and their powerful personalities, which on principle were anti any kind of compromise. Reger knew that Walsh had gone way out on a limb to make the compromise, and he asked the crowd to take it. But this was a "democracy," which meant that everyone in the room could vote, although those who voted were not necessarily the same ones who had been there at the beginning of the meeting. The Walsh offer lost by two votes.

Faced with an injunction, the students decided to leave. A girl polished Reiss's secretary's desk with Pledge, saying, "This place isn't that much of a mess, but they're going to try to get us on anything they can."

As the four hundred occupants filed out and handed their IDs to Marty Meade, they declared the university on strike. FORDHAM ON STRIKE signs, with a raised fist printed in red, went up on the trees around Edwards Parade. Sympathetic faculty were invited to offer their classes in the "Free University" space in the Campus Center rather than in their classrooms. As far as Walsh was concerned, since the students had rejected his compromise, the Friedland case was "finished," but to a cross section of students and faculty, including administrators and Jesuits, the other issues of participation and communication were still very much alive.

The next several days were a steady round of rallys and student-faculty discussions, with classes canceled on April 22 so that everyone could get involved. There was also another antiwar rally, a spring festival, and an ecology day.

The strike ended as a "resounding success," according to the Ram, because at last it got people at Fordham "to talk to each other frankly and honestly." The main instrument of the new communication would be the Rose Hill Campus Council, made up of twenty-one faculty, sixteen students, and ten administrators, to "develop educational policies" and foster communication on the Bronx campus. The most lasting impact of those weeks, for those who took part, was the discovery of a "concerned" community of faculty and students who respected one another and were glad to labor through hard days and sleepless nights to make a few inches of progress toward mutual understanding.

In early April, a Ram reporter made an unscientific survey to determine the ten most influential people on campus and came up with this list.

1. Fr. Walsh

2. Robert Reger

3. Fr. Joseph Fitzpatrick

4. Roger Wines, a history professor who had served on virtually every "riot" committee and participated in all the deliberations

5. Bill Toppeta, USG president and student spokesman

6. Dr. Joe Cammarosano

7. Bill Arnone, spokesman for the student left

8. Robert Himmelberg, history chair and Handbook Committee chair

9. Marty Meade

10. Fr. George McMahon, college dean, who had credibility with students and faculty alike.

Thirty years later, it is interesting to observe how well the list has held up. Meade, worn down, soon left for a dean of students position at Ottawa University; the faculty on the list stayed at Fordham and continued to grow in stature over the years. Arnone was an articulate advocate in regular *Ram* columns; he admitted (*Ram,* April 17, 1970) that in rifling through Walsh's files during the "peaceful" building occupation, he had found a "form letter" Walsh might use in sending a note of condolence. For Arnone, this proved Walsh a "villain" with a perspective "no wider than a dollar bill." In no way would Reger endorse that judgment.

V ⚊

Peace did not last long. On April 30, President Nixon, having watched the movie *Patton* again to steel his nerves, ordered the invasion of Cambodia and defended his decision in a belligerent TV address to the nation. Campuses across the country erupted in protest. At Kent State, in Ohio, students flung bottles at police cars and burned down the ROTC building. On May 4, some in a crowd of five hundred protesters threw rocks at National Guardsmen, whom the governor had sent in to restore order. Some guardsmen opened fire, killing four students, none of them radicals, and wounding nine. The news inspired angry demonstrations at over 350 campuses, involving 2 million students, or 25 percent of the students in the country. More than seventy-five campuses closed for the rest of the year.

On May 7, I returned to my room after a long discussion with students following my nightly midnight Mass in the Thomas More Chapel beneath the University Church. Some Fordham students had turned their last-minute term papers into passionate cries of alienation, and others had gone home for the study days before exams. A wild fringe group of SDS who called themselves "Ryppies" had burned a flag and thrown rocks through windows. At an SDS meeting a week before, I had heard one of them say, "The only way to get attention here is to burn a building."

Suddenly my dark room was illuminated by the glow of a red light throbbing like a telltale heart in the night. I looked out the window and saw that the Campus Center was on fire. Firemen with hoses hustled through the luminous smoke that billowed out the back and through the front doors. The fire, set by what the *Ram* termed an "unbalanced person," burned for four and a half hours. On Friday, the faculty met to debate what to do about exams. Cancel them? Close the university and go home? Give them on a pass/fail basis? Make exams optional? Faculty who had given tests and papers all semester were prepared to evaluate students without a final; those who based everything on the final exam had nothing to work with. Rather than close down, Fordham more or less staggered through to the end of the term with students and faculty using a variety of means to come up with final grades. It was an ignominious end to a year that had inflicted many wounds, but it left scars that symbolized the strength of hard-won maturity.

It rained that year at graduation, forcing the ceremony into the overcrowded old gym. Cammarosano, always ready for trouble, had the 52nd Police Precinct station a contingent in the locker room downstairs, ready to sweep out onto the floor if a riot broke out. Nothing happened. The speaker, Daniel Patrick Moynihan, lamented the "breakdown of trust" that had come to characterize the relationship between the government and the people.

VI

Mike Walsh stayed another two years, consolidating McLaughlin's gains without shifting basic direction. The Schweitzer Chair returned and Bundy money was approved. The Friedland case and several others taught Reiss that Fordham lacked strong and clear tenure procedures other than the norms established by the AAUP. He set to work developing procedures based on the AAUP norms, but adapted them to Fordham's situation, so that a faculty handbook committee could submit them to the faculty senate. Some Friday nights, the senate would begin deliberations at 7:00 and not end until 1:00 A.M.

This coincided with what Cammarosano considered, along with the fiscal crisis and student uprisings, to be one of the three great challenges of his time: a 1971 move within the faculty to unionize. The administration and its faculty supporters opposed unionization for a variety of reasons. Teachers who saw the university as modeled on a community could not imagine themselves depriving students of classes by going on strike, and those who considered themselves superior teachers and scholars wanted salary increments to be determined by merit, not by union negotiators across the board. At the beginning, however, a strong majority favored the union. They had been angered by what they considered the administration's softness toward student demonstrators and the exaggerated authority that McLaughlin had given to student leaders. He had backed the idea of a university senate, a governing body that would include student representatives and undermine the authority of the faculty senate.

To Walsh and his advisers, Fordham's identity was at stake. So Walsh systematically invited key faculty members to small group sessions with himself in which he painstakingly and quietly laid out his position: because the faculty, through the senate, committees, and departmental meetings were already so intimately involved in governance, a separate collective-bargaining agent, according to the norms of the NRLB, was neither necessary nor appropriate.

The union was narrowly defeated by fourteen votes. In a second attempt in 1975 after the University Statutes had been implemented, the proposed union, the AAUP, was defeated by a 3-2 margin.

Ron Friedland's novel was published, as with many first novels, to little notice. It was about a white English professor teaching at a black college who lost his job and was considered a racist because he demanded quality work from his students. Like most first novels, it was autobiographical, based on Friedland's experience at a black college before coming to Fordham. Friedland died shortly afterward and Bob Reger attended his memorial service.

A decade after the "revolution," an article in *Point* (February 1980) asked, "Where Have All the Radicals Gone?" One of the Fordham Five, Leo Parascondola, was a bus driver and still politically active. He had just protested the arrival of the shah of Iran for medical treatment in the United States. He would consider it "repugnant to give money to Fordham." Reger, a graduate of the University of Virginia Law School, was at the Wall Street firm of Reid and Priest, backing George Bush in the 1980 race. He was still dedicated to Fordham.

VII ⌐

The Walsh years included one more drama, a relatively minor one on the scale including the Vietnam War and the burning of the Campus Center, but unforgettable to those who always believed that Fordham would be "great" when it had a "great" football or basketball team.

Part of the excitement of 1968 was about the return of Ed Conlin, '55, Fordham's greatest basketball player, who had spent seven years in the NBA and had a successful career selling insurance. He arrived as assistant to Johnny Bach in 1967–68, and later replaced him. Bach, who had coached Conlin, had been at Fordham for eighteen years serving as athletic director before leaving Fordham for Penn State. This cleared the way for the arrival of Peter J. Carlesimo, class of '40, who had played football in the Crowley years.

A rotund Scrantonian of medium height, Carlesimo enjoyed a reputation as a roll-'em-in-the-aisles after-dinner speaker on the sports circuit. He recycled his stories, changing the names so that even those who had heard his basic pitch several times could still muster a smile. When a *Ram* interviewer, Michael Burke (March 13, 1970), asked him about his philosophy of sports, he began his reply with the familiar idea that they enhanced "traditional values" by student participation in intramurals. Then he said what he really thought. "Sports, more than anything else, draw the alumni back to Fordham." The formula was that Fordham's name in the papers plus winning teams draw in alumni money and "their sons and the sons of their friends."

Concluding that to Carlesimo sports was mainly a business, Burke posed some of the same questions to Conlin in his office in the gym basement, as Conlin, who looked straight at him, puffed on a cigar but was careful to keep the smoke out of the reporter's eyes.

Fordham was adding Notre Dame and Marquette to the schedule; this would help recruiting, Conlin said, but recruiting took time and money. Yes, Conlin knew that his 1969–70 10-15 record—following his 1968–69 19-8 record, with a loss to Louisville in the NIT—had been a bad year. He welcomed the boos at the games, he said, as they were much better than apathy. "I just have to be patient."

Burke left Conlin's office liking him a lot, saying that "if he had been selling me insurance, I would have bought a million dollars' worth." Conlin must have known during the interview that Carlesimo was not willing to "be patient" and that he was on his way back to his insurance career, where, in Carlesimo's opinion, he was already spending too much time.

A few days latter, the athletic governing board discussed Conlin's situation for four and a half hours. Three weeks after that, Carlesimo called a press conference at Lincoln Center to announce that University of Pennsylvania assistant coach Dick Phelps—also known as Digger, because his father was an undertaker—had signed a four-year contract. The popular radio comedy mortician Digger O'Dell on *The Great Gildersleeve* had the laugh line, "I'll never let you down." Phelps, a twenty-eight-year-old graduate of Rider College in Trenton with a strong reputation as a recruiter, said he was going to "sell New York for what it is—the greatest city in the nation."

For many, the 1970–71 basketball season was one of those brief shining moments in which a community that had undergone some pain and suffering gets to come together and feel good about itself again. Those in the Jesuit community who felt that Fordham had sold its soul three years previously were reassured to see the whole basketball team, under Phelps's direction, file into the Loyola Hall Jesuit community chapel to huddle solemnly around the altar for a private Mass before every game. Phelps built a personal following among alumni by talking about morality in his pep talks and lectures. A Catholic coach seemed to be restoring the identity a Jesuit president had given away.

Using players whom Conlin had recruited—Charlie Yelverton, Bill Mainor, Ken Charles, Tom Sullivan, and John Burik—Phelps did give the alumni something to talk about, a winning 26-3 season, sold-out crowds for Notre Dame and Marquette games at Madison Square Garden, and a postseason appearance in the NCAA tournament. He was a hot coach and team for the New York press to write about, and Fordham was back in 1937.

Then Fordham saw the other side of Digger Phelps. He had signed a four-year contract, but in his first year, Walsh soon picked up rumors that he had been looking around. The *Ram* pursued reports of his negotiations with other schools. Walsh gave Phelps a $3,000 bonus for getting Fordham into the second round of the NCAA. Today, the practice of breaking a contract to take a better offer has become more common, but in a 1970 Fordham it was a violation of integrity that turned the community sour.

The day the *Ram* printed a scathing editorial on Phelps's quitting Fordham to go to Notre Dame, I, who had once said Mass for the team, met him when he was leaving Walsh's office and I was going in. "They don't understand, Father," he said. "This is something that I've wanted all my life."

15.

The Bronx Is Burning

Dawn Cardi, TMC, '73, is a Manhattan criminal lawyer. When we spoke in November 1999, she had just finished setting up a witness-protection program not just for a witness but for his whole family. She lives happily with her second husband and their two sons and daughter in Riverdale, a few miles and thirty years—though emotionally a split second—from the Fordham campus, where, as a graduate of Mary Louis Academy in Queens, she arrived at Thomas More College in 1969.

Dawn's parents were seventeen and fifteen when they were married, and her father was one of those fathers who did not believe girls should be educated. So from the beginning, Dawn was on her own, working three jobs to put herself through.

She was also part of a "wild" generation of women, including some who went to Fordham, who were just starting to throw off all the rules. The fifty girls in Spellman Hall, a former Jesuit house of studies designated as a woman's dorm, had just voted out all restrictions, and about a dozen of them, including Dawn, moved their boyfriends in to live with them. Dawn and Greg, who was two years ahead of her, married in her sophomore year, and they moved off campus to an apartment on Bainbridge Avenue, between 194th and 195th Streets.

Dawn's was not the ordinary Fordham experience.

But the extraordinary part was not so much her marriage, which like the marriages of many of her contemporaries, ended within a few years, but that several faculty, such as Jesuit classicists Richard Doyle and William Grimaldi, knowing that she was poor, gave her money for food and books. Most memorable was her English teacher, Claire Hahn, a brilliant, beautiful, exuberant Dominican nun in secular clothes, who carried herself so erect that students thought she was six foot two and who talked of the poet Yeats with such familiar authority that they were convinced she knew him personally. Hahn, who referred to her students affectionately as "kids," never sat down in class but strode back and forth reciting from memory and acting out parts in Chaucer's poems or reciting Yeats in a melodious voice that evoked the music in the verse.

One sophomore, Joe Ross, who did not take naturally to Middle English, cringed on the first day when Hahn urged them to read Chaucer "in the original," but he resisted the instinctive urge to drop the course. He never quite met Hahn's standards—"Joooooooe," she would coo, "don't tell me the story . . . analyze the text"—but he took her again the next semester for *The Canterbury Tales*. One day, their noses in the text probing for "hidden meanings" in "some lady in black character," no one in Joe's class seemed to notice that Hahn was "all decked out in black." Later that day, a student came upon her sitting despondently in the cafeteria. "No one noticed," she said. She had come to class dressed as the character, and no one noticed.

Through and with Claire Hahn, Dawn came to notice a world much bigger than either her home or her classroom. Both taught at the new experimental college, Malcolm-King, sponsored by Fordham, Marymount Manhattan, and Mount St. Vincent's. It was a free (up to thirty credits) feeder college for adult Harlemites who might otherwise never have finished high school or dreamed of a college education. Hahn was one of those who helped Dawn financially, and Dawn was tutoring as a way of "giving back."

On a fall afternoon in 1970, Claire stopped by my room in A house, ecstatic with some news. She was in love. She was to leave the Dominicans and be married at Thanksgiving to Jack Becker, a Jesuit from Kansas City, who was leaving the Society. I did not learn until later the years of emotional and spiritual turmoil that had preceded this moment.

They had met when he was a Ph.D. student at Yale, living in a small Jesuit community across from the Dominican Albertus Magnus College in New Haven, where she, a Fordham Ph.D., was teaching in 1963. He said Mass at their convent, making quite an impression with his "new theology" interpretations of the Scripture, and she began coming to him for spiritual direction.

Over the next several years, both had a series of emotional upheavals, traceable perhaps to both their personal histories and to the controlled passion of their relationship within the bounds of their religious commitments. Jack and Claire clung to one another as religious superiors, for various reasons, stationed them in different parts of the country. All the while, they were determined that they would remain in religious life, and they made a "no touching" rule to protect their vows. Finally, one of Jack's Jesuit friends advised him to leave and marry Claire.

I knew that Claire was apprehensive because she was coming up for tenure and feared that the "scandal" of an ex-nun marrying an ex-priest might enter the deliberations. I did not know, as she shared her joy, that she had been diagnosed with the breast cancer that had claimed her mother's life.

To her students, Claire's married life was a window into the new world of the intellectual salon, which offered delights they had never tasted. Jack taught American literature at Fairleigh Dickinson in New Jersey, and literature filled their evenings as well. At their Riverdale apartment, Dawn met the shy, beloved Erwin Geissman and the exotic Marguerite Young, a creative writing teacher and author of reputedly the longest novel in the English language, *Miss MacIntosh, My Darling.* Young swept across the Fordham campus in her long black cape and puffed incessantly on cigarettes at parties.

As news of Claire's illness spread, students signed up for her classes expecting to face a teacher about to die, but found her very much alive. I was book editor of *Commonweal* during the 1970s and brought her on board as a regular poetry reviewer. In her feature article on the relationship between culture and belief, she wrote, "Perhaps if we look steadily enough at this emerging face of contemporary man we can learn to love and compassionate his image and hear the Word spoken in time" (November 15, 1974).

Any good teacher also teaches students how to live, and as her illness progressed, Claire became more outspoken in sharing her life and attitudes with students. Reports that she told students that "Chaste makes waste" and that she wanted her Mass card at her death to depict her with a lifted middle finger as a final "F—— you" message to death offended some, but few knew how much these expressions emerged from a life of sexual self-denial and a defiance of the death that the herald of cancer often announces.

In 1975, I visited Claire in New York Hospital, feeling worn down myself over my own battle for tenure. She had some tubes in her, and her bed, one of six in the room, was nearest the door. Her cancer was inoperable, but she was hoping for a remission; she was determined to return to the classroom in January. She told me that her suffering had renewed her faith and liberated her from the pain of her earlier life experiences. I kissed her, thinking I would never see her again, but knowing that she had liberated me, at least for a while, from some less important suffering of my own.

She lived to teach three more years, to go on writing, to encourage other writers, and to win promotion. That meant a lot to her even when she could hardly pull herself along the hall. For the first time in her life, she had to teach sitting down. She told her class, "I'm not as much fun as I used to be." But she was wrong. She was, as one student said, "Like a basket of loaves and fishes that never emptied once you started giving it away." One day when she was talking to a friend, Professor Mark Caldwell, a student who had undergone a religious conversion dropped by and enthusiastically promised Claire that she could be cured if she would only announce that she was in the hands of God. Claire smiled and said that the announcement would be superfluous. She was already in the hands of God, and both she and God knew it.

II —

James C. Finlay, forty-nine years old, didn't want to be president of Fordham, as he had said many times. A Regis graduate, he had gone to Fordham for two years before entering the Jesuits. He knew that he had been an effective graduate dean and had administrative skills, but fundamentally, he wanted to teach.

As for becoming president, he almost got his wish.

When Mike Walsh took board chair Felix Larkin aside in 1971 and told him that he wasn't feeling well, that he had a heart condition and wanted to return to Boston, Larkin was determined that the new president, the first chosen by an independent board, should be a Jesuit. So he named himself chair of the search committee, polled the other Jesuit presidents for suggestions, and whittled down seventy-two names to a short list that included the former provincial, Robert Mitchell; Thomas Fitzgerald, vice president of Georgetown; Donald Monan, dean of LeMoyne College; and Finlay, who had told Larkin several times he was not interested.

Mitchell was removed from the list early by intervention from a group within the Jesuit community that resented a number of Mitchell's provincial decisions—known as the Demong Drive decisions, named for the Syracuse address where they were made—to close or downgrade several province schools. They said they wanted a candidate from "inside Fordham."

The race came down to Finlay and Monan, both of whom said they did not seek the job. They both gave such impressive, well-prepared presentations that the board could not make up its mind. Finlay said he would have three goals: to mend relations with alienated alumni, to reemphasize Fordham's Catholic identity, and to identify Fordham more closely with its neighbors in the Bronx. One of Monan's strengths was as a planner, as he had an ability to think ahead and build for the future; he thought Fordham had not done enough with its Lincoln Center campus, and there is a possibility that, had he become president, the "real" Fordham would have shifted downtown.

The board went through six votes, unable to reach a two-thirds majority, with several members, including Walsh, switching their preferences back and forth. When they finally settled, Finlay was not hanging by the phone but in the hospital visiting his secretary, who was ill. Father Mitchell eventually became president of the University of Detroit and LeMoyne; Fr. Fitzgerald became president of Fairfield and St. Louis University; and Mike Walsh found in Monan a new president for Boston College.

When Finlay left office in 1984, a writer for *Fordham* magazine predicted that a future historian would judge his years as "steady, calm, and
productive." They were calm compared to 1970, but they were years of
cultural and social upheaval that carried their own share of stress.

While Walsh was content to talk work all the time, Finlay, who
had other interests—such as his love of his native Ireland, golf, reading, and long drives and evening walks with Jesuit friends—guarded
zones of work-free privacy in the Jesuit community or at Mitchell
Farm. In style and philosophy he was conservative, but not ideological;
in appearance, like McGinley, dignified and gentle, with prematurely
silver hair and a pleasant, unlined face that projected kindness and
integrity. His secretary, Stella Moundas, who served and revered three
presidents, recalls that on Walsh's last day in office she and Fr. Walsh
embraced and wept, and Finlay came in and found them in tears.
Because of his even disposition, Finlay was the easiest to work for. It
was a trait that he would need, especially in his many frustrated efforts
to get the Bronx neighbors to work together for their common good.

III ⌐

"I used to say I would never come back to this place. I used to say that
no matter how rich I became, I would never give Fordham a penny,
and for twenty years I never did." Robert Daley, journalist, novelist,
and crime writer, class of '51, spent nine years at Fordham, including
the prep and a year of graduate school, and like many in his generation, hated it. His feelings are strikingly similar to those of Robert
Gould Shaw a century before; his problem was the Jesuits and their
rules. His article, written twenty years after he graduated, "Fordham
Now: The Shock of Nonrecognition" in *New York* (May 31, 1971) is a
fair gauge of the campus when Finlay took charge. It is highly proba-
ble that Finlay read it as he prepared his presentation for the trustees.

"In my day the Jesuits controlled everything, even our thoughts,"
says Daley. He had some of those bad incidents that embitter someone for life. When a security guard gave Daley a beating, two black
eyes, and a torn philosophy robe for a traffic violation, and Daley
complained to McGinley, demanding justice, the president, he says,

told him to keep his mouth shut if he wanted to graduate. He remembered the president as a tyrant and could remember only four teachers who communicated any love of their subjects.

But on his return visit he was stunned to find his own books in the Duane Library, including *A Priest and a Girl,* a novel about a Fordham boy who becomes a priest and leaves to marry. The uncensored *Ram* had printed an article on the ambivalence of the Mass of the Holy Spirit, "the Ghost of Fordham past," with twenty-five Jesuit concelebrants "in full battle array," "a contradiction that underscored the confused state of Fordham . . . falling all over itself in urgency to junk the old, to rely on feelings and emotion, to start from scratch." It was written by Barbara Gibbs, who was, at the time, a nun, but who later left and married a fellow student journalist.

At the *Ram* office, where both Daley and his father, Arthur Daley, legendary sports columnist for the *New York Times,* had written the column "Looking 'Em Over," young Daley found that the current columnist had never heard of him. In the 1950s, everyone knew the biographies of their predecessors.

Enormous oil portraits of Cardinal Spellman and Fr. Gannon grace the *Ram* office walls, but they are jokes. The editors don't even know that Gannon was once Fordham's president. Says one, "He's the guy who goes around giving holy rosary speeches. They should shut that guy up. He's not what they want connected with Fordham."

Daley had dinner with editor Jim Knickman and a group of students in Knickman's Decatur Avenue apartment. A junior told Daley she knew four girls who had been raped in the neighborhood. Daley had spent much of the day listening to his old Latin teacher, Dr. James Brady, who still remembered where Robert sat in the classroom, and then to George McMahon, Elbert Rushmore, and Mike Walsh. To his astonishment, he found them to be wise, tolerant, and understanding priests who knew they could not turn back the clock and that, in this generation, religion could not be forced. They could only do their best to create an atmosphere, a community, where students would at least learn to think about God.

Daley felt as if a hundred, rather than twenty, years had passed as he sipped scotch with Knickman: "I wish I could have attended his Fordham instead of mine."

The elder Daley had resolved he would never contribute to Fordham because it was "no longer Catholic." The son had not given because religion had alienated him; now he was coming back, if not to the religion, then at least to the school.

IV ⟋

Many of Finlay's accomplishments were in the day-to-day maintenance, belt tightening, and prudent development that held an institution together. Others were in facing problems of personnel and governance, such as the growing role of women faculty and the administration of tenure policies in hard cases, which build up until they surface in controversy. The Friedland case had begun to educate students, most of whom had little idea of what tenure was or why it was necessary, to the notion that tenure decisions affected their educations; meanwhile the administration and faculty were challenged to achieve both the appearance and the reality of justice in personnel decisions.

Other problems surged up from cultural situations, such as attitudes toward sex, drugs, and violence. Students brought these with them from high school and the student-affairs staff had to train RAs and win the trust of the student leadership to deal with them. On all these issues, students expected to have a say, and during these years it happened that the student press—the *Ram,* the newly founded *the paper,* and the new opinion magazine *Point*—had exceptional staff members, many of whom went on to win awards and become reporters and editors at the best publications in the country. As with the original *Ram* staff, many who didn't become journalists became lawyers; a few became both.

On the president's administrative staff, Paul Reiss became executive vice president in 1975, and historian Joseph F. X. McCarthy, from the school of education, became academic vice president in 1976. Philosopher Robert Roth became college dean in 1974. He initiated the Values Program as a way to reemphasize the college's commitment to moral education and, in a sense, to offset the alleged "secularization" of the years before. Roth also put in motion a much-needed curriculum revision, wherein the student took five three-credit courses rather than the four-four in the first two years of "core" work. His successor, Jim Loughran, finished the job and put the curriculum into effect.

In the early 1970s, under dean George Shea, the new identity of the liberal-arts college at Lincoln Center took form. In 1973, although the campus had a capacity for 2,000 students, enrollment was down to 970. Shea responded on two fronts. He introduced a new curriculum and reorganized the school into four interdepartmental divisions: the arts, science and mathematics, social sciences, and the humanities. Then he developed more programs to attract older students, expanding the EXCEL program aimed at people over twenty-five working in the business world, and College at Sixty, which attracted students aged fifty-eight to eighty-three. By the end of the decade it was clear that for stability and community it needed, Lincoln Center also had to build a dorm.

In 1975, Finlay appointed Vincent Novak, S.J., as dean of the new Graduate School of Religion and Religious Education. He transformed what had been a graduate program in religious education in the School of Adult Education into a thriving Rose Hill M.A. In 1976, Fordham opened a new campus for graduate courses at Marymount College in Tarrytown, and on the Bronx campus, built the $5 million Vincent T. Lombardi Memorial Center, with a new pool, indoor track, tennis and basketball courts, and weight rooms, all intended for student and faculty use, not for the varsity teams.

In a 1975 interview, at a time when other Jesuits were learning not to ask a female student to sew on buttons for them and were wondering whether it was right or wrong to hold a door for a female, Finlay said he had been "incensed when he came to realize the obstacles that women were facing." He thought that Fordham had to emphasize the importance of providing career opportunities for women. In 1970, 21 percent of the university's full-time faculty were women, about the same as the national percentage among faculty, but partly because of the still-large Jesuit faculty, women were only 12 percent of the Fordham College–Thomas More faculty group.

When psychology professor Anne Anastasi came to Fordham from Queens College in 1947, there were only three other women on the Rose Hill faculty—Elizabeth Salmon in philosophy, Dorothea

McCarthy in psychology, and Ruth Witkus in biology. As department chair (1966–74) Anastasi unified the department, dealt with student activists by talking to them as if they were rational adults, and helped poorly prepared minority students by tutoring rather than by lowering standards. When a black Ph.D. candidate told Anastasi that keeping standards high helped him believe in himself, she concluded that that was what made a lifetime of teaching worthwhile. By the time she reached emeritus status in 1979, she was one of the most distinguished Fordham professors, a veteran of the faculty senate and many committees, and author of three influential textbooks—*Differential Psychology, Fields of Applied Psychology,* and *Psychological Testing*—which had gone through many editions.

But Anastasi's career is atypical of the experience of most Fordham women, partly because the major influx of women faculty did not begin until the 1970s; 80 percent of the women faculty in 1981 had joined within the previous ten years. In 1981, the percentage of women on Rose Hill rose to 16.5 percent; and according to extensive *Ram* interviews in 1978 and 1981, after Fordham had hired a full-time affirmative-action coordinator, most women felt at home. Nevertheless, a good number were sensitive to subtle signs of discrimination (one mentioned the lack of a Kotex machine in the ladies room), were strongly critical of the absence of women in high administrative positions, and were sensitive to real and perceived salary inequities. Finally, they were insecure about tenure at a time when the faculty was shrinking, and with a newly imposed tenure quota, tenure for everyone was harder to get.

Ram surveys documented the rise in drug use and the progress of the sexual revolution and for several years printed the text of a Planned Parenthood pamphlet with detailed information on birth control and venereal disease. On January 25, 1979, it devoted a special section to abortion, including interviews with five Fordham women who had terminated their pregnancies. Of the five, four felt overwhelming relief and one was coping with guilt. In an editorial, the editors said that no member of the editorial board favored abortion on demand, but they were divided as to what legislation could control it.

Gay liberation first surfaced as a public issue in 1973 when the social-thought program sponsored a forum featuring philosophy professor Charles Kelbley, philosopher Quentin Lauer, theologian Herbert Rogers, who was moderator of the Gay Liberation Front, and dean of students William Crawley, who had forced the issue of homosexual rights by denying a meeting room to the GLF. Crawley was in a difficult position during his entire eight-year tenure because he had to play the role of cop in a decade when cops and students didn't get along. With over two hundred in the audience and some shouting obscenities, the discussion drifted from the basic right of homosexuals to be accepted as human beings, which both Rogers and Lauer defended without approving of homosexual activity, to an argument over the definition of "recognition," which Crawley said the university would not grant. The issue was not resolved and did not die. It returned in the 1990s when a gay-rights club called GROUP sought, and was denied, official "recognition."

V ⤴

It is a rare university administrator who does not pick up the student publications with a feeling of dread. If he has given a reporter an interview, he fears he will be misquoted; if he has not, he will be condemned for his silence. But Finlay and the *Ram* were pals every once in a while, particularly on the issue of Fordham's weak classroom standards.

Some of the problem might have been the result of declining enrollments, especially in Fordham College, although the College of Business Administration was growing. The slide was attributable to several causes: the Bronx's economic and social collapse, especially in the perception of a high crime rate; the closing of many New York Catholic high schools as the Irish and Italian middle class fled to the suburbs; the high tuition in a weak economy; competition from CUNY's open admissions policy; and Fordham's failure to expand housing in the 1960s. Because of this, Fordham accepted less qualified students. This included those with reasonably high SATs, but weak grades, and marginal, poorly motivated students who had money and talent, but no will to work. Students such as these were more likely to whine and rebel, and to retaliate in negative course evaluations when faculty made what they considered to be too many demands.

The other explanation for low standards was lazy faculty. At the 1973 faculty convocation (*Ram,* October 23), Finlay called for more-stimulating teaching and a more challenging undergraduate experience. A *Ram* investigation (April 9, 1975) of the average student workload found that the standard course required a midterm, a paper and/or a final, and three or four books. There were few quizzes or short papers and few attendance requirements. Many courses required no reading beyond the textbook, and students could fulfill the requirements for a four-credit course by studying two and a half hours a week. Many handed in the same paper for several courses, and some of these were written by someone other than themselves. Almost 70 percent of the grades that year were A's or B's. Teachers told the *Ram* that they didn't assign more work because it meant more work for them. The four-four had failed, and it was time for a new curriculum.

At the faculty convocation of October 1977, Finlay called for an end to "academic huckstering," "gut courses," and "thin scholarship." Two days later, in an address to the graduate-school faculty, he called on them to face some unpleasant truths. The State Department of Education had determined that, in the shrinking academic job market, graduate programs would have to be upgraded, changed, or closed. In the last three years, seven Fordham programs had been reviewed by the state, and only two, so far, French and philosophy, had been approved. Fordham's self-evaluations, said Finlay, had been "late," "poorly written," and marked by "self-deception." The graduate dean, Harry Sievers, S.J., had suddenly dropped dead shortly after a discussion with Finlay on the school's "clouded future." Finlay appointed Joe Frese in his place and set up a small blue-ribbon task force to determine the graduate programs' future.

Then he sent his director of public relations to the *Ram* office with the text of his address, with word that this was "important." The *Ram* printed the whole text and cheered him on in an editorial: "Fordham has to stop eking out its existence, praying that it will survive one more year. We need aggressive leadership. We need Father Finlay to follow the lead he forged for himself this week" (October 27, 1977).

Finlay's task force included familiar names—Cammarosano, Anastasi, Joe Grennan of English, and John McLaughlin of biology. The graduate programs in chemistry, physics, mathematics, and part of history were lost. The task force urged that the graduate school run a tighter, smaller, and higher quality operation. Reconsidering that decision in 1990, Cammarosano thought he should have eliminated more programs, holding on to theology and philosophy as distinctive to Fordham's mission.

VI

When Joe Fitzpatrick was a naive young priest in his hospital pastoral training in 1944, he knew so little about Puerto Rico that he thought that Hernandez and Gomez were Italian names. One day, he administered the sacrament of the sick to a Puerto Rican, Mrs. Gonzales, whose child was about to be delivered by cesarean section.

About eight hours later, he was called to minister to a woman near death and found it to be the same Mrs. Gonzalez. As the baby was delivered, the mother had gone into shock and the blood transfusion equipment was broken. She died as Fr. Fitz prayed.

The next day, the maternity-ward nurse took young Fitzpatrick aside and told him, "There was no need for that cesarean." The doctor responsible had done more cesareans in a year than they had in the ten years before he arrived. "He's getting a lot of practice," she said, "but Mrs. Gonzalez is dead." This was the beginning of Fitzpatrick's basic conviction that Puerto Ricans often suffered as helpless victims.

After teaching at Xavier High School during the day and the Xavier Labor School at night, and after his Harvard Ph.D., Fitz started teaching at Fordham in 1949. The more he studied the patterns of immigration, the more he became convinced that Puerto Rican immigrants were recapitulating the experience of the nineteenth-century Irish. He thought that they were subject to the same prejudices and that, if they got the proper support, they could move into the American mainstream. The Puerto Rican special problem, however, was that Puerto Rican and New York cultural values clashed; Puerto Rican teenagers, who were accustomed to chaperones at high school dances, were on their own in the Bronx. With no consistent norms, they drifted into delinquent behavior.

In response to Fitzpatrick's influence, Cardinal Spellman established an Office of the Puerto Rican Apostolate and sent half his seminarians for Spanish language training. Ivan Illich, a Spellman confidant, was director of the Center for International Documentation in Cuernevaca, Mexico, which trained American priests for the Spanish-speaking apostolate. Through Illich, Fitz met Dorothy Dohen, editor of *Integrity*, the intellectual journal of the lay apostolate, who invited him to do his first major article, "Catholic Responsibility and New York's Puerto Ricans" (*Integrity*, July, 1955). Dohen became his student, fellow Fordham sociology professor, and friend for life. Meanwhile, their mutual friend, editor William Lynch, got Fitzpatrick writing on the same themes for *Thought*.

At Fordham in the 1970s, Fitzpatrick was already the author of several books and a renowned scholar. Though physically a small man, slightly stooped, with graying hair, he was also a giant, a cyclone of seemingly inexhaustible energy who said yes to every request and lined up with the defenders whenever someone was or seemed to be the victim of injustice.

Like Quentin Lauer and Claire Hahn, he said yes to my request to serve as a mentor in the open curriculum, a 1970s experimental independent-study community for highly motivated students. It tried to combine the imaginative freedom of Bensalem with the protective structure, such as regular evaluation, of Fordham College.

For Fitz, the appointment of Professor Lloyd Rogler as the Schweitzer Chair professor in 1974 and Rogler's establishment of the Hispanic Research Center in 1977 rooted Fordham's commitment to the Bronx neighborhood in scholarship as well as in community action.

At public meetings, Fitz had an uncanny skill of figuring out which way the discussion was going and holding back his opinion, then coming on strong at the end with a spellbinding, clearly enunciated speech that went something like: "I've been listening very carefully to what's been said, and it seems to me that this group can either _____ or _____. If it does ____, it may seem to solve the immediate problem, but if it does not do ____, it will betray the principles that have inspired this group from the beginning."

Every other night for several years, he would join our small group that met for nightly midnight Mass. We would sit in a circle on the chapel floor, discuss the readings, and proceed with the Eucharist. After Mass he would share a beer with the young priests and scholastics, then retire to his room in Faber Hall, so cluttered and crammed with research papers and documents that he could hardly find his desk or his bed. Then he would rise at dawn and go back to work.

VII ⟿

It was raining hard that late September night in 1977 when I stepped off the Metro North train at Conrail's Fordham Station and made my way through the downpour along the platform to an old hole in the fence, a shortcut onto the campus that saved us the trouble of going up through the station and in through Third Avenue Gate.

Suddenly two Hispanic men descended from the old trestle, about fifty yards north of the station, which crossed the tracks over to Webster Avenue.

They were upon me in a second, each pressing a blade of a big knife against my throat and into my chest.

"I'm a priest," I said, foolishly imagining that they might be too superstitious to kill a man of God. They replied with one word, "Money!" They took my wallet, watch, and keys and then fled into the night.

I tried to follow them, not knowing what I'd do if I caught them. I did find two policemen eating pizza on Webster Avenue; they took me to the precinct headquarters, where I went through volumes of mug shots and picked out some familiar faces, but I never heard from them again. I told a *Ram* reporter that although I "didn't think physical fear was part of my makeup," it did occur to me that this might be "the end." But my main reaction was a smoldering anger that, if I let this assault get to me, I could not be at home in "my city." This I refused to accept.

In the 1970s, on and off campus, we watched "our city" crumble before our eyes. Two beloved Italian restaurants on Webster—Sera-Nata's, which had displayed Fr. Victor Yanitelli's poster-sized photo in the kitchen as if he were a patron saint, and the Capri, where Nick and

Mary DeMeo, the proprietors, created special dishes for special customers—mysteriously burned down.

In March 1978, a student, Anne Moravick, found a crumpled, bloodied man a few yards from the college gate, a Fordham professor of business law, mugged on his way to class. In 1973, on three occasions, three or four neighborhood teenagers carrying pistols invaded a suite in G house and held up students who themselves were campus drug dealers in marijuana, hashish, and LSD. Students suspected that the drug dealing was related to a recent rape in Martyrs' Court. In 1974, McDonald's, Burger King, and other fast-food outlets opened on Fordham Road, providing more sites for drug dealers to hang out and spewing tons of plastic, styrofoam, glass, and paper litter onto the sidewalks and gutters.

During the 1978 World Series, fans watching the Yankee game on TV could see the red glow and billowing smoke of buildings on fire outside Yankee Stadium. In 1979, a speeding car being chased by the police careened down the steep 194th Street hill, hoping to turn onto Webster Avenue and escape. But the driver lost control and charged straight ahead, right into the iron fence over the New York Central tracks. He smashed through the bars and tumbled over the cliff onto the tracks in a ball of fire. Student journalist Jim Dwyer watched it burn and saw it as a symbol of what had been happening to the whole community for years.

In a few pungent sentences, Henry G. Waltemade, chair of the Dollar Savings Bank and of the Fordham Road Area Development Corporation, summed up the frustration of local businesses impatient with the government's dragging its feet on the Fordham Plaza renewal project. Writing to the Environmental Protection Agency, he complained that their "asinine pollution survey" had taken three months. "Most importantly, the money spent by your department could be better used by employing more police officers and firemen. As a native Bronxite, I have never heard of anyone dying from the environment, yet our citizens are dying daily by bullets in the head, slit throats, and strangulation by felons who roam the streets."

The long process that led to the slit throats began in the population shift of the 1950s and reached flood level in the 1970s. By 1980, the overall Bronx population had fallen 20 percent to 1,169,000, more than twice the rate of New York's decline. By the end of the decade, as whites fled, the population was 34 percent Latino and 30 percent black. During these years, the national and overall New York City economy suffered as well, and the Bronx unemployment rate more than doubled to 9.3 percent, higher than the rest of the city's. When Co-op City, with its 15,375 apartments, opened in 1968 at the far eastern end of the Pelham Parkway, this hideous high-rise architecture drained as many as 60,000 white residents from other neighborhoods, including many Jews from the Grand Concourse. Meanwhile, better-off black and Latino families joined the flight to lower Westchester towns such as Yonkers, New Rochelle, and Mount Vernon.

The drama of President Jimmy Carter's unannounced visit to the rubble of Charlotte Street in 1977 gave fleeting but illusory hope that the federal government might redeem the borough, but the government's intervention had neither the scale nor the imagination to stem the tide. By the time of the 1981 police movie *Fort Apache: The Bronx,* the borough had become a national symbol for urban decay. Originally, "South Bronx" denoted the Western area below 161st Street. Next, the barrier was the Cross-Bronx Expressway. As the mass exodus progressed, leaving abandoned buildings behind, the "South Bronx" had lost 60 percent of its population, and the plague had reached Fordham Road and the university's front gate.

The empty apartments were razed at the city's order by the wrecker's ball or burned by arsonists for insurance or by gangs for fun. Why did the disaster of abandonment and burning happen so quickly? Some historians attribute the phenomenon to a combination of the city's rent-control laws, which prevented landlords from raising rents enough to meet inflationary costs, and to the tension between elderly Jewish landlords and militant, politically organized, younger minority tenants. In some cases, landlords encouraged old tenants to leave so that they could replace them with welfare clients who needed housing and whose higher rents would be paid by government checks. Irresponsible landlords, "slumlords," neither maintained services nor paid their taxes, and the ruined buildings became city property. In 1976, Roger Starr, Mayor Abraham Beame's housing-and-development administrator, suggested a policy of "planned shrinkage," hastening the population decline in the South Bronx and Brooklyn's Brownsville so as to more efficiently distribute city services. The following month, banker Felix Rohatyn suggested that blighted areas of the city, such as the Bronx, be bull-dozed, blacktopped, and developed as industrial sites. In other words, let the Bronx destroy itself, to be rebuilt later when the low cost of real estate would make it a profitable takeover.

Paradoxically, the one nostalgic oasis of civility in the neighbor-hood was the old Eldorado Bar on Third Avenue, right under the Third Avenue El. The El was scheduled for demolition by 1972. The bar, which had been a tavern since 1890, had a high, plank ceiling supported by a row of wooden posts, with the big rotating fans that later became fashionable in Manhattan watering holes. It had a pool table with a ripped felt cover, and it served Italian hero sandwiches and ham-burgers thrown together in a dingy kitchen in back. The proprietor was Nick DeMaio, five-foot-six and stocky, in his late seventies, wearing a tie and sometimes an apron. He muttered unintelligible wisdom in a gruff voice with a cigar butt stuck in the side of his mouth.

Nick had bought the place in 1922. Faking it as a flower shop in front, the place had been a speakeasy during Prohibition, but more than anything, with its long, solid mahogany bar and the mirror behind it, it resembled a saloon in the cowboy movies. If Gary Cooper had strode in and ordered a whiskey or if Hopalong Cassidy had sashayed up to the bar and ordered sarsaparilla, no one would have been surprised. Word has it that the Seven Blocks of Granite and the New York Yankees used to stop by in the 1930s.

In 1969–70 it was a "radicals" hangout; at a corner table one might hear that "a world war would be a terrible tragedy, but it would be disastrous for the capitalists." As the ranks of radicals thinned, their places were taken for a time by druggies, and at another time by student-government types, journalists, and writers, by little groups of students and faculty who wanted to keep talking about a book after class over a few beers, and on Holy Thursday by those who wanted to share food and wine after Mass.

VIII ⌐

Fordham's new dedication to the neighborhood began when Mike Walsh appointed Paul Brant, a Chicago Province Jesuit scholastic studying for a Ph.D. in philosophy, as his liaison to the neighborhood. Brant's involvement began when he and some Jesuit graduate students living on Marion Avenue, appalled by the trash in the street and in an open lot, cleaned the streets up themselves. At Fordham from 1968 to 1975, Brant played an active part in organizations such as the Morris Heights Neighborhood Improvement Association and the Community Planning Board 5 as he moved back and forth between the classroom and the streets, as a student, catalyst, and leader.

In time, he was joined by other young Jesuits, who were trained in community organizing by Chicago activist Saul Alinsky; by graduate students such as Brian Byrne, whom Finlay later made his assistant for urban affairs and his point man on the Fordham Plaza project; and by Joe Muriana. There were also undergraduate students from the interdisciplinary sociology, philosophy, and political science departments' new social-thought program.

Their goal was to develop grassroots organizations to address the housing problems of the entire Northwest Bronx. With Finlay's help, Brant, Auxiliary Bishop Patrick Ahern, the vicar of the Bronx, and Msgr. John C. McCarthy brought together seventeen pastors to found the Northwest Bronx Community and Clergy Coalition. At a 1973 meeting in the boardroom of the Dollar Savings Bank, the group confronted Henry Waltemade and asked for a $25,000 gift to fund their organization. The banker replied that the bank had "never given $25,000 to charity before." At that, Ahern leaned over and said, "Henry, this isn't charity. This is protection." Waltemade came up with $15,000.

A key element in the plan to rescue the declining area was the dream of Fordham Plaza, which was to be cosponsored by the City of New York Office of Development, the federal government, and private developers. The plaza would consist of an office building, a department store, a parking garage, and shops on two blocks across Fordham Road from the campus. They hoped this would provide an anchor similar to the role of Loehman's department store on Jerome Avenue as well as becoming a hub of commercial excitement and a barrier against the creeping blight.

For over ten years, Finlay had tirelessly lobbied senators, congressmen, cabinet officers, and mayors to get the postmaster general, whose department owned the land, to put his proposed new post office somewhere else and sell the land at a reasonable cost to the city. The city would make it available to a realty company, who they hoped would bring it to life. If the New York postmaster had carried out the original plan of putting a new post office across the street, with trucks roaring in and out, blocking traffic day and night, the effect on the campus and neighborhood would have been horrendous.

In October 1974, frustrated by a stalemate in the negotiations, Finlay made a bold threat. NYU had left their Bronx campus two years before. Now, in a letter to Senators Jacob Javits and James L. Buckley and Congressman Jonathan Bingham, and cosigned by Finlay and Waltemade, Fordham threatened to leave the Bronx and "relocate their undergraduate campus to a site they presently own in Westchester County. Such a move from the area would have a devastating effect on citizen morale and future commercial development in Bronx County" (*Ram,* October 16, 1974).

Finlay's ploy, which seemed uncharacteristic for a leader generally considered cautious, might be described as a bold move or as an imprudent bluff. A *Ram* editorial (October 16) spelled out the negative aspects. The administration did not seem to have fully researched whether it could actually "pack its bags and move." The possible new sites in Westchester were the failed seminary at Shrub Oak and the Calder Estate, Fordham's 114-acre environmental research center at Armonk, which it had acquired in 1968.

At the moment, the university was scrambling to raise funds for the Vincent T. Lombardi Memorial Center, attached to the old gym. Did Fordham have the will to drop the Lombardi Center and Keating Hall as well as historic sites such as St. John's Hall and the chapel with which the alumni identified? Would it construct an instant modern campus another hour or two away from Manhattan and the Lincoln Center campus? Perhaps it was misguided for Finlay to imagine a future for Fordham in Westchester when its real future was in Manhattan. And what would it do to Fordham's image in history to identify itself with the white middle class who left the Bronx behind?

Somehow, as the months and years went by, less was heard about moving to Westchester. The plaza plans were scaled down, minus the department store, to an office building with shops on the first floor.

Yet the threat had been heard. The public had gotten the message that Fordham would leave only if forced out by the indifference of public officials. In 1978, the Arlen Realty Corporation, parent of the Korvettes department store chain, pulled out of their original commitment. But Finlay refused to give up. In 1979, New York's Urban Development Corporation (UDC) took over and found a new developer. Finally, Finlay went to Washington and sat down with the postmaster general, William F. Bolger. In 1982, the Postal Service agreed to transfer the land, and in 1984 ground was finally broken.

Next, Finlay's urban team, led by Brian Byrne, picked up a suggestion from Msgr. Charles Fahey, director of Fordham's Third Age Center. With the help of Finlay's friend Congressman Mario Biaggi, who got the federal funding, they converted an abandoned patch of land behind Fordham Prep on Southern Boulevard into a home for the elderly disabled. The neighborhood was looking up.

Today, a student studying on the fourth floor of the new library can look out and see a modernistic fourteen-story office building, a sort of cylindrical ziggurat with wings, with a few storefronts, mostly medical clinics from local hospitals, on the ground floor. Theodore Roosevelt High School, which the developers wanted to tear down at one stage, still stands to its east. On Third Avenue over the Central tracks is a new bus-station park, marking the corner's role as a transportation hub. Only a few old-timers from the 1970s remember this as the site of the Old El-D.

IX ⟋

It's five o'clock, December 7, 1999. The sun is setting on Manhattan outside our windows, and all 150 or so of us are packed neatly into the twelfth-floor lounge of the Lowenstein building, Lincoln Center campus. Cameramen from *60 Minutes* are ready to roll; the president, Fordham College–Lincoln Center dean, Robert Grimes, S.J., and a trustee sit perched in the front row; two student leaders pose on either side of an empty plush leather chair, and security chief John Carroll, in a dark blue blazer, stands guard at the entrance, all awaiting the appearance of Fordham's most famous alumnus.

The hosts have delivered their introductions; they're moving into their last lines. Standing in the back against the wall, I peer down the corridor and there's no distinguished person in sight, only a young black guy hanging out, baseball cap over his eyes, slouching in an oversized basketball jacket and blue jeans, probably hoping to get a glimpse of Denzel Washington, movie star, when he glides in with his entourage.

Born in Mount Vernon in 1954, he grew up in a mixed neighborhood of Irish, blacks, West Indians, and Italians, right on the northern border of the Bronx, feeling the effects of the population shift of the 1960s and living on streets that offered the ideal training ground for an actor who needed insight into all kinds of people and cultures.

His father was a Pentecostal minister, a remote man who did not communicate well with his children and who held two jobs during the week and preached on Sunday. His mother was a former gospel singer and beautician who owned several beauty parlors. His parents were strict. The father wouldn't allow the children to watch movies, except biblical epics and Disney cartoons, and Denzel knew his mother would "kill him" if he got into trouble the way the neighborhood boys did—some of whom ended up in jail.

Denzel's parents' divorce when he was fourteen was a terrific blow. He took out his anger by picking fights at school until his mother sent him upstate to Oakland Academy in New Windsor, where he excelled in baseball, football, basketball, and track, but wasn't much of a student. From there he entered Fordham in 1972.

It took Denzel a while to find himself. He played freshman basketball, and the coach, P. J. Carlesimo, son of the athletic director, drove him and drove him, running the team till their tongues were hanging out so they would be better and faster and not give out in the second half. Twenty years later, Denzel would have some sense of how Latrell Sprewell felt when he and Carlesimo clashed, but coaching his daughter's team and with his own son on the court, Denzel would train them in much the same way.

Academically, however, things weren't clicking. He thought he'd be a doctor, but his biology grades killed that. Maybe he'd be a lawyer, but political science didn't hold him. Maybe a journalist? Sent to cover a city-council meeting for his reporting class, he fell asleep.

While he was living at "555," the new apartment-style dorm now named for Mike Walsh, he got a part-time job in Manhattan at a camera-equipment store. One day he missed work to have a tooth pulled, the same day someone broke into the store and stole equipment. The next day his employers showed up at 555 to see if he was really sick, and even examined his mouth to the see the hole from which the tooth had been pulled. When he recalls the insults he endured for being black, Denzel takes solace in being rich, for in America, to be rich is to be somebody. Years later, he revisited his suspicious old employers just to let them know he had overcome their bigotry with his wallet. When white taxi drivers pass him up because he is black, he knows he could literally buy their cabs.

But what of his education? Having failed as a journalist, he took an acting class. Vaughn Deering, in the mid-1970s, was in his mideighties, though no one knew how old he really was. Those of us in the audience knew he had coached Jessie Royce Landis, Bela Lugosi, and Lucille Ball. He had nursed Fordham theater through *Once upon a Midnight* and *O My People,* and had coached the presidents on how to deliver annual reports, and students such as myself on how to be interviewed on radio during half-time at basketball games.

Deering's rockbed conviction was that anyone who really wanted a life in the theater should drop out of college and work full time getting parts on the stage. Denzel Washington didn't drop out of college, but in his junior year, he transferred to Lincoln Center because they had a theater program. There, under his new mentor, Robinson Stone, he won the leads in Eugene O'Neill's *The Emperor Jones* and in *Othello.* José Ferrer came to see these plays and predicted a brilliant future for Denzel.

As his career took off, he concentrated on live drama because that was the real test of an actor's mettle, and he resisted movie roles that played off of offensive black stereotypes. His part in the 1980s TV hospital series *St. Elsewhere* earned him a broader reputation. He was never flooded with offers, but he carefully chose parts—such as Steve Biko in *Cry Freedom* and the title role in *Malcolm X*—that deal with moral issues and human redemption. He was at Fordham that evening to promote his new film, which the students had seen the night before. *Hurricane* is the story of the middleweight boxer, Rubin "Hurricane" Carter, unjustly sentenced in the 1970s for murders he insisted he did not commit, who turned his nineteen-year prison sentence into a redemptive experience of forsaking hate for love.

As his name is called, Denzel Washington, in blue jeans and purple sweatshirt with his T-shirt hanging out, strolls in. "I thought I'd come like a student," he says. He's a forty-five-year-old man passing for a twenty-year-old kid and the students love it. He is one of them. They stand and cheer. He beams a super smile and, like celebrities on TV, joins in the clapping.

Most of the questions are about the film, since that is what this event is supposed to be about. The students wonder how he got his forty-five-year-old body in shape for the cameras, how they film fight scenes (body blows are real, head punches are fake), and how he consulted with the still-living Hurricane Carter on what each scene meant.

But soon it is clear that something else is at work. Denzel Washington, who loves live acting in New York but cannot do it because it would take him away from his wife and four children in Los Angeles, has, in a very subtle way, become a messenger, a preacher, his father's son.

As if he were their father, the students ask him to give direction to their lives. He falls naturally into the father role. First he tells them about faith, about belief in God. "It all started at this school," he says. "That's why I'm here today. I believe in God." Every person has a choice to be good or bad, to be part of the solution or part of the problem, he tells them. It's a choice everyone in the room has to make.

Second, he challenges them to act, to take chances, to risk failure now in a big way. That's what college is for. Vaughn Deering died in 1978, but Robinson Stone, suffering from cancer, was in his eighties and Denzel had visited him the day before. We can hear their voices alive in their student who has become a teacher today. If you want to be an actor, then act, act, act. "Where you sit now, I sat twenty-two years ago. You can be anyone you want to be."

I know that Denzel had researched the history of black regiments in the Civil War for his role as the defiant ex-slave in *Glory*, the story of the black Massachusetts regiment that Robert Gould Shaw led both to "glory" and to death, and I wanted to ask him if he knew, during the filming, that his "commander," played by Matthew Broderick, had gone to Fordham too.

X ⌐

Again, it is October 1999, and in the Bronx's St. Angela Merici School, a classroom of twenty-two eighth graders, all either black or Hispanic, look up at a big, prosperous-looking sixty-five-year-old man whom they have been told is an important person, a member of the school's board of advisers, and who has spoken to them at this morning's Mass and assembly, and is now right here in front of their eyes.

He grew up in their neighborhood, played touch football in their streets, served Mass in their church, and graduated from their school.

"How many of you want to be lawyers?" he asks.

Eight raise their hands. "I want to be a lawyer because they're heroes," one boy says.

"They can save someone's good name."

Another asks how often he, John Feerick, dean of Fordham law school, had to take the bar exam.

Saint Angela Merici, as a parish, has been at 161st Street and Morris Avenue in Morrisania, the farmland through which Michael Nash's train passed in 1846, for a hundred years. In the 1940s, the parish school trained middle-class Irish such as Feerick. Today, Feerick is telling children what he does. In an attempt to explain to the class what arbitration is, he recalled the case of Latrell Sprewell, the basketball player who had been sanctioned two years before for choking and threatening to kill his coach, Peter J. Carlesimo Jr. As arbitrator Feerick rendered a decision that, in time, got Sprewell back in basketball, playing for the Knicks. He also authored a book on presidential succession.

When Feerick arrived at Fordham in 1953, Leo McLaughlin took him aside and warned him that students from his high school, Bishop DuBois, had not done well, so "he had better work hard." So he did work hard, and he worked on his political skills as well. As sophomore class representative, though he himself did not consume spirits at the time, he organized beer parties at the Rhinelander Restaurant on 86th Street that attracted hundreds. He chose Fordham law school under the influence of political science professor William Frasca, an admirer of the dean, William Hughes Mulligan. His work on the law review earned him a place with Skadden, Arps, State, Meagher, and Flom. Father Finlay put him on the board of trustees, and when Dean Joseph M. McLaughlin stepped down in 1981, Feerick was named his successor.

The law school had had only seven deans since its founding, and only two—Mulligan in 1956 and McLaughlin in 1971—since Feerick graduated from the college. Two weeks before this meeting with the students, he had handed in his annual report to Fr. O'Hare. In it he observed that whereas the school had started with only 9 men in 1905, the 1998–99 class of 366 day and 121 evening students had been selected from 4,458 applicants, was 48 percent women, 25 percent minorities, and from twenty-six different states, the District of Columbia, Puerto Rico, and France.

Today in his old grammar school, all 625 students at the school Mass in their maroon-and-white uniforms (except for two white girls, one from Hungary and one from Albania) are minorities—African Americans, Africans, Puerto Ricans, Dominicans, South American immigrants, and others. He too, Feerick says, had been in their position. His parents were immigrants from Ireland. Where you sit now, he tells them, is "where I sat forty years ago." Dream, strive, reach high, and you will be dean of Fordham law school.

In another classroom a floor below, Colette Higgins, one of six Fordham graduates on the faculty, is teaching the concepts of multiculturalism and diversity to eighth graders. She puts the buzz words—such as *prejudice, racism, discrimination, assimilation, sexism, classism,* and *homophobia*—on the board and, recalling her American studies classes with Fr. Mark Massa, gets the class to go to the roots of the words and to make distinctions in their meanings. She invites students to come to the head of the class and tell stories of their family trees. A boy tells of his sharecropper uncle and a grandmother who was half Blackfoot Indian. A shy girl is too nervous to go on, but Colette links her arm in the girl's and coaxes her to continue.

Around the corner, Pat Kelly, with Ansel Adams's *Canyon* and Fritz Eichenberg's etching of *Christ of the Breadline* on his walls, sits in the orderly mess of his office. This is his eighth year as principal, and these boys and girls are the first group he has seen through their whole grammar-school education. A chess set stands poised ready for action on a side table, along with a set of same-and-different wooden Montessori cylinders and cubes used as a quick assessment of children's conceptual skills.

On the desk is a flier for a fourth-grade student who is slowly dying, in need of a bone-marrow transplant, and the plans for a new Bronx County Court Complex to be built right across the street. Three blocks long, it will be the largest building in the Bronx, one of those massive projects that will redo—some say ruin—the neighborhood, already so congested that it can take ten minutes to drive three blocks. For those Angela Merici students who said they wanted to be lawyers, the complex will include a High School for Law and Justice, which also means that after school over three thousand young people will flood the streets.

Growing up in an Irish-Italian family in Brooklyn, Pat had often wondered whether God wanted him to be a priest. At sixteen, to think about his life, he visited the Mount Savior Monastery in Elmira, New York, and sought out a monk, whose prayerful demeanor he had noticed at table, for advice. One afternoon, while the monk was working in the fields, Pat told him he was wondering about a vocation to the priesthood or to monastic life.

"How old are you?" the monk asked.

"I'm sixteen."

"Put it out of your mind. If God wants you, he'll have you."

At Fordham, Pat enrolled in the Values Program, the 1970s experiment that clustered three required courses—such as history, philosophy, and communications—around a common theme. The teachers cooperated in planning the syllabi, and they attended one anothers' classes. For Pat, it worked. He learned, he wrote later, that "the world could be embraced and be elevated in the embrace," that the life of the mind and the life of the soul were not at odds with each other. He also learned mercy, an awareness of the "infinite vicissitudes in the lives of learners."

Pat survived a tough bout with depression and graduated in 1980. Had he not taken one Jesuit, who never gave him higher than a

B+, three times, he would have graduated with honors. He passed up graduate school for a while and worked as a roofer, then decided to teach. He chose to teach in the Bronx because Fordham had not abandoned it, and so neither should he.

After ten years of teaching social studies at St. Simon Stock at Valentine Avenue and 182nd Street, he got a master's in educational administration from Manhattan College and became principal of St. Angela Merici in 1992. There, he reached out to ask John Feerick to become chair of his advisory board. A few years later, he mercifully added to the board the Jesuit who never gave him an A.

XI ⚊

There were other memorable moments in the 1970s. The glee club celebrated its fiftieth anniversary in 1973. Track coach Artie O'Connor, who had run for Fordham in 1928, retired in 1973. Ed Walsh, "the Chief," died at seventy-three, having joined the faculty after twenty-five years as a newspaperman. The day after he died, my American character course, which met in the seminar room next to his office, was discussing obstacles to love in the competitive American culture. "But," one student asked, "if Americans cannot love, how do you explain Mr. Walsh?" His best friend, Vaughn Deering, died at approximately eighty-seven in 1978, after directing seventy plays and teaching for twenty-eight years, the last ten of them without pay.

When Thomas A. Murphy, chair of General Motors, spoke at the Fordham commencement in 1977, it was one of those moments that made Fordham look at itself and ask if the man they had honored by inviting him to speak shared the values that Fordham stood for. Joe Fitzpatrick, for one, went away shaking his head. He and others who had listened carefully had heard a glorification of rugged individualism, an attack on "twisted egalitarianism," and an encomium to a ruthless capitalism that leaves the noncompetitive poor in the dust. Kevin Doyle, a student who had grown up on 193rd Street and thought Fordham was a "progressive place," was stunned as Murphy put down the Third World countries who wanted to "play varsity," who were "third stringers" trying to claim a starting position. Doyle critiqued the speech in *Point*. He wondered both why Fordham had honored Murphy and why Georgetown had hired a war criminal such as Henry Kissinger. But he took hope from news that although a Jesuit who had worked for the poor in El Salvador had been assassinated by a fascist death squad, the other Jesuits were determined to stay.

Before his death in 1992, I visited Finlay in the Murray-Weigel infirmary the same day I visited Leo McLaughlin. Although, as usual, he had not been looking for power jobs, he had served for several years as dean of LeMoyne, and although he was barely seventy, his engine was running down. Barbara Stolz, who had fought him hard on closing Thomas More College, called him regularly, telling him not to die because after Fr. Grimaldi's death she could not handle another. He held on and promised her that when he went, she would be the first to know.

He and I because of temperament, I guess, had not been close friends, which made it all the more impressive when, after the communications department denied me tenure in 1976, he declared the decision unjust. Calling on a statute never used before, he personally went before the faculty senate and asked them to override the department and grant me tenure. One of his assistants told me that it was a matter of honor with him and that he would have resigned if they had not done so. They met on Election Day 1976. The *New York Times* carried the story on an inside page—with Jimmy Carter on page one.

In his infirmary bed, he was obviously weak. It was his heart, he said. He used to claim that he never read the *Ram*—which we did not believe—and knowing that the *Ram* writers were my students and friends, he quipped, "I know the *Ram* would deny that I even had a heart." But we knew his heart well. He had worn it out serving Fordham and trying to save the Bronx, and I cannot think of him without tears.

16.

Identity Reconsidered

We don't know who he is. We do know he is up to no good. He drives cautiously up the New York State Thruway toward a state park in Rockland County, a nightmarish thirty-five-mile trip in the night with the snow "beating relentlessly against the windshield." A state trooper has rushed by him, lights flashing, but certainly the police have no reason to suspect that in his trunk, under a pile of luggage, "wedged in a space-defying squeeze against a spare tire," is "a plastic bag containing the body of a prominent sixty-one-year-old writer, Ethel Lambston." She has been dead nearly fourteen hours and a sweet odor has begun to emanate from the corpse. A year ago, he had found a natural opening behind a boulder and a pile of rocks just off the bridal path—a perfect place to stash Ethel away, to be rid of her at last.

Mary Higgins Clark, known as the queen of suspense, had found that rock and hole one day during her riding lesson when the ornery horse had run away with her down a steep incline, and she had seen something protruding from the rock pile that did indeed look like a human hand. Yes, she would use that bridal path and rock in her next novel.

While My Pretty One Sleeps (1989) is the story of Neeve Kearny—an attractive young woman who runs a fashionable dress shop, her father, Myles, a retired police commissioner whose wife was slain a few years before—and of the murder of Ethel Lambston, one of Neeve's customers whose body is discovered, her hand sticking out from a pile of rocks, by a rider whose horse has run away with her in the state park.

Myles Kearny grew up in the Bronx and went to Fordham on the G.I. Bill. His best friend from their Bronx boyhood is Bishop Devin Stanton, who is like an uncle to Neeve. The bishop has copper-color hair tinged with gray, and "behind his silver-rimmed glasses, his mild blue eyes" radiate warmth and intelligence. He seems to read Neeve's mind and likes what he reads. His favorite dish is pasta *al pesto,* and by the end of the book he will be named cardinal of the see of Baltimore. Unlike Bishop Stanton, Fordham President Joseph A. O'Hare is no longer thin and he has no copper in his hair, but when Mary Higgins Clark created Stanton, she was thinking of Fr. O'Hare.

Clark grew up in the Bronx, where her father, Luke Joseph Higgins, owned the elegant Irish pub, Higgins' Bar and Grill. After her father's death when Mary was ten, her mother Nora took in boarders and worked as a baby-sitter. All of her life, Mary, a scholarship student at Villa Maria Academy, worked—as a telephone operator, as a secretary in advertising at Lord & Taylor, and as a flight attendant—until she married airline executive Warren F. Clark, a Fordham graduate, in 1949. When her husband died in 1964 after a long illness during which their love became stronger than ever and Mary was left a thirty-four-year-old widow with five children to support, she turned herself into a professional writer. She wrote radio scripts, a novel about George Washington, and finally, the suspense thriller *Where Are the Children?* (1975) inspired by the case of Alice Crimmins, a New York woman convicted of murdering her two children.

All of her life she had wanted to go to college, and the money from *Children* now made it possible. At forty-five, Mary started evening classes at Fordham Lincoln Center in the fall of 1974. Though she had thought she would be an English major, a course on St. Augustine and her experience of reading his *Confessions* swung her to philosophy. Determined to get good grades, she rented an apartment in New York where she could study rather than commute every day to and from her New Jersey home.

Though studies were her priority, she kept working on her next novel, *A Stranger Is Watching* (1978). While *Children* was being filmed, her producer met her on the street one day and started talking business; Clark had to put him off with, "Sorry, I have a midterm." When a poor grade in Fr. John Adam's logic class took her by surprise, she hurried over to Barnes and Noble's and stacked up on logic books, determined to master this structured mode of thinking, which turned out to be useful in organizing her plots. Working on *The Cradle Will Fall* (1980), the story of a murderous obstetrician, she sat down with her biology professor and picked his brain on in vitro fertilization to authenticate a plot twist. One reviewer in the *Library Journal* (April 1, 1980) called the book "rubbish," but a *Newsweek* reviewer (June 30, 1980) confessed, "I stayed up late to turn the last page, and I did not hate myself—or Mary Higgins Clark—in the morning."

Ms. Clark graduated summa cum laude in 1979 and received an honorary degree (one of her fourteen) in 1988. Joe O'Hare, who met Ms. Clark at the American Irish Historical Society, put her on the board of trustees when the big issue before the board was the relationship between Rose Hill and Lincoln Center. She felt that the Lincoln Center campus had been treated like a stepchild and became its eloquent advocate. Her classes had been filled with mature people who wanted to be there, who brought their life experiences into discussion of Augustine and C. S. Lewis, who came from all professions—including a woman who had performed in burlesque. Besides, it was a beautiful campus, and after class there was still time to catch the second act at the Metropolitan Opera. Today, very happily remarried, her five children established in business, writing, and law, with many millions of copies of her seventeen novels and her short-story collection in print, she serves on the board of St. Peter's College, is active in charities, and writes, and writes, and writes.

II —

Like Mary Higgins Clark, Joe O'Hare, son of a mounted policeman and a schoolteacher, grew up in the Bronx a few minutes from the campus he would someday lead. As a teenager on hot summer afternoons he would come on campus with his friends and play basketball on the one outdoor court between Hughes and Loyola Hall. He occasionally encountered the dignified Fr. Gannon on his rounds. When he joined the Jesuits at seventeen from Regis High School in 1948, his model was the "waterfront priest," Jesuit John Corridan, who also inspired the movie *On the Waterfront*.

In a 1998 profile of O'Hare, a *New York Times* writer described the Fordham he inherited in 1984 as "somewhat academically sleepy." By 1999, Fordham's applications had doubled. O'Hare had built the new William D. Walsh Family Library, and he was known as a New York civic leader, the chair since 1988 of the Campaign Finance Board. He was making various journalist's lists—such as the *World of Hibernia*'s "Shining Stars of the Irish Diaspora" (September 1998), *Irish America*'s "Top 100 Irish Americans" (March/April 1998), and Jack Newfield's "Top 50 Movers and Shakers" (number 44) in the *New York Post.*

In his inaugural address, O'Hare quoted Fr. Kohlmann, who had lost his contest against Georgetown in 1915 to concentrate Jesuit manpower in New York. New York, wrote Kohlmann, "will always be the first city in America," and New York State, "of greater importance to the Society than all the states together." O'Hare would tap this theme as he attempted to reinterpret Fordham's identity in a rapidly changing urban culture.

A 1979 fund-raising feasibility study had spelled out some of Fordham's strengths, such as the Jesuit tradition, and some weaknesses. These included the Rose Hill–Lincoln Center split, a feeling among the 121 opinion leaders interviewed that the future was downtown, and weak financial support among both trustees and alumni.

The temptation was strong for Fordham to change course, according to Johnson and Johnson executive and Fordham business school 1955 graduate Robert E. Campbell, who joined the board at the beginning of O'Hare's presidency. "Things weren't working." Enrollment was falling, the alumni office had still not developed an up-to-date address list, and the city still presented a menacing face to the world. When O'Hare told the board that he wanted to build the library Fordham had been needing for years, some rolled their eyes in disbelief. He had determined that Fordham would stay where and as it was, and act as if it were going to grow.

It grew in several ways.

First—with the addition of Sesquicentennial Hall, behind Spellman, in 1986; and the freshmen residence halls, Alumni Court North and South, behind Queen's Court, in 1987; and the Lincoln Center residence, named for George McMahon, in 1993—Fordham became a predominantly residential community. This included a total of 3,305 residents, with 2,300 on the Rose Hill campus.

This has allowed the university to attract an increasingly national and diverse student body, with the result that in the class of 2002, 23 percent of Fordham College at Rose Hill and 21 percent of Lincoln Center come from outside the New England–Washington, D.C., corridor. This enriched both the opportunities and the challenges of the campus culture.

These were years when students considered the movie *Animal House* to be a reinforcement for their own behavior. In the late 1970s and early 1980s, it was common practice to throw bottles out of windows and an accepted ritual to scream hysterically every Thursday night from dormitory windows as if this "primal scream" were a "release" from terrible tensions. Certainly the "tensions" were not intellectually inspired.

In his first report to the faculty in February 1985, O'Hare attacked the "*Animal House* culture" in the dormitories and the dichotomy between student and academic affairs that perpetuated vandalism and academic mediocrity. Thus, a key project for the 1980s and 1990s—under student affairs vice presidents Jay McGowan, John Shea, S.J., and Jeff Gray—would be to improve the quality of life, ensure order in the dorms, and reduce drug and alcohol consumption.

Second, undergraduate education was renewed by a new curriculum that included required courses on global and multicultural topics and an interdisciplinary-values seminar in senior year.

Most important, in a process begun by Academic Vice President Jim Loughran and continued by Robert Carruba, the faculty and core curricula of Rose Hill and Lincoln Center were integrated, both colleges were oriented to traditional college-age students, and the adult, part-time, and evening students on both campuses were concentrated in a new entity, the College of Liberal Studies, formally known in the Bronx as Ignatius College.

This didn't happen without protest. Some Rose Hill faculty complained that Lincoln Center standards were lower, and some Lincoln

Center students and faculty objected that older and younger students in the same class were a livelier intellectual mix. But the goal was to enable Fordham to present a clear, unified image to its public, including a common curriculum with the shared standards symbolizing one "Jesuit" education.

At Rose Hill, the college dean, Joseph McShane, S.J., emphasized high standards by cultivating an elite group of student leaders through a carefully structured honors program, the Fordham Club, and the Matteo Ricci Society, which prepared top scholars to compete for Rhodes, Marshall, Fulbright, and other prestigious scholarships. Their efforts bore fruit in a steady increase in awards, including New York City Urban Fellowships, Fulbrights, and a Marshall in 1999. At the same time, the ethos among all the undergraduate deans in all the colleges was to treat every student—the stars, the athletes, the disappointments, the mixed-up, the seekers, those struck by family tragedy—as precious individuals to be nurtured toward graduation or sent elsewhere when they declined to measure up.

Third, to recognize research and scholarship, Fordham established a number of endowed chairs, most notably the Laurence J. McGinley Chair in Religion and Society, held from 1988 by the theologian Avery Dulles, S.J. A prolific author who had taught philosophy as a scholastic at Rose Hill in the 1950s, Dulles had become for many Catholics the proper guide to just where the church was on ecclesiological questions. In January 2001, Pope John Paul II named Dulles to the college of cardinals, thus honoring, said Dulles, both American theology and the Society of Jesus.

In 1998, the university appointed three outstanding scholars to the rank of distinguished professor: Sister Elizabeth Johnson in theology, Merold Westphal in philosophy, and Dominic Salvatore in economics.

Fourth, many lesser things still counted. In 1985, a freshman left fielder, Jack Allen, broke Frankie Frisch's 1918 record by stealing forty-six bases in one season; in 1992, the basketball team made the NCAA for the first time since 1971; in 1990, a new seven-thousand-seat grandstand rose on the football field; and each year both campuses became more beautiful, with more flowers, sculpted gardens, and newly planted trees. In an effort to preserve the seventy endangered old elms and the history they symbolize, the grounds-keepers have injected them with a serum to ward off the Dutch elm disease. Compared to today's effulgence, the early century's Rose Hill was a bleak and barren place.

An occasional special moment linked the 1990s generation to Fordham's past. The archeological team of professors Roger Wines and Alan Gilbert kept publishing the results of their dig for the foundation of the original seventeenth century Rose Hill manor. The 1840 home of William Rodrigue, architect of the chapel and St. John's Hall, was redesignated as Rodrigue's Coffee House and Cafe. The *Ram* published a long grim chronology of what had happened to each of the twenty-seven rams honored with the royal title King Rameses, I to XXVII. Three, alas, had been ewes and one a mother. With few exceptions, they had suffered countless kidnappings, tortures, mutilations, poisonings, and beheadings at the hands of students from rival schools who found cruelty to an animal that symbolized Fordham to be amusing (November 15, 1990).

In October 1996, on the fiftieth anniversary of their 1936 season, the five living members of the Seven Blocks of Granite—John Druze, Al Babartsky, Alex Wojciechowicz, Ed Franco, and Leo Paquin—came back for Homecoming Weekend and posed in front of their photo mural in the Lombardi Center.

And the *New York Times* (August 12, 1996) reported that WFUV, after fifty years on the air with a unique, home-generated mix of programming—including artists other stations don't play anymore, a broad definition of popular "classics," plus ethnic music and nostalgia on Saturday and Sunday nights—has, even with only 185,000 listeners, become one of the most respected stations in the area.

In 1999, novelist and culture critic Tom Wolfe, whose 1980s bestseller *The Bonfire of the Vanities* aptly caught the terror of a Manhattan executive whose car breaks down in the Bronx, spoke at the Lincoln Center campus honoring the life and ideas of Marshall McLuhan and the anniversary of his year at Fordham.

During the 1980s and 1990s, the Bronx did not exactly bloom, but it did make a comeback. The unemployment rate remained much higher than that of the rest of New York City. The population remained stable, and the Latino share rose to 48 percent, with newer immigrants from the Caribbean and Latin America. But, writes Robert Worth in the *Washington Monthly* (April 1999), the South Bronx was saved by a combination of factors, including a commitment of Mayor Edward Koch, after his reelection in 1985, to pour $5.1 billion, with the Bronx as a priority, into a well-thought-out rebuilding of neighborhoods.

This meant rehabilitation rather than demolition, maintaining a mixed-income population rather than jamming the homeless into one place, and rebuilt low-density blocks with ranch-style houses, picket fences, front yards, and tree-lined streets. Worth acknowledges the damage the Robert Moses expressways have done and how bus depots and trucks have poisoned Bronx air, but, he says, with the drop in the crime rate, many of those who flew in the 1970s are coming back. In 1999, the old Loews Paradise theater on the Concourse was restored to its original glory as a concert hall and boxing arena. The media ran pieces on Fordham's "Little Italy," the Belmont blocks. Though there are fewer than a thousand Italian families, Fordham students and their families and friends love a convivial evening in the Arthur Avenue restaurants as much as if they were on downtown's Mulberry Street—or even in Naples, Italy.

In 2001, Fordham also reached north and merged with the women's college Marymount College in Tarrytown, giving Fordham its third residential campus.

III ~

O'Hare's reign has not always enjoyed a smooth ride. The 1994 *Self-Study for Reaccreditation* for the Middle States Association of Colleges and Schools, while noting the "two campus" problem, gives an overall positive picture of the institution. Its chapter on faculty identity and concerns describes a "malaise," a "serious morale problem," in that faculty feel the administration does not sufficiently include them in the decision process. "The typical Fordham faculty member," it says, "is not a happy camper." Some complained that the administration didn't listen, some questioned its competence, some felt so alienated that they wanted to unionize.

The bad feeling was due to several factors. There had been a year when enrollments were so low that there was no salary increase, O'Hare had appointed a dean of faculty whose selection met opposition, and the faculty discovered a proposal, on which they had not been consulted, to pare down the number of graduate programs. To save money, the travel budget had been cut, and the integration of the two campuses was under way, a major change that inevitably offended some of those affected. O'Hare, who obviously enjoyed his job, was visible at games and social events, and was eloquent and pastoral. He could also, as one senior faculty member described his personality, "have an edge."

The "malaise" passed when enrollment, the financial situation, and New York's reputation all brightened; when the administration loosened up on some austerities and restored travel money; when the president, vice presidents, and deans employed their diplomatic skills; when the integration of the two campuses began to jell; and when the faculty saw their new library. As Roger Wines put it, "The guy raises a $100 million and builds a new library. What can you say?" The Committee on Undergraduate Education, which had been reshaped by Loughran and revived by Vice President for Enrollment Peter A. Stace, met weekly with vice presidents and deans all in attendance to set enrollment strategy. A handsome new set of brochures exploited Fordham's fresh face—urban, competitive, Jesuit, and diverse.

Not that the millennium's "peaceable kingdom" had arrived to stay. Faculty want a lighter teaching load, five rather than six courses a year, to free them for more research. They see a decline in motivation among their students, who expect the faculty to do more of the work for them. Historian Elaine Crane, who assigns seven short books to sophomores, has found students wanting more class discussion of the books because they have not read them themselves. Classics professor George Shea, who graduated from Fordham College in 1956 and was dean of Lincoln Center for fifteen years, finds the current faculty much stronger and still personally concerned, but he feels that too many students have no desire to learn. In the curriculum he regrets the loss of rigorous study of "the word," the poetic text—whether in language, literature, philosophy, or theology—that was originally central to Jesuit teaching.

A lot of faculty and some administrators are disappointed and frustrated by the decline of community and communication. Twenty-five years ago, faculty, with the Faculty Wives Club as a catalyst, socialized more, entertained at home, lingered in the faculty dining room, had picnics in the park, and sponsored intellectual discussions and spiritual retreats. Today, one might not see colleagues for months; as Roger Wines described it, they meet on campus like residents of a big apartment house who nod to one another in the foyer on the way to work.

Although the deans' offices have live persons answer their calls, the university's internal communications system, in which voice mail has replaced human beings even in offices that deal with the public, makes it extremely difficult to get a prompt answer to a question. The graduate dean was once told by another department to "send a fax" if he wanted a reply. Others wait days to have a call returned.

Even while the university is doing well in so many ways, there is the lingering question of "roads not taken," opportunities lost. Fordhamites sometimes ask, "Why aren't we better than we are?"

Some factors were foreordained, such as the historical mission of moving the children of first-generation immigrants out of the Catholic ghetto and the burning of the Bronx, which frightened the now middle-class graduates of the 1940s and 1950s into sending their sons and daughters to Fairfield, Scranton, and Holy Cross.

There were also failures of imagination and will, such as the narrow anti-intellectualism of the 1940s and 1950s; 1950s dean Thurston Davis was driven out partly because of opposition from Jesuits who thought it absurd for him to require reading several books. The student residence known as 555 was built facing 191st Street rather than the campus because Fordham lacked the confidence that students would fill it, and it might have to be sold as another Bronx apartment building. Most critical, as Himmelberg observes, was the long pattern of laxness in the uniform enforcement of standards. Faculty and administrators have been too tolerant of mediocrity, both in their evaluation of one another and in the goals set for students.

IV ⤚

O'Hare told the millennium edition of the *Ram* (December 9, 1999), "We are probably in better financial shape than we have ever been before." Fordham has operated with a balanced budget for the past thirty years; it finished a successful $150 million fund-raising drive in 1998 and started a bigger one the following year. The endowment (as recorded by the *Chronicle of Higher Education* on April 13, 2001) is $237,756,000, which is not large enough to keep the yearly finances from being tuition-dependent. This means that Fordham must get enrollments high and keep them there.

Applications to Fordham College, have almost doubled over the past five years, and enrollment has risen from 577 for the class of 1997 to 838 for the class of 2002. The quality of students, as measured by SAT scores, has gone up but not spectacularly. The mean SAT score for those years went from 580/552 to 597/576. The face of the student body has changed in other ways. About 70 percent of the Fordham College students are white, and 18 percent represent minorities. About 74 percent are Catholics. The percentage ratio of men to women at Fordham College is 40 to 60, in the College of Business Administration, 56 to 44, and at Fordham College at Lincoln Center, 27 to 73.

Inevitably, these proportions raise questions about future fund-raising. For a long while, men, more than women, have controlled wealth. Now Fordham, consistent with Finlay's hope, is educating a leadership class of women, particularly at Lincoln Center. They will also have to assume leadership in Fordham's fund-raising.

The hope, as Fordham grows, would ideally be to become more residential and more selective without losing the commuter base, and still maintain diversity. This is a complicated formula. In general, schools with a high percentage of alumni givers are residential, with a full-time, relatively homogeneous student body, who made strong friendships during the college years, identified emotionally with the campus, and want to keep those relationships alive. Competing with the other three Jesuit schools that now attract the best Catholic students—Georgetown, Boston College, and Holy Cross—will be difficult for both students and faculty for two reasons.

First, of the twenty-eight Jesuit colleges and universities, seven have a higher endowment than Fordham. Boston College, for example, had $1,044,542,000 in 2001, five times what Fordham's endowment is. Fordham has big plans—including a monumental $500 million, two-tower law school and graduate school of business, plus another residence hall for Lincoln Center; but it will be a struggle to overcome the negative legacy of alumni who left neither their hearts nor their gifts on campus. Recent graduates show increasing loyalty, but the overall giving rate is 16 percent, whereas Boston College's is 25 percent, and Georgetown's 29 percent.

Second, the Society of Jesus is shrinking. In the 1960s, Fordham had 135 Jesuits; when O'Hare arrived, about 70; in the 1990s, about 40, a half dozen of whom are semiretired or close to it. The New York Province alone has three colleges—Canisius in Buffalo, LeMoyne in Syracuse, and St. Peter's in Jersey City—and Fordham University. Each year one or two Jesuits will finish their higher studies and become available, making the rounds and hoping one of these schools will hire them. Inevitably, the Society will have to ask the same question that was raised in the 1950s and 1960s: Since there are not enough Jesuits to staff all their colleges and universities, shouldn't one be given priority so that it can become "great"? Unfortunately, even if the Jesuits wanted to cooperate and pool resources, they probably couldn't. The power to hire is in the hands of lay faculty; they would have to decide that the Jesuit character was central to the school's identity and survival and act decisively to preserve it.

This means that faculty and administrators would have to actively recruit both Jesuit and lay faculty, Catholic or non-Catholic, who are committed to the dialogue between faith and reason and to the other principles of Jesuit identity Fordham has embraced.

V ⁓

Meanwhile, with a shortage of Jesuits, how important is a Jesuit president to Jesuit identity? When Georgetown appointed its first lay president in 2001, O'Hare assured the public that his own successor would be a Jesuit.

What is the Jesuit identity for this new century? For Archbishop Hughes, the key concepts were Catholic and Irish. From 1846 to 1968, they would be Catholic and Jesuit. Now they are Jesuit and New York. The external trappings of 1950s Catholicism—such as mandatory daily Mass and the heavy overload of scholastic philosophy—are gone, but I, for one, do not find the campus less Catholic, perhaps because I have lived through the cultural changes in student dorms in several Jesuit universities. But today every university's Catholicism is more difficult to define.

This is so, first, because of the changes of separate incorporation and nonsectarian status. Second, Pope John Paul II's 1990 decree *Ex corde ecclesiae,* with its policies for application ratified by the American bishops in 1999, has attempted, with new controls, to force a uniform definition of a "Catholic" institution throughout the world. The document says that a majority of trustees and faculty must be committed Catholics, that presidents must take an oath of fidelity, and that Catholic teachers of theology must request from the local bishop a "mandate" that is "fundamentally an acknowledgment that a Catholic teacher of a theological discipline is in communion with the Church and will refrain from putting forth as Catholic teaching anything contrary to the Church's magisterium."

Even though couched in conciliatory diplomatic language like "as far as possible," the decree puts a damper on faculty spirit, both in institutions where faculty may be anticlerical and in those where they may love the school but don't want a bishop looking over their shoulders.

O'Hare, as president of both the American Jesuit Colleges and Universities (AJCU) and of the American Catholic Colleges and Universities (ACCU) has been a chief spokesman in crafting their response to the papal statement. They have maintained that *Ex corde ecclesiae* itself is in many ways an inspiring and useful document in its articulation of the principles of Catholic education, but that its implementation must allow for the differences of historical culture, including American pluralism, freedom of expression, separation of church and state, and the reliance of most universities on government support. The 1990 document was helpful in clarifying identity; it provided a Christological perspective to university activities and an ethical perspective to professional education in areas such as law, business, and health care. But the Vatican requirement that the majority of faculty be Catholic O'Hare considered a "dangerous and impractical strategy."

In 1994, the bishops approved a set of applications that the presidents supported, but in 1997, Vatican officials required another draft with more juridical links between the universities and the hierarchy. To the presidents' disappointment, the bishops approved the tougher version in 1999.

O'Hare's position, spelled out at an ACCU business meeting (February 3, 1999) was that over thirty years the United States bishops, in a process of which the Land O'Lakes statement was part, had developed a model of a university that was juridically independent, but in which the universities considered themselves Catholic by reason of an institutional commitment made and sustained by their lay boards. This was consistent with the Vatican II call for lay leadership.

In many ways, the turning point in Catholic identity took place in the 1970s after Fordham's Fr. Canavan had warned that to give up control of the hiring process was to give up the university and when there was a market glut of bright Ph.D.'s desperate for work, many of whom were already published and from the best universities. They applied to Jesuit universities that were anxious to raise their profiles by hiring the "best," but which failed to ask whether the new faculty were committed to a Jesuit Catholic university's goals. Jesuit applicants, older men with slightly shorter resumes, could lose to the "stronger" candidates who had applied to Holy Cross because it was "near Cambridge" or to Fordham because it was in New York.

Or as a secular scholar described the same phenomenon from another point of view,

> The shortage of jobs, along with federal affirmative action regulations and pressure from women and African American scholars, transformed the process of academic recruitment. Jobs were openly advertised; the "old boy" network lost legitimacy and its former power to place students. Not only did this change promote greater equality of opportunity among job candidates, but it also reduced the advantage of a small cluster of traditionally powerful departments in each discipline.

The new social groups in academe fixed attention on issues of race, class, and gender and created a more fragmented academic culture, less able to speak with one voice.

This meant, on one level, that the schools are now stuck with some senior faculty either oblivious to or hostile to religion. They are also, like their peers at other universities, more dedicated to their professions than to their institutions. They want to build their reputations through participation in the Modern Language Association or the American Political Science Association and to write articles that will get noticed—on race, class, and gender. The incentive to write about "Catholic" topics, such as the moral dimensions of poverty, world trade, or advertising is limited.

On the positive side, however, Catholic universities have attracted Jewish, Protestant, and secular humanist intellectuals even more dedicated to some important values—such as social justice, varieties of spirituality, and intellectual excellence—than traditional Catholics tend to be.

Elaine Crane, for example, is more dedicated to Fordham's Jesuit identity than to its Catholic identity. To her, "Catholic" has connotations of dogmatism. Not a Catholic, she disagrees with the church's position on abortion and knows many faculty, including Catholics, who feel the same. She has never sensed any limitation on her academic freedom, but to faculty she knows, *Ex corde* is cause for concern.

Though she backs off in some ways from the word *Catholic,* she does identify with the Jesuit tradition of intellectuality and academic standards. She loves to teach graduates of Jesuit high schools, and she would like to see Fordham establish a separate Institute of Catholic Studies. To some, this would emphasize the Catholic character; to others, it would marginalize discussion of the faith.

VI ⁓

In the nineteenth century, Fordham's Jesuit identity came from two sources: the control, the seminarylike discipline and piety that established a way of life for the boys, and the *Ratio*'s method of teaching by preparation, repetition, and "eloquent" expression. For most of the twentieth century, as the seminary atmosphere subsided under pressure from war veterans and urbanization, Jesuit identity came from influential Jesuit and lay faculty—such as Connolly, Remini, Liegey, Telfair, and others—and from the curriculum, the equivalent of a required major in philosophy, which, as many alumni fondly recall, "taught them how to think." Yet a cold eye on the content of those courses suggests that, whatever their positive influence, they were replaced just in time. The reduction of required philosophy and theology, beginning in the 1960s, to two courses each in order to make room for science, the social sciences, and a strong major meant that identity could not spring from the curriculum alone.

Since the 1970s, Catholic universities, partly in response to marketing pressures, have employed a variety of strategies to reassert their religious identities. One is the "back to the future" scenario, a retrieval of the "Catholic culture"—the romantic medievalism of the *Thirteenth, Greatest of Centuries* and great Catholic literary figures of the 1930s and 1940s such as Maritain, Chesterton, and Belloc—plus stricter rules in the residence halls and a president who makes a public show of taking an oath of fidelity to the Vatican.

Some participate in *Colloquium,* a program that pairs young Ph.D.'s with mentors, such as Fordham sociologist James R. Kelly, to encourage the young scholars to see teaching and scholarship not just as a career but as a spiritual vocation.

Alternative strategies emphasize campus ministry, public worship, and retreats. Others enrich the curriculum with a "values" approach or with Catholic studies as an interdisciplinary major or minor analogous to American studies or peace studies. Many emphasize the commitment to social justice and service.

The November 16, 1989, murder of six Jesuits and their cook and her daughter at the University of Central America (UCA) in El Salvador by a military death squad was a turning point in the history of the consciousness of American Jesuits and their students. The murderers made their intentions clear; they deliberately blew out the Jesuits' brains. Their brains were the enemy of the power of the state. They were killed, said their colleague Jon Sobrino, because through their intellectual research they told the truth about the "massive, cruel, and unjust poverty of the mass of the people . . . because they believed in the God of the poor and tried to produce this faith through the university." As David O'Brien wrote in his classic study of Catholic identity, *From the Heart of the American Church,* "The event sparked outrage, expressions of solidarity, and renewed attention to academic responsibility for poverty, violence, and injustice. The slain Jesuit scholar-educators embodied ideas about the 'service of faith and promotion of justice' much discussed on Jesuit campuses, particularly the idea of former Jesuit General Pedro Arrupe that the task of the educational apostolate is to form 'men and women for others.'"

American Jesuits could now look at one another as men willing to die for a principle, and students could suddenly see their Jesuit teachers as brothers of contemporary martyrs. They also knew of Archbishop Oscar Romero and the four American churchwomen who had been killed by the same death squads a few years before. Throughout the country, students at Jesuit schools protested against the United States government's support of the Salvadorian regime that had engineered the killings. In December, over twenty-two Fordham students, faculty, and administrators, participating with five hundred demonstrators at the El Salvadorian Consulate in Manhattan, were arrested for civil disobedience. One, theology professor Dean Brackley, S.J., was one of the many Jesuits to volunteer to replace their slain brethren, and as this is written, he is there now.

In 1990, O'Hare, with a small delegation of Jesuit presidents, flew to El Salvador to investigate the murders. Today the annual commemoration of their deaths is not just a ritual of remembrance but an utterance of Fordham's Catholic and Jesuit identity.

In his *New York Newsday* column (January 6, 1993), Jim Dwyer meditated on the passing of three older Jesuits identified with Fordham—Tim Healy, historian Francis X. Curran, and Victor Yanitelli—who all died within a few days of one another. The ranks were thinning. Then, at Healy's funeral, Dwyer's eyes turned to the altar mural in St. Ignatius Church of the battle-wounded saint as his thoughts turned to the El Salvador martyrs and O'Hare's words at their memorial. "For us to forget them or to decide that the costs of justice are too high for us to pay would be to betray not only their memory but our faith that this is God's world and that He is the Lord of justice."

In the concluding essay of Fr. Hennessy's *Fordham: The Early Years,* James R. Kelly takes the level of student volunteer-service activities as a "concrete test of Fordham's Jesuit culture." This volunteer, or "missionary," spirit developed slowly. In the 1950s, we took up "mite box" collections for the missions, and some Jesuits, such as J. Franklin Ewing, Edward Dowling—who was the college dean during Finlay's administration—and O'Hare, had served in the Philippines; campus minister Joseph Currie, S.J., served in India for many years. But it took Vatican II to unleash the spirit of service. The Mexico Project was the first step. Today 350–400 students, only a small percentage of those who apply, will participate over a four-year period in Global Outreach's ten programs all over Latin America, India, and the United States.

In fall 1998, preparing a report for a 1999 Jesuit conference on justice in higher education, Kelly studied the breadth and depth of Fordham's commitment. He found the campus very much alive with lectures, community-service programs, internships, and discussions responding to current events. The forty-one faculty and administrators who responded to his questionnaire for the most part experienced questions of justice as integral to their work. Their motivation varied, however, and it was not clear that their commitment was inspired or challenged by Catholic or Jesuit institutional ideals. Thus, however rich and sincere this element of Fordham's identity may be, it is not yet the explicitly defining element.

In O'Hare's view, identity is not determined so much by how the institution settles controversies, but on its contribution to the dialogue between faith and reason and its promotion of the Catholic intellectual tradition, even though, depending on the context, issues such as whether to sanction a pro-choice or a gay/lesbian student group or whether all theologians are 100 percent orthodox can be very important. For O'Hare, more important than an abstract philosophy of Jesuit education are the three themes of Ignatian spirituality that, he says, provide a "unifying thread."

First is Catholic humanism, a "secular mysticism" linked to the Ignatian principle of finding God in all things. Second, this contemplation of God in the world must lead to action, with students committing themselves to a wider community as "men and women for others."

David O'Brien tells the story of the Paraguayan Jesuit, Cesar Jerez Garcia, who, on receiving an honorary degree at Canisius College in 1978, asked the graduates,

> Do you plan to use your degree for your own profit, be it profit in the form of money or power, status or respect? Will you end up with General Motors or Morgan Trust, with Chase Manhattan or Abbot Laboratories, with Goodyear or Boeing. . . . Will you become people who use your knowledge for the furtherance of justice . . . or live the good life of manipulated, unconcerned people in suburbia who grant honorary degrees to people from the Third World but refuse to join them in the fight for justice and liberty for the poor of the world?

Finally, the Ignatian "magis" means "What more can I do for the kingdom?" In practice, that concept, says O'Hare, "challenges those comfortable with the status quo and inspires the desire to deal creatively with the inevitability of change." That inevitability of change means that a statement of Fordham's identity, even though it has a mission statement, is not easily etched in stone or nailed to the wall. It all depends on whether or not these ideas are made concrete on the grassroots level, in syllabi and in dorm behavior.

A senior Jesuit scholar says that Fordham's identity is rooted in its history of taking the sons of immigrants and moving them into the mainstream of society, and its future is in creating a sophisticated intellectual Catholic people and, through synthesis of the gospel and secular culture, bringing forth a community of intelligent and convinced Catholics. Robert Campbell adds that the work with immigrants is not finished. Many will not be Catholics, but some from Latin America and Eastern Europe will have Catholic traditions on which to build.

VII ~

In the archives on the top floor of the Walsh Library, I close the manuscripts of two Fordham oral histories—one of a young man conducted in 1990, the other of an old man done in 1982—and slip them into their folders and boxes to be returned to the shelves.

The young man, Joseph "Jay" McGowan, came to Fordham with only half a Jesuit education. From St. Joseph's Prep in Philadelphia, he had gone to Notre Dame, and then to Columbia for a Ph.D. in education. When he arrived at Fordham as assistant dean of students to Marty Meade, he and his wife, Maureen, had twins on the way. Jay was—and is—basically a people person, a handsome young Irishman with a much-too-good Elvis impersonation he was all too ready to demonstrate.

One of his first duties as Marty Meade's second was to receive the IDs of the students who had occupied the Administration Building during the Friedland fight as they filed out in compliance with the threat of injunction. Most of the students who surrendered were his personal friends. As assistant to deans George McMahon and Bob Roth, he organized the Values Program. Then, as dean of students and later as vice president for student affairs, succeeding Bill Crawley, he had to put a human, credible face on the student-affairs office and yet not come across as too much of either a "cop" or a "nice guy."

In 1990, he became part of a tradition of which O'Hare is proud: a good number of Fordham administrators go on to become presidents of other universities. Jim Loughran, S.J., became president of Loyola Marymount in Los Angeles, acting president of Brooklyn College, interim president of St. Mary's in Emmitsburg, where Archbishop Hughes got his start, and president of St. Peter's College. Economist John Piderit, S.J., who turned Queens Court into an exclusive residential college where freshmen learned table manners as well as civil discourse, became president of Loyola University-Chicago. John Shea, S.J., McGowan's successor as vice president, went to John Carroll University. Gerry Reedy, S.J., who had run the honors program, lived in Walsh Hall, and had been dean and academic vice president, became president of Holy Cross, and Joe McShane, president of Scranton University. Donna Carroll, university secretary, went to Dominican University. Jay McGowen took over Bellarmine College in Louisville, Kentucky, and sang an Elvis song at his inauguration banquet.

In his oral-history interview, Jay remembers the times he wanted to run Joe Cammarosano off campus and the times he wanted to hug him. He calls Paul Reiss "one of the best men I ever met." He remembers

Mike Walsh's clearheadedness in crisis and his ability to be strong without trampling on people. He feels for the students of the 1980s and 1990s, swamped by the entertainment industry, the pressures of their peer culture, and "the tremendous value of friendliness" that can overwhelm, and sometimes undo them, at a happy place like Fordham. He is convinced, however, that the distinguishing mark of students of the 1980s is their commitment to service . . . "their tremendous amount of activity and love."

He passes over tragic stories and tells some funny ones, such as the one about the student at registration who was arguing with the dean about getting into a class, and the point was that he couldn't get into the class because it was closed. So he pushed it. The dean said, "No, you can't get into the class. There are already too many in the class. The student limit is thirty, and there are already thirty-five in there."

The student kept pushing.

Finally, the dean said, "We can't do it, there's simply not enough room."

And the kid said, in all seriousness, "Oh. That's not a problem. I never go to class. I just don't go."

Oh.

Jay remembers the peace vigil during the Vietnam war, the march through the Bronx, and the times the whole community came together in tragedy, particularly when a student had died.

How has he changed?

"I think I have become much more serious about what I am doing as I have come to realize its importance and also its difficulty. I think I've gotten at Fordham, through my experience, the understanding of what integrity means, and what love means, and how difficult it is to be an integrated person, how difficult it is to love."

The old man was Larry McGinley. In the interview it is clear that his short-term memory is slipping—he's not sure with whom he had breakfast—but he remembers what was said. Pressed by George Shea, a student with me in the 1950s when McGinley was president, he reflects on changes in student attitude. In the 1950s, we had discipline and wore our philosophy gowns with pride, "but it was not from within." In the 1970s, McGinley was saddened because "everybody was mad at everybody" and the anger sprang from an inner agony. Students of the 1980s were more open. They lacked discipline because parents feared their children. But they were "great kids."

He had advice for those planning the future of the Lincoln Center campus: dream a lot, cultivate beauty—he's very proud of the campus green space—and be "very person-oriented."

From the balcony outside the archives, I look down at a brilliant copper beach tree between the library steps and the old Duane Library, which, according to plans, will be renovated, restored, and transformed into a visitors' center.

I try to imagine a grand ritual that was suggested but did not take place: a solemn procession from the old library to the new in which the faculty, in full academic robes, would each carry on high the book that he or she had written and deposit it in its new abode—a good idea that might not have worked. Some had written a dozen books and some had written none. Could they carry their journal articles, newspaper reviews, class notes, letters from students whose lives they had saved or changed? Is it right to expect great things from a university, or only that it do ordinary things well?

If the new library has not replaced the intersection between Edwards Parade and the Campus Center as the campus hub, it is becoming the campus heart, with its 2,500 visitors a day (4,000 during exams), its modern gothic design making it at home both on campus and in the Bronx, its technology center at the service of Bronx high school students. All this would not have been available without the Leo McLaughlin separate incorporation, the New York State $9 million, the William D. Walsh, FC '51, $10 million, and the trustees and donors who put it there.

Charles Osgood, in his best WFUV/WCBS voice on the October 1997 dedication day, had this to say about the components used in the creation of the new library: "Brick and mortar, a lot of stone, metal and glass. But there are other elements—faith in this university and what it stands for, hope reinforced by prayer, dedication, and love. It took a lot of love to make this building . . . and money, which wouldn't have come without love."

Epilogue:
A Millennium's Last Class

The New York Province used to send Jesuit scholastics who were teaching high school to summer graduate classes at Fordham. In 1962, I took a course on John Henry Newman from Francis X. Connolly. I did not know then that Connolly had been at Fordham since the 1930s, that he had been a major figure in the Catholic Renaissance of those years, or that his 1948 anthology textbook, *Literature: The Channel of Culture,* would, after many of the norms and values it championed had been discarded, stand unused on the library shelf as an artifact, a remnant of a lost vision. But I did know that inside that handsome gray head and behind that gentle, courtly manner, was a flame lit from the first torch ever lit and passed along at Fordham. I knew that I should experience it before it flickered out.

Connolly's anthology was an innovation in its own time in that, contrary to New Criticism, which emphasized the literal, objective content of a literary text over its philosophical or historical contexts, Connolly looked at literature in the way that Jesuits viewed philosophy, as a guide to life. Without a philosophical and historical frame of reference, says Connolly in the preface to his anthology, "literary delight may well become a riot of fancy and an invitation to anarchy." He acknowledges that his selections—Maritain, Gilson, Newman, and contemporary priest-writers such as John LaFarge and Thomas Merton—are weighted toward a particular worldview, but assumes that "the average young American of every persuasion needs more awareness of the continuity of history and the coherence of truth than he does of the change and chaos that floats in the intellectual sphere like bomb dust over a ruined city."

His first section, "The Idea of the University," with excerpts from Pope Pius XI, Maritain, Newman, and Fordham political scientist George Bull, establishes that education can "be ideally perfect only when it aims to form the true Christian and the useful citizen." This is contrary, he says, to John Dewey's "progressive" position that "social utility rather than wisdom is the end of education."

My final paper for Connolly's course that summer tried to show that, for Newman, the student-teacher relationship was at the heart of the educational experience. Connolly, I think, was the first person to alert me to the famous line in President James A. Garfield's address at Williams College in 1871, that all one needs for an education is a "simple bench" with Williams's president Mark Hopkins on one end and the student on the other. Personal influence was for him, even more than books, the essence of education. What matters is the intellectual friendship. "For truth to live in the student," I wrote in my paper, "he must catch it from someone in whom it lives already."

II —

I don't think that is the first thought in the minds of the twenty students in my Fordham freshman English on the first day of class, January 1999. Nor in mine. I am laying down rules—no food, no water bottles, no gum, no absences or lateness, no late papers (not even one minute), no book bags on the desk, no hats, no stacking books before the class is dismissed—all meant to drive home the idea that literature is extremely important and that the work we are doing together demands every atom of our concentration. For the first time in many years, to force myself to break from familiar material I've taught before, I've put myself at the mercy of a standard textbook, *Elements of Literature*. We meet at 10:30, three times a week, in a cinder-block seminar room on the first floor of Dealy Hall, the same building, built in 1867, where I took my first English course forty-eight years ago. For the editors of my new text—Robert Scholes, Nancy R. Comley, Carl H. Klaus, and Michael Silverman—"literature enriches our lives because it increases our capacities for understanding and communication. It helps us to find meaning in our world and to express it and share it with others."

Of the one hundred authors in Connolly's text, only sixteen appear in *Elements of Literature.* The only clearly identifiable Catholics are Flannery O'Connor and Gerard Manley Hopkins, but there are works by those other writers I most love to teach: Thoreau, E. B. White, Virginia Woolf, George Orwell, James Baldwin, Joan Didion, James Joyce, Ernest Hemingway, and Langston Hughes.

While Connolly, guided by his religious vision, designed his texts to teach not only literature but Christian virtue to Catholic men, these editors have collaborated to produce a marketable product that must do three things: continue the canon, those writers such as Shakespeare, Tennyson, and Fitzgerald, without whom, presumably, no educated person can open his or her mouth in public; contain enough explanatory material to compensate for the teacher's inade-quacies; and teach the new secular virtue—multiculturalism—with enough works by blacks, women, and various minorities to satisfy a teacher who wants to build a whole course around a political issue.

The biggest change in English teaching over thirty years, says a professor who revered Connolly, is the imposition of political agendas on literary texts, agendas that both distort the texts and rob students of the opportunity to discuss the more fundamental questions about human life that the original authors pose. On the first day of class we have a 1,500-page anthology with no up-front ideology, but 114 authors from Sophocles to John Lennon, with little sense of what we and it will yield in the fourteen weeks that follow.

The twenty-one of us are crammed close together around long tables placed in a rectangle, so we have to look at each other all the time. There are twelve women and eight men, four of whom have gone to Jesuit high schools. Seven are in the business school. Two are varsity athletes—one in baseball and one in football. The ethnic-racial mix includes two Puerto Ricans, an Albanian, one African American, a Ukrainian, a Nicaraguan, and the usual component of Italian and Irish. The Albanian, Lek Berishaj, resists removing his heavy leather jacket—a sign, I explain to him, that he does not intend to stay. At this point in the semester, he considers himself more Albanian than American.

For about thirty years, I've taught journalism, American studies, and literature at five Jesuit universities. In recent years, partly to test myself and to prove to my students that I can write, I have traveled to international hot spots such as South Africa, Syria, Iraq, Vietnam, Cuba, and Indonesia and published articles and photographs on my adventures. In Indonesia last summer I looked out the train window at miles of rice patties, lush forests, mountains, and poverty-stricken farmers on the way from Jakarta to Yogyakarta and was overwhelmed by the realization of how differently God treats us all. If I had been born the son of an Indonesian rice farmer rather than the son of a Trenton, New Jersey, journalist, I'd be standing in a rice field in mud up to my knees, not even looking up to see this train go by, rather than knowing the joys of Beethoven's *Fidelio,* of French bread, cheese, and wine, of Tolstoy and Walden Pond, and of teaching generations of students like those in this room.

If my personal history repeats itself, one or two of these students may take a course from me again, become my friend, my running or biking partner, my dinner guest and host, write to me for years and maybe even invite me to perform a wedding and baptize a child. Or I may bury a parent or spouse. Someone else will finish the course bitter, angry at a low grade or some other offense of which I may have been unaware.

I must miss the second class in order to preach at a friend's wedding in St. Augustine, Florida, and so, for the long weekend, I assign nine essays, fifty-nine pages. Two drop the course immediately.

III —

One day when she was twelve, Clarilibeth Torres, looking out her South Bronx windows about thirty blocks south of Fordham, waved to her friend Hector, who was on his way home from his job. He waved and smiled; then suddenly a gang of men appeared with baseball bats and beat him to the ground. They slashed his face, pounded him, ripped his shirt, and left him facedown in a pool of blood. They had stolen the gold chain Clara's mother had given him for his birthday. The next day she read in the paper that Hector had provoked the fight.

Now Clara, a freshman at Fordham, age twenty, sits directly across from me, determined to master the media, write poetry, and have her own Web page and her own magazine. Born in Puerto Rico, she spent the first five years of her life shuttling between various aunts and grand-parents in Puerto Rico and the Dominican Republic. She has never met her father, although she once called him on the phone, then hung up before he could answer. Years passed without her seeing her mother, who does not even know her birthday. Her two older brothers and three younger sisters have different fathers. When she moved to America in 1989, her mother and her mother's current boyfriend dragged her from Albany to Philadelphia to all over Florida because the authorities in each town were just a few steps behind the boyfriend.

Today she divides her addresses between two Bronx "aunts," who are really cousins, commutes to lower Manhattan, where she works thirty hours a week as a receptionist at Barnes and Noble, and at Fordham does her best to compete with students with more stability in their lives than she has had in hers.

At the Bayard Rustin Humanities High School in Manhattan she was a star. She won a Shakespeare recital contest, worked in an antidrug program, joined the photo club and the softball and volley-ball teams, worked on the yearbook and newspaper, and edited her own magazine. The faculty loved her and encouraged her creativity, but they did not teach her intellectual discipline, spelling, or grammar, which is not necessarily their fault.

Surrounded by Spanish speakers most of the day, she has settled into something she calls "Spanglish." Her favorite poet is Sylvia Plath, and she has read the *Confessions* of St. Augustine twice on her own, but there's an enormous gap between what's bursting out of her creative soul and what she can say in Sylvia Plath's native tongue.

When she arrived at Fordham for the HEOP (the federally funded Higher Education Opportunity Program) remedial summer courses, she loved it, the beautiful campus, and students like herself. But September, when the other 3,800 students arrived, threw her into a funk. To her eyes, she was swamped in a sea of preppies, all cool in their J. Crew and Gap designer garb. All the middle-class white people and the minorities split into their own cliques, and only the resident students were in on the fun. Those high-school A's and B's slipped to a 2.6. But somehow, though she is not formally religious, she believes in God's plan; she loves her courses and almost all of her teachers, and she adapts.

She fights me. When I take ten points off her quiz because she says that Robert Frost's classic poem "Stopping by Woods on a Snowy Evening"—"Whose woods these are I think I know / his house is in the village though"—is about "escaped slaves," because there's no evidence for that in the text, she stays after class to argue: that's *her* interpretation.

When we do four films at the end, I assign *High Noon* (they have never heard of Gary Cooper!) and John Cunningham's story "Tin Star," on which it is based. The class unanimously prefers the story, in which the sheriff—contrary to the film's lone hero, who wins a shoot-out with four killers—dies, deliberately taking a bullet aimed at his deputy. But to Clara, Gary Cooper's Will Cain, the 1950s liberal's ideal man of courage, is a "coward," because he went around trying to raise a posse rather than handle it himself.

It is the most astonishing idea I have ever heard from a student. Perhaps her imagination is so distorted by *Lethal Weapon,* Arnold Schwarzenegger, Sylvester Stallone, and kung-fu movies, where comic-book heroes armed with automatic weapons—and somehow never touched by the thousands of bullets that splatter earth, sand, walls, and glass around them—blow away their adversaries with machine gun bursts and flying kicks.

Or rather, perhaps she reads all literature totally through the prism of her own experience. She is an escaped slave looking for a house in the snow. No posse or armed committee of townsfolk have ever done anything for her, and she has survived. So Gary Cooper should quit whining and take care of himself.

When class goes well, it is 90 percent lively discussion; I sit with my prepared discussion outline, broken into five- or ten-minute segments, in front of me and a long No. 2 pencil in my hand, look around to call on quiet people who resist getting involved, and strain with my army-artillery-damaged ears to hear what to me are mumbles and whispers.

But sometimes I go to the board and outline the things I think we should have learned so far. This is important stuff, I say. And most of them sit back with their arms folded, either remembering it all or unconvinced that what I say is worth remembering. How do I look to them, talking emphatically and scrawling illegibly with my chalk?

In my first semester nonfiction writing course, a bright sopho-more, Amanda, took notes on me.

> The pencil is his heartbeat: the blood of his life gushes on his
> student's papers in a series of X-filled circles and marks where he
> must have tap, tap, tapped in contemplation. The nod is the invite
> to enter his universe. He is the center of this universe, pulling
> each student onto his planet with an invisible cord that comes
> with the penetrating eyes that stare from behind his glasses.
> Sitting ramrod straight, his lean body clothed in a collared shirt
> and tie, he is relaxed and ready for action. If it is cold he wears a
> cardigan sweater, and he is reminiscent of the quintessential
> grandfather: strong, trusting, and yet powerfully authoritative.

But I am not ready to look like a grandfather. And if I am "authorita-tive," why aren't they all paying rapt attention? Do they not know that I see their every move? Clara is doodling. Now she's talking to the boy next to her. I never reprimand in public, so I speak to her after class. To my embarrassment, she has been drawing a portrait of me. I am a hideous prune with big ears, deep eyes, wrinkled bony cheeks, bald head, and a ridged brow like those Klingons on *Star Trek*.

IV ⌁

In a rare small experiment with democracy, rather than assign my old standbys such as Thomas Gray's "Elegy in a Country Churchyard," I ask the class to read ahead and pick poems they want to study. Some light on my favorites, such as Langston Hughes's "Theme for English B," about a black student at Columbia, overlooking Harlem, who tells his instructor in a paper, "You are white—yet a part of me, as I am a part of you." Several pick Shakespeare's sonnet 130, "My mistress' eyes are nothing like the sun," in which the speaker loves his mistress, though her hair is like wire, her cheeks are colorless, and her breath reeks. They are reflecting, I think, their own insecurity about their looks in a culture where, one tells me, no young woman can look in the mirror and find herself thin enough, and young men take steroids and pump iron for hours a day to chisel their pecs and abs.

They focus too on Adrienne Rich's "Rape," in which a violated woman graphically describes her humiliation—"the maniac's sperm still greasing your thighs"—and implies that the policeman to whom she must report the crime is the very man who degraded her. And they pick Gwendolyn Brooks's "The Mother," in which a woman laments, though not necessarily regrets, her several abortions. At the end, she addresses her dead children: "Believe me, I loved you all." As Brooks has presented her, I doubt any reader is meant to believe her, and she may not believe herself.

In his anthology, Connolly included Hemingway's bullfighter story, "The Undefeated," perhaps because it represents spiritual triumph in physical defeat, but our book has "Hills Like White Elephants," in which, without using the word, a selfish young man intending to end his relationship talks his girl into having an abortion. *Elements of Literature* has no stated ideology, yet the themes of race and women's issues have naturally emerged. And though I did not know him well enough to be sure, I think Connolly would approve.

V ⁓

Joseph C. DeBarbrie, tall, smooth-complexioned, and gentlemanly, usually sits four seats to the left of Clara. A year before, as a senior at St. Ignatius Prep in San Francisco, he sat in a musty, wood-paneled room at the Jesuit retreat house outside Palo Alto, sipping Earl Grey tea and wondering what was so great about *kairos* and *agape,* the buzz words that annually floated home from the senior retreat. Then a retreat leader knocked, came in, and handed him an envelope bearing St. Ignatius's picture and stuffed with surprise letters from family, teachers, and friends showering him with love and praise.

Joe is the kind of boy adults find easy to praise. His family— insurance-broker father and teacher mother, who met at Santa Clara University and married right after graduation, his older brother, and younger sister—are so happy and supportive that he sometimes sat around just enjoying them rather than studying. When surgery following a freshman-year injury to his back ended his varsity sports career in high school, he threw himself into four years of those extracurricular activities that allow the Jesuit student to thrive: manager and trainer for five teams, the yearbook and newspaper, the liturgy, cheerleader, social action, and, above all, the theater. Appearing in plays and musicals—*Inherit the Wind, Our Town,* and *Carousel*—for four years, as a senior he won the male lead in *Shadowlands.*

Not that every moment was smooth. The more than six weeks of recuperation in freshman year took him out of circulation longer than an adolescent can endure without losing out on friendships and the group. As a sophomore, he drifted into the wrong bunch of friends. One night when the gang was hanging out smoking cigarettes by the San Francisco reservoir overlooking the Pacific, his "friends" turned on him, told him bluntly that they didn't like him and that he was out of the gang. Go home. Emotionally crushed, he staggered home in the rain.

He rebuilt himself in school activities, particularly on a school-sponsored summer "faith tour" living and working in Belfast and Dublin. In Dublin he lived at Gonzaga College and worked in a summer camp for eight- to ten-year-old boys strung out on dope. In Ireland, he says, the campaign against drugs resembles the American campaign against cigarettes—graphic posters of young people with rotting teeth. His little boys liked to show off the track marks between their fingers where their older brothers and pals had given them a hit. On walks, he would cut through a graveyard where the boys had left their needles strewn between the tombstones.

So on retreat he relished the notes of praise, but he was most struck by the letter from his drama coach, who told him "it's time to exit stage left at the prep"; rather than applaud, his director challenged him to go on and "become a good man."

He picked Fordham because Jesuits "take care of their students," because he liked the pretty campus with the pretty girls, because he liked the student body's economic diversity, and because he thought he "could handle New York." Though it took him a few months to be sure he had come to the right place, he soon came on strong in residence-hall leadership, a role in the Mimes and Mummers' production of *Moon over Buffalo,* and a focused dedication to study that moved his high-school B average to a Fordham A-. In his theology course, famed feminist theologian Elizabeth Johnson changed his image of God from the more simple, personal, someone-I-can-talk-to encounter of his high-school retreat to a God who is many things, masculine and feminine, still real, yet incomprehensible.

On Thursday nights he occasionally enjoys the local bar scene, which he sees as just one aspect of Fordham's generally healthy social milieu. True, some students party too much, but that depends on the attitude they bring with them, and better to visit the local pubs than drink on campus. Besides, he says, the neighborhood is safe. On weekends he loves to ride the "awesome" D train to Manhattan and, coming home, doesn't mind the twelve-minute walk from the subway down Fordham Road.

Joe's final paper focused on three films—*Citizen Kane, Casablanca,* and *The Four Feathers*—in which strong men either compromise or sustain their integrity. I teach Zoltan Korda's 1939 British Empire epic *Four Feathers* both because it is a wonderful work of art and because its thinking and rationale, its lofty concept of duty and commitment, are so foreign to 1990s young people, who are reluctant to commit themselves to anything beyond Saturday night's date, which they will also break if something better comes along.

It's also one of the first films I remember seeing, and as the son of a World War I hero who wiped out a German machine-gun nest on his own and who personified courage and integrity all his life, I must have identified with the hero, young Harry Faversham, who joined the army just to please his Crimean War–veteran father and was terrified that his father would ever consider him a coward. As everyone over fifty—plus some of my college classes—knows, Harry resigns from the army after his father's death, just as his regiment is on the way to the Sudan. When his friends send him white feathers as a sign of cowardice, he disguises himself, goes to the Sudan and saves their lives. For Joe, Harry's true courage was in refusing to follow the army career; his war exploits were merely a brave gesture to regain the respect of his friends and fiancée.

VI 〜

Other things happened this semester. Tornadoes killed more than forty persons in Oklahoma and Kansas. The Yugoslav army drove one million Albanians out of Kosovo. NATO bombings killed anywhere between four hundred and one thousand innocent Serbian and Kosovar civilians by mistake. High-school students gunned down their classmates. Fordham College's new dean, Jeffrey von Arx, S.J., a historian who had been at Princeton, Yale, and Georgetown, spelled out the trustees' plan to move Fordham to the national prominence that Georgetown and Boston College have enjoyed.

During Black History Month someone smeared racial and sexual insults on a door in Finlay Hall, prompting weeks of self-examination on the possibility of racism in our midst. Three of the five students we helped prepare for Fulbright Fellowships won—to France, the Philippines, and an alternate to Indonesia. A series of Fordham *Ram* surveys sampling fifty students reveal that 86 percent drink and 42 percent had missed class at some time because of drinking; 88 percent could name three Shakespeare plays, but only 22 percent could name three of the twelve apostles. The *Ram* ran a series of articles on *Ex corde ecclesiae*, Pope John Paul II's 1990 guidelines for an authentic Catholic university; most writers seemed relatively content with Fordham's Catholic character, whatever it may be.

With the help of students and alumni—plus a rambunctious gang of student happy hecklers called "the Sixth Man"—who packed the gym for home games, basketball caught fire. Fr. Avery Dulles, S.J., who celebrated his eightieth birthday and tenth year in the McGinley Chair, lectured to a crowd of seven hundred on "Can Philosophy Be Christian?" The last week of the year I visited a student friend, a senior, in the hospital. After early-morning words exchanged in a local pub, he had been outnumbered on the way home and beaten senseless. They have punched in his face and could have killed him. In the final month we, as a nation, have been overwhelmed by the shock of American middle-class boys with guns who somehow release the demons that plague them by shooting down their classmates. This madness seemed far away, in the West or South. But this attack on my friend was done not by neighborhood troublemakers, but by Fordham freshmen. He is victim of the alcohol culture, surely, but also of whatever it is in American mores that says men should settle their differences by resorting to violence in any form. But we can hope those freshmen will not be back, and the senior received his diploma in person to a standing ovation.

VII ~

I close up my deserted sophomore dean's office a little before 5:30, trying to decide which I need more, daily Mass or a quick swim. Tonight I'll go to the wake of a sophomore's father who died in a fall. At a student Mass in my residence-hall room on Monday night we prayed for those whose lives come apart in the last weeks of class and during exams. During the semester about a half dozen withdrew from classes for a while with depression. On the way to the gym I pass John—hospitalized two years ago, now one of our successes. His philosophy professor calls him a star; his mother says any other school would have forgotten about him.

In the campus center and Vince Lombardi Sports Complex, the newly installed network of around-the-clock TV monitors in the lobby, cafeteria, lounge, and weight rooms has given the area the atmosphere of an airport waiting room or a sports bar without the beer. On the screen, commercials, news trivia, and MTV: actors kiss, their tongues meet, they unbutton their clothes. In the Jesuit graveyard, I make the rounds of the tombstones and try to decipher the names, many of which time, air pollution, and New York winters have washed away. The plan is to destroy the old stones before the elements reduce them to rubble and replace them with a little bronze plaque for each man and a statue of St. Ignatius. A fitting memorial, to be sure, but not an old-fashioned college graveyard with whatever those stones have to teach the young.

It begins to rain. The skies open. The earth is drenched. Three students—two guys and a girl—cavort onto Edwards Parade and send their Frisbee sailing through the torrent. They leap, tumble, and roll, laughing and splashing in the lush green grass.

VIII ~

On the last day of class I give students a short slide show, pictures I've taken over the years, but mostly within the last few months. Nineteenth-century Fordham: Dealy Hall, in which we sit, and Hughes Hall, in which several of us live, when they first went up. The baseball bleachers no longer on Edwards Parade. For the group photo of the 1857 Jesuit faculty, I point out Fr. Tissot, the Civil War chaplain; Fr. Doucet, the friend of Edgar Allan Poe; Fr. Daubresse, who taught moral philosophy but did not know English; and Fr. Legouais, the funny-looking fellow with the face of an angry goat, the dwarf whom students loved. (I don't tell the anecdote about Legouais on a walk with students when a rude fellow by the side of the road made fun of his appearance and a burly Fordham boy resolved the situation by pummeling the wise guy with his fists.) The Third Avenue El passing by the campus in 1916. Myself swimming in Walden Pond and sitting by Thoreau's grave. Hemingway posing with a dead leopard in Africa and kicking a can in Idaho shortly before killing himself. The campus in fall and in spring.

And finally themselves. The class photo—my last class of the millennium—very few of them the same persons who sat looking at me and one another in January. Lek, though he still hates poetry and old movies, makes an exception for *Four Feathers*. It may help him stand up to his father who wants him to move back to Albania. The baseball player has quit the team. The football player thought of quitting, but stayed. Two of the eighteen in the picture have failed the course.

Joe could go one of two ways. This summer he works for Gap in San Francisco. With a Colombian grandmother, he speaks Spanish well. Some day, as a Gap executive, he could go to Latin America and convince his company to apply Jesuit social-justice principles to their factories there. Or he could take some risks, take communications courses, stay in New York, "make it here," and end up host of the *Today Show*.

Clara ends the year evicted by her aunt and split from her boyfriend, but with a solid average Fordham grade. Her favorite essay is James Thurber's short fable "The Moth and the Star," about a young moth who ignores his parents' commands to flutter around the street lamps like the other moths and get his wings singed. Rather, every night for years, he tries to fly to a star, as if it were right beyond the treetops. He never reaches it, of course, but he begins to think he did and lives a long life happy with his imagined accomplishment. His parents, brothers, and sisters all burned to death when they were young.

Chronology of Fordham

1540   St. Ignatius and his companions take their first vows, forming the company of Jesus

1599   Publication of the *Ratio Studiorum*

1639   Jonas Bronck, Dutch settler, settles at 132 St. and Lincoln Ave.

1669   John Archer buys 3,900 acres from Mohegan Indians

1671?   Gov. Francis Lovelace grants Archer 3,900 acres. Archer names it Fordham, meaning "wading place (for crossing a ford)"

1692   Original Rose Hill Manor built

According to legend, used by George Washington as headquarters during the American Revolution; cf. John Fenimore Cooper, *The Spy*

College infirmary until demolition in 1890s

Kings Bridge opens, first link between Bronx and Manhattan

NB: Today's Bronx consisted of two towns, Westchester and Eastchester, and four manors: Pelham, Morrisania, Fordham, and Philipsburgh

1773   Suppression of the Society of Jesus

1814   Restoration of the Society of Jesus

1832   Revised *Ratio Studiorum* published

1834   Jesuits from Bardstown take over St. Mary's, Marion County, Kentucky

1838   Present Rose Hill Manor built; gets two one-story extensions, replaced in 1870 by present north and south wings. Wings once extended from back of building toward Keating Hall

John Hughes comes to New York as coadjutor bishop (bishop 1839; archbishop, 1850) to M. R. John Dubois; looks for site for seminary and college

1839 Hughes purchases Rose Hill Manor, then a farm of about 100 acres, bordering on Bronx River and including part of present Botanical Gardens, for about $30,000

1840 Alumni House built. Believed to be work of architect William Rodrigue, brother-in-law of John Hughes, who lived there during construction of adjacent church and resident hall

St. Joseph's Seminary opens at Rose Hill with approximately fourteen transfers from Lafargeville and seven new admissions. After it closed in 1859, seminarians were sent to St. Joseph's Seminary in Troy, later in Yonkers

1841 New York and Harlem Railroad is extended to Webster Avenue. and what is now Fordham Road

1841–42 CARDINAL McCLOSKEY, president of Fordham

24 June (Feast of St. John the Baptist), St. John's College opens with six students

First president, John McCloskey, became first bishop of Albany, then archbishop of New York, and later first American cardinal

Bishop Levi Silliman Ives (former Episcopal bishop of South Carolina, convert to Catholicism in Rome) teaches rhetoric

1842–43 AMBROSE MANAHAN, president of Fordham

1843–45 JOHN HARLEY (27) (+) 1846, president of Fordham

1845–46 JAMES ROOSEVELT BAYLEY, president of Fordham

1845 Seminary church built, named Our Lady of Mercy. Stained-glass windows, given by King Louis Philippe of France to John Hughes for old St. Patrick's Cathedral, were the wrong size, so they were transferred to St. John's

Hughes and French Jesuits sign agreement. France moves personnel from mission in Kentucky to New York to take over St. John's and, in 1846, St. Joseph's Seminary

1846 Edgar Allen Poe moves to the Bronx

1846–51 AUGUSTUS J. THEBAUD, S.J., president of Fordham

10 April, governor signs act granting St. John's College a university charter

15 July, Jesuits begin to arrive from Kentucky. Hughes deeds college to Jesuits for $40,000, but retains title to the seminary, about nine acres with buildings

1847   18 July, New York *Herald* story of second commencement, held 2 July

Guests arrived by New York and Harlem Railroad. There was a tent on the lawn and 2,000 persons attended

1849   Poe writes "The Bells"

1851-54 JOHN LARKIN, S.J., president of Fordham

1852   Our Lady of Mercy parish organized. Services in college chapel, until Our Lady of Mercy Church built in 1890 off campus

1854   1854-59 REMIGIUS TELLIER, S.J., president of Fordham

Debating Society established

1855   First drama productions: *Henry IV* and *The Seven Clerks*

1856   Orestes Brownson's address

1858   First lab fees, $5.00 for use of chemical apparatus

1859–63 AUGUSTUS J. THEBAUD, S.J., president of Fordham

November, first regular baseball team: Rose Hill Baseball Club. First college game in U.S. with nine on a side. Rose Hill 33, Xavier 11

1859   Seminary closes; theologians gone

1860   Hughes sells seminary to Jesuits for $45,000

Alumni Society founded

1863   Woodlawn Cemetery established

1863–65 EDWARD DOUCET, S.J., president of Fordham

1864   Gatehouse built at Third Ave and Fordham Road entrance to test quality of stone from local quarry. Later moved to become Alpha House

1865 PETER TISSOT, S.J., president of Fordham for four months

1865–68 WILLIAM MOYLAN, S.J., president of Fordham

1867–90   Belmont Stakes run at Jerome Park racetrack. Moved to Morris Park in 1890, and to Nassau in 1905

1867   East section of the first-division building built. West front built in 1891. In 1935, building is named for Patrick F. Dealy, S.J., president, 1882–85

1869   Jesuits open Woodstock College in Maryland for theological studies

    1869–74 JOSEPH SHEA, S.J., president of Fordham

    1874–82 WILLIAM GOCKELN, S.J., president of Fordham

1874   Maroon selected as official school color

    1882–85 PATRICK DEALY, S.J., president of Fordham

1882   *The Monthly* begins publication

1883   26 November, football team organized. Lost first game to Xavier, 21-6

    1885–88 THOMAS E. CAMPBELL, S.J., president of Fordham

1885   Military cadet battalion established

1886   Science building built. Later named Thebaud Hall in 1935 for Augustus Thebaud, S.J., president, 1846–51, 1859–63

    1888–91 JOHN SCULLY, S.J., president of Fordham

1888   The Third Avenue El extended to 132nd Street beginning a new age of prosperity in the Bronx

    Land bought for Bronx Park, later divided into Bronx Zoo, Botanical Gardens, etc.

1890   The Grand Concourse designed and built

    Present Fordham Cemetery opened. Bodies moved from first property, now belonging to Botanical Garden. Last burial in 1909

    1891–96 THOMAS GANNON, S.J., president of Fordham

1891   24 June 1891, Golden Jubilee

    Botanical Garden opens

    Second-division building built. Named Hughes Hall in 1935. Housed Fordham Prep until 1972

    24 June, statue of John Hughes presented by Alumni Association. Restored 1941

1893   4 December, University Church, Our Lady of Mercy, blessed and formally opened

1896–1900 THOMAS E. CAMPBELL, S.J., president of Fordham

1897   Cap and gown introduced for commencement

1898   Bronx consolidated into Manhattan; 23rd and 24th Wards become Bronx Borough

1900–04 GEORGE A. PETTIT, S.J., president of Fordham

Restoration of classical curriculum

1900–59 Shopping district develops along Fordham Road. Alexander's added in 1928. New apartment buildings, five-story walk-ups and six-story buildings with elevators. Middle-class Jews, Irish, Italians from Manhattan: second-generation immigrants

1900   Third Avenue El extended to Fordham Plaza

1902   First intercollegiate basketball game against Brooklyn Poly. Fordham lost 18-10

1904–06 JOHN J. COLLINS, S.J., president of Fordham

Fordham moves to university status with a law school and a medical school

1904   First Avenue Subway connects Bronx and Manhattan under 149th Street to Third Avenue El

The "Hub" develops, with theaters, Alexander's Department Store in 1928

Hundreds of thousands of Italians and other immigrant groups move from Manhattan to Bronx for new Bronx apartment buildings

Collins Auditorium built. Named for John J. Collins, S.J., president 1904–06, later apostolic vicar of Jamaica

J. Ignatius Coveney writes "The Fordham Ram"

1905   28 September, medical school opens in science building (will close in 1921); law school, with thirteen students and Paul Fuller first dean, opens in Collins

1906–11 DANIEL J. QUINN, S.J., president of Fordham

1906   Law school moves to 42 Broadway. Case method introduced by Prof. Ralph W. Gifford

1907   Amendment to original charter. Name changed to Fordham University

Fordham Hospital opens

Fordham University Press established

1908   Law school moves to 20 Veset Street with forty-six students

1910   First seismograph installed in basement of Administration Building by Fr. Edward P. Tivnan, S.J.

1911–15 THOMAS J. McCLUSKY, S.J., president of Fordham

1911   New medical-school building completed. After closing of medical school, building becomes chemistry building (later Old Chemistry Building, and then New Hall. Named Finlay Hall in 1990)

1912   Law school moves for fourth time, to 140 Nassau St. More than four hundred students

Carl Jung series of lectures at medical school

College of pharmacy established. Closed in 1971

1913   Medical school moves to new building, completed in 1911

1914   *Fordham Law Review* founded. Publication suspended in 1917 for World War I

1915–19 JOSEPH A. MULRY, S.J., president of Fordham

Twenty-eighth floor of Woolworth Building becomes law school for next twenty-eight years

1916   12–14 June, Celebration of Diamond Jubilee; 8,000 attend

6 November, Graduate School of Arts and Sciences, teachers college, and School of Social Service organized and located in Woolworth

First publication of the *Maroon*

1918   Jerome Avenue El opens

7 February, first *Ram*

Student Army Training Corps initiated

1919–24 EDWARD P. TIVNAN, S.J., president of Fordham

1920   Department of Education of the graduate school opens

          School of Business Administration opens as School of Accounting. Moves to Rose Hill, 1947

          14 November, stone pillars at Third Avenue gate dedicated as gift of Alumni Association; 1941 memorial plaques added

1921   Accreditation from Middle States Association of Colleges and Universities

1922   Messenger of Sacred Heart Building erected. Converted to Murray-Weigel Hall, residence of scholastics, in 1965

1923   Yankee Stadium built at 161st Street

          Kohlman Hall constructed as headquarters for New York Province. Named for Anthony Kohlman, S.J., founder of the New York Literary Institution (1808–14)

          Ignatius M. Wilkinson, S.J., named dean of law school. Serves until death in 1953

          1924–30 WILLIAM J. DUANE, S.J., president of Fordham

1924   4 December, University Gym completed

          Seismic Observatory, donated by William Spain, dedicated on present site of Loyola Hall. Moved to site of Keating Hall in 1927, and to present site east of Freeman in 1931

1926   Duane Library built and named for William J. Duane, S.J., president 1924–30

          Larkin Hall (biology building) named for John Larkin, S.J., president, 1851–54

1928   Loyola Hall built. Faber Hall added, 1960

1929   Loews Paradise opens: $4 million, 4,000 seats

          1930–36 ALOYSIUS J. HOGAN, S.J., president of Fordham

1930   Freeman Hall opens (physics building) named for science teacher Thomas J. A. Freeman, S.J.

1931   10 May, first annual faculty convocation. Seven faculty and administrators awarded Bene merenti

          19 November, charter change enables change of the collegiate department from St. John's College to Fordham College

1932   First comprehensive exams in graduate school

1933   Grand Concourse Subway opens

1934   School of Sociology and Social Service given its present title and expanded to offer grad courses and degrees

1935   *Fordham Law Review,* suspended for WWI, resumes publication

1936–49 ROBERT I. GANNON, S.J., president of Fordham

May, law school receives provisional approval from ABA

Keating Hall, named for Joseph Keating, S.J., university treasurer from 1910–48, completed. Though originally constructed for the seniors of Fordham College, Gannon changes purpose and houses Graduate School of Arts and Sciences

Accreditation by the Association of American Law Schools

The juniorate of St. Andrew-on-Hudson is affiliated with Fordham College

1936–37 Jim Crowley football coach

The Seven Blocks of Granite—John Druze, Al Babartsky, Vincent Lombardi, Alex Wojciechowicz, Nat Pierce, Ed Franco, Leo Paquin—coached by "Sleepy" Jim Crowley, one of the "Four Horsemen of Notre Dame," dominate Fordham football

1937   Association of American Universities admits Fordham to the circle of Complex Organization

1938   1 August, teachers college merges with the Department of Education of the graduate school to become the School of Education, offering both graduate and undergraduate degrees

Hillaire Belloc in residence in history department during spring semester

Dr. Victor Hess, Nobel prize winner in physics for discovery of cosmic rays, joins physics department, teaches until 1956

Constitution Row, thirteen red maple trees dedicated by class of '41

1939   Working model of seismic station, designed by director J. Joseph Lynch, the only exhibit by an individual university at New York World's Fair

Delegates of Pax Romana hold their first American congress at Fordham

Quad renamed Edwards Parade for Gen. Charles Edwards, former commander of Fordham ROTC

1940   St. John's Hall expands into Our Lady's Court (Queen's Court) with construction of Bishop's Hall and St. Robert's Hall, named for Robert Bellarmine

27 September, 400th anniversary of the Society of Jesus; celebration held in Keating Hall

Fordham assumes publication of *Thought* from America Press

1940–41   28 September, yearlong Centennial Celebration begins, and Fordham Century Fund Appeal launched for $1,000,000

1941   1 January, Fordham loses Cotton Bowl to Texas A&M, 13-12

1942   1 January, Fordham wins Sugar Bowl against Missouri, 2-0

School of Sociology and Social Service moves to 134 E 39th Street

University Church hosts Cardinal Spellman at consecration of new reredos and triptych in connection with installation of new altar. The inlaid marble altar, given in 1878 by diocesan clergy to St. Patrick's Cathedral, is donated to Fordham by Cardinal Spellman

Parkchester Apartments completed, population 40,000

1943 $122,000 paid for Vincent Building, 302 Broadway, home for law school, School of Education, Fordham College–Manhattan Division

1944   Adult and evening programs begin, develop into School of General Studies in 1969

1945   Population change after WWII: 170,000 blacks and Puerto Ricans, displaced by slum clearance in Manhattan, move to South Bronx

1946   11 May, Charter Centenary, President Harry S Truman rings for first time ship's bell of aircraft carrier *Junyo*, presented by Admiral Chester W. Nimitz, blessed by Spellman as memorial to "dear young dead of WWII"

Fordham institutes department of communication arts

26 October, Spellman dedicates WFUV

Spellman Hall opens for Jesuit graduate students

1948   23 May, WWI memorial in University Church dedicated by Spellman

1949–63 LAURENCE J. McGINLEY, S.J., president of Fordham

1950s–60s New highways: Cross-Bronx Expressway, Major Deegan, and Bruckner

1950–80 Traditional Bronx residents move to the suburbs. Now Puerto Ricans, Latin Americans, blacks from South Bronx take their places. Buildings abandoned. Northwest Bronx Community and Clergy Coalition formed. 1980s: Dominicans, Jamaicans, Albanians, Koreans, Vietnamese

1950–51 Martyrs' Court erected. Named for French Jesuits slain by Iroquois on Mohawk River in 1640s: Isaac Jogues, Rene Goupil, Jean LaLande

September 1951, author arrives, lives in Dealy Four

1952–53 Author's Junior Year Abroad

1954 Varsity football dropped

1955 Coffey Field dedicated, for Jack Coffey's 33rd anniversary as baseball coach

College of Philosophy and Letters, Shrub Oak, affiliated with Fordham. Closes in 1969

1956 Tom Courtney, at Olympic Games in Melbourne, wins gold medal in 800-meter track competition

1958 30 June, organizational meeting of board of lay trustees

Fordham acquires approximately 320,230 square feet (7 acres) of property as collegiate sponsor in Lincoln Center Urban Renewal Project under Title 1 of the Housing Act of 1949. Cost $2,241,610. Also acquires Third Avenue El property at this time

1959 Campus Center constructed. Later named for Laurence McGinley, S.J., president 1949–63

1960s–70s In Bronx, rampant arson by landlords for insurance and by tenants to gain priority in housing

1961 New law-school building opens at Lincoln Center. Robert F. Kennedy, attorney general, speaks and gets honorary degree

1962 1 March, Tau Chapter of Phi Beta Kappa installation ceremonies

1963–65 VINCENT T. O'KEEFE, S.J., president of Fordham

1964 Thomas More College opens as coordinate college for women

Club football established

1965–69 LEO J. MCLAUGHLIN, S.J., president of Fordham

First meeting of faculty senate, Joe Cammarasano (FC '47) elected first president

1966   14 September, first meeting of combined Jesuit and lay board of trustees

Faculty Memorial Hall converted from a five-story loft building. Plaques in lobby for Sam Telfair and others

Yearlong observance of 125th anniversary of founding of Fordham University. Theme, "The University in the American Experience," culminates with visit of Fr. Pedro Arrupe, general of the Society of Jesus

5 April, honorary doctorates to five men committed to religious liberty

1967   Experimental Bensalem College opens. Closes 1974

Fordham selected for Schweitzer Chair. Dr. Marshall McLuhan, University of Toronto, accepts

Louis Calder Foundation transfers 114-acre estate to Fordham as Louis Calder Conservation and Ecology Study Center

1968–70   Co-op City opens, population 60,000; largest housing development in the world

1968   Humanae vitae

1969–72   MICHAEL P. WALSH, S.J., president of Fordham

1969–70   Two strikes, building occupations, Cambodia, Kent State, McGinley fire

1969   Leo McLaughlin removed, replaced by Mike Walsh, S.J.

Undergraduate liberal-arts college at Lincoln Center opens

Graduate School of Education, Social Service, and Business Administration move into Lowenstein Center

16 November, John Mulcahy Hall, the chemistry building, opens

Joseph A. Martino Graduate School of Business Administration, named for trustee emeritus, established at Lincoln Center

First meeting of board of trustees in new form with Jesuits and and laymen

1970   Administration Building, St. John's, and chapel designated landmark buildings by Landmarks Preservation Commission

Calder Conservation and Ecology Center, Armonk, New York, founded on 114 acres

1971   School of Pharmacy closes

1972–84 JAMES C. FINLAY, S.J., president of Fordham

1972   Fordham Prep moves from Hughes Hall to new building, separated from university

Thirteen-story residence opens on E. 191st Street called 555 and named for Mike Walsh, S.J., president 1969–72

1973   Inception of women's tennis

1974   First Archbishop Hughes Medals awarded to administrators for twenty years' service

Thomas More College merges with Fordham College

1975   Graduate School of Religion and Religious Education develops out of education programs begun in 1969

1976   Vincent T. Lombardi Memorial Center built

Graduate Center on campus of Marymount College in Tarrytown opens, with courses in business administration, education, and social service

1977   South Bronx known nationally as symbol of urban blight. *Fort Apache: The Bronx*

Hispanic Research Center established by Lloyd Rogler, director, Schweitzer Chair professor of humanities

1978   All-University Center on Gerontology established

Fordham Hospital property (4.3 acres) purchased at auction from City of NY for $400,000

1979   Law-school student team wins National Moot Court Competition

1981   Alumni House designated landmark building

1982   First 1841 Awards presented to physical plant and clerical staff for twenty years' service

1984   JOSEPH A. O'HARE, S.J., 1984–, president of Fordham

1986   Completion of Rose Hill Apartments, Fordham-sponsored, federally subsidized residence for senior citizens and handicapped on strip of abandoned park land adjacent to Fordham Prep

       Sesquicentennial Residence Hall built

1987   Alumni Court residence halls built

1990   30 September, Sesquicentennial Year, theme "Keeping Faith with the Future," opens with Mass of the Holy Spirit and convocation

       2 October, New Hall renamed Finlay Hall after president 1972–84

1991–92   Yearlong celebration of Sesquicentennial

1996–97   Leo McLaughlin, who had been living in Murray-Weigel Hall, dies

       Quentin Lauer, S.J., dies

       William D. Walsh Family Library opens

2001   Avery Dulles, S.J., Fordham McGinley Professor, named cardinal of the Roman Catholic Church

       Fordham merges with Marymount College in Tarrytown

Notes and Sources

Abbreviations

FA Fordham University archives
FOH Fordham sesquicentennial oral histories
FM Fordham Monthly
FEY Fordham: The Early Years
JCB "Jesuit and Catholic Boyhood"
RAS Raymond A. Schroth
UP Up to the Present
WL Woodstock Letters

In these notes I will not necessarily refer to a book or article if the reference is already in the text. As often as seems appropriate I have included references in the text to campus publications such as the *Ram,* the *Maroon* yearbook, and the *Monthly,* particularly when the reporting of the story is part of the story itself. All these are available in the Fordham University Archives (FA). The *Ram* is a weekly, but during crises it publishes several times a week.

Full bibliographic information on books, periodicals, manuscripts, and other materials is in the selected bibliography. Any references to a work in the notes will simply be to the author and/or title of the work and will include page numbers when appropriate. All other documents and letters that are not cited in the bibliography are in FA or in my possession (RAS). I also personally witnessed many of the events described for 1950–55, 1969–79, and 1996–99.

There are four major works that cover the history of Fordham University in some detail. The best known is Robert I. Gannon, S.J.'s *Up to the Present: The Story of Fordham* (*UP*), which quotes liberally from contemporary documents such as the *Fordham Monthly* (*FM*) and reflects former Fordham president Gannon's own views on American Catholic higher education. Thomas G. Taaffe's *A History of St. John's College, Fordham, New York* was published in 1891 to celebrate Fordham's fiftieth anniversary. Christa R. Klein's "The Jesuits and Catholic Boyhood in Nineteenth-Century New

The most recent biography of Archbishop John Hughes is Richard Shaw's *Dagger John: The Unquiet Life and Times of Archbishop John Hughes of New York*. My interpretation of his career and the history of the Irish in New York relies partly on Charles R. Morris, *American Catholic: The Saints and Sinners Who Built America's Most Powerful Church*. The story of Hughes's earlier attempts to found a seminary is in Thomas J. Shelley, "Fordham before the Jesuits: Bishop John Hughes and St. John's College, 1838–1846," in *FEY*, pp. 51–74. Hughes's address to the Leopoldine Society is in *The Complete Works of the Most Rev. John Hughes, D.D.*, edited by Lawrence Kehoe, pp. 459–64. On the earlier Jesuit schools see Golda G. Standler, "Jesuit Educational Institutions in the City of New York, 1683–1860." Material on the Society of Jesus in France comes from John Padberg, S.J., *Colleges in Controversy: The Jesuit Schools in France from Revival to Suppression, 1815–1880*, and "The Restored Society of Jesus in France, 1814–1830: Why French Jesuits Came to America in 1831," in *FEY*, pp. 11–29.

The reference to "staging areas" for the expansion of Jesuit education is from JCB, pp. 3–5, and is based on a concept in Philip Gleason's "The First Century of Jesuit Higher Education in America: An Overview," a lecture he gave to the American Catholic Historical Society in Dayton, Ohio, on 26 March 1976. R. Emmett Curran's *The Bicentennial History of Georgetown University* summarizes the early expansion of American Catholic higher education.

For the decision to move from Kentucky to New York, see James Hennesey, S.J., "The Coming of the French Jesuits to Fordham: An Overview," in *FEY*, pp. 1–10. An earlier essay is Gilbert J. Garraghan's "Fordham's Jesuit Beginnings." The description of the campus upon their arrival is based on Nash's recollections and old maps and drawings in FA. For the history and archeology of the property, see Harry C. W. Melick, *The Manor of Fordham and Its Founder*, and Allan S. Gilbert and Roger Wines, "From Earliest to Latest Fordham: Background History and Ongoing Archeology," in *FEY*, pp. 135–67. For Thebaud's life, see the biographical sketch by Thomas J. Campbell in Augustus J. Thebaud, S.J., *Forty Years in the United States of America, 1839–1885*, vol. 3, a posthumous collection of Thebaud's partly autobiographical writings. Volumes 1 and 2 contain reflections on recent French history. Volume 3 includes his arrival in Kentucky and reflections on American Catholicism. Brother Mace's obituary is in *WL* 18 (1887): 385–87.

2. A Visit from Mr. Poe

The description of Poe's life around Fordham is drawn from Mary Gove Nichols, *Reminiscences of Edgar Allan Poe*, the reprint of a *Colliers* magazine article; Mary E. Phillips, *Edgar Allan Poe: The Man*, vol. 2, pp. 1115–29, 1133–41, 1200–27, 1240–71, 1547–55; "Some Fordham Poets," an anonymous letter by "A Villager" in *FM;* and "An Ancient Member of the Faculty Interviewed," an interview with Fr. Doucet.

The analysis of the early Jesuit community and the biographies of the men are based on Hennessy's chapter, "The First Jesuits," in *FEY*. The material on Larkin also draws from several references to him in *FM,* including John H. G. Hassard's "Fr. Larkin," 1891; and Francis J. Nelligan, "Fr. John Larkin, S.J., 1801–1858," in *Canadian Messenger*

York City: A Study of St. John's College and the College of St. Francis Xavier, 1846–1912" (JCB) focuses on the curriculum and the moral training of the young men. *Fordham: The Early Years (FEY)*, edited by Thomas C. Hennessy, S.J., collects definitive essays by eight scholars on the histories of the early Fordham Jesuits from their departure from France up to the Civil War.

An important source for the mid-twentieth century is a collection of oral histories from interviews conducted between 1980 and 1990 with faculty, administrators, alumni, and trustees as part of the sesquicentennial celebration. The Fordham oral histories (FOH), of varying length and quality, are in three boxes in FA. A selection of these histories, edited by Jerry Buckley, was published in 1991 under the title *As I Remember Fordham*. The project was organized by Stella Moundas, secretary to three presidents.

For histories of American Catholic higher education, see Edward J. Power, *Catholic Higher Education in America: A History,* and Philip Gleason, *Contending with Modernity: Catholic Higher Education in the Twentieth Century.* The Fordham archival sources consist of Fordham catalogues; the Minister's Diary (1846–1912) of the early fathers; reports by Fordham Jesuits published in *Woodstock Letters (WL)* (1872–1969); reminiscences in the *Fordham Monthly* (1882–1960s); the *Maroon,* Fordham's yearbook; and the *Fordham Ram* (1918–present).

Prologue

All the material in the prologue comes from my experiences and observations and from interviews with the participants: Eric Montroy, Eileen Markey, Vincent Augello, Nicola Pitchford, and Joseph A. O'Hare, S.J.

1. Michael Nash Arrives

The story of Michael Nash's arrival is in "Reminiscences of Fr. Michael Nash," *WL.* His obituary is in the same volume. Thomas C. Hennessy summarizes Nash's life in "The First Jesuits at St. John's College" in *FEY,* pp. 116–17.

For St. Mary's College and St. Joseph's College, see Walter Hill, "Some Reminiscences of St. Mary's College, Kentucky," and "Some Facts and Incidents Relating to St. Joseph's College, Bardstown, Kentucky," in *WL.* The most recent and thorough summary is Cornelius Michael Buckley, S.J.'s "French Jesuits at St. Mary's College, Marion County, Kentucky, 1831–1846," in *FEY.* Also see "The History of St. Mary's College, 1821–1871," in *Memorare: St. Mary's College, 150 Years,* Chester Gawronski and David Hilier, editors.

of the Sacred Heart, (1957), 68, 37–43, 102–10, 181–87. The stories about his role in the founding of Xavier College are in Michael Nash's "Reminiscences." Descriptions of the early curriculum are in *UP* and JCB. The material on the goals of Jesuit education comes from John W. O'Malley, S.J., *The First Jesuits,* and Padberg's *Colleges in Controversy.* The alumnus's comment on Daubresse is by H. H. Dodge in "Reminiscences of a Forty-Niner," *FM* (1891), 77–8.

3. Brownson, Hughes, and Shaw

The details of Robert Gould Shaw's life and all the citations from his war letters are from the introduction to *Blue-Eyed Child of Fortune: The Civil War Letters of Colonel Robert Gould Shaw,* edited by Russell Duncan. The references to Fordham are from his earlier letters, published in Robert Gould Shaw, *Letters,* in the New York Public Library. The references to Georgetown are from R. Emmett Curran's *Bicentennial History. The Goose Quill, The Critic,* and *The Collegian* are in FA. There is a tribute to Hassard by General M. T. McMahon in *FM* (May 1888) and a biography in *National Cyclopedia of American Biography,* vol. 3. For the complete story of the conflict between Hughes and the Jesuits, see Francis X. Curran, S.J., "Archbishop Hughes and the Jesuits: An Anatomy of Their Quarrels," in *FEY* and Thomas J. Shelley, *Dunwoodie: The History of St. Joseph's Seminary, Yonkers, New York,* pp. 13–29.

For an overview of Orestes Brownson's place in American Catholic history, see Morris and the chapter on Brownson in Ross Labrie, *The Catholic Imagination in American Literature.* The most thorough biography is Thomas R. Ryan, C.Pp.S, *Orestes A. Brownson: A Definitive Biography.* Ryan narrates Brownson's encounters at St. John's with Hughes in 1856, 1860, and 1861 in great detail. He also draws heavily on Henry Brownson's *Later Life,* which quotes letters from his father. In Ryan, see pp. 400, 547, 552–53, 556–57, 616–17, and 713. Henry F. Brownson's *Orestes A. Brownson's Later Life: From 1856–1876,* by Brownson's son, refers to his father's attitude toward Jesuits. James M. McDonnell's *Orestes A. Brownson and Nineteenth-Century Catholic Education* is my source for Brownson's educational philosophy and the story of the son at Holy Cross. McDonnell draws on Brownson's correspondence with his sons at the time. See p. 193, nn. For Thebaud on slavery, see his *Forty Years,* pp. 60ff. For Hughes on slavery, see Shaw, *Dagger John.* For a view which argues that Brownson and Hughes were closer in their positions on Americanization than is generally acknowledged, see Charles P. Connor, "The American Catholic Political Position at Mid-Century: Archbishop Hughes as a Test Case."

4. Michael Nash Goes to War

For general background on the Civil War, I used the following sources: James M. McPherson, *Battle Cry of Freedom: The Civil War Era;* a narrative by Bruce Catton in *The*

American Heritage Picture History of the Civil War; and for regimental histories, Frederick H. Dyer, *A Compendium of the War of the Rebellion,* vol. 3. *FM* is the main source for the Civil War activities of Fordham men. Articles include: "How the Colors Were Lost," on the gallantry of the McMahon brothers; "Reminiscences of General James R. O'Beirne"; "General Martin McMahon, '55"; and a series on chaplains in the Civil War, including Thomas Oulette, S.J., Peter Tissot, S.J., and Michael Nash. Peter Tissot, S.J.'s memoir, based on his diary, ran for five issues in 1900. "Our Soldier Dead" is an incomplete list of casualties on both sides. James R. O'Beirne's "Reminiscences in War Times" tells his story again. Richard S. Treacy's "Reminiscences: Early Sixties," describes the home front. Michael Nash, S.J., wrote eleven letters between June 1861 and February 1862 that were published in *WL,* volumes 14 through 19.

5. Jimmy Walsh Gets Started

A good summary and analysis of James J. Walsh's career is Harry W. Kirwin, "James J. Walsh: Medical Historian and Pathfinder." Mary Anastasia Smith (Sister Mary Marcella) for her "James J. Walsh: American Revivalist of the Middle Ages," had the advantage of access to a Walsh autobiographical memoir now lost. The personal Fordham material is based on Walsh's letters, 1878–92, in the archives of St. Charles Borromeo Seminary in Philadelphia, Pennsylvania. These include letters by Joseph Walsh. Additional unpublished personal material made available to me by Walsh's son, James Walsh, includes: "Ordinary Facts in the Life of James J. Walsh," three pages, undated, probably from 1943; "Further Events in the Life of Dr. James J. Walsh by Dr. Joseph Walsh," (December 7, 1943); "The Boys of a Country Mining Town," seven pages, undated; and an autobiographical summary by James J. Walsh, six pages, 1935–38.

The material on the various presidents and on the beginnings of athletics is from *UP,* supplemented by reminiscences in *FM* and reports in *WL.* Most of the information on the buildings, while some of it is in *UP,* is based on Allan S. Gilbert and Roger Wines, "From Earliest to Latest Fordham," in *FEY.* This includes the details of ritual in the dining hall and of the menu. *FM,* December 1888, has an interview with Fr. Freeman, and June 1889 has one with Fr. Dealy. The account of the founding of Catholic University is based on C. Joseph Nuesse, *The Catholic University of America: A Centennial History.* The decision to move New York University is from Thomas J. Frusciano and Marilyn H. Pettit, *New York University and the City: An Illustrated History.*

6. Becoming a University

Edward P. Gilleran's unpublished manuscript, "Five to Fifty-Five: Recollections of Fordham during Its First Fifty Years as a University," compiled in 1958, is in the FA. It includes reminiscences on a sodality picnic, on the first movie filmed at Rose Hill (1908), and on various presidents. It also includes detailed descriptions of the interiors of Hughes Hall, St. John's Hall, and the Administration Building in 1905. Gilleran graduated from the prep in 1909 and the college in 1913. The information on Ignatius Coveney is in two *FM* articles: Stanley Quinn, "Obituary," and Robert J. King, "A Singer and His Song."

The historical background on the turn-of-the-century reform of Catholic higher education relies on Gleason, pp. 21–61; on Power; and on JCB, particularly the final chapter on both Fordham and Xavier in which the distinction is made between the high school and the college. The reference to the 1885 Jesuit province evaluation is on pp. 169–70. Power's assessment of the motivation for colleges is on p. 48.

For the year-by-year growth or decline of student enrollment, see *WL*. The Fordham Varia section includes commencement details, religious ceremonies, enrollment statistics, etc. The Minister's Diary and other internal Jesuit documents also sometimes mention student statistics. For example, see *WL* 16 (1887): 114; 17 (1888): 400; and 23 (1893): 441–42, the last of which adds, "The college is blessed in having no lay teachers, all the classes being under the direction of Ours."

The reports on Catholic attendance at non-Catholic colleges are in Gleason, pp. 22–24; the reference to conservative Jesuits, on p. 58; and Klein's figures on students not completing the Jesuit program, on p. 188. Fordham turns down half of its Latin American applicants, *WL* 34 (1905): 436–37. The Richard Harding Davis comment, *WL* 36 (1907): 385, from *Colliers Weekly*.

For the evidence of changes in the students' behavior, see the following notebooks and ledgers in FA: Prefect's Book of Rules and Customs during 1860s; Minister's Diary, 1889–1890; Diary, 1902–1910; Notes about Various Students for the Use of Rev. Fr. Rector, 1891–1896; Diary of Presidents 1885–1906; Consultors, 1890–1938. The opening of the tobacco shop is recorded in the Diary of the Prefect of the First Division, September 9, 1892. The Jamie O'Neill story is in Edward L. Shaughnessy, "Elle, James, and Jamie O'Neill."

These references to James J. Walsh, *The Thirteenth, Greatest of Centuries,* originally published by the Catholic Summer School Press (1907), are to the Eleventh Memorial Edition (1943) because it contains additional testimonies from historians. The critical response to the book is summarized in Sister Mary Marcella's Ph.D. dissertation, "James J. Walsh: American Revivalist of the Middle Ages." Walsh's comment on St. Thomas is on p. 278. The details of Walsh's European travels and of his return to and departure from Fordham are in Kirwin; the Walsh quote on taking risks when young is in Walsh's lost autobiographical manuscript seen by Kirwin. For the history of the early years of Catholic medical schools, see Power, pp. 210–20, and on Georgetown, R. Emmett Curran, pp. 149–55. For the Collins presidency, see *UP,* pp. 120–28. The Fordham medical school's innovative teaching practices are in *WL* 36 (1907): 159–60 and *WL* 42 (1913): 126. The student's comparison of Walsh to Chesterton is in an unpublished letter from Thomas Feeney, in Marcella, p. 123.

I have drawn primarily from three sources on Terence Shealy, S.J.,: his obituary in *WL* 52: 86–104; Gerald C. Treacy, S.J., ed., *Fr. Shealy: A Tribute;* and Michael Earls, S.J., ed., *Fr. Shealy and Marymount: His Lectures and Conferences.* The "sweat blood" quote is in Treacy, p. 75. The various opinions are from "Sententiae," in Earls, pp. 116–28. The material on the teachers college relies on Joseph F. X. McCarthy, *Learning in the City: The Graduate School of Education Reviews Its Seventy-five Years in New York, 1916–1992.*

7. "We'll Do, or Die"

The text of the 1917 baccalaureate sermon is in the *FM* 35: 468–74, but the celebrant is not named. How Fordham participated in the war is summarized in *UP,* pp. 149–56 and in the *Centurion,* the 1941 yearbook. The details of the Ambulance Corps dinner are in *FM* 35: 445–52. Charles A. Curtin's story is in the 1920 *Maroon. UP* and *WL* 47 (1918): 429–32 describe the S.A.T.C. operation and the football game against St. John's of Brooklyn. *UP,* p. 156, describes Mulry's end. The first *Ram* is in *UP,* p. 148, and *WL* 47: 268–69. Frank Frisch is in the 1920 *Maroon* and the *New York Times* obituary, March 13, 1973. The description of Francis X. Connolly comes from a letter, Richard Hurzeler to RAS, September 27, 1998, and William M. Halsey, *The Survival of American Innocence: Catholicism in an Era of Disillusionment, 1920–1940,* pp. 105, 112–15. The summary of the accomplishments of the postwar presidents is based on *UP,* pp. 156–66, 173–89. The history of the chemistry department relies on an unpublished manuscript in FA by Ronald A. Burdo, '67, "A History of Chemistry at Fordham, 1841–1967," which was based on articles in the *Retort,* the department publication. Details on the reopened seismic observatory come from "Seismic Observatory Reopened as Research and Learning Center."

Power's quote is on pp. 279–80 of his *Catholic Higher Education.* Edward F. Gilleran Jr.'s "One Last Look," an unpublished history of Fordham athletics, is the principal Fordham source for the material on Frank Cavanaugh, Jim Crowley, and the Seven Blocks of Granite. Most of the story on Cavanaugh comes from "Francis William Cavanaugh," an obituary by Joseph W. Gannon. The anecdotes on Vince Lombardi's behavior are from *Lombardi,* a collection of reminiscences edited by John Wiebusch, pp. 66–8. The most authoritative analysis of Lombardi's career is David Maraniss's biography, *When Pride Still Mattered,* chapters 2 and 3, pp. 56, 65–6. The Coffey material is in Maraniss and in Coffey's obituary in the *Ram.*

The story of the reform of Jesuit education is in Gleason, pp. 124–28, 136–42, and in William P. Leahy, S.J., *Adapting to America: Catholics, Jesuits, and Higher Education in the Twentieth Century.* Ross J. S. Hoffman's conversion is narrated in *Restoration,* pp. 14, 35. Statistics on enrollment in Jesuit institutions and Tivnan's judgments on Jesuit schools are from Leahy, pp. 35–36. The initiatives of Jesuit superiors to reform their colleges are from Leahy, pp. 43–46, and *UP,* pp. 195–200. I rely on *UP* for Hogan's policy on athletics, the building of Keating Hall, and Hogan's attitude toward accrediting agencies. I have also read the correspondence between Hogan and the accrediting agencies in the FA. Hogan's statue story is in "The Statue of Christ in Keating Hall" in *WL,* 66, 430-42. George Bull's address is in Francis X. Connolly's *Literature: The Channel of Culture,* pp. 21–24. There are other references to Bull in Halsey, p. 55. Gleason treats the evaluation of the graduate program on p. 174. Fr. Richard Tierney's evaluation of Jesuit writers is in Leahy, p. 37. Halsey discusses Pollock, pp. 78–81, and I have seen Pollock lecture at Woodstock.

8. Gannon Takes Charge

Father Gannon gives a personal interpretation of his own presidency in *UP* and of his early life and career at St. Peter's College in *The Poor Old Liberal Arts.* Thomas E. Curley Jr.'s Ph.D. dissertation, "Robert I. Gannon, President of Fordham University, 1936–1949: A Jesuit Educator," is based on interviews with Gannon and on materials in FA. Wherever possible, I have checked the original documents for verification of the Gannon and Curley accounts. The texts of the speeches to which I refer are in *After Black Coffee* and *After More Black Coffee.* Peter McDonough's analysis of Gannon as an icon of 1950s Catholicism is in *Men Astutely Trained,* 322–33. Curley is the principal source for my summary of Gannon's educational ideology.

Fr. Edward McGlinchy, S.J., described the early days of St. Peter's College to me. Other than Curley's interview, according to the Jacques Maritain Center at Notre Dame University, there does not seem to be other information on Fordham's invitation to Maritain. For background on Maritain see Bernard E. Doering, *Jacques Maritain and the French Catholic Intellectuals,* and Deal W. Hudson and Matthew J. Mancini, eds., *Understanding Maritain.* Details of Cardinal Pacelli's visit are from Gannon's *The Cardinal Spellman Story* as well as from the *Ram.*

Eugene Rogers sent me his class notes, which will remain in the FA, and I interviewed Rogers and John Clauss in 1999.

A copy of the Zacheus Maher memorial is in my files. For a biographical essay on J. Harding Fisher, see Edward A. Ryan, S.J., and William F. Graham, S.J., "John Harding Fisher (1875–1960)."

For the story of John LaFarge's efforts on behalf of Hudson J. Olliver and his interaction with authorities in the Society of Jesus, see David W. Southern, *John LaFarge and the Limits of Catholic Interracialism, 1911–1963,* pp. 160, 176, 194, 204–5, and 233. The relevant letters—LaFarge to Ledochowski, December 20, 1934; Memorandum on Negroes at Fordham University College, May 20, 1934; LaFarge to Zacheus J. Maher, August 16, 1944; LaFarge to Maher, August 24, 1944; and Maher's own "On the Acceptance of Negro Candidates into the Province of the Assistancy," May 3, 1945— are in the LaFarge Papers, Georgetown University archives. Catherine de Hueck Doherty's account of the Fordham incident is in *Fragments of My Life,* pp. 154–56, and is repeated uncritically in Albert Schorsch II, "'Uncommon Woman and Others': Memoirs and Lessons from Radical Catholics at Friendship House." I have copies from de Hueck's diaries through the courtesy of Lorene Hanley Duquin, author of *They Called Her the Baroness: The Life of Catherine de Hueck Dohertry.*

For the surveys of Negroes in Catholic colleges see John T. Gillard, S.S.J., *Colored Catholics in the United States,* and Francis K. Drolet, S.J., "Negro Students in Jesuit Schools and Colleges, 1946–1947: A Statistical Interpretation." McDonough, n. 27, p. 534, concludes that the first African American to join the Society of Jesus in the United States was Carl Shelton, who began his novitiate in the Missouri Province in 1945–46. RAS interviewed Roy Brown in June 1999.

9. From *Oedipus* to Dachau

Gannon's account of Roosevelt's visit is in *UP,* pp. 232–34. For background see Doris Kearns Goodwin, *No Ordinary Time,* pp. 184–87; Kenneth S. Davis, *FDR: Into the Storm, 1937–1940,* pp. 618–21; and the *New York Times* October 27–30, 1940. The full text of Roosevelt's remarks, along with a few letters to Gannon commenting on the visit, are in FA. The letter of Charles C. Tansill to Gannon (September 7, 1940), Gannon's reply (October 3, 1940), and Senator Edward R. Burke to Gannon (October 1, 1940) are in FA.

Preparation for the *Oedipus* production is described in the *Ram* throughout the 1940–41 year. Virgil Thomson recalls the production in his autobiography, *Virgil Thomson,* pp. 350–51. Laurence H. Reilly was interviewed by RAS in July 1999. The opening night was reviewed in the *New York Times,* May 10, 1941. Esther (Basuk) Smith wrote to RAS on June 8, 1997.

The wartime enrollment statistics are from *UP,* pp. 234 and 242, and from the *Ram,* August 6, 1943, and October 24, 1944. Richard E. Priday's story is from his letter to RAS of June 1997 and an RAS interview in August 1999. The statistics for postwar enrollment and Gannon's reaction to the Commission on Higher Education report are in *UP,* p. 245; Curley, pp. 176–77; and the *Ram,* February 20, 1948. Different sources give different estimates of the enrollment. *UP* lists a 1949 "all-time high" of 13,200. Curley, based on Gannon's Report of the President, gives a breakdown of the 1947–48 total of 12,218, including ten colleges (one of which is the Jesuit novitiate at St. Andrew's with forty-six) and summer school. But a *WL* 77 (July 1948), p. 356, item states that Fordham had become the largest Catholic institution of learning in the world with 14,000 students.

The Healy-Lombardi friendship is in the Healy interview, FOH. George Roach's D day experience is in Stephen E. Ambrose, *D-Day, June 6, 1944: The Climactic Battle of World War II,* pp. 182–83 and 329–30, and in an interview with RAS, 1999. John F. Manning's unpublished autobiography, "As I Remember It," along with his Holocaust photos are in FA. Also, there was an RAS interview, 1999.

Documents consulted on WFUV and the communications department in the Gannon Papers in FA include: Gannon to the Trustees of the Michael P. Grace Trust, December 19, 1946; the Department of Communications Arts, Introduction, 1948; and Alfred J. Barrett, S.J., to Fr. Grady, March 27, 1947. *UP* and Curley summarize this period.

10. Lou Mitchell Meets G. Gordon Liddy

The "Boys, go straight home" story is in Edward A. Ryan, S.J., and William F. Graham, S.J., "J. Harding Fisher (1875–1961)." The description of Catholic culture's strength is from Morris, chapter 8, and James T. Fisher, "Catholicism Ascendant: American

Popular Culture in the 1950s." The summary of Bronx history from 1900 to 1960 is based on standard sources and especially: Jill Jonnes, *We're Still Here: The Rise, Fall, and Resurrection of the South Bronx,* chapters 2–10; Edward J. Flynn, *You're the Boss: The Practice of American Politics,* pp. 17–20; Gary Hermalyn and Lloyd Ultan, "One Hundred Years of the Bronx,"; and Robert A. Olmstead, P.E., "Transportation Made the Bronx." The contrasting interpretations of Robert Moses's impact are from Robert Caro, *The Power Broker,* and Ray Bromley, "Not So Simple! Caro, Moses, and the Impact of the Cross-Bronx Expressway."

The Lou Mitchell story is drawn from his memoirs, "A Journey through a Journal"; from manuscripts in the Mitchell Papers in FA; from RAS interviews with Joseph Coviello, Bob Beusse, Joseph Landy, S.J., and G. Gordon Liddy; and from my personal recollections. The Joseph Donceel material is in Mitchell, in various *Ram* articles, in the Donceel interview in FOH, and from my personal recollections.

G. Gordon Liddy's story is from his autobiography, *Will,* pp. 36–37, and RAS interviews with Liddy, Charles Currie, S.J., Bob Beusse, Joseph Coviello, and Thomas Liddy.

The description of Fr. Laurence McGinley is based on my experience and discussions with numerous Jesuits, including Malachi Fitzpatrick, S.J., who assisted him when he signed diplomas. McGinley's opening statement to the press is in *WL* 78 (1949): 203–4. The description of Thurston Davis, S.J., is from personal experience, conversation with Joseph R. Frese, S.J., and various *Rams*. For an analysis of Davis's *Jesuit Educational Quarterly* article, see McDonough, pp. 205–13. The opening of the Russian Institute is in J. Franklin Ewing, "Fordham's Institute of Contemporary Russian Studies."

The activities of the Mimes and Mummers come from the *Rams* of 1951–52, the *Maroon,* 1952, and personal recollections. The earlier complaints are in a memo from Gannon to Fr. Tynan, dean of men, dated May 25, 1942, Gannon Papers in FA. The *FM* article is Peter Caupisens, "Fordham Theater Quo Vadis." Barrett's memo to McGinley is from June 11, 1952, McGinley Papers in FA; Quain's are July 21, 1952, and July 22, 1953. The John Leonard material is from an RAS interview with Fr. Leonard. The obituary, "Fr. Barrett," is by Joseph O'Neill, S.J.

11. Football Loses, Courtney Wins

Margaret Garvey's story is from her letter to RAS, June 12, 1997. The Miss Fordham event is in the *Ram* annually, with Pat Shalvey's experience, October 29, 1953. Aletta Lamm was written up often in the *Ram,* including on Sept 27, 1951, and I knew her well.

The Junior Year Abroad experience of 1953–54 is recounted in my regular *Ram* reports during the year and in my journal for the year. Prof. Telfair's quote on the football team is in Patrick McGowan, "Mr. Telfair: Tarheel Thucydides."

McGinley's conditional support is quoted in the *Ram,* February 21, 1952. For the Hyatt story, see the *Ram,* October 9, 1952. Jacob Freeman retells his "firing" story in the Seventy-fifth Anniversary *Ram,* April 30, 1993. McGinley's letter to Cardinal Spellman,

December 14, 1954, is in the McGinley Papers, FA. The student letter on the Senator McCarthy story is included in Donald F. Crosby, S.J., *God, Church, and Flag: Senator Joseph R. McCarthy and the Catholic Church, 1950–1957,* pp. 218–19. I was one of the authors of the published letter.

I interviewed Rupert Wentworth and knew Wentworth and Courtney and some of their friends. For Tom Courtney stories, see the *Ram* (March 16, 1954; December 9, 1954; November 19, 1956) and the *New York Times* and New York *Herald Tribune* (December 15, 1956). I interviewed Msgr. John Catoir, and Prof. Walsh showed me Don DeLillo's paper.

Father McGinley's quote on the importance of the Lincoln Square project is in McGinley to Dr. Howard A. Berman, March 24, 1948, McGinley Papers, FA. The Spellman quote, the fact about McGinley's grandfather, the conversation with Present, and the Rockefeller support are in the McGinley FOH interview. The basic background papers on Fordham's role in the project are "Fordham and Lincoln Square: History and Background," undated report; "Background: Fordham University in Lincoln Square," a six-page discussion paper on the housing controversy, March 22, 1957; "Fordham at Lincoln Square," notes for presentation to the Ford Foundation, six pages, February 1959; "Facts Related to Fordham University That Might Be of Interest to the Ford Foundation," three pages, all in McGinley Papers, FA. The *New York Times* and *Herald Tribune* had major stories on Fordham's role in the plan on January 21, 1959. Robert Caro's interpretation of how Fordham's needs matched Moses's plans is in the *Power Broker,* p. 1013. The controversy over Msgr. Egan's unpublished article, the galleys of which are in FA, is recorded in the following letters: Robert Moses to Thurston N. Davis, S.J., March 27, 1958; Moses to McGinley, March 27, 1958, which includes McGinley's notation, "Fr. Davis decided not to publish," March 28, 1958; Thomas J. Shanahan to McGinley, April 7, 1958; M. J. Sheehan to Thomas J. Shanahan, April 8, 1958, all in FA.

12. Jesuits and Women

For the story of the opening and a description of the buildings of Loyola Seminary, see Francis X. Curran, S.J., "Loyola Seminary at Shrub Oak." All the material on the deliberations, such as the McGinley memo from Woodstock, correspondence between Cardinal Spellman and Fr. Francis McQuade, S.J., and the ballots of the final deliberations, are in the Shrub Oak box in the archives of the New York Province. Details of student life in the early 1960s are from my recollections and discussions with other Jesuits. The description and price of the property are in Spellman to McQuade, May 10, 1946. The appointment of professors is in Quain to Rector, September 22, 1955, FA.

Father Vincent O'Keefe's appointment and goals are in his oral history interview, FOH. John Donohue, S.J.'s reflections are also in his FOH. The summary and conclusions of the self-study are in Francis J. Donohue, "The Self-Study of Fordham University. A Report Presented for the Consideration of the Commission on Institutions of Higher Education of the Middle States Association of Colleges and Secondary Schools,"

Fordham University, the Bronx, January 1963. The internal studies done in preparation for this report—e.g., the profiles of the faculty and seniors, and Donohue's reflections on the faculty survey—are in eight volumes of papers in the self-study box in FA.

Most of the *Ram* background stories on Thomas More are indicated in the text. I interviewed Susan Barrera and Barbara Stolz. Stolz's letter to the trustees, the minutes of the campus council, and Academic Vice President Paul Reiss's memo on how the Thomas More students viewed the school in 1972 are in FA.

13. Leo

The characterization of 1968 comes from personal recollections and from Kim McQuaid, *The Anxious Years: America in the Vietnam-Watergate Era,* p. 11. The summary of the six trends within the church and university draws on my own article, "Catholic Universities: Identity Lost and Found." The full text of the Land O'Lakes statement can be found in Neil G. McCluskey, S.J., *The Catholic University: A Modern Appraisal.* For the debate within the Society of Jesus, see *The Society of Jesus and Higher Education in America: Proceedings of the Woodstock Institute, October 9–11, 1964,* Woodstock College, 1965, and Robert S. Fitzgerald, S.J., ed., "Jesuits and Higher Education: A Symposium." The text of Fr. Arrupe's address is in *WL.*

Pete Fornatale told his story in an interview with RAS. The summary of Marshall McLuhan's experience at Fordham comes from W. Terrence Gordon's *Marshall McLuhan: Escape into Understanding: A Biography,* John Culkin's "A Schoolman's Guide to Marshall McLuhan," discussions with people who knew McLuhan and Culkin, and various issues of the *Ram.* In general, wherever necessary, I have included the date of the *Ram* in the text. During the period discussed in this chapter, the *Ram,* normally a weekly, would appear almost daily to keep current on a crisis. I was a summer editor of *America* when we published Frank Canavan's "To Make a University Great." The financial statistics were in the full texts of McLaughlin's addresses, which were published in the *Ram.* The rumors on Fordham's future were in the *Ram,* April 26, 1968.

I based my description of the Lincoln Center college's early history on interviews with Fr. Arthur Clarke, S.J., and with Fr. Daniel Mallette; on the FOH interviews with Paul Reiss and Joseph Cammarosano, FA; and on *Ram* stories in the December 13, 1967; February 7, 1968; and September 10, 1968 editions. The Bensalem section draws from my own "College as Camelot." In my research for that article I had access to the dossiers of the students in the registrar's files.

For the Gellhorn report, I used Walter Gellhorn and R. Kent Greenawalt, *The Sectarian College and the Public Purse: Fordham—a Case Study;* Alice Gallin, O.S.U., *Independence and a New Partnership in Catholic Higher Education;* James Jerome Conn, S.J., *Catholic Universities in the United States and Ecclesiastical Authority;* and the *Ram.* On the last days of McLaughlin and the situation within the Jesuit community, I consulted "Report of the Special Committee on Fordham University," in *WL;* the FOH interviews with Timothy Healy, S.J., and James Hennesey, S.J.; and personal interviews with James Hennesey, S.J.,

Frederick Dillemuth, S.J., Robert Mitchell, S.J., Francis Canavan, S.J., Edmund Ryan, S.J., and Eugene "Gib" O'Neill, former financial vice president.

14. The War at Home

The text of Daniel Garde's letter to the *Ram* is from October 20, 1965. I also interviewed Garde. Information on Armin Merkle is from a research paper by Brian Lyman, '99, and from my interview with Merkle. The description of Michael Walsh, S.J., is based on my observations and the James Hennesey, S.J., Paul Reiss, and Joseph Cammarosano FOH interviews. Felix Larkin's role is described in the Larkin FOH. I owe most of the observations on the emergence of lay-faculty leadership and the relations between lay professors and Jesuits, such as George McMahon, S.J., to a memo: Roger Wines to RAS, November 14, 1999, 7 pages, in my possession. The events of November 12 are based on *Ram* accounts; my interview with a security guard, Mr. Elwood Tuck; the Reiss and Cammarosano FOHs; and my recollections.

The Friedland controversy is based on the *Ram,* on my recollections, on interviews with Robert Reger and *Ram* reporter James Knickman, and on the Reiss and Cammarosano FOHs. Accounts of Digger Phelps's year at Fordham are in the *Ram* and the Carlesimo and Cammarosano FOHs.

15. The Bronx Is Burning

The Claire Hahn story is based on interviews with Dawn Cardi and Jack Becker; on a letter from Joe Ross to RAS, September 20, 1999; an unpublished manuscript, "Claire," by Jack Becker; a memorial booklet, "Everything We Look Upon Is Blest: Claire Hahn Becker, 1924–1978"; and my recollections, including "Loaves and Fishes, Remembering Claire Hahn."

The Finlay election is in the James C. Finlay and Felix Larkin FOH interviews. I interviewed Edmund Ryan, S.J., who participated as a trustee, and Donald Monan, S.J., who was a candidate.

The best summary of Finlay's accomplishments, published when he left office, is in *Fordham* magazine, in 1984. His *New York Times* obituary is December 7, 1992. The *Ram* studies on women at Fordham appear February 4, 1972; December 14, 1978; and April 30, 1981. Anne Anastasi's story is in her FOH interview.

Any list of individual students and their accomplishments inevitably risks leaving someone out, but in the period discussed in this chapter, much information was provided by the highly competent writers and editors of the *Ram; the paper,* which was founded by Mike O'Neill and Rita Ciolli; and *Point,* founded by Joe Russo and later edited by Dave Herndon, Jim O'Grady, Mike Sweeney, and Jerry O'Sullivan. Other *Ram* editors and writers include Jim Knickman, Joe DiSalvo, Loretta Tofani (Pulitzer Prize, *Washington Post*), John Holl, Jim Cavanaugh, Tom Curran, Kevin Hayes, Jim Dwyer (Pulitzer Prize, *New York Newsday*), Jerry Buckley, Malcolm Moran, Neil Grealy, Tom Maier, Herman Eberhardt, Carolyn Farrar, Thom Duffy, Bill Bole, Rosemary McManus (Pulitzer Prize, shared, *Newsday*), Chris Keating, and Bart Jones. A survey of sexual attitudes is from Loretta Tofani's "Morality Twisting to the Trends," *Ram* (November 3, 1972). Tom Curran's "The Meeting" analyzes the gay-liberation debate (*Ram*, February 9, 1973). The abortion article was by Carol Coyne, January 25, 1979.

I interviewed Richard T. Waldron, admissions director, on admissions trends, and I studied internal reports over ten years, e.g., Office of Admissions, Research Report No. 1, November 1979. Fordham College had 952 students (651 male, 301 female) in the class of 1976, and 820 (421 male, 399 female) in the class of 1983. The SATs (verbal/math) went from 569/591 to 519/539 (male) and from 555/550 to 524/526 (female). The standards study is by Cathy Carson, "Little Work, High Grades Decrease Standards." The text of Finlay's address to the graduate faculty and the *Ram*'s analysis and story by Charlie Kelly and Rita Ferrone are in the October 27, 1977, edition of the *Ram*. Cammarosano's reflection is in his FOH interview.

Joe Fitzpatrick tells his own story in *The Stranger Is Our Own,* pp. 3–90. The images of the Bronx's decline come from personal experience; an interview with Jim Dwyer; Jim Cavanaugh, "Details Emerge on Drug Dealing," and "Fast Food Outlets Dirty the Neighborhood"; Rick Marsico, "The Generation of Difference"; and the letter from Henry G. Waltemade to Donald F. Mohr, January 18, 1977. The statistics and history are based on Jill Jonnes's *We're Still Here* and Emmanuel Tobier's "The Bronx in the Twentieth Century: Dynamics of Population and Economic Change." The Roger Starr story is in the *New York Times,* March 17, 1976; the Felix Rohatyn plan is in the *New York Times,* February 3, 1976. Two sources on the Eldorado Bar are Kevin Lynch, "SDS at Home," and Dan Hayes, "A Man, His Bar, and the Bronx."

The story on Fordham's role in the neighborhood is from Joseph P. Muriana's unpublished paper, "'Institutional Witness' as a Practical Basis for the Promotion of Justice by a Jesuit University in Its Institutional Dimension as 'Public Citizen' within a Local Urban Setting: A Fordham Case Study," and from the Finlay, Cammarosano, and Paul Brant FOH interviews. Very helpful *Ram* articles include Thom Duffy, "A Neighborhood Graduates to Poverty"; Herman Eberhardt, "Bronx Coalition Fights Decline," and "Fordham Plaza Important to Area's Future." The Fordham student activists who played leading roles assisting the neighborhood were Roger Hayes and Jim Mitchell, who were, at that time, Jesuits, and Bill Frey, Peter Bourbeau, Jim Buckley, and Lois Harr.

Background articles on Denzel Washington include John Edgar Wideman, "The Man Can Play"; Rick Lyman, "The Spotlight Shifts to the Ring"; and *Current Biography*. The day in St. Angela Merici grammar school is based on my interviews with Pat Kelly, on an essay by Kelly, on an interview with John Feerick, on Feerick's 1998–99 Dean's Report, and on Feerick's FOH interview.

I was blessed during my tenure appeal to be represented before the senate by Fr. Charles Whalen, S.J., an associate editor of *America* and professor at Fordham law school. Through him, I learned what the word *advocate* fully means and, through that experience, that no one may remain silent in the face of an injustice.

16. Identity Reconsidered

The opening scene is from the first pages of Mary Higgins Clark's *While My Pretty One Sleeps.* The biographical material is from *Current Biography* and an interview with Clark. The biographical data on Joseph A. O'Hare, S.J., and the main events of his administration to date are from material supplied by Fr. O'Hare's office, the annual President's Reports as published in *Fordham*.magazine, and particularly the President's Ten-Year Report, 1984–1994.

For general background and historical perspective on this chapter, I interviewed six persons with long experience at Fordham as students, faculty, and/or trustees: Robert Himmelberg, Elaine Crane, Roger Wines, Robert Campbell, John Donohue, S.J., and George Shea. I am grateful to Don Gillespie of the office of institutional research for the Fordham Fact Book, 1998–1999, admissions-office reports over the 1970s and 1980s, and the Class of 2002 Profile, published in 1998. The Feasibility Study Report was based on 121 personal interviews and prepared by the firm of Marts and Lumly, Inc., May 1979, to determine capital-fund-raising potential.

The update on the Bronx is based in part on Robert Worth, "Guess Who Saved the South Bronx? Big Government." The faculty "malaise" is based on Self-Study for Reaccreditation, Susan Ray, chair of the Steering Committee, 1994, in FA.

For some of O'Hare's thinking on identity and *Ex corde ecclesiae,* see "Are We Compromising the Catholicism of the Institution? The Debate on Student Groups on Campus: Civil and Ecclesiatical Considerations," "Application of *Ex Corde Ecclesiae* to the United States," "*Ex Corde Ecclesiae:* Background Issues," and "What Are the Odds of Jesuit Higher Education Surviving in America?" The three qualities of Ignatian spirituality are listed in "What Are the Odds?"

The secular university description of the hiring process in the 1970s is from Thomas Bender, "Politics, Intellect, and the American University," in *American Academic Culture in Transformation,* p. 40. For the impact of the El Salvador martyrs, see David O'Brien, *From the Heart of the American Church*, p. 188, and Daniel Cardinali, S.J., "Jesuit Martyrs in El Salvador." The arrest of the demonstrators is in the *Ram,* December 7, 1989. The James R. Kelly report is "Love of Learning, Love for Justice." The Jay McGowan story is from FOH and my experience. Charles Osgood's remarks are quoted from *Fordham,* President's Report, 1996–1997.

17. Epilogue: A Millenium's Last Class

All the material is from my experience and interviews with Joseph DeBarbrie and Clarilibeth Torres. This chapter appeared in a slightly different form in the *National Catholic Reporter,* September 24, 1999. Joe and Clara read the chapter before publication.

Selected Bibliography

Books and Manuscripts

Alland, Alexander. *Jacob A. Riis: Photographer and Citizen.* Millerton, N.Y.: Aperture, 1974.

Ambrose, Stephen E. *D-Day, June 6, 1944: The Climactic Battle of World War II.* New York: Simon and Schuster, 1994.

As I Remember Fordham. New York: Fordham University Office of the Sesquicentennial, 1991.

Becker, Jack. "Claire." Unpublished manuscript.

Bednar, Gerald J. *Faith as Imagination: The Contribution of William F. Lynch, S.J.* Kansas City, Mo.: Sheed and Ward, 1996.

Bender, Thomas, and Carl E. Schorske, eds. *American Academic Culture in Transformation: Fifty Years, Four Disciplines.* Princeton, N.J.: Princeton University Press, 1998.

Brownson, Henry F. *Orestes A. Brownson's Later Life: From 1856–1876.* Detroit: Brownson, 1900.

Burdo, Ronald A. "A History of Chemistry at Fordham, 1841–1967." Unpublished manuscript in FA.

Caro, Robert A. *The Power Broker: Robert Moses and the Fall of New York.* New York: Knopf, 1974.

Catton, Bruce. *The American Heritage Picture History of the Civil War.* Edited by Richard M. Ketchum. New York: American Heritage Publishing Company, 1960.

Clark, Mary Higgins. *While My Pretty One Sleeps.* New York: Simon and Schuster, 1989.

Conn, James Jerome, S.J. *Catholic Universities in the United States and Ecclesiastical Authority.* Rome: Editrice Pontificia Università Gregoriana, 1991.

Connolly, Francis Xavier, S.J. *Literature: The Channel of Culture.* New York: Harcourt, Brace, 1948.

Connor, Charles P. "The American Catholic Political Position at Mid-Century: Archbishop Hughes as a Test Case." Ph.D. diss., Fordham University, 1979.

Crosby, Donald F., S.J. *God, Church, and Flag: Senator Joseph R. McCarthy and the Catholic Church, 1950–1957.* Chapel Hill: University of North Carolina Press, 1978.

Cudahy, Brian J. *Under the Sidewalks of New York: The Story of the Greatest Subway System in the World.* 2nd rev. ed. New York: Fordham University Press, 1995.

Curley, Thomas E. Jr. *Robert I. Gannon, President of Fordham University 1936–1949: A Jesuit Educator.* Ph.D. diss., New York University, 1974.

Curran, Francis X., S.J. *The Return of the Jesuits.* Chicago: Loyola University Press, 1966.

Curran, Robert Emmett. *The Bicentennial History of Georgetown University.* Vol. 1, *From Academy to University, 1789–1889.* Washington, D.C.: Georgetown University Press, 1993.

Davis, Kenneth S. *FDR: Into the Storm, 1937–1940: A History.* New York: Random House, 1993.

Doering, Bernard E. *Jacques Maritain and the French Catholic Intellectuals.* Notre Dame, Ind.: University of Notre Dame Press, 1983.

Doherty, Catherine de Hueck. *Fragments of My Life.* Notre Dame, Ind.: Ave Maria Press, 1979.

———. *Friendship House.* New York: Sheed and Ward, 1946.

———. "The Passion in the Slums." In *This Is My Passion.* Edited by William J. Flynn. New York: Alba House, 1962.

Duquin, Lorene Hanley. *They Called Her the Baroness: The Life of Catherine de Hueck Doherty.* New York: Alba House, 1995.

Dyer, Frederick H. *A Compendium of the War of the Rebellion.* Des Moines, Iowa: The Dyer Publishing Co., 1908.

Earls, Michael, S.J., ed. *Fr. Shealy and Marymount, His Lectures and Conferences.* Worcester, Mass.: Harrigan Press, 1924.

FitzGerald, Paul A., S.J. *The Governance of Jesuit Colleges in the United States, 1920–1970.* Notre Dame, Ind.: University of Notre Dame Press, 1984.

Fitzpatrick, Joseph P., S.J. *The Stranger Is Our Own: Reflections on the Journey of Puerto Rican Migrants.* Kansas City, Mo.: Sheed and Ward, 1996.

Flynn, Edward J. *You're the Boss: The Practice of American Politics.* New York: Collier, 1962.

Flynn, Gerard. *The Bronx Boy.* Huntington, W.V.: University Editions, 1993.

"Fordham in the Year 2000." Committee Report, John Healey, chair, undated, in FA.

Frusciano, Thomas J., and Marilyn H. Pettit. *New York University and the City: An Illustrated History.* New Brunswick, N.J.: Rutgers University Press, 1997.

Gallin, Alice, O.S.U. *Independence and a New Partnership in Catholic Higher Education.* Notre Dame, Ind.: University of Notre Dame Press, 1996.

Gannon, Robert I., S.J. *After Black Coffee.* New York: Declan X. McMullen Co., 1946.

———. *After More Black Coffee.* New York: Farrar, Straus, 1964.

———. *The Cardinal Spellman Story.* Garden City, N.Y.: Doubleday, 1962.

———. *The Poor Old Liberal Arts.* New York: Farrar, Straus, and Cudahy, 1961.

———. *Up to the Present: The Story of Fordham.* Garden City, N.Y.: Doubleday, 1967.

Gellhorn, Walter, and R. Kent Greenawalt. *The Sectarian College and the Public Purse: Fordham—a Case Study.* Dobbs Ferry, N.Y.: Oceana, 1970.

Gillard, John Thomas, S.J. *Colored Catholics in the United States.* Baltimore: Josephite Press, 1941.

Gilleran, Edward P. "Five to Fifty-Five. Recollections of Fordham during Its First Fifty Years as a University." Unpublished manuscript in FA, 1958.

Gilleran, Edward P., Jr. "One Last Look"; a history of Fordham athletics. Unpublished manuscript in FA, written in the 1980s.

Gleason, Philip. *Contending with Modernity: Catholic Higher Education in the Twentieth Century.* New York: Oxford University Press, 1995.

Goodwin, Doris Kearns. *No Ordinary Time: Franklin and Eleanor Roosevelt: The Home Front in World War II.* New York: Simon and Schuster, 1994.

Gordon, W. Terrence. *Marshall McLuhan: Escape into Understanding.* New York: Basic Books, 1997.

Halsey, William M. *The Survival of American Innocence: Catholicism in an Era of Disillusionment, 1920–1940.* Notre Dame, Ind.: University of Notre Dame Press, 1980.

Hennessy, Thomas, S.J., ed. *Fordham: The Early Years.* New York: Something More Publications, 1998.

Hoffman, Ross J. S. *Restoration.* New York: Sheed and Ward, 1934.

Holbrook, Francis X., and August A. Stellwag. *When September Comes . . . . : A History of Fordham Preparatory School, 1841–1991.* Seven Graphics.

Hudson, Deal W., and Matthew J. Mancini, eds. *Understanding Maritain: Philosopher and Friend.* Macon, Ga.: Mercer University Press, 1987.

Hughes, John. *The Complete Works of the Most Rev. John Hughes, D.D.* Edited by Lawrence Kehoe. New York: Kehoe, 1866.

Jonnes, Jill. *We're Still Here: The Rise, Fall, and Resurrection of the South Bronx.* Boston: Atlantic Monthly Press, 1986.

Klaus, Carl H., Nancy R. Conley, Robert Scholes, and Michael Silverman, eds. *Elements of Literature,* 4th ed. New York: Oxford University Press, 1991.

Klein, Christa Messmeyer. "The Jesuits and Catholic Boyhood in Nineteenth-Century New York City: A Study of St. John's College and the College of St. Francis Xavier, 1846–1912." Ph.D. diss., University of Pennsylvania, 1976.

Labrie, Ross. *The Catholic Imagination in American Literature.* Columbia, Mo.: University of Missouri Press, 1997.

Leahy, William P., S.J. *Adapting to America: Catholics, Jesuits, and Higher Education in the Twentieth Century.* Washington, D.C.: Georgetown University Press, 1991.

Liddy, G. Gordon. *Will.* New York: St. Martin's Press, 1980.

Mangum, Claude. "The Coming of Age of the Black Catholic Community in New York." In *One Faith, One Lord, One Baptism.* Edited by Ruth Doyle. New York: Office of Pastoral Research, 1988.

Manning, John F. "As I Remember It." Unpublished autobiographical manuscript in FA, 1999.

Maraniss, David. *When Pride Still Mattered: A Life of Vince Lombardi.* New York: Simon and Schuster, 1999.

McCarthy, Joseph F. X. *Learning in the City: The Graduate School of Education Reviews Its Seventy-five Years in New York, 1916–1992.* New York: Fordham University Graduate School of Education, 1992.

McCluskey, Neil G., S.J., ed. *The Catholic University: A Modern Appraisal.* Notre Dame, Ind.: University of Notre Dame Press, 1970.

McDonnell, James M. *Orestes A. Brownson and Nineteenth-Century Catholic Education.* New York: Garland, 1988.

McDonough, Peter. *Men Astutely Trained: A History of the Jesuits in the American Century.* New York: Free Press, 1992.

McLynn, Frank. *Carl Gustav Jung.* New York: St. Martin's Press, 1997.

McPherson, James M. *Battle Cry of Freedom: The Civil War Era.* New York: Oxford University Press, 1988.

McQuaid, Kim. *The Anxious Years: America in the Vietnam-Watergate Era.* New York: Basic Books, 1989.

Melick, Harry C. W. *The Manor of Fordham and Its Founder.* New York: Fordham University Press, 1950.

Mitchell, Lou. "A Journey through a Journal." Unpublished autobiographical manuscript in FA, n.d.

Morris, Charles R. *American Catholic: The Saints and Sinners Who Built America's Most Powerful Church.* New York: Times Books, 1997.

Muriana, Joseph P. "'Institutional Witness' as a Practical Basis for the Promotion of Justice by a Jesuit University in Its Institutional Dimension as 'Public Citizen' within a Local Urban Setting: A Fordham Case Study." Unpublished manuscript in FA.

Murphy, Jean Mary. *Analysis of the Curriculum of Thomas More College: A Historical Perspective.* Ph.D. diss., Fordham University, 1984.

Nichols, Mary Sargeant Gove. *Reminiscences of Edgar Allan Poe.* New York: Haskell House, 1974.

Nuesse, C. Joseph. *The Catholic University of America: A Centennial History.* Washington, D.C.: Catholic University of America Press, 1990.

O'Brien, David J. *From the Heart of the American Church: Catholic Higher Education and American Culture.* Maryknoll, N.Y.: Orbis Books, 1994.

O'Malley, John W. *The First Jesuits.* Cambridge, Mass.: Harvard University Press, 1993.

Padberg, John W., S.J. *Colleges in Controversy: The Jesuit Schools in France from Revival to Suppression, 1815–1880.* Cambridge: Harvard University Press, 1969.

Phillips, Mary E. *Edgar Allan Poe: The Man.* Vol. 2. Chicago: John C. Winston Co., 1926.

Power, Edward J. *Catholic Higher Education in America: A History.* New York: Appleton-Century Crofts, 1972.

Riis, Jacob A. *The Making of an American.* New York: Macmillan Co., 1901.

Ryan, Thomas R., C.Pp.S. *Orestes A. Brownson: A Definitive Biography.* Huntington, Ind.: Our Sunday Visitor, 1976.

Shaw, Richard. *Dagger John: The Unquiet Life and Times of Archbishop John Hughes of New York.* New York: Paulist Press, 1977.

Shaw, Robert Gould. *Blue-Eyed Child of Fortune: The Civil War Letters of Colonel Robert Gould Shaw.* Edited by Russell Duncan. Athens: University of Georgia Press, 1992.

———. *Letters.* New York: Collins, 1876 (in New York Public Library).

Shelley, Thomas J. *Dunwoodie: The History of St. Joseph's Seminary, Yonkers, New York.* Westminster, Md.: Christian Classics, 1993.

———. *The New History of the Archdiocese of New York.* Strasbourg: Editions du Signe, 1999.

Southern, David W. *John LaFarge and the Limits of Catholic Interracialism, 1911–1963.* Baton Rouge: Louisiana State University Press, 1996.

Smith, Mary Anastasia (Sister Mary Marcella). "James J. Walsh: American Revivalist of the Middle Ages." Ph.D. diss., St. John's University, 1944.

Taaffe, Thomas Gaffney. *A History of St. John's College, Fordham, New York.* New York: Catholic Publication Society Co., 1891.

Thebaud, Augustus J., S.J. *Forty Years in the United States of America, 1839–1885.* With a biographical sketch by Rev. Thomas J. Campbell, S.J. Edited by Charles George Herbermann. New York: United States Catholic Historical Society, 1904.

———. *Three Quarters of a Century, 1807–1882: A Retrospect.* 3 vols. New York: The United States Catholic Historical Society, 1904–1913.

Thomson, Virgil. *Virgil Thomson.* New York: Alfred A. Knopf, 1966.

Treacy, Gerald Carr, S.J., ed. *Father Shealy: A Tribute.* Fort Wadsworth, N.Y.: Mount Manresa, 1927.

Ultan, Lloyd. *The Beautiful Bronx, 1920–1950*. New Rochelle, N.Y.: Arlington House, 1979.

Ultan, Lloyd, and Gary Hermalyn. *The Bronx: It Was Only Yesterday, 1935–1965*. Bronx, N.Y.: Bronx County Historical Society, 1992.

Walsh, James J. *The Popes and Science*. New York: Fordham University Press, 1908.

———. *The Thirteenth, Greatest of Centuries*. Memorial edition. New York: Fordham University Press, 1943.

Wiebusch, John, ed. *Lombardi*. Chicago: Follett, 1971.

Manuscripts in Fordham University Archives on Early Jesuit Community

Fordham Oral History

Prefect's Book of Rules and Customs, 1860s

Minister's Diary, 1889–1900

Notanda Collegii, 1846–1904

Photograph Album, mid- to late-nineteenth century

Periodicals

"An Ancient Member of the Faculty Interviewed." *Fordham Monthly* (November 1888): 28–29.

Arrupe, Pedro, S.J. "Address at Fordham University." *Woodstock Letters* 96 (1967): 65–74.

Barry, W. J. "Dr. Arnold and Catholic Education." *Brownson's Quarterly Review* (July 1860): 302–29.

Bromley, Ray. "Not So Simple! Caro, Moses, and the Impact of the Cross-Bronx Expressway." *Bronx County Historical Society Journal* 35 (spring 1998): 5–29.

"Brother Julius Mace." *Woodstock Letters* 18 (1887): 385–87.

Canavan, Francis, S.J. "To Make a University Great." *America* (July 15, 1967): 57–60.

Cardinali, Daniel, S.J. "Jesuit Martyrs in El Salvador." *Ram* (November 15, 1990).

Carson, Cathy. "Little Work, High Grades Decrease Standards." *Ram* (April 9, 1975).

Caupisens, Peter. "Fordham Theater Quo Vadis." *Fordham Monthly* 69: 29–30.

Cavanaugh, Jim. "Details Emerge on Drug Dealing." *Ram* (September 25, 1974).

———. "Fast Food Outlets Dirty the Neighborhood." *Ram* (October 16, 1974).

Culkin, John, S.J. "A Schoolman's Guide to Marshall McLuhan." *Saturday Review* (March 18, 1967).

Curran, Francis X., S.J. "Loyola Seminary at Shrub Oak." *Woodstock Letters* 87: 36–42.

Curran, Tom. "The Meeting." *Ram* (February 9, 1973).

Daley, Robert. "Fordham Now: The Shock of Unrecognition." *New York Magazine* (May 31, 1971): 24–30.

Dodge, H. H. "Reminiscences of a Forty-Niner." *Fordham Monthly* (1891): 77–78.

Drolet, Francis K., S.J. "Negro Students in Jesuit Schools and Colleges, 1946–1947: A Statistical Interpretation." *Woodstock Letters* 76: 299–309.

Duffy, Thom. "A Neighborhood Graduates to Poverty." *Ram* (May 27, 1979).

Eberhardt, Herman. "Bronx Coalition Fights Decline." *Ram* (February 22, 1979).

———. "Fordham Plaza Important to Area's Future." *Ram* (November 6, 1980).

Ewing, J. Franklin. "Fordham's Institute of Contemporary Russian Studies." *Woodstock Letters* 81: 24–28.

Feasibility Study Report, prepared for Fordham by Marts and Lumly, Inc., May 1979, in FA.

Fisher, James T. "Catholicism Ascendant: American Popular Culture in the 1950s." *Culturefront* (winter 1998–99): 58–60, 75–76.

Fitzgerald, Robert S., S.J., ed. "Jesuits and Higher Education: A Symposium." *Woodstock Letters* 94: 245–74.

Fleming, Thomas J. "Fordham, Trying to Be Catholic with a Small c." *New York Times Magazine* (December 10, 1967).

Fordham University Fact Book, 1998–1999. Office of Institutional Research.

Gannon, Joseph W. "Francis William Cavanaugh: Obituary." *Dartmouth Ninety-Nine* (March 1934): 6–16.

Garraghan, Gilbert J. "Fordham's Jesuit Beginnings." *Thought* (March 1941): 17–39.

"General Martin McMahon, '55." *Fordham Monthly* 14, no. 5 (1896): 74–75.

Hayes, Dan. "A Man, His Bar, and the Bronx." *Ram* (April 20, 1978).

Hermalyn, Gary, and Lloyd Ultan. "One Hundred Years of the Bronx." *Bronx County Historical Society Journal* 35 (fall 1998): 63-69.

Hill, Walter. "Some Facts and Incidents Relating to St. Joseph's College, Bardstown, Kentucky." *Woodstock Letters* 26 (1897): 90–105.

———. "Some Reminiscences of St. Mary's College, Kentucky." *Woodstock Letters* 20 (1891): 25–38.

Hogan, Aloysius J., S.J. "The Statue of Christ in Keating Hall." *Woodstock Letters* 66: 430–32.

"How the Colors Were Lost." *Fordham Monthly* 1, no. 9 (1883): 95.

Kelly, James R. "Love of Learning, Love for Justice." Report to the Conference on the Commitment to Justice in Jesuit Higher Education, Boston College, October 29–31, 1999.

King, Robert J. "A Singer and His Song." *Fordham Monthly* 57: 72–77.

Kirwin, Harry W. "James J. Walsh, Medical Historian and Pathfinder." *The Catholic Historical Review* 45, no. 4 (January 1960): 409–435.

Lyman, Rick. "The Spotlight Shifts to the Ring." *New York Times* (November 14, 1999).

Lynch, Kevin. "SDS at Home." *Ram* (March 17, 1970).

Marsico, Rick. "The Generation of Difference." *Ram* (November 6, 1980).

McGowan, Patrick. "Mr. Telfair: Tarheel Thucydides." *Ram* (April 30, 1948).

Nash, Michael, S.J. "Reminiscences of Fr. Michael Nash." *Woodstock Letters* 26, (1897): 257–86.

O'Beirne, James R. "Reminiscences in War Times." *Fordham Monthly* 34, no. 9 (1916): 51.

———. "Reminiscences of General James R. O'Beirne." *Fordham Monthly* 5, no. 6 (1887): 88.

O'Hare, Joseph A., S.J. "Application of *Ex Corde Ecclesiae* to the United States." ACCU Business Meeting, Washington, D.C., February 3, 1999.

———. "Are We Compromising the Catholicism of the Institution? The Debate on Student Groups on Campus: Civil and Ecclesiastical Considerations." Catholic Higher Education Symposium, Los Angeles, Calif., June 26, 1992.

———. "*Ex Corde Ecclesiae:* Background Issues." Workshop with the Board of Trustees, Gannon University, Erie, Pa., January 11, 1991.

———. "What Are the Odds of Jesuit Higher Education Surviving in America?" AJCU Conference, Jesuit Education 21, St. Joseph's University, June 25–29, 1999.

Olmstead, Robert A. "Transportation Made the Bronx." *Bronx County Historical Society Journal* 35 (fall 1998): 166–80.

———. "A History of Transportation in the Bronx." *Bronx County Historical Society Journal* 26 (1989): 68–91.

"Our Soldier Dead." *Fordham Monthly* 21 (1902): 22.

O'Neill, Joseph E., S.J. "Father Barrett." *Woodstock Letters* 87 (February 1958): 63–80.

President's Ten-Year Report, 1984–1994. *Fordham Magazine.*

Quinn, Stanley. Obituary of John Coveney. *Fordham Monthly* 30: 73–75.

"Report of the Special Committee on Fordham University." *Woodstock Letters* 98 (1969): 242–52.

Ryan, Edward A., S.J., and William F. Graham, S.J. "John Harding Fisher, S.J." *Woodstock Letters* 94 (summer 1965): 333–58.

Schorsch, Albert, II. "'Uncommon Women and Others': Memoirs and Lessons from Radical Catholics at Friendship House." *U.S. Catholic Historian* 9:371–86.

Schroth, Raymond A., S.J. "Catholic Universities: Identity Lost and Found." *culturefront* (fall 1998): 39–46.

———. "College as Camelot." *Saturday Review* (November 11, 1972): 52–58.

———. "Loaves and Fishes: Remembering Claire Hahn." *Commonweal* (February 2, 1979).

"Seismic Observatory Reopened as Research and Learning Center." *Inside Fordham* 21, no. 6 (March 10, 1999).

Shaughnessy, Edward L. "Elle, James, and Jamie O'Neill." *The Eugene O'Neill Review* 15 (1991): 5–93.

Standler, Golda G. "Jesuit Educational Institutions in the City of New York, 1683–1860." *Historical Records and Studies* 24 (1934): 209–75.

Tobier, Emmanuel. "The Bronx in the Twentieth Century: Dynamics of Population and Economic Change." *The Bronx County Historical Society Journal* 35 (fall 1998): 69–102.

Tofani, Loretta. "Morality Twisting to the Trends." *Ram* (November 3, 1972).

Treacy, Richard S. "Reminiscences: Early Sixties." *Fordham Monthly* 34, no. 9 (1916): 68–71.

Walsh, Francis. "The Story of the Conference." *Interracial Review* 9:150–52.

Wideman, John Edgar. "The Man Can Play." *Esquire* (May 1998).

Worth, Robert. "Guess Who Saved the South Bronx? Big Government." *Washington Monthly* (April 1999): 26–33.

Index

A

B